D1105579

Subjective Well-Being

AN INTERDISCIPLINARY PERSPECTIVE

INTERNATIONAL SERIES IN EXPERIMENTAL SOCIAL PSYCHOLOGY

Series Editor: MICHAEL ARGYLE, *University of Oxford*

Subjective Well-Being

AN INTERDISCIPLINARY PERSPECTIVE

Edited by

Fritz Strack, Michael Argyle and Norbert Schwarz

PERGAMON PRESS

Member of Maxwell Macmillan Pergamon Publishing Corporation

OXFORD · NEW YORK · BEIJING · FRANKFURT
SÃO PAULO · SYDNEY · TOKYO · TORONTO

U.K.	Pergamon Press plc, Headington Hill Hall, Oxford OX3 0BW, England
U.S.A.	Pergamon Press, Inc., Maxwell House, Fairview Park, Elmsford, New York 10523, U.S.A.
PEOPLE'S REPUBLIC OF CHINA	Pergamon Press, Room 4037, Qianmen Hotel, Beijing, People's Republic of China
FEDERAL REPUBLIC OF GERMANY	Pergamon Press GmbH, Hammerweg 6, D-6242 Kronberg, Federal Republic of Germany
BRAZIL	Pergamon Editora Ltda, Rua Eça de Queiros, 346, CEP 04011, Paraiso, São Paulo, Brazil
AUSTRALIA	Pergamon Press (Australia) Pty Ltd., P.O. Box 544, Potts Point, N.S.W. 2011, Australia
JAPAN	Pergamon Press, 5th Floor, Matsuoka Central Building, 1-7-1 Nishishinjuku, Shinjuku-ku, Tokyo 160, Japan
CANADA	Pergamon Press Canada Ltd., Suite No. 271, 253 College Street, Toronto, Ontario, Canada M5T 1R5

Copyright © 1991 Pergamon Press plc

All Rights Reserved. No part of this publication may be reproduced, stored in a retrieval system or transmitted in any form or by any means: electronic, electrostatic, magnetic tape, mechanical, photocopying, recording or otherwise, without permission in writing from the publishers.

First edition 1991

Library of Congress Cataloging in Publication Data

Subjective well-being / edited by Fritz Strack,
Michael Argyle, and Norbert Schwarz. — 1st ed.
p. cm. — (International series in experimental social
psychology; v. 21)
Includes bibliographical references.
1. Happiness. I. Strack, Fritz, 1950–
II. Argyle, Michael.
III. Schwarz, Norbert, Dr. phil. IV. Series.
BF575.H27S82 1990   158—dc20   90–34742

British Library Cataloguing in Publication Data

Subjective well-being. — (International series in
experimental social psychology)
1. Happiness
I. Strack, Fritz II. Argyle, Michael *1925*
III. Schwarz, Norbert IV. Series
152.4

ISBN 0–08–037264–3

Front cover illustration by Penny Berry Paterson

Printed in Great Britain by BPCC Wheatons Ltd., Exeter

BF
575
.H27
S82
1990

Contents

Subjective Well-Being in its Social Context

List of Contributors

Editors

MICHAEL ARGYLE, Department of Experimental Social Psychology, University of Oxford, South Parks Road, Oxford, OX1 3UD, England.

NORBERT SCHWARZ, Zentrum für Umfragen, Methoden und Analysen, ZUMA, Postfach 122155, 6800 Mannheim, West Germany.

FRITZ STRACK, Max-Planck-Institut für psychologische Forschung, Leopoldstr. 24, 8000 München 40, West Germany.

Contributors

HERMANN BRANDSTÄTTER, Institut fur Psychologie, Johannes-Kepler-Universität, A-4040 Linz, Austria.

MIHALY CSIKSZENTMIHALYI, Department of Behavioral Sciences, University of Chicago, 5848 S. University, Chicago, Illinois 60637, USA.

ED DIENER, Department of Psychology, University of Illinois, 603 E. Daniel Street, Champaign, Illinois 61820, USA.

SIGRUN-HEIDE FILIPP, Fachgebiet Psychologie, Universität Trier, Tarforst, Gebäude D, 5500 Trier, West Germany.

ADRIAN FURNHAM, Department of Psychology, University College of London, Gower Street, London, WC1E 6BT, England.

WOLFGANG GLATZER, FB Gesellschaftswissenschaften, Johann Wolfgang Goethe Universität, Robert-Mayer-Str. 5, 6000 Frankfurt, West Germany.

BRUCE HEADEY, Department of Political Science, University of Melbourne, Parkville, Victoria 3052, Australia.

PETER LEWINSOHN, Department of Psychology, University of Oregon, Straub Hall, Eugene, Oregon 97403, USA.

AMOS TVERSKY, Department of Psychology, Stanford University, Stanford, California 94305, USA.

RUUT VEENHOVEN, Erasmus Universiteit Rotterdam, Postbus 1738, 3000 DR Rotterdam, The Netherlands.

1

Introduction

FRITZ STRACK, MICHAEL ARGYLE and NORBERT SCHWARZ

The happiness of the human species has always been at the focus of attention of the humanities. Its manifestations were prime topics for literary and poetic descriptions. Its possibility has been an issue in philosophy ever since Plato and Seneca. The great religions gained their attraction partly from their recipes for reaching this goal. Political ideologies centred around the ideal society that would guarantee ultimate happiness. Economists developed quantitative measures to describe a whole nation's well-being (see Chapter 5) while social scientists, noting the shortcomings of economic indices, concerned themselves with various social indicators to describe the quality of life.

And psychology? Most interestingly, psychology has been preoccupied less with the conditions of well-being, than with the opposite: the determinants of human unhappiness (cf. Diener, 1984). Why? Was it because psychology was often more concerned with the dark side of human nature? Was it because psychology was only called upon when people were suffering and needed help? Was it because negative states and events elicit a stronger need for causal explanations than positive experiences (cf. Bohner, Bless, Schwarz and Strack, 1988)? The answer will remain speculative.

However, psychology has made up for this apparent deficit during the past twenty years (cf. Argyle, 1987). Subjective well-being has meanwhile become an established topic of research that has received attention from both basic and applied perspectives. The cognitive and affective mechanisms have been studied extensively (see Chapter 5), and integrating theoretical models have emerged from this endeavour. The psychological importance of happiness has been recognized for most aspects of social and private life. As a consequence, the topic has attracted interest from several fields of psychology. The conditions of happiness and satisfaction are being studied within the domains of clinical as well as cross-cultural psychology, in social as well as in industrial/organizational and in personality psychology, to name only a few areas.

Given this growing interest in the topic and its apparent interdisciplinary nature, the idea of inviting representatives from different areas of psychology (and the neighbouring social sciences) to contribute their perspectives on the joint theme was clearly desirable. It is the intention of the present volume to document these divergent perspectives on the common issue of subjective well-being and to foster communication between these areas.

The book starts out with a series of fundamental questions that are pertinent to all research perspectives. In his discussion, Veenhoven raises several conceptual and methodological issues that have been important for the study of subjective well-being. In the next chapter, Schwarz and Strack demonstrate that reports of happiness and satisfaction can be viewed as judgments that are influenced by various affective and cognitive mechanisms. On the basis of a series of experimental findings, they suggest a theoretical model to account for these influences. Headey, on the other hand, uses ideas and concepts from economics to explain his findings of temporal stability and change of reported subjective well-being.

The second part of the book focuses on more specific research issues that are important for a better understanding of the general phenomenon. Argyle and Martin give a comprehensive review of empirical findings that elucidate the causal role of different life domains, especially social relationships, work and leisure. Tversky and Griffin generate some provocative conclusions on the basis of the observation that a hedonically relevant event can exert two opposing influences on judgments of well-being. They argue that the same event may make a person both happy and unhappy and describe a dilemma in which humans tend to choose courses of action that may decrease their happiness. Diener, Sandvik and Pavot look at hedonic experiences as a source of happiness. They provide results showing that the frequency of affect is more important than intensity for individuals' well-being. Lewinsohn, Redner and Seeley report data that allow them to triangulate "life satisfaction" in relation to other psychosocial variables, above all in its relation to depression.

The third part of the book emphasizes the social context in which people experience and report their happiness and satisfaction. Brandstätter describes findings that demonstrate how aspects of the social situation and personality interact in their influence on positive and negative emotions. The cultural context of subjective well-being is the focus of a comparative study by Csikszentmihalyi and Mei-Ha Wong. These authors compared the personal and situational concomitants of happiness for American and Italian teenagers and speculate about universal and culture-specific features of subjective well-being. Filipp and Klauer studied people's ability to maintain their sense of well-being under situations that are least conducive for generating happiness—stressful life events, like terminal illness. Furnham's chapter reviews theories about work and its relationship to leisure (see Chapter 5) and shows the causes of job satisfaction. The chapter by Glatzer gives a report of subjective well-being at a national level. On the basis of reports from a representative sample of respondents, it provides a comprehensive picture of the quality of life experienced in West Germany.

The present book is based on a conference that was held in Bad Homburg in 1987. The editors would like to express their sincere thanks to the Werner-Reimers-Foundation for its generous funding of this conference. Special gratitude goes to Kerstin Matthias for her invaluable support in proof reading and editing the final manuscript and to Claudia Halvorson for preparing the indices.

References

ARGYLE, M. *The psychology of happiness.* London: Methuen, 1987.

BOHNER, G., BLESS, H., SCHWARZ, N. and STRACK, F. What triggers causal attributions? The impact of valence and subjective probability. *European Journal of Social Psychology*, 1988; **18**, 335–345.

DIENER, E. Subjective well-being. *Psychological Bulletin*, 1984; **235**, 542–575.

General Perspectives

2

Questions on happiness: classical topics, modern answers, blind spots

RUUT VEENHOVEN[1]

Introduction

Happiness is a longstanding theme in Western thought. It came under scrutiny in the following three periods: (1) Antique Greek philosophy; (2) Post-Enlightenment West-European moral philosophy, Utilitarianism in particular; and (3) Current Quality-of-Life research in the rich welfare states. Printed reflections on all this contemplation now fill a hundred metres of bookshelves.

This paper takes stock of the progress made on seven classical topics. Are we now any wiser? Or is Dodge (1930) right in his contention that "the theory of the happy life has remained on about the same level that the ancient Greeks left it"? This inventory will differ from the usual review articles. The focus will not be on current technical research issues, but rather on the broader questions that prompted the enquiry. Furthermore, the aim is not only to enumerate advances in understanding, but also to mark the blind spots.

The following issues will be considered:

1. What is happiness?
2. Can happiness be measured?
3. Is unhappiness the rule?
4. How do people assess their happiness?
5. What conditions favour happiness?
6. Can happiness be promoted?
7. Should happiness be promoted?

These scientific issues do not emerge in a social vacuum, but are rooted

7

in broader moral and political debates. Questions 1 and 7 are part of an ongoing ethical discussion about value priorities. Which values should guide us? How should we rank values such as "wisdom", "equality", "justice", "freedom" and "happiness"? Together with question 5, these issues also figure in the related political debates about socio-economic priorities. Should the emphasis be on national economic growth or on individual well-being? Who are the deprived in our society? How can their suffering best be reduced?

Questions 2 to 6 further link up with the discussion about the possibilities and dangers of socio/political technocracy. Will our understanding of human and social functioning ever allow the deduction of optimal policies? Will the political system ever be able to put such policies into practice? If so, will not the remedy be worse than the disease, and bring about a "Brave New World"? Questions 3 to 6 relate to the broad argument between pessimists and optimists. They are all issues in the discussion as to whether current society is rotten or not, and whether social development holds any promise for a better one. Questions 4 and 5 are relevant in the debate on human nature. Is happiness the result of rational consideration or of following blind instincts? Has human happiness anything to do with the real good or can we be happy in any condition? Finally, question 3 is an issue in the ongoing discussion about the legitimacy of the political order. If most people feel happy under the current régime, why change it? For that reason, conservatives tend to claim that we are happy, while revolutionaries try to prove we are not.

What is happiness?

The history of happiness research is the history of confusion. The term has carried many different meanings and has thereby hindered productive thinking enormously. Nowadays, the discussion has largely escaped from this deadlock. In fact, the greatest advance achieved is at the conceptual level.

Part of the problem is not specific to the subject matter but results from the variety of meanings the term happiness has in common language. Because of the lack of conceptual discipline, that confusion of tongues has been continued into the scientific debate. An additional problem is that the seemingly technical discussion about the proper use of words in fact covers up an ideological debate about value priorities. In many arguments the term "happiness" is used as a synonym for "the good". "Defining" happiness is then propagating an ideology. Therefore, a consensus on the use of the word has never emerged.

Recent conceptual differentiation

In the 1950s the use of concepts such as "welfare", "adjustment" and "mental health" had much in common with the traditional confusion about "happiness". Yet in the last few decades social scientists have largely escaped from these deadlocks and have thereby allowed a breakthrough in the conceptualization of happiness. It is now generally agreed that there are many varieties of goodness, which do not necessarily concur. A classification of current concepts is presented by Table 2.1.

TABLE 2.1 *Classification of well-being concepts*

	Objective well-being	Subjective well-being	Mixed conceptions
Individual well-being			
personal qualities	self-appraisals	
— aspect	Wisdom, stability, hardiness, creativeness, morality, etc.	job satisfaction, self-esteem, control belief	ego strength, identity
— overall	need gratification, self-actualization, effectance	life satisfaction*, contentment, hedonic level.	(mental) health, adjustment, individual morale
Collective	Societal qualities	social (opinion) climate	
— aspect	coherence, justice, equal chances, stability, etc.	acceptance of political order, mutual trust, belief in national progress	social integration, anomy
— overall	viability, capacity	group morale	livability
Mixed conceptions			
— aspects	economic prosperity, safety, freedom, equality, etc.	emancipation	
— overall	welfare, progress	alienation	well-being in broadest sense

*Focus of this article.

In the table some examples are presented in italics. The reader should bear in mind that the enumeration is illustrative rather than exhaustive. Furthermore, most of the terms mentioned are used with other meanings as well and could therefore be classified differently. Elsewhere I have elaborated this classification in more detail (Veenhoven, 1980).

Focus on life satisfaction

This paper will focus on happiness in the sense of life satisfaction. We cannot answer the seven questions for all concepts. Therefore, a choice is required. I choose the overall self-appraisal of life for four reasons: (1) This concept can be fairly precisely defined (see below); (2) the phenomenon thus defined can be measured fairly well (to be demonstrated in the next paragraph); (3) there are empirical data on this matter which allow answers to the questions raised; (4) focusing on an "objective" conception of happiness would involve *a priori* answers to several of the questions under discussion.

Life satisfaction is conceived as the *degree to which an individual judges the overall quality of his life-as-a-whole favourably*. In other words: how well he likes the life he leads. The term "happiness" will be used as a synonym.

Next to this "overall" evaluation, this paper will refer to two aspect appraisals of life-as-a-whole [an affective aspect (hedonic level) and a cognitive aspect (contentment)]. Hedonic level is the degree to which the various affects a person experiences are pleasant; in other words: how well he usually feels. Contentment is the degree to which an individual perceives his aspirations to have been met. In other words: to what extent one perceives oneself to have got what one wants in life. These distinctions will prove fruitful in answering the questions asked here. The concepts are described in more detail in Veenhoven, 1984a, chapter 2.

Can happiness be measured?

During the last century frequent discussions have taken place as to whether happiness can be measured. These debates were part of the discussion about the utilitarian moral philosophy, which required some kind of hedonic book-keeping in order to assess the happiness revenues of alternative courses of action. A great deal of that discussion is not relevant for this paper, because it concerns conceptions other than life-satisfaction.

When happiness polls began to be used during the last few decades, the discussion focused on whether subjective appreciation of life can be assessed validly. The following issues figured in that discussion: (1) Can happiness be measured "objectively" or only "subjectively" by questioning? (2) If questioning is the only way, do interviews tap an existing state of mind or do they merely invite a guess? (3) If people do indeed have an idea about their enjoyment of life, do their responses to questions reflect that idea adequately? These questions have instigated a great deal of empirical research and can now be fairly well answered.

"Measurement" was long understood as "objective", "external" assessment, analogous to the measurement of blood-pressure by a doctor. It is now clear that life satisfaction cannot be measured that way. Steady physiological concomitants have not been discovered and modern insights into the complexity of psycho-physiological interactions do not suggest that they ever will be. Neither have any overt behaviours been found to be linked reliably to inner enjoyment of life. Like all attitudes, happiness is reflected only partly in social behaviour. Though an "active", "outgoing" and "friendly" appearance is more frequent among the happy, it is observed among unhappy persons as well. Even unconscious body language has been found to be only weakly related to the inner appreciation of life (Noelle-Neumann, 1977, p. 244). Consequently, ratings of someone's happiness by his peers or teachers are only weakly related to self-reports (research reviewed in Veenhoven, 1984a, pp. 83–84). The case of suicide was long considered to be an exception. This kind of behaviour was thought to indicate extreme unhappiness. However, the abundant research in that field has made it clear that dissatisfaction with life is at best one of the motives and that there is a great cultural and personal variation in one's capacity to cope with unhappiness, other than by committing suicide.

Assessment by questioning

Inference from overt behaviour being impossible, we must make do with questioning: either direct or indirect and in a personal interview or by an anonymous questionnaire. Great doubts have been expressed about the validity of such self-reports of happiness. However, empirical checks of these suspicions have not revealed great distortions (see Chapter 3 for a different perspective).

One of the doubts raised is that most people would have no opinion at all about their life satisfaction. Answers to questions on that subject would reflect other things: in particular prevailing norms of self presentation. However, people appear quite aware of their enjoyment of life. Eight out of ten Americans think of it once a week or more often (Shaver and Freedman, 1975, p. 70). Consequently, responses on happiness items tend to be prompt, the non-response is low and temporal stability high. Stereotypical responses are not the rule (evidence reviewed in Veenhoven, 1984, pp. 40–42).

It is often claimed that people present themselves happier than—deep in their heart—they know they are. Both ego-defensive and social desirability effects would be involved. This distortion should give itself away in the often observed overrepresentation of "very happy" people, in the fact that most people perceived themselves as happier than average and in the finding that psychosomatic complaints are not uncommon among persons who characterize themselves as being happy. Yet these facts provide no proof. As we will see in the next paragraph, it is quite comprehensible that a positive appreciation of life prevails. There are also reasons why most people could honestly imagine themselves happier than average, and reasons why the presence of psychosomatic complaints does not exclude a positive appreciation of life. The proof of the pudding is a demonstration of distortion itself. Several clinical studies have tried to do so, but failed to find evidence for a general overstatement of happiness (research reviewed in Veenhoven, 1984a, pp. 44–51).

Although there is no proof of systematic desirability distortion, there is evidence that responses to questions on happiness are liable to various situational influences, such as the site of the interview, the interviewer, the weather, one's mood, etc. (see Chapter 3). These differences can be considered as essentially random error, because they tend to disappear in repeated observations of the usual one-time-one-item measurement. More systematic measurement error is involved as well. Responses are influenced by the precise wording of questions, answer formats, sequence of questions and context of the interview (see Strack and Martin, 1987).

Andrews and Whithey (1976, p. 216) estimated that error produces about half the variance in happiness reports. Several reasons for this vulnerability seem to be involved. Firstly, some people may not have a definite opinion in mind and engage in an instant (re)assessment which is then influenced by situational characteristics (see Chapter 3). Secondly, those who do have a definite opinion will mostly hold a rather global idea of how happy they are and will not think in terms of a ten points scale. Hence, their precise score may vary. Thirdly, the process of retrieval involves some uncertainty as well.

Is unhappiness the rule?

Social critics of all times have bemoaned the miseries of life. Most people are believed to be basically dissatisfied and real enjoyment of life is to be projected in past paradise or future utopia. Such claims have always been denounced by optimists but the discussion has always been inconclusive. During the last few decades many surveys have been carried out (see Chapter 13), some drawing on world samples: so is it now finally possible to draw a conclusion?

The first representative surveys were carried out in Western countries and showed an uneven distribution of happy and unhappy citizens: the happy outweighing the unhappy by about 3 to 1. This finding raised much doubt about the validity of survey questions (discussed earlier). Later cross-national studies have reproduced this pattern in less affluent non-Western countries as well, but not in the Third World nations where a large proportion of the population lives at subsistence levels (see Figure 2.1). This latter finding took away many of the validity doubts: a universal tendency to claim happiness in the face of misery is not involved.

Various social critics have discounted such findings as sullen adjustment. Rather than really enjoying their life, people would just give up hope for a

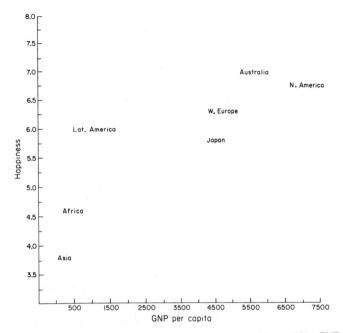

FIG. 2.1. Veenhoven (1984a:149): Happiness in seven parts of the world by GNP per head in 1975.

better one and try to make the best of it (e.g. Ipsen, 1978, p.49). Various defensive strategies would be used for that purpose: simple denial of one's misery; downward comparison (Wills, 1981) and a tendency to see things rosier than they are (Ostroot and Snyder, 1982). This view is supported in experiments suggesting "depressive realism" (Alloy and Abramson, 1979). Two counter-arguments can be mentioned:

(1) Such resignation must give itself away in a discrepancy between the "constructed" judgment of life and "raw" affective experience: in my terms between "overall happiness" and "hedonic level". Hedonic level is less vulnerable to cognitive adaptation, because it is a direct experience and is less open to defensive distortion, because it is less threatening to admit that one feels bad sometimes than to admit to being disappointed in life. Various surveys in Western nations have assessed both overall happiness and hedonic level and found these highly correlated (research reviewed in Veenhoven, 1984a pp. 106–113).[1] Studies focusing on daily variations in mood have also found that pleasant affect dominates unpleasant affect (e.g., Bless and Schwarz, 1984 for a meta-analysis of eighteen studies).

(2) Elaborate comparisons between actual living conditions and subjective appreciation of life have shown that the pattern of high

life satisfaction in the face of relatively bad living conditions is the exception rather than the rule (Glatzer and Zapf, 1984, pp. 282–397).

Together these findings suggest that people tend to enjoy their lives once conditions are not too bad. From an adaptive biological point of view this does not seem strange. Nature is unlikely to have burdened us with characteristic unhappiness, because evolution is unlikely to result in a species that does not fit its characteristic environment subjectively. Like "health", happiness would seem to be a normal condition.

One argument for this latter theory is that happiness has a certain survival value. As we will see in more detail later, enjoyment of life fosters "activity", strengthens "social bonds" and preserves "health".

There is a little evidence for a biological substrate of this capacity for happiness. In the human brain more areas seem to produce positive experiences than negative ones (25 per cent to 5 per cent, according to Fordyce, 1975, p. 191).

The prevalence of satisfaction with life-as-a-whole does not wash away the multitude of suffering and complaints. As noted in the foregoing paragraphs, even the happy are not without complaints. The German Welfare Survey, conducted in 1978, found that half of the "highly satisfied" report frequent worries (Glatzer and Zapf, 1984, p. 180).

If not due to response distortion, what else can explain these anomalies? One first thing to note is that happiness and complaining do not exclude each other logically. One can be fairly satisfied with life as a whole, but still be aware of serious deficits. In fact, both stem from a reflection on life. Secondly, bad feelings and perception of problems may to some extent contribute to overall happiness. Only through realistic acknowledgement of pains can people cope effectively with the problems of life and thereby maintain a positive overall balance.

How do people assess their happiness?

What goes on in people when they evaluate their life? This inner manufacturing of happiness is a subject full of controversies: whether happiness is the product of "thinking" or of "emotion"; whether it is a "state" or a "trait"; whether it results entirely from "comparison" or results from the gratification of "needs", etc. The issue was a major theme in antique philosophy about happiness and enjoys a renewed interest nowadays. It is not just curiosity about the inside of the black box that draws one's attention, but rather the far-reaching consequences of the different points of view. If happiness were indeed to result entirely from comparison, it is likely to be essentially relative and hence insensitive to ameliorations of the (objective) quality of life. A better society will not make happier people. If happiness is a fixed "disposition", efforts to improve living conditions will not contribute to greater enjoyment either. However, if happiness draws on "need satisfaction", there is a point in trying to identify basic human urges and to facilitate their fulfilment. If personal cognitive "constructs" are involved, we might sometimes relieve suffering by changes in thinking.

The discussion has yielded many facts and a lot of theories, which are difficult to oversee. A simple partition may help to sketch the field. Most questions and speculations about the inner fabrication of happiness concern mental processes. Yet it is widely acknowledged that a physical substrate is involved as well. Likewise, most of the discussion focuses on the processes that produce variable states, while there is no doubt that processes of stabilization into traits are involved as well. Together these two distinctions

TABLE 2.2. *Major questions about the inner processing of happiness*

	Substrates	
	Mental	Physical
Assessment of states	1 – emergence of pleasant affect? – comparison processes – striking the balance of life	3 – neuromechanics of pleasant experience – biochemical defects
Stabilization into traits	2 – how stable? – "freezing" and "unfreezing": why, when, how?	4 – humans born for happiness? – temperamental differences? – biochemical imprinting?

produce the four cell scheme in Table 2.2. It allows an ordering of issues, provides a view on current emphasis and may to some extent correspond with the realities involved.

Traditionally, the processes in cell 1 of the scheme have received the most attention, in particular the cognitive processes of comparison and making overall judgments. The growth of cognitive psychology in the last few decades has triggered a great deal of new ideas on these matters. Theories on (social) comparison have been refined and new perspectives have been opened on how people may put things together. Elsewhere I have reviewed current views (Veenhoven, 1989). The mental mechanisms that underlie the emergence of (raw) pleasant affect are still largely a mystery.

Less progress has been made in answering the questions in cell 2. The classical trait-state discussion still drags on: nowadays mostly presented as the bottom-up/top-down controversy. At the empirical level remarkable demonstrations have been provided for both views, yet understanding has advanced little, attention being focused too much on either/or answers.

Consideration of the conditions in which appraisals of life "freeze" and "unfreeze" would seem to be more productive. It could draw on a wide body of knowledge about attitude formation and personality.

The physiology of happiness depicted in cell 3 is still largely terra incognita. In the 1960s the discovery of pleasure centres in the brain seemed to promise a breakthrough (Olds, 1956). That promise has become somewhat bleak by now. There are more than one pleasure centre and their links with thinking and experience remain unclear. Pharmacological research has not yet resulted in great progress either. Various mood elevating chemicals have been identified but their working is only dimly understood.

The issues in cell 4 are generally acknowledged as highly relevant but empirical research on the matter is difficult and expensive. The 1930s witnessed some minor attempts to demonstrate temperamental differences in happiness proneness. In the last decade more serious research has been launched in the related field of depression in the tradition of "biological psychiatry". With the exception of "manic depression", no clear biological basis has been identified as yet.

What conditions favour happiness?

This question lies at the heart of various moral and political debates. What lifestyle is most satisfying in the long run? What society allows the greatest happiness for the greatest number? Scientific answers could provide the consensus ideologists fail to achieve and could legitimize social reform. Although quite relevant, the study of conditions for happiness is still in its infancy. As yet at least one thousand empirical studies have considered the influences between happy and unhappy persons. Elsewhere I have a meta-analysis of part of that research (Veenhoven, 1984a and 1984b). This analysis concerned 245 studies in 32 countries.

At the risk of simplifying too much, one could characterize the results as follows: happy persons are more likely to be found in the economically prosperous countries, where freedom and democracy are held in respect and the political scene is stable. The happy are more likely to be found in majority groups than among minorities and more often at the top of the social ladder than at the bottom. They are typically married and get on well with families and friends. In respect of their personal characteristics, the happy appear relatively healthy, both physically and mentally. They are active and openminded. They feel they are in control of their lives. Their aspirations concern social and moral matters rather than money making. In matter of politics the happy tend to the conservative side of the middle.

Do these findings allow a conclusion in the above mentioned debates? Unfortunately they do not, at least not yet. The following limitations stand in the way: The variables related to happiness as yet are largely easy to measure. Several equally relevant variables are absent: probably because of methodical problems. One such white spot is the "cultural climate" in society: the "meaning" the prevailing belief system provides; the "expression" it allows; the amount of "conformism" it requires, etc. At the individual level we miss data on various antecedents of happiness such as: "style of upbringing" and "stress in early youth".

Most of the studies are simple, correlational ones. The statistical relations they yield can be artifactual. In particular spurious distortion can be involved: e.g. when happiness appears related to income, that may be due to the fact that the happy tend to be better educated, rather than from a genuine effect of income. Only some of the studies have checked such distortions systematically.

Uncertainty about causal effects

Correlates of happiness are generally considered as "causes" of happiness. Yet statistical links can result from reversed effects as well. If happiness appears related to income, this cannot just be interpreted as signifying that a good income contributes to the appreciation of life. Happiness could affect income level as well: e.g. because enjoyment of life stimulates "energy" and "doing". Unravelling causes and effects is difficult and often not feasible. It requires longitudinal and experimental studies, which are rare in this field.

Investigators typically aim at identifying "the" conditions for happiness. However, the assumption of general "laws" is not very fruitful. By bitter experience we have learned that many of the regularities we observe are highly conditional. The field of happiness research is no exception. The best way to identify such contextual variations is to perform large longitudinal and cross-national surveys. A meta-analysis of existing data is a cheap alternative.

Can happiness be raised?

Much of all this consideration of happiness is prompted by the hope of finding ways to a more satisfying life. Traditionally, moral philosophers have sought guidelines at the individual level. Which life goals are most gratifying in the long run? What lifestyle most satisfying? What character tendencies harm happiness, what traits should be cultivated? Currently the emphasis is on the collective level. What should governments do to allow their citizens the best life? What socio-economic and educational policies have the highest happiness revenues?

Yet many people doubt whether happiness levels can be changed at all. This doubt is rooted in the belief that happiness is too variable and elusive to allow manipulation, and in theories about happiness which imply that it cannot be changed anyway.

Can happiness be influenced at all?

Two theories of happiness imply that enduring change is not possible. Attempts to improve happiness would be in vain.

Zero sum?

One theory is that happiness is cyclical: happy periods are always followed by unhappy periods. In the longer run these swings are believed to neutralize each other (zero sum). Hence, attempts to improve happiness may lengthen or heighten a positive swing, but their effect is invariably nullified by a depression soon after. This classic idea has been reinvented by Unger (1970) and figures currently in a psycho-physical form in Solomon's (1980) Opponent-Process Theory. This theory does not apply to happiness as defined here. Observations of mood and life satisfaction across time do not show any cyclical pattern (e.g. Fordyce, 1972, pp. 151–153). Neither has the zero sum prediction been proved true. As we have seen previously, most people feel positive about their life rather than neutral.

Fixed trait?

The other theory is that happiness does not even vary in the short run, but remains the same throughout life. This inertia has been attributed to neurological make up as well as to processes of attitudinal stabilization. The latter view has already been discussed.

As we have seen there, appreciation of life indeed tends to change little through adulthood. Yet high stability observed in most cases does not imply inchangeability at all times. Firstly, we must keep in mind that the investigations concerned elderly populations. Happiness is probably less stable in adolescence and young adulthood, when living conditions are more variable and opinions about life less crystallized. Secondly, various studies have shown that happiness is not left unaffected by major life changes. Thirdly, the investigations figure in a socio-historical context characterized by stability. Things might have been different if a Third World War had taken place in the sixties.

Rather than saying happiness "is" fixed, we should say that it "tends to get" fixed. In adolescence and young adulthood the attitude towards life is likely to be most open to change. In later phases of life it is likely to change only under the pressure of rather drastic life changes, especially if these involve a wider reorientation of the self.

Can happiness be learned?

Since antiquity there have been books on how to become happier. Since the

1970s happiness-trainings have appeared on the scene (*inter alia*, Fordyce, 1977). Both presume that happiness can be learned. A common objection to these practices is that the rather uniform recipes involved do not work, mostly because people are too different. A second objection is that good advice seldom works, people being too inflexible, the unhappy in particular.

Antique moral philosophers mostly recommend a sober and contemplative lifestyle, a positive philosophy of life and a disciplined character. Nowadays, that idea is still held in respect in that various "learned" qualities are believed to predispose one for a happy life. However, current opinion holds that there is no one "ideal" model. Rather, present-day pedagogues, educationalists and therapists emphasize that developmental goals must be tailored to personal preferences and capacities and situational opportunities. Individual trainings are better suited to that purpose than general books of good advice.

Irrespective of these possibilities for individual treatment, there are many learnable qualities that generally predispose one to lead a happy life. "Ignorance", "hate" and "lack of control" will at least reduce chances for gratifying experiences in most cases. Not only does human nature set universal developmental demands (e.g. the innate need for contact requiring sociability), but also general existential conditions (we must all live with others and therefore need capacities to establish stable relations). Empirical identification of such generally useful qualities is possible. As we have seen previously, empirical happiness research has considered various personality and lifestyle variables. Characteristics found over-represented among the happy are: "identity integrity", "ego-strength", "mental maturity", "inner control", "social ability", "activity" and "perceptual openness". Not surprisingly, these characteristics are typical concomitants of mental health, and goals in many psychotherapies.

Antique prescriptions are confirmed in that material aspirations appear under-represented among the happy. However, the classic notion that sober and planned living is most rewarding is not confirmed, nor the idea that intelligence and psychological differentiation favour happiness.

The classical prescriptions for greater happiness by personal improvement presumed "rational" people, who are both willing and able to change themselves. Their critics have argued that stupidity and inflexibility are rather the rule. Moreover, personality building is largely accomplished in early youth within the uncontrollable realm of the family, leaving only marginal room for psychological engineering by formal institutions such as schools and mental health care. Several facts can be introduced to support these arguments: e.g. the earlier mentioned finding that happiness tends to be remarkably stable and the common lamentation that psychotherapy does not work.

There is certainly a great deal of truth in these objections, but the point should not be exaggerated. Firstly, research has shown that special educational programmes can foster the development of desirable characteristics such as self-esteem, autonomy and control. Secondly, psychotherapy has proved to work for at least some kinds of problems. Thirdly, the early socialization in families is not entirely "uncontrolled", but figures in the context of a belief system that is not entirely insensitive to influence.

The proof of the pudding is of course experimental demonstration. During the last decade a few small scale experiments have been reported. Firstly, several experiments checked whether happiness can be raised by the teaching of specific qualities, such as focusing on "satisfying activities" (Reich and Zautra, 1981), "reviewing one's life" (Fergusson, 1980), "assertiveness" (Johnson, 1981) and "cognitive self-control" (Jeziarsky, 1982). The observed effects on happiness are generally small or nonexistent. Secondly, some studies on the effectiveness of general psychotherapy programmes have considered happiness as one of the outcome variables (e.g. Morgan, 1978; O'Dowd, 1978; Naskeff, 1980). Slight positive effects appear. Lastly, two comprehensive attempts to influence happiness by cognitive retraining have been reported (Lichter et al., 1980; Fordyce, 1977). These "happiness courses" required subjects to practice self-suggestion of happiness, to lower their aspirations and to engage more in behaviour already proven to be beneficial, such as socializing. Experimental groups showed improvement in happiness over control groups. None of these follow ups cover more than a few months. Hence, it is not yet clear whether happiness can be boosted permanently in this way.

Can social improvements raise happiness?

The expectation that planned social improvements can raise human happiness is one of the ideological foundations of current welfare states. Yet this idea is subject to much doubt. Sociologists have objected that planned improvement of society is illusional, the political process being irrational (Van Doorn and Schuyt, 1978). Psychologists have added that possible improvements do not materialize in greater satisfaction. Firstly, social "improvements" would be largely irrelevant, happiness drawing on "inner" sources rather than on "outer" ones. Secondly, relevant improvements would often be nullified by social comparison processes. Thirdly, the few possible gains would soon be washed away by the inevitable adjustment of standards. Below I will consider these claims in more detail.

Conditions irrelevant?

Down the ages mystics and ascetics have preached that happiness cannot be found in the outside world, but depends entirely on one's "inner life". Currently this view is echoed in interpretations of modern empirical research, in particular the finding that happiness tends to be quite stable through time and that happiness relates more strongly to psychological variables than to socio-economic ones (as discussed previously).

Yet these results can be interpreted in a different way: as argued earlier, the apparent stability of happiness does not imply that it is entirely insensitive to weal and woe. Further, low correlations with some socio-economic variables do not mean that external conditions are always irrelevant to happiness. As we have seen, bad economic conditions in most African and Asian countries have a devastating effect on happiness. Moreover, there are more "outer" conditions than just "economic affluence" and "social position": the political system under which one lives; macro-cultural traits such as current beliefs and modes of expression; interpersonal networks, etc. These conditions do appear important, the latter in particular. Happiness depends heavily on ties with spouse, family and friends, in Western societies especially (research reviewed in Veenhoven, 1984a, pp. 232–258).

Apart from these empirical proofs to the contrary, the idea that outer conditions do not count must be rejected on other grounds as well: stable attitudes towards life, once established, may be largely insensitive to living conditions, but while being established they clearly depend on them. Likewise, the effect on happiness of "inner" sources such as wisdom and vigour depends largely on their interaction with "outer" variables: they enable the individual to cope more effectively with the problems of life. Again it is also unlikely that the human species could have survived if its happiness were unresponsive to the environment.

Social comparison only?

Another objection is that the appreciation of life would depend on the degree to which one considers oneself to be "better off" than other people. Then all-round improvement would not contribute to happiness: the distance to reference persons would remain the same. Several striking findings have been interpreted as proof of this theory: e.g. the finding that Americans did not become much happier in the post-war decades in spite of a doubling of income per head (Easterlin, 1974) and the observation that seriously handicapped persons maintain a reasonable appreciation of life by comparing themselves to fellow sufferers (Cameron, Van Harck, and Kostin, 1971).

There is little doubt (though no convincing proof) that social comparisons are involved in the evaluation of life, but the available data also make clear that their effect is not all important. Firstly, Michalos (1985) has demonstrated that more standards of comparison are involved than just social ones. In fact, comparisons to other persons appear to be not even the most important standard. Further, there is evidence that they affect happiness only in specific conditions, e.g. when differences are regarded as unjustified (Glatzer and Zapf, 1984, p. 242). Secondly, we have seen earlier that the evaluation of life also draws on affective experience, which is largely dependent on the gratification of basic bio-psychological needs. These needs are essentially non-relative. Consequently, serious deprivations at this level by "war", "hunger" and "social disorganization" do lower the enjoyment of life drastically, notwithstanding the fact that everybody is hurt equally (evidence reviewed in Veenhoven, 1984, p. 400).

As in the above case, one could ask how evolution could possibly have resulted in a way of assessing life that fixes the individual on surpassing his fellow beings rather than focusing the attention on real weal and woe.

Inflation of aspirations?

Another theory implying that happiness is relative holds that we tend to get used to everything. The effects of improvement or deterioration of living conditions on happiness are hence short-lived. This theory was already advocated by the ancient Stoics. Currently, it is phrased in terms of "psycho-physical adaptation level" theory and cognitive "adjustment of aspirations" (Brickman and Campbell, 1971). As in the above case, several remarkable findings have been presented in support of this theory: the fact that lottery winners appear to be hardly happier than average; and the observation that quadriplegics tend to become reconciled to their fate (Brickman et al., 1978, pp. 917–927).

Yet again it is obvious that humans cannot adjust to any situation. Like the "absolute thresholds" in psycho-physics there are "minimum levels" of need gratification. A few anomalies apart, nobody can adjust to "starvation", "loneliness" and "injustice".

In summary, there is sense in trying to improve human happiness. Better living conditions and wiser, more sensible living can contribute to more enjoyment in life. Though not all recipes work, many improvements are possible. The challenge for future research is not to question the obvious any longer, but to find out which improvements promise the greatest yields.

Should happiness be promoted?

If happiness levels can be raised, should they be raised? For the nineteenth-century Utilitarian social philosophers this question did not exist. Their moral axiom was that happiness is the greatest good and that we should promote it as much as possible (Greatest Happiness Principle). Yet there have always been philosophies that idealized suffering and questioned the desirability of life satisfaction.

For a long time such issues were largely a matter of conviction, value priorities being beyond discussion. However, as we get a better view of the reality consequences of various values, we become more aware of incompatibilities with other values we endorse. As a result, we are now better able to predict which mix of values promises the most results. Calculating ideological programmes on the basis of empirically verified information about reality consequences is in its infancy. Bay's (1965) study about the effect of and the preconditions for various sorts of "freedom" provides an encouraging example. Let us follow that lead and consider the consequences of promoting happiness. Will happiness contribute to other values such as "peace", "wisdom" and "morality" or will undesirable effects prevail (egotism, apathy)?

Presumed consequences of happiness

Traditionally, anti-hedonists have argued that enjoyment of life has adversive consequences and thereby destroys itself in the long run. Happiness is said to lead to "apathetic easy going" and "irresponsible optimism", thus ringing in economical and political decline. Happiness is also expected to give way to "individualism" and "egotism", which weaken moral consciousness and disrupt social bonds. Another objection is that the social technology needed to bring about public happiness will bring us a "Brave New World".

On the other hand, several traditions in modern psychology predict positive effects: humanist psychologists believe that happiness frees the way to "active involvement", "creativity" and "better personal relations". Current stress theory holds that positive attitudes such as happiness "buffer" the impact of negative life events. Similarly, an accepted view in psychosomatic theory is that chronic dissatisfaction increases vulnerability to disease and premature death!

Observed effects

As yet no empirical investigations have focused on consequences of happiness. Nevertheless, some indications can be found in the results of a few longitudinal investigations on life satisfaction and experimental studies on mood. These results suggest that a positive appreciation of life tends to broaden perception rather than paralyse it, to encourage active living rather than induce apathy and to foster social contact rather than lead to selfish individualism. There are strong indications that happiness fosters health and even lengthens lives somewhat (research reviewed in Veenhoven, 1988).

These findings do not conclude the whole discussion of whether happiness should be promoted or not; they simply do away with the argument that happiness is harmful.

Conclusions

Centuries of thought about happiness have not been without effect: we are now closer to an answer to seven longstanding questions:

1. Major progress has been made in the conceptualization of happiness. We are now more aware of the varieties of well-being. This enables more precise observation and consideration of the variable under discussion: i.e. life satisfaction.
2. The invention of survey research has allowed the quantitative measurement of life satisfaction. Though not very precise, current interview techniques seem to measure happiness reasonably validly.
3. We are now able to answer the longstanding question of whether people are characteristically dissatisfied or not. Positive appreciation of life appears to be the rule.
4. In spite of great advances, we are largely in the dark about how people make up their mind about their life-as-a-whole. Various plausible theories have been proposed about the cognitive processes involved. The origins of affective experience are still mysterious as we do not know much about the neural physiology of happiness either. The promising issue of "freezing" and "unfreezing" of attitudes towards life has hardly been explored at all.
5. In spite of a wealth of correlational research, we know very little about the conditions that foster a positive appreciation of life. What is lacking are follow up studies that can demonstrate causal effects and meta-analyses that show variations across time and culture. For the time being, it seems that people feel at their best when they live in a free, affluent and peaceful society, when they are part of an intimate network and are physically and mentally healthy.
6. Current evidence does not support the old idea that happiness levels cannot be raised permanently. Happiness is not a zero sum matter, nor a fixed trait, nor entirely relative. Planned promotion of the general public happiness is possible in principle.
7. There is no evidence for the idea that happiness is harmful. Happiness does not numb or lead to apathy. Rather, it seems to activate people, to foster social contacts and to benefit health. Therefore, happiness is a matter worth promoting.

References

ALLOY, L.B. and ABRAMSON, L.Y. Judgments of contingency in depressed and non-depressed students. Sadder but wiser?, *Journal of Experimental Psychology-General*, 1979; **108**, 441-485.

ANDREWS, F. M. and WITHEY, S.B. *Social Indicators of Well-being*, New York: Plenum Press, 1976.

BARROW, R. *Happiness*, Oxford: Robertson, 1980.

BAY, C. *The structure of freedom*, California: Stanford University Press, 1965.

BLESS, H. and SCHWARZ, N. *Ist schlechte Stimmung die Ausnahme? Eine Meta-Analyse von Stimmungsuntersuchungen*, University of Heidelberg, unpublished paper, 1984.

BRICKMAN, P. and CAMPBELL, D.T. *Hedonic relativism and planning in the good society*, London: Academic Press, 1971.

BRICKMAN, P., COATES, D. D. and JANOFF–BULMAN, R. Lottery winners and accident victims: is happiness relative? *Journal of Personality and Social Psychology*, 1978 **36**, (8), 917–927.

CAMERON, P., VAN HARCK, D., WEISS, N. and KOSTIN, M. Happiness or life-satisfaction of the malformed. *Proceedings of the 79th Annual Convention*, 1971 **6**, (2), 641–642.

DIENER, E. and LARSEN, R.J. Temporal stability and cross-situational consistence of affective behavioral and cognitive responses. *Journal of Personality and Social Psychology*, 1984 **4**, 871–883.

DODGE, R. *Autobiography*, Worcester: Clark University Press, 1930, pp. 99–121.

VAN DOORN, J.A.A. and SCHUYT, C.J.M. (eds.), *De stagnerende verzorgingsstaat*. Assen: Boom, 1978.

EASTERLIN, R.A. *Does economic growth improve the human lot? Some empirical evidence*. California: Stanford University Press, 1974.

FERGUSSON, J.D. *Reminiscence counseling to increase psychological well-being of elderly women in nursing homes*. Unpublished dissertation, University of South Carolina, Columbia, 1980.

FORDYCE, M.W. *Happiness, its daily variation and its relation to values*. California: United States International University, 1972.

FORDYCE, M.W. *What psychologists know about your personal happiness*. Unpublished manuscript, 1975.

FORDYCE, M.W. Development of a program to increase personal happiness. *Journal of Counseling Psychology*, 1977; **24** (6), pp. 511–521.

FREEDMAN, J. and SHAVER, P. What makes you happy-Questionnaire. *Psychology Today*, 1975; **9** (5), pp. 66–72.

GLATZER, W. *Lebenszufriedenheit und alternative Masse subjektiven Wohlbefindens*. Frankfurt: Campus Verlag, 1984.

GLATZER, W and ZAPF, W. *Lebensqualität in der Bundesrepublik: Objektive Lebensbedingungen und subjektives Wohlbefinden*. Frankfurt: Campus Verlag, 1984.

IPSEN, D. Das Konstrukt Zufriedenheit. *Soziale Welt*, 1978; **29**, (1), pp. 44–53.

JEZIARSKI, R.M. *The effects of a cognitive self-control treatment and its components on depression, locus of control and general morale in the elderly*. Unpublished doctoral dissertation, University of San Francisco, California, 1982.

JOHNSON, P.D. *Effects of increased personal and interpersonal control upon the well-being of institutionalized geriatrics*. Unpublished doctoral dissertation, Arizona State University, Arizona, 1981.

LEVENKRON, J.C., COHEN, J.D., MUELLER, H.S. and FISHER, E.B. Modifying the Type-A coronary-prone behaviour pattern. *Journal of Consulting and Clinical Psychology*, 1967: **51**, pp. 192–204.

LICHTER, S., HAYE, K. and KAMMANN, R. Increasing happiness through cognitive retraining. *New Zealand Psychologist*, 1980; **9**, pp. 57–64.

MCKENNEL, A. Cognition and affect in perceptions of well-being. *Social Indicators Research*, 1978; **5**, pp. 389–426.

MCKENNEL, A. *Cognition and affect in judgement of subjective well-being*. Institute for Social Research, London, unpublished paper, 1973.

MICHALOS, A.C. Multiple Discrepancy Theory. *Social Indicators Research*, 1985: **16**, pp. 347–413.

MORGAN, J. *The effect of insight-oriented group therapy and task-oriented group-therapy on coping style and life satisfaction of nursinghome elderly*. Unpublished doctoral dissertation, University of Maryland, Maryland, 1978.

NASKEFF, A.A. 1980, *The effect of group therapy on affective states, social distance, interpersonal locus of control, life satisfaction and word behavior among institutionalized aged*. Unpublished doctoral dissertation, University of Toronto, Toronto.

NOELLE–NEUMANN, E. Politik und Glück. In H. Baier (Ed.), *Freiheit und Sachzwang*, pp. 208–262, 1977.

O'DOWD, L.A. *An investigation of the effectiveness of counseling technique employed with elderly clients*. Unpublished doctoral dissertation, Wayne State University, Michigan, 1978.

OLDS, J. Pleasure centers in the brain. *Scientific American*, 1956; **193**, pp. 105–116.

OSTROOT, N., SHIN, and SNYDER, W. Quality of life perceptions in two cultures. *Social Indicators Research*, 1982; **11**, pp. 113–138.

REICH, J.W. and ZAUTRA, A. Life events and personal causation: some relationships with satisfaction and distress. *Journal of Psychology and Social Psychology*, 1981: **41**, (5), pp. 1002–1012.

SOLOMON, R.L. The opponent-process theory of acquired motivation: the costs of pleasure and the benefits of pain. *American Psychologist*, 1980; **35**, pp. 691–712.

STRACK, F. and MARTIN, L.L. Thinking, judging and communicating: A process account of context effects in attitude surveys. In: H. J. Hippler, N. Schwarz and S. Sudman (eds.), *Social information processing and survey methodology*, New York: Springer, 1987.

UNGER, H.E. The feeling of happiness. *Psychology*, 1970; **7**, (1), pp. 27–33.

VEENHOVEN, R. *Wat heet welzijn?* Unpublished working paper, Erasmus University, Rotterdam, 1980.

VEENHOVEN, R. *Conditions of happiness*. Dordrecht and Boston: Reidel, 1984a.

VEENHOVEN, R. *Databook of happiness*. Dordrecht and Boston: Reidel, 1984b.

VEENHOVEN, R. The utility of happiness. *Social Indicators Research*, 1986; **20**, p. 333–4.

VEENHOVEN, R. *Striking the balance of life*. Unpublished paper, Erasmus University, Rotterdam, 1989.

WILLS, T.A. Downward comparison principles in social psychology. *Psychological Bulletin*, 1981: **92**, (2), pp. 245–271.

Notes

1. Still there are discrepancies that are worth studying. Current attempts to do so are hindered by inept indicators (e.g. McKennel, 1978).

3

Evaluating one's life: a judgment model of subjective well-being

NORBERT SCHWARZ and FRITZ STRACK

Introduction

Much of what we know about individuals' subjective well-being is based on the findings of a great number of representative surveys that asked respondents to report how happy and satisfied they are with their life-as-a-whole and with various life domains (see Chapters 2 and 13). These so-called *subjective social indicators* are used in social science research as measures of the subjective quality of life to supplement measures of the objective standard of living, which have dominated welfare research in the social sciences for a long time.

As Angus Campbell (1981, p. 23), one of the pioneers of subjective social indicator research, points out, the "use of these measures is based on the assumption that all the countless experiences people go through from day to day add to . . . global feelings of well-being, that these feelings remain relatively constant over extended periods, and that people can describe them with candor and accuracy." As this research progressed, however, it became increasingly obvious that these assumptions are highly problematic. In particular, the relationship between individuals' experiences and objective conditions of life and their subjective sense of well-being was found to be weak and sometimes counterintuitive. Most objective life circumstances account for less than 5 per cent of the variance in measures of subjective well-being, and the combination of the circumstances in a dozen domains of life does not account for more than 10 per cent (Kammann, 1982). Some dramatic examples from various domains of life include that poor people are sometimes happier than rich ones (Easterlin, 1974), that patients three years after a cancer operation were happier than a healthy control group (Irwin, Allen, Kramer and Danoff, 1982), or that paralysed accident victims were happier with their life than one might expect on the basis of the event (Brickman *et al.*, 1978). These examples, and additional ones from other life domains, provide drastic illustrations inconsistent with a simple and straightforward relationship between external conditions and internal state.

Moreover, measures of well-being have been shown to have a low test-retest reliability, usually hovering around .40, and not exceeding .60 when the same question is asked twice during the same one hour interview (Glatzer, 1984). In addition, these measures were found to be quite sensitive to influences from preceding questions in a questionnaire or interview (Schuman and Presser, 1981).

A judgmental perspective

While these findings have been deplored by researchers who consider subjective social indicators to reflect rather stable inner states of the respondents (e.g. Campbell, 1981), they are less of a surprise to researchers in the area of social judgment. From this perspective, reports about happiness and satisfaction with one's life are not necessarily valid read-outs of an internal state of personal well-being. Rather, they are judgments which, like other social judgments, are subject to a variety of transient influences. As Sherman and Corty (1984) noted, judgments which researchers ask respondents to make "don't passively tap into or elicit thoughts that are already in the subject's head". Rather, "it is often the case that the judgment is developed at the time the question is asked. Whatever information is available at the time and whatever principle of judgment happens to be employed will determine the nature of the judgment. Many judgments can thus be considered constructions to a particular question posed at a particular time", rather than reflections of underlying stable attributes of the respondent (p. 218).

During recent years, we have applied this perspective to explore how individuals evaluate their subjective well-being. In this research we have not been interested in *what* makes a person happy, but rather in *how* people determine whether they are happy or not. From a "social cognition" perspective (cf. Bodenhausen and Wyer, 1987; or Strack, 1988, for general introductions), we investigated the mechanisms of information processing that result in the reports economists and sociologists use as subjective social indicators.

Accessibility of information

Which information is considered?

How do respondents go about it if they are asked "How are you?" or, more technically, "Taking all things together, how would you say things are these days? Would you say you are very happy, pretty happy, not too happy?".

Unfortunately, "taking all things together" is a difficult mental task. In fact, as an instruction to think about all aspects of one's life, it requests something impossible from the respondent. How can a person conduct a complete review of "things these days", particularly in a survey interview in which the average time to answer a question is frequently less than one minute (Groves and Kahn, 1979)? Therefore, the person will certainly not think about all aspects but probably about some of them. The question is: about which?

One of the most central principles in social cognition research predicts that it is the most accessible information that enters into the judgment. Individuals rarely retrieve all the information that potentially bears on a judgment, but truncate the search process as soon as enough information has come to mind to form the judgment with a reasonable degree of subjective certainty (cf. Wyer, 1980; Bodenhausen and Wyer, 1987; Higgins and King, 1981, for reviews). Accordingly, the judgment reflects the implications of the information that comes to mind most easily. One determinant of the accessibility of information is the frequency and recency with which it is used. Applied to judgments of subjective well-being, prior use of relevant information may increase the likelihood that this information enters into the happiness judgment.

This reasoning was tested in a study in which we manipulated the accessibility of relevant information. We asked people to think about their present life and asked them to write down three events that were either particularly positive and pleasant or were particularly negative and unpleasant (Strack, Schwarz and Gschneidinger, 1985, Exp. 1). This was done under the pretext of collecting life events for a life event inventory, and the dependent variables, among them "happiness" and "satisfaction", were said to be assessed in order to "find the best response scales" for that instrument.

As predicted, subjects who had previously been induced to think about positive aspects of their present life described themselves as happier and more satisfied with their life-as-a-whole than subjects who had been induced to think about negative aspects.

In another study (Strack, Martin and Schwarz, 1988), the same idea was tested with a somewhat more subtle priming manipulation. Respondents were led to think about a relevant life domain simply by asking a specific question before they had to report their general happiness. Generating an answer should render this specific information more accessible for subsequent use and therefore influence the judgment. In this study, we asked

American students how frequently they go out for a date, which is known to be relevant to general happiness for that population (Emmons and Diener, 1985). We asked the dating question either before or after the general happiness question and assumed that the correlation between the two measures would be increased if the specific question was asked first. Empirically, this was the case. When the general happiness question was asked prior to the dating frequency question, both measures correlated $r = -.12$; a correlation that is not significantly different from zero. Asking the general happiness question after the dating frequency question, however, increased the correlation to $r = .66, p < .001$ ($z = 5.04, p < .001$ for the difference in the correlations obtained under both conditions). We would obviously draw very different conclusions about the impact of dating frequency on happiness with one's life, depending on the order in which the two questions are asked.

Taken together, these findings indicate that it is not sufficient to experience positive and negative events, it is also necessary that these experiences are cognitively accessible at the time of the happiness report. And whether they are accessible or not may depend on transient influences, such as the nature of the preceding questions in a research interview.

Is accessible information always used?

Accessible information is not always used in forming a judgment. Rather, the communicative context of a conversation or a research interview may induce individuals to disregard highly accessible information under some conditions. One of the key norms of social discourse holds that speakers should be informative and should avoid redundancy (Grice, 1975). In particular, speakers are expected to provide information that is "new", and should not provide information that the listener already has. This principle is known in psycholinguistics as the "given-new contract" (cf. Clark, 1985), and can be fruitfully applied to survey situations as suggested by Strack and Martin (1987; see also Schwarz and Strack, 1988).

* As an example, consider the following question/answer sequences:

Conversation A
    Q: How is your family?
    A: . . . . . .
Conversation B
    Q: How is your wife?
    A: . . . .
    Q: And how is your family?
    A: . . .

While the question about the well-being of the family includes the well-being of the wife in *Conversation A*, this is not the case in *Conversation B*.

In the latter case, the question about the family refers to the well-being of the remaining members of the family because information about the well-being of the wife was already "given" in response to the previous question.

The same given-new principle was found to underlie the use and disuse of information when forming a judgment. Above, we reported an experiment in which asking respondents about their dating frequency, prior to assessing their happiness with life-as-a-whole, dramatically increased the impact of dating frequency on reported subjective well-being, as shown in Table 3.1 (Strack *et al.*, 1988).

TABLE 3.1. *Correlations between "general happiness" and "frequency of dating"*

Control	"Priming"	"Conversation"
general dating	dating general	dating general + context
$r = -.12$	$r = .66$	$r = .15$

Note: $N = 60$/cell. a vs. b: $p < .001$; b vs. c: $p < .001$; a vs. c: $p > .05$.
Adapted from Strack, F., Martin, L. L. and Schwarz, N. Priming and communication: Social determinants of information use in judgments of life satisfaction. *European Journal of Social Psychology*, 1988; **18**, 429–442. Reprinted by permission.

While this question order effect indicated that respondents were more likely to consider their dating behaviour in evaluating their lives when information about dating was activated by the preceding question than when it was not, another condition of this experiment demonstrated that this is not always the case. For some subjects, we attempted to place the dating question and the happiness question into the same communicative context. This was accomplished by a lead-in that read, "Now we would like to learn about two areas of life that may be important for people's overall well-being." This introduction was followed by the same questions that were used in the other conditions of the study, namely "(a) How often do you normally go out on a date? (b) How happy are you with your life in general?"

As is shown in Table 3.1, placing the dating and happiness questions into the same communicative context, resulted in a dramatic decrease in the correlation, as compared with the same question order without the above lead-in. In fact, establishing one communicative context for both questions completely eliminated the impact of question order. This suggests that respondents who were asked the dating question prior to the happiness question were not more likely to consider their dating frequency in evaluating their life, despite its high accessibility, than respondents for whom the accessibility of dating information was not increased to begin with.

In summary, this and related findings (cf. Strack, Martin and Schwarz, 1987, 1988; Ottati *et al*., in press) demonstrate that highly accessible information will not be used in forming subsequent judgments if it is already "given", because the norms that govern the conduct of conversation request speakers to be informative and to avoid redundancy.

How is accessible information used?

We now need to consider *how* individuals use accessible information, if they do so. In the preceding examples, the accessible information provided the basis of the judgment and influenced the answer in the direction of the valence of the experience. This, however, is not necessarily the case. There are conditions under which accessible information influences the judgment in the opposite direction.

In the first study mentioned above (Strack *et al*., 1985, Exp. 1), not only the hedonic quality of the life event was varied, but also the time perspective. Some participants had to think about a recent event, others, however, about an event that had occurred several years ago. The consequences were quite different, as is shown in Table 3.2.

TABLE 3.2. *Subjective well-being: the impact of valence of event and time perspective*

Time perspective	Valence of event	
	Positive	Negative
Present	8.9	7.1
Past	7.5	8.5

Note: Mean score of happiness and satisfaction questions, range is 1 to 11, with higher values indicating reports of higher well-being.

Adapted from Experiment 1 of Strack, F., Schwarz, N. and Gschneidinger, E. Happiness and reminiscing: The role of time perspective, mood, and mode of thinking. *Journal of Personality and Social Psychology*, 1985; **49**, 1460–1469. Reprinted by permission.

Thinking about hedonically relevant past events did not only fail to influence well-being judgments in the direction of their valence, but actually had a reverse impact. Respondents who thought about a negative past event reported higher well-being than respondents who thought about a positive past event ($F(1,48) = 8.42, p < .005$ for the interaction of valence of event and time perspective).

In combination, these findings indicate that highly accessible information will influence the judgment in the direction of its hedonic quality, resulting in assimilation effects, if it pertains directly to one's present living conditions. If the accessible information bears on one's previous living conditions, on the other hand, it will serve as a salient standard of comparison, resulting in contrast effects (see Chapter 6).

These experimental results are further supported by correlational data (Elder, 1974) that indicate for senior US citizens, that the "children of the great depression" are more likely to report high subjective well-being, the more they had to suffer under adverse economic conditions when they were adolescents. The cumulation of negative experiences during childhood and adolescence apparently established a baseline against which all subsequent events could only be seen as an improvement (cf. Filipp, 1982). Portraying the other side of the coin, Runyan (1980) found that the upwardly mobile recollected their childhood as less satisfying than did the downwardly mobile, presumably because they used their current situation in evaluating their past.

While the above findings bear on the impact of temporal distance of the event *per se*, subsequent research (Strack, Schwarz and Nebel, 1987) demonstrated that it is not temporal distance by itself that moderates the use of accessible information but rather the subjective perception of whether the event one thinks about pertains to one's current conditions of living or to a different episode of one's life. Specifically, we asked students to describe either a positive or a negative event that they expected to occur in "five years from now". For half of the sample, we emphasized a major role transition that would occur in the meantime, namely leaving university and entering the job market. Theoretically, this should increase the probability that respondents would assign the expected event to a "different" phase of their life, and would therefore use it as a standard of comparison. The results support this reasoning. When the role transition was *not* emphasized, subjects reported higher happiness and life satisfaction when they had to describe positive rather than negative expectations. When the role transition *was* emphasized, this pattern was reversed, and subjects reported higher well-being after thinking about negative rather than positive future expectations.

In summary, these findings indicate that the impact of an event depends upon whether or not the event is cognitively accessible at the time of judgment. Moreover, the direction of its impact depends on whether the event is perceived to bear on one's current situation or is assigned to a different phase of one's life. In the former case, the accessible information will result in assimilation effects, but in the latter, it will serve as a standard of comparison, resulting in contrast effects (see also Chapter 6). Accordingly, it is not surprising that the overall relationship between objective conditions of living and subjective well-being is weak: the same event may influence subjective well-being in opposite directions, depending on its perceived "distance" to one's current situation.

Social comparison processes

All of the preceding examples pertained to the use of accessible information about one's own life. However, the same principle of accessibility applies to the use of information about the living conditions of others. Much as the subjects in the above experiments used highly accessible information about their own previous experiences as a standard of comparison, subjects were also found to use salient information about others as a comparison standard. Accordingly, they evaluated their own life more favourably when they were exposed to a description of past adverse living conditions in their hometown (Dermer *et al.*, 1979), met a handicapped confederate (Strack, Schwarz, Chassein, Kern and Wagner, in press, Exp. 2), or listened to a confederate who described how a severe medical condition interferes with his enjoyment of life (Strack *et al.*, in press, Exp. 1). In the latter study, the impact of the confederate's description was found to be more pronounced when the seating arrangements rendered the confederate visible at the time of the later happiness report, than when they did not, a finding that further emphasizes the role of temporary accessibility in the choice of comparison standards.

However, respondents' choice of comparison standards is not only affected by their exposure to the rather extreme living conditions of others. Rather, subtle variations in question form, that frequently go unnoticed in survey research, may also exert a profound influence on respondents' judgments. Frequently, social researchers attempt to assess respondents' experiences, their objective conditions of living, or the frequency with which they engage in a certain behaviour, by asking them to check the proper alternative from the list of response alternatives provided for them. While researchers assume that the respondents' answers inform them about the respondents' behaviours or experiences, they frequently overlook that the list of response alternatives may also constitute a source of information for the respondent.

As a number of studies indicated (see Schwarz, 1988a, in press a; Schwarz and Hippler, 1987, for a review), respondents assume that the list of response alternatives designed to assess their behavioural frequency reflects the researcher's knowledge of the distribution of the behaviour. That is, they assume that the "average" or "usual" behavioural frequency is represented by values in the middle range of the scale, and that the extreme values of the scale reflect the extremes of the distribution. Accordingly, they use the range of the response alternatives as a frame of reference in estimating their own behavioural frequency. Moreover, they extract comparison information from their own location on the scale for use in subsequent comparative judgments.

A study on leisure time satisfaction illustrates this phenomenon (Schwarz, Hippler, Deutsch and Strack, 1985). In this study, we asked respondents to report their daily TV consumption in an open answer format or on one of the two scales that are shown in Table 3.3, along with respondents' behavioural reports.

TABLE 3.3. *Reported daily TV consumption and leisure time satisfaction as a function of response alternatives*

Low frequency alternatives		High frequency alternatives	
Up to ½ h	11.5%	Up to 2½ h	70.4%
½ h to 1 h	26.9%	2½ h to 3 h	22.2%
1 h to 1½ h	26.9%	3 h to 3½ h	7.4%
1½ h to 2 h	26.9%	3½ h to 4 h	0.0%
2 h to 2½ h	7.7%	4 h to 4½ h	0.0%
More than 2½ h	0.0%	More than 4½ h	0.0%
Leisure time satisfaction	9.6		8.2

Note: N = 79.
   Leisure time satisfaction was assessed as an 11-point bipolar scale (I = very dissatisfied, I wish there were more variety, II = very satisfied, I don't want more variety).
   Adapted from Experiment 2 of Schwarz, N., Hippler, H. J., Deutsch, B. and Strack, F. Response scales: Effects of category range on reported behaviour and comparative judgments. *Public Opinion Quarterly*, 1985; **49**, 388–395. Reprinted by permission.

As expected, the range of the response alternatives affected respondents' reports. More respondents reported watching TV for more than 2½ hours per day when given the high than when given the low frequency range scale (cf. Schwarz and Bienias, in press, for a fuller analysis of the underlying processes). More germane to the present issue, respondents extracted comparison information from their own placement on the scale. Given a modal daily TV consumption of slightly more than 2 hours in the Federal Republic of Germany (Darschin and Frank, 1982), many respondents endorsed a value in the lower range of the high frequency scale, suggesting to them that they watch *less* TV than "usual". Accordingly, respondents who reported their TV consumption on the high frequency scale subsequently evaluated their satisfaction with the variety of things they do in their leisure time more favourably than respondents who reported their TV consumption on the low frequency scale. Respondents who provided their reports in an open answer format, which does not provide relevant comparison information, reported intermediate satisfaction.

In combination, these findings indicate that the use of comparison standards follows the same principle of cognitive accessibility as the use of other information (for additional findings see Schwarz and Scheuring, 1988, 1989). Most notably, the selection of comparison standards is not primarily determined by relatively stable attributes of the respondent, which may be expected to change only slowly over time, such as his or her orientation at an enduring reference group (e.g. Hyman and Singer, 1968; Runciman, 1966), adaptation level (e.g. Brickman and Campbell, 1971), or aspiration level (e.g. Michalos, 1985)—contrary to what sociological theorizing would suggest.

The impact of mood states

So far, we considered which information respondents use to evaluate their well-being, and how they use it. However, judgments of well-being are not only a function of what one thinks about, but also of how one feels at the time of judgment (see also Chapter 7). As we are all aware, there are days when life seems just great and others when life seems rather dreadful, even though nothing of any obvious importance has changed in the meantime. Rather, it seems that minor events that may affect our moods may greatly influence how we evaluate our life. Not surprisingly, experimental data confirm these experiences. Thus, we found that finding a dime on a copy machine greatly increased subjects' reported happiness with their life-as-a-whole (Schwarz, 1983), as did receiving a chocolate bar (Münkel, Strack and Schwarz, 1987), spending time in a pleasant rather than an unpleasant room (Schwarz, Strack, Kommer and Wagner, 1987, Exp. 2), or watching the German soccer team win rather than lose a championship game (Schwarz *et al.*, 1987, Exp. 1).

Mood congruent recall or mood as information?

The psychologically interesting question is how the impact of mood at the time of judgment is mediated. Two possible processes deserve particular attention. On the one hand, it has been shown that moods increase the accessibility of mood congruent information in memory (cf. Blaney, 1986; Bower, 1981; Isen, 1984 for reviews). That is, individuals in a good mood are more likely to recall positive information from memory, whereas individuals in a bad mood are more likely to recall negative information. Thus, thinking about one's life while being in a good mood may result in a selective retrieval of positive aspects of one's life, and, therefore, in a more positive evaluation.

On the other hand, the impact of moods may be more direct. People may assume that their momentary well-being at the time of judgment is a reasonable and parsimonious indicator of their well-being in general. Thus, they may base their evaluation of their life-as-a-whole on their feelings at the time of judgment and may evaluate their well-being more favourably when they feel good rather than bad. In doing so, lay people may follow the same logic as psychologists who assume that one's mood represents the global overall state of the organism (e.g. Ewert, 1983) and reflects all the countless experiences one goes through in life (e.g. Bollnow, 1956). According to this perspective, which has a long tradition in European phenomenological psychology, our moods are an integrative function of all the experiences we have. If people share this perspective, they may evaluate their life on the basis of their mood at the time of judgment, a strategy that would greatly reduce the complexity of the judgmental task.

In fact, when people are asked how they decide whether they are happy or not, most of them are likely to refer explicitly to their current affect state, saying, for example, "Well, I feel good". Accordingly, Ross, Eyman and Kishchuk (1986) report that explicit references to one's affective state accounted for 41 per cent to 53 per cent of the reasons that various samples of adult Canadians provided for their reported well-being, followed by future expectations (22 per cent to 40 per cent), past events, (5 per cent to 20 per cent), and social comparisons (5 per cent to 13 per cent).

We conducted a number of laboratory and field experiments to explore the judgmental processes that underlie the impact of respondents' current mood on reported well-being: Is the impact of moods mediated by mood congruent recall from memory or by the use of one's mood itself as an informational basis? In one of these studies (Schwarz and Clore, 1983, Exp. 2), we called respondents on sunny or rainy days and assessed their well-being in telephone interviews. As expected, respondents reported being in a better mood, and being happier and more satisfied with their life-as-a-whole, on sunny than on rainy days.

To test the hypothesis that the impact of mood on reported well-being is due to respondents' use of their perceived mood as a piece of information, some respondents were induced to attribute their current mood to a transient external source which was irrelevant to the evaluation of one's life. If respondents attribute their current feelings to transient external factors, they should be less likely to use them as an informational basis for evaluating their well-being in general, and the impact of subjects' current mood should be greatly reduced. In the weather study, this was accomplished by directing subjects' attention to the weather. In one condition, the interviewers pretended to call from out of town and asked, "By the way, how's the weather down there?". With this manipulation, we wanted to suggest to respondents that their mood may be due to the weather and may therefore not be diagnostic for the quality of their life. What we wanted to suggest to respondents in a very indirect way is, "Don't worry about it, everybody feels lousy these days."

Table 3.4 shows the results. While good or bad weather resulted in a pronounced difference in reported well-being when the weather was *not* mentioned, this difference was eliminated when respondents' attention was directed to the weather as an irrelevant external source of their current mood.

TABLE 3.4. *The informative function of mood*

	Weather	
	Not mentioned	Mentioned
Differences due to weather	2.1	0.2

Note: The difference in well-being (mean score of happiness and satisfaction; range is 1–10; 10 = high well-being) reported on sunny and rainy days is presented.

Adapted from Experiment 2 of Schwarz, N. and Clore, G. L. Mood, misattribution, and judgments of well-being: Informative and directive functions of affective states. *Journal of Personality and Social Psychology*, 1983; **45**, 513–523. Reprinted by permission.

In addition, a measure of current mood, assessed at the end of the interview, was not affected by the attention manipulation, which suggests that the manipulation did not affect respondents' current mood itself but only their inferences based upon it. Accordingly, the mood measure was more strongly correlated with reported well-being when the weather was *not* mentioned than when it was mentioned.

In summary, these results (which have been replicated in a laboratory experiment; Schwarz and Clore, 1983, Exp. 1) demonstrate that respondents use their affective state at the time of judgment as a parsimonious indicator of their well-being in general, unless the informational value of their current mood is called into question. Moreover, the discounting effects obtained in the present study, as well as in our follow-ups, rules out an alternative explanation based on mood-congruent retrieval. According to this hypothesis, respondents may recall more negative information about their life when in a bad rather than a good mood, and may therefore base their evaluation on a selective sample of data. Note, however, that the impact of a selective data base should be independent of respondents' attributions for their current mood. Attributing one's current mood to the weather only discredits the informational value of one's current mood itself, but not the evaluative implications of any positive or negative events one may recall. Inferences based on selective recall should therefore be unaffected by salient explanations for one's current feelings. Thus, the present data demonstrates that moods themselves may serve informative functions. This hypothesis has meanwhile received considerable support in different domains of judgment (cf. Schwarz, 1987, 1988b; Schwarz and Clore, 1988; Schwarz, Servay and Kumpf, 1985), and has provided a coherent framework for conceptualizing the impact of affective states on cognitive processes (Schwarz, in press b).

When do people rely on their mood rather than other information?

So far, we have seen that individuals may evaluate their well-being on the basis of comparison processes or on the basis of their affective state at the time of judgment. This raises the question under which conditions they will rely on one rather than the other source of information.

General life satisfaction versus specific life domains

On theoretical grounds, we may assume that people are more likely to use the simplifying strategy of consulting their affective state, the more burdensome the judgment would be to make on the basis of comparison information. After all, humans have frequently been shown to be "cognitive misers" (Taylor, 1981) who prefer simple strategies to more complex ones whenever they are available. In this regard, it is important to note a basic difference between judgments of happiness and satisfaction with one's life-as-a-whole versus judgments of specific life domains. Evaluations of general life satisfaction pose an extremely complex task that requires a large number of comparisons along many dimensions with ill-defined criteria and the subsequent integration of the results of these comparisons into one composite judgment. As noted earlier, one may evaluate one's current situation by comparing it with what one expected, with what others have, with what one had earlier, and so on. And which domains is one to select for these comparisons? Health, income, family life, the quality of your environment, and what else? And after making all these comparisons, how should one integrate their results? Which weight does one want to give to each outcome? Facing this complex task, people may rarely engage in it. Rather, they may base their judgment on their perceived mood at that time, unless the informational value of their current mood is discredited.

Evaluations of specific life domains, on the other hand, are often less complex. In contrast to judgments of general life satisfaction, comparison information is usually available for judgments of specific life domains and criteria for evaluation are well-defined. An attempt to compare one's income or one's "life-as-a-whole" with that of colleagues aptly illustrates the difference. Moreover, one's affective state is not considered relevant information in evaluating many domains. Therefore, judgments of domain satisfaction are more likely to be based on inter- and intra-individual comparisons rather than on the heuristic use of one's affective state at the time of judgment. In line with this reasoning, we found that the outcome of the 1982 championship games of the German national soccer team affected respondents' general life satisfaction but not their satisfaction with work and income (Schwarz, Strack, Kommer and Wagner, 1987, Exp. 1).

The hypothesis that judgments of general well-being are based on respondents' affective states, while judgments of domain satisfaction are based on comparison processes, raises the intriguing possibility that the same event may influence evaluations of one's life-as-a-whole and evaluations of specific domains in opposite directions. For example, an extremely positive event in domain X may induce a good mood, resulting in reports of increased global well-being. However, the same event may also increase the standard of comparison used in evaluating domain X, resulting in judgments of decreased satisfaction with this particular domain. Such a differential impact of the same objective event may in part account for the weak relationships between global and specific evaluations, as well as measures of objective circumstances that have frequently concerned sociological researchers in the subjective social indicators tradition (Campbell, 1981; Glatzer and Zapf, 1984).

This possibility was explored by testing subjects in either a pleasant or an unpleasant room, namely a friendly office or a small, dirty laboratory that was overheated and noisy, with flickering lights and a bad smell. To the extent that these rooms affect subjects' mood, subjects should report lower life satisfaction in the unpleasant than in the pleasant room. However, to the extent that the rooms serve as salient standards of comparison, subjects in the unpleasant room should also report higher housing satisfaction than subjects in the pleasant room. The results (Schwarz, Strack, Kommer and Wagner, 1987, Exp. 2) confirmed this prediction as shown in Table 3.5.

TABLE 3.5. *Global well-being and housing satisfaction: the impact of one's current environment*

	Type of room	
	Pleasant	Unpleasant
Global well-being	9.4	8.1
Housing satisfaction	7.4	8.6

Note: Global well-being presents the mean score of happiness and satisfaction with one's life-as-a-whole. Range of scores is 1–11, with the higher scores indicating higher well-being or housing satisfaction, respectively.

Adapted from Experiment 2 of Schwarz, N., Strack, F., Kommer, D. and Wagner, D. Soccer, rooms and the quality of your life: Mood effects on judgments of satisfaction with life in general and with specific life-domains. *European Journal of Social Psychology*, 1987; **17**, 69–79. Reprinted by permission.

The relative salience of mood and competing information

As we have seen before, however, the use of comparison information is not limited to evaluations of specific life domains. Rather, we also found clear evidence for comparison processes in judgments of general well-being. Most importantly, respondents used events that they recalled from their own past as standards of comparison and reported lower current well-being when they recalled negative rather than positive past events (Strack *et al.*, 1985, Exp. 1). How is this finding compatible with the assumption that people prefer to evaluate their general well-being on the basis of their mood at the time of judgment?

The available data suggests that individuals rely on their mood state if their mood is pronounced, but use other salient information about their life in the absence of pronounced mood states. The best evidence for this assumption comes from two experiments in which we manipulated the emotional involvement that subjects experienced while thinking about past life events. In one experiment (Strack *et al.*, 1985, Exp. 2), we asked subjects to give either a short description of only a few words or to provide a vivid account of one to two pages in length. In the other study (Strack *et al.*, 1985, Exp. 3), subjects had to explain *why* the event occurred, or *how* the event proceeded. Explaining *why* the event occurred or providing a short description did not affect subjects' current mood, whereas *how* descriptions and vivid reports resulted in pronounced mood differences between subjects who reported positive and negative experiences.

When no pronounced mood state was induced, recalling negative past events resulted in reports of higher general well-being than recalling positive past events, thus replicating the contrast effects found earlier, as shown in Table 3.6. When the recall task did induce a pronounced mood state, on the other hand, mood had an overriding effect; in that case, subjects who described negative past events reported lower well-being than subjects who described positive past events, replicating the mood effects found in other studies.

In combination, these studies demonstrate that the impact of an event is a joint function of its hedonic quality, its temporal distance, and the person's emotional involvement while thinking about the event. That the relationship between objective events and subjective well-being is as weak as the subjective indicator literature demonstrated, is therefore not surprising. Knowing the hedonic quality of an event does not allow a prediction of its impact on reported well-being in the absence of knowledge about other judgmental variables.

TABLE 3.6. *Subjective well-being: the impact of style of thinking*

	Valence of Event	
	Positive	Negative
Detailed versus Short descriptions		
Detailed	9.1	7.9
Short	6.8	8.4
"How" versus "Why" descriptions		
How	8.2	6.3
Why	7.8	8.9

Note: Mean score of happiness and satisfaction questions, range is 1 to 11, with higher values indicating reports of higher well-being.

Adapted from Experiments 2 and 3, respectively; Strack, F., Schwarz, N. and Gschneidinger, E. Happiness and reminiscing: The role of time perspective, mood, and mode of thinking. *Journal of Personality and Social Psychology*, 1985; **49**, 1460–1469. Reprinted by permission.

Reporting the judgment

Once respondents have formed a private judgment, either based on their mood or based on a comparison process, they face the task of communicating this judgment to the researcher. Depending on the nature of the response situation, self-presentation and social desirability considerations may bias reports at this stage. Smith (1979) provided meta-analytic evidence that higher well-being is reported in face-to-face interviews than in mail surveys. Experimental research confirmed this finding (Strack *et al.*, in press) and indicated that self-presentation effects are moderated by interviewer characteristics.

Specifically, respondents reported higher well-being in personal interviews than in self-administered questionnaires. Moreover, this difference was more pronounced when the interviewer was of the opposite sex but was not obtained when the interviewer was severely handicapped. Subjects obviously hesitated to tell someone in an unfortunate condition how great their own life is. In contrast, when the handicapped confederate did not serve as an interviewer, but was only present in the room as another subject, filling out his own questionnaire, his presence did increase subjects' reported well-being, presumably because the handicapped confederate served as a salient standard of comparison, as discussed previously.

In summary, this research indicates that public reports of well-being may be more favourable than respondents' private judgments. These findings, in combination with the usually low correlations between measures of well-being and measures of social desirability, which rarely exceed $r = .20$ (cf.

Diener, 1984), moreover, suggests that respondents' editing of their reports may be more affected by characteristics of the interview situation than by individual differences between respondents.

A judgment model of subjective well-being

Figure 3.1 summarizes the findings presented in this chapter. If respondents

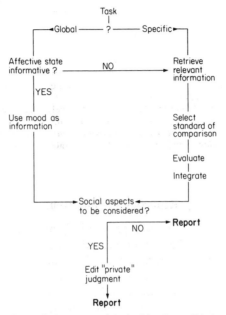

FIG. 3.1. A judgment model of subjective well-being.

are asked to report their happiness and satisfaction with life-as-a-whole, they are likely to base their judgment on their current affective state, which greatly simplifies the judgmental task. If the informational value of their affective state is discredited, or if their affective state is not pronounced and other information is more salient, they are likely to use a comparison strategy, which is also the strategy that is most likely to be used for evaluations of specific life domains.

When using a comparison strategy, both the selection of information about one's life and the selection of a comparison standard follow the principle of cognitive accessibility: whatever comes to mind first, and is relevant to the judgment at hand, is most likely to be used, unless the conversational context renders the use of information that has already been "given" inadequate. Whether information that comes to mind, and is used, serves as a standard of comparison or as descriptive information depends on whether it appears to bear on one's own current living conditions or not. Information that appears as distinct, because it pertains to a different episode of one's life or to a distant person, is used as a comparison standard and results in contrast effects. Information that directly bears on one's current living conditions, on the other hand, is used as descriptive information and results in assimilation effects.

Finally, after having formed a judgment on the basis of comparisons or on the basis of their affective state, respondents have to report their judgment to the researcher. At this stage they may or may not edit their report to conform to social expectations, depending on the nature of the situation.

This model, along with the research that bears on it, emphasizes that reports of well-being, which are used by social scientists as subjective social indicators, are subject to a number of transient influences. Like other social judgments they can be considered constructions in response to particular questions posed at a particular time rather than reflections of stable underlying attributes of the respondent. In particular, these judgments depend on the subset of potentially relevant information that is most accessible at the time, and they are strongly likely to be affected by news events (e.g. the outcome of soccer games), seasonal variations (e.g. the weather) or the specific succession of questions in an interview, as well as other aspects of question context. Moreover, the impact of retrieved information about the objective circumstances of life is dependent on respondents' time perspective and emotional involvement. Thus, the same objective event may affect respondents' reported well-being in opposite directions depending upon its temporal distance and respondents' mode of thinking about the event. Low test-retest reliabilities and a low explanatory power of objective conditions of life are therefore unavoidable consequences of the judgmental nature of reported well-being.

While some of these influences may be controlled for under some conditions (cf. Schwarz, 1987, Chapter 8), they usually undermine the comparability of data across time and studies. Unfortunately, this comparability is a key prerequisite for most applied uses of subjective social indicators, as well as other survey data. If we want to avoid misinterpretations of method effects as substantive effects in this, as well as other areas of psychological and social research, we will have to learn more about the cognitive processes that underlie the reports that our respondents provide. Hopefully, the recently initiated collaboration between survey researchers and cognitive psychologists (for first results see Hippler, Schwarz and Sudman, 1987) will advance our knowledge of these important aspects of social and psychological research.

References

BLANEY, P.H. Affect and memory: A review. *Psychological Bulletin*, 1986; **99**, 229–246.
BODENHAUSEN, G.V. and WYER, R.S. Social cognition and social reality: Information acqui-

sition and use in the laboratory and the real world. In H.J. Hippler, N. Schwarz and S. Sudman (eds.), *Social information processing and survey methodology*. New York: Springer Verlag, 1987.

BOLLNOW, O.F. *Das Wesen der Stimmungen*. Frankfurt: Klostermann, 1956.

BOWER, G.H. Mood and memory. *American Psychologist*, 1981; **36**, 129–148.

BRICKMAN, P. and CAMPBELL, D.T. Hedonic relativism and planning the good society. In M. H. Appley (ed.), *Adaptation-level theory*. New York: Academic Press, 1971.

BRICKMAN, P., COATES, D. and JANOFF-BULMAN, R. Lottery winners and accident victims: Is happiness relative? *Journal of Personality and Social Psychology*, 1978; **36**, 917–927.

CAMPBELL, A. *The sense of well-being in America*. New York: McGraw-Hill, 1981.

CAMPBELL, A., CONVERSE, P.E. and RODGERS, W.L. *The quality of American life*. New York: Russell Sage, 1976.

CLARK, H.H. Language use and language users. In G. Lindzey and E. Aronson (eds.), *Handbook of social psychology, Vol. 2*, pp. 179–232. New York: Random House, 1985.

CLARK, H.H. and CLARK E.V. *Psychology and language*. New York: Harcourt, Brace, Jovanovich, 1977.

DARSCHIN, W. and FRANK, B. Tendenzen im Zuschauerverhalten. Teleskopie-Ergebnise zur Fernsehnutzung im Jahre 1981. *Media Perspektiven*, 1982; **4**, 276–284.

DERMER, M., COHEN, S.J., JABOBSEN, E. and ANDERSON, E.A. Evaluative judgments of aspects of life as a function for vicarious exposure to hedonic extremes. *Journal of Personality and Social Psychology*, 1979; **37**, 247–260.

DIENER, E. Subjective well-being. *Psychological Bulletin*, 1984; **235**, 542–575.

EASTERLIN, R.A. Does economic growth improve the human lot? Some empirical evidence. In P.A. David and M.W. Reder (eds.), *Nations and households in economic growth*. New York: Academic Press, 1974.

ELDER, G.H. *Children of the Great Depression*. Chicago: University Press, 1974.

EMMONS, R.A. and DIENER, E. Factors predicting satisfaction judgments: A comparative examination. *Social Indicators Research*, 1985; **16**, 157–167.

EWERT, O. Ergebnisse und Probleme der Emotionsforschung. In H. Thomae (ed.), *Theorien und Formen der Motivation. Enzyklopädie der Psychologie*, C, IV, Vol. 1. Göttingen: Hogrefe.

FILIPP, S.H. Kritische Lebensereignisse als Brennpunkte einer angewandten Entwicklungspsychologie. In R. Oerter and L. Montada (eds.), *Entwicklungspsychologie*. München: Urban und Schwarzenberg.

GLATZER, W. Lebenszufriedenheit und alternative Masse subjektiven Wohlbefindens. In W. Glatzer and W. Zapf (eds.), *Lebensqualität in der Bundesrepublik*. Frankfurt: Campus Verlag, 1984.

GLATZER, W. and ZAPF, W. Lebensqualität in der Bundesrepublik. In W. Glatzer and W. Zapf (eds.), *Lebensqualität in der Bundesrepublik*. Frankfurt: Campus Verlag, 1984.

GRICE, H.P. Logic and conversation. In P. Cole and J.L. Morgan (eds.), *Syntax and semantics, 3: Speech acts*. pp. 41–58. New York: Academic Press, 1975.

GROVES, R.M. and KAHN, R.L. *Surveys by telephone: a national comparison with personal interviews*. New York: Academic Press, 1979.

HIGGINS, E.T. and KING, G. Accessibility of social constructs: Information processing consequences of individual and contextual variability. In N. Cantor and J.F. Kihlstrom (eds.), *Personality, cognition, and social interaction*. Hillsdale NJ: Erlbaum, 1981.

HIPPLER, H.J., SCHWARZ, N. and SUDMAN, S. (eds.), *Social information processing and survey methodology*. New York: Springer Verlag, 1987.

HYMAN, H.H. and SINGER, E. (eds.), *Readings in reference group theory and research*. New York: Free Press, 1968.

ISEN, A.M. Toward understanding the role of affect in cognition. In R.S. Wyer, Jr. and T.K. Srull (eds.), *Handbook of social cognition, Vol. 3*. Hillsdale NJ: Erlbaum, 1984.

IRWIN, P.H., ALLEN, G., KRAMER, S. and DANOFF, B. Quality of life after radiation therapy: A study of 309 cancer survivors. *Social Indicators Research*, 1982; **10**, 187–210.

KAMMANN, R. *Personal circumstances and life events as poor predictors of happiness*. Annual Convention of the American Psychological Association, Washington, DC, 1982.

MICHALOS, A. Multiple discrepancies theory. *Social Indicators Research*, 1985; **16**, 347–413.

MÜNKEL, T., STRACK, F. and SCHWARZ, N. *Der Einfluß der experimentellen Honorierung auf*

Stimmung und Wohlbefinden: Macht Schokolade glücklich? 29th Tagung Experimentell Arbeitender Psychologen, Aachen, FRG, 1987.

OTTATI, V.C., RIGGLE, E., WYER, R.S., SCHWARZ, N. and KUKLINSKI, J. (in press). The cognitive and affective bases of opinion survey responses. *Journal of Personality and Social Psychology.*

ROSS, M., EYMAN, A. and KISHCHUCK, N. Determinants of subjective well-being. In J.M. Olson, C.P. Herman and M. Zanna (eds.), *Relative deprivation and social comparison.* Hillsdale NJ: Erlbaum, 1986.

RUNCIMAN, W.G. *Relative deprivation and social justice.* London: Routledge & Kegan Paul, 1966.

RUNYAN, W.M. The life satisfaction chart: Perceptions of the course of subjective experience. *International Journal of Aging and Human Development*, 1980; **11**, 45–64.

SCHUMAN, H. and PRESSER, S. *Questions and answers in attitude surveys. Experiments on question form, wording and context.* New York: Academic Press, 1981.

SCHWARZ, N. Stimmung als Information: Zum Einfluß von Stimmungen auf die Beurteilung des eigenen Lebens. In G. Lüer (ed.), *Bericht über den 33. Kongreß der Deutschen Gesellschaft für Psychologie in Mainz 1982.* Göttingen: Hogrefe, 1983.

SCHWARZ, N. *Stimmung als Information: Untersuchungen zum Einfluß von Stimmungen auf die Bewertung des eigenen Lebens.* Heidelberg: Springer Verlag, 1987.

SCHWARZ, N. Was Befragte aus Antwortvorgaben lernen: Zur informativen Funktion von Antwortvorgaben bei Verhaltensberichten. *Planung und Analyse*, 1988a; **15**, 103–107.

SCHWARZ, N. Stimmung als Information. Zum Einfluß von Stimmungen auf evaluative Urteile. *Psychologische Rundschau*, 1988b; **39**, 148–159.

SCHWARZ, N. Assessing frequency reports of mundane behaviours: Contributions of cognitive psychology to questionnaire construction. In C. Hendrick and M. Clark (eds.), *Review of Personality and Social Psychology*, **11**. Beverly Hills CA: Sage, in press a.

SCHWARZ, N. Feelings as information: Informational and motivational functions of affective states. In E.T. Higgins and R. Sorrentino (eds.), *Handbook of motivation and cognition: Foundations of social behavior*, **2**. New York: Guilford Press, in press b.

SCHWARZ, N. and BIENIAS, J. What mediates the impact of response alternatives on frequency reports of mundane behaviours? *Applied Cognitive Psychology*, in press.

SCHWARZ, N. and CLORE, G.L. Mood, misattribution, and judgments of well-being: Informative and directive functions of affective states. *Journal of Personality and Social Psychology*, **45**, 513–523.

SCHWARZ, N. and CLORE, G.L. How do I feel about it? Informative functions of affective states. In K. Fiedler and J. Forgas (eds.), *Affect, cognition, and social behavior.* Toronto: Hogrefe International, 1988.

SCHWARZ, N. and HIPPLER, H. J. What response scales may tell your respondents. In H.J. Hippler, N. Schwarz, and S. Sudman (eds.), *Social information processing and survey methodology.* New York: Springer Verlag, 1987.

SCHWARZ, N., HIPPLER, H.J., DEUTSCH, B. and STRACK, F. Response categories: Effects on behavioral reports and comparative judgments. *Public Opinion Quarterly*, 1985; **49**, 388–395.

SCHWARZ, N. and SCHEURING, B. Judgments of relationship satisfaction: Inter and intraindividual comparisons as a function of questionnaire structure. *European Journal of Social Psychology*, 1988; **18**, 485–496.

SCHWARZ, N. and SCHEURING, B. Die Vergleichsrichtung bestimmt das Ergebnis von Vergleichsprozessen: Ist-Idealdiskrepanzen in der Beziehungsbeurteilung. *Zeitschrift für Sozialpsychologie*, 1989.

SCHWARZ, N., SERVAY, W. and KUMPF M. Attribution of arousal as a mediator of the effectiveness of fear-arousing communications. *Journal of Applied Social Psychology*, 1985; **15**, 74–78.

SCHWARZ, N. and STRACK, F. The survey interview and the logic of conversation. *ZUMA-Arbeitsbericht* 1988; **3**.

SCHWARZ, N., STRACK, F., KOMMER, D. and WAGNER, D. Soccer, rooms and the quality of your life: Mood effects on judgments of satisfaction with life in general and with specific life-domains. *European Journal of Social Psychology*, 1987; **17**, 69–79.

SHERMAN, S.J. and CORTY, E. Cognitive heuristics. In R.S. Wyer and T. Srull (eds.), *Handbook of social cognition, Vol. 3.* Hillsdale NJ: Erlbaum, 1984.

SMITH, T.W. Happiness. *Social Psychology Quarterly*, 1979; **42**, 18–30.

STRACK, F. "Social Cognition": Sozialpsychologie innerhalb des Paradigmas der Informationsverarbeitung. *Psychologische Rundschau*, 1988; **39**, 72–82.

STRACK, F. and MARTIN, L.L. Verfügbarkeit und Verwendung selbstbezogener Informationen in der Befragungssituation. In M. Amelang (ed.), *Bericht über den 35. Kongreß der Deutschen Gesellschaft für Psychologie in Heidelberg 1986.* Göttingen: Hogrefe, 1986.

STRACK, F. and MARTIN, L.L. Thinking, judging, and communicating: A process account of context effects in attitude surveys. In H.J. Hippler, N. Schwarz, and S. Sudman. (eds.), *Social information processing and survey methodology.* New York: Springer Verlag, 1987.

STRACK, F., MARTIN, L.L. and SCHWARZ, N. The context paradox in attitude surveys: Assimilation or contrast? *ZUMA Arbeitsbericht* 1987; **7**.

STRACK, F., MARTIN, L.L. and SCHWARZ, N. Priming and communications: Social determinants of information use in judgments of life satisfaction. *European Journal of Social Psychology*, 1988; **18**, 429–442.

STRACK, F., SCHWARZ, N., CHASSEIN, B., KERN, D. and WAGNER, D. The salience of comparison standards and the activation of social norms: Consequences for judgments of happiness and their communication. *British Journal of Social Psychology*, in press.

STRACK, F., SCHWARZ, N. and GSCHNEIDINGER, E. Happiness and reminiscing: The role of time perspective, mood, and mode of thinking. *Journal of Personality and Social Psychology*, 1985; **49**, 1460–1469.

STRACK, F., SCHWARZ, N. and NEBEL, A. *Thinking about your life: Affective and evaluative consequences.* Conference on "Ruminations, Self-Relevant Cognitions, and Stress". Memphis: State University, 1987.

TAYLOR, S.E. The interface of cognitive and social psychology. In J. H. Harvey (ed.), *Cognition, social behavior, and the environment.* Hillsdale NJ: Erlbaum, 1981.

WYER, R.S. The acquisition and use of social knowledge: Basic postulates and representative research. *Personality and Social Psychology Bulletin*, 1980; **6**, 558–573.

4

Subjective well-being: a stocks and flows framework

BRUCE HEADEY and ALEXANDER WEARING

Introduction

Some people enjoy higher levels of subjective well-being than others, and people who are happier at one point in time tend to be happier at later times. However, considerable change can occur in levels of subjective well-being, so we need to know what accounts for change. The twin aims of this paper are: (1) to describe the relatively stable personal characteristics which account for the fact that some people are generally happier than others and (2) to describe the satisfying and distressing life events which account for change in levels of subjective well-being. In thinking through these issues we find it helpful to use terms borrowed from economics. Stable personal characteristics—including social background, personality traits and social networks—may be thought of as *stocks* (the capital account). The satisfactions and distress arising from life events in a particular time period may be thought of as *flows of psychic income* (the current account). Subjective well-being is analogous to an individual's *wealth* or net worth. The three dimensions of subjective well-being analysed here are life satisfaction, positive affect (positive moods) and negative affect (negative moods). We shall integrate our account of stocks and flows into a theory of stability and change in subjective well-being.

Essentially the theory says that for most people, most of the time, subjective well-being is fairly stable. This is because stock levels, psychic income flows and subjective well-being are in *dynamic equilibrium*. Over the years the same people, due to their "stocks", keep experiencing the same kinds of life events. Some people have many satisfying experiences (e.g. job promotions; close friendships) and few distressing experiences (e.g. unemployment; trouble with their children). Other people keep experiencing just the reverse pattern; few satisfying and many distressing events. A third group experience many satisfying and many distressing events, while a fourth group experience few events of either kind (see Chapter 7). In other words, history repeats itself in people's lives. Provided an individual's "normal" (equilibrium) pattern is maintained, subjective well-being is not affected. It is only when events and experiences deviate from the equilibrium pattern that a person's level of subjective well-being changes.

From a psychologist's standpoint perhaps the most striking claims made in this paper are that history tends to repeat itself in people's lives—the same kinds of events keep happening to the same people—and that this is due to stable personal characteristics which we term stocks. Previously, psychologists have treated life events as if they were exogenous, unpredictable shocks. Confronted with evidence that the same people keep reporting the same events a psychologist wonders whether this could just be due to selective perception of the recent past. Personality or mood could well bias reports of events (Bower, 1969; Diener, Larsen and Emmons, 1984; Schroeder and Costa, 1984; Teasdale and Fogarty, 1979; Cohen, Towbes and Flocco, 1988). In order to check on this possibility we have run all analyses with (a) a complete list of life events and (b) a list restricted to those events which appeared so "objective" and so salient (e.g. wife died, job promotion) that there seemed little danger of biased reporting (see also Maddi, Bartone and Puccetti, 1987; Rowlison and Felner, 1988).

Evidence comes from the Victorian Quality of Life Panel study. The Victorian Quality of Life study has involved recording the life events and changes in subjective well-being of panel members who have been interviewed on four occasions between 1981 and 1987. The first section of the paper describes the panel study. The second section sets out a series of propositions about the causes of stability and change in subjective well-being, and gives results which are consistent with a dynamic equilibrium model. The concluding section compares this model with three alternative models put forward by other researchers. These are adaptation models which suggest that life events and experiences have no more than a fleeting impact on subjective well-being (Brickman, Coates and Janoff-Bulman, 1978), personality models which suggest that subjective well-being is stable because it depends on stable personality traits (Costa and McCrae, 1980, 1984, 1985) and static equilibrium models in which all life events and experiences are regarded as exogenous shocks which disturb an existing equilibrium state. The concluding section also elaborates on the stocks-flows framework borrowed from economics and indicates some interesting questions for future research which are suggested by this framework.

The Victorian Quality of Life Panel Study

The main purpose of the Victorian Quality of Life study is to try and account for *change* in levels of subjective well-being. Most previous research has relied on cross-sectional data; data collected at one point in time. Such data provide a snapshot of relationships between subjective well-being and other variables, but are of limited value in accounting for change. Accounting for change (by definition) requires measures taken at several time points. Panel data also improve the prospects of distinguishing causes (or antecedent variables) from effects (or dependent variables). A key requirement for establishing cause and effect is to show that changes in antecedent variables preceded changes in dependent variables. With cross-sectional data this is often problematic. Serious difficulties remain with panel data (Kessler and Greenberg, 1981), but it is sometimes possible to be reasonably sure that particular changes (e.g. life events) occurred prior to other changes (e.g. changes in subjective well-being) and that people to whom certain events happened displayed different patterns of change in subjective well-being from people to whom the events did not happen.

In order to try and explain change in subjective well-being our basic strategy was to measure subjective well-being at each time point and also to measure relatively stable personal characteristics (stocks) which might be associated with subjective well-being: social background characteristics, personality traits and social networks. In addition we asked panel members, each time they were interviewed, to record the life events and experiences that had happened to them since the last interview. This was done by asking them to complete a life events inventory: a standard list of ninety-four events which might or might not have occurred in their lives. For each event which had happened respondents recorded scores, indicating how satisfying or distressing the event was to them personally. These scores were summed up to provide a measure of psychic income accruing from events in the period in question. The aim was to assess the impact of psychic income—and of changes in income—on subjective well-being.

Sample

The data come from the first four waves of a panel study conducted in Australia's most densely populated state, Victoria. Respondents were inter- viewed in 1981, 1983, 1985 and 1987. In 1981 panel members ($N=942$, aged 18–65) were selected according to stratified probability sampling methods, using a Kish grid to designate one respondent at each selected household (Kish, 1965). The sample proved to be representative of the local govern- ment areas from which it was drawn, particularly with regard to income, education, occupational and marital status. Women were somewhat over- represented, but not seriously so (women 54 per cent, men 46 per cent).

By 1987, 649 members remained in the panel. We maintain contact by means of regular study reports and requests for change of address infor- mation. House movers are usually traced; over 350 panel members moved house between 1981 and 1987. Even so, panel loss is inevitably fairly substantial. However, checks indicate that, unlike most panel studies, attrition rates among younger and lower socio-economic status respondents have not been higher than among older and higher status respondents (although of course panel members are now six years older than they were in 1981.)[1]

Measures of subjective well-being

Evidence will be presented relating to three dimensions of subjective well-being: cognitive life satisfaction, positive affect and negative affect. Several recent reviews have concluded that these three dimensions need to be distinguished (Andrews and Withey, 1976; Andrews and McKennell, 1980; Argyle, 1987). This conclusion is by no means uncontroversial. Indeed advocates of one dimensional (Fordyce, 1986; Kamman, Christie, Irwin and Dixon, 1979; Stones and Kozma, 1985) and two dimensional solutions (Bradburn, 1969; Warr, 1978; Warr, Barter and Brownbridge, 1983; Watson and Tellegen, 1985) can also be found. We ourselves have recently suggested that a four dimensional approach, based on dividing negative affect into anxiety and depression, is useful for some purposes (Headey, Kelley and Wearing, 1989). However, the three dimensions mentioned initially have been measured in all four waves of the Victorian Quality of Life survey, so on practical grounds, as well as in deference to current scholarly views, these are the dimensions included.

The "Life Satisfaction Index" comprised six items, all asked on a 9-point Delighted-Terrible scale (Andrews and Withey, 1976; Headey, Holmstrom and Wearing, 1985). Two of the items involved asking respondents, "How do you feel about your life-as-a-whole?" One item was placed near the beginning of the interview schedule, the other towards the end ($r = 0.67$). The other four items were "How do you feel about 'the sense of purpose and meaning in your life?' . . . 'what you are accomplishing in life?' . . . 'how exciting your life is?' . . . 'the extent to which you are succeeding and getting ahead in life?' ". All correlations among the six items were over 0.4 and were averaged to form the life satisfaction index. The index had a Cronbach alpha of 0.92.

It could be questioned whether the items tap cognitive life satisfaction or whether they also include a substantial affective element (Andrews and McKennell, 1980). We accept that the life satisfaction index may no longer be the most "pure" measure of life satisfaction available. However, it is strongly correlated ($r = 0.70$) with Diener, Emmons, Larsen and Griffin's (1985) Satisfaction With Life Scale, which was added to the 1987 Victorian Quality of Life survey. Factor analyses also confirm that the index is much more closely related to cognitive than to affective measures.

The measures of positive and negative affect included in the Victorian Quality of Life surveys were Bradburn's "Positive" and "Negative Affect" scales. Each scale is based on five "yes-no" items asking about affects experienced during the last few weeks. In the 1987 Victorian Quality of Life survey the scales had Cronbach alphas of 0.64 and 0.65, respectively.

The Bradburn scales were the only measures available in 1981 and continue to be widely used. They have been shown in a recent review to have somewhat lower convergent and construct validity than other more recently developed measures (Larsen, Diener and Emmons, 1985).

In the Victorian Quality of Life (1987) the correlations between the life satisfaction index (1), positive affect (2) and negative affect (3) were $r_{12} = .39$, $r_{13} = -.40$, $r_{23} = -.16$.

Measures of stocks

Individuals have many kinds of "stocks" which could influence psychic income and subjective well-being. The three kinds measured in the Victorian Quality of Life study were social background, personality traits and social networks. Other potentially important stocks include buildings, equipment and facilities available for work, family life and leisure, individual skills and abilities, and aspects of the social and economic environment.

Social background

The three social background variables included are sex (male = 1, female = 2), age (measured in years) and socio-economic status. This last measure gives equal weights to family income, the main breadwinner's occupational status and the respondent's level of formal educational attainment.

Personality

Three personality traits affecting subjective well-being were included in the Victorian Quality of Life surveys: extraversion, neuroticism and openness to experience. The "Eysenck Personality Inventory" Form B, which measures extraversion and neuroticism, has been our main personality instrument (Eysenck and Eysenck, 1964). However, in searching for an improved explanation of why some people report more events of all kinds, we conjectured that "openness to experience" might be implicated. Costa and McCrae (1985), following Norman (1963) and Coan (1974), regard "openness to experience" as a third major domain of personality. One specific facet of this domain, "openness to feelings", was included in the 1987 survey. This was measured by eight items (e.g. "I rarely experience strong emotion"; "I find it easy to empathise—to feel myself what others are feeling") with a Cronbach alpha of 0.76. Since the measure was not taken until 1987, its inclusion as a "predictor" of events in earlier periods rests on Costa and McCrae's (1985) evidence that it is a stable personality trait.

Social networks

The measures of social networks used in the Victorian Quality of Life study were "availabilty of intimate attachments" and "availability of friendships" (Henderson, Byrne and Duncan-Jones, 1981). Both are three item, short versions of longer scales, developed at the Social Psychiatry Research Unit, Canberra. The former scale has a Cronbach alpha of 0.60 and the latter an alpha of 0.68 (1987).

Measures of life events and psychic income

The experiences which happened to respondents in each time period (1981–3, 1983–5, 1985–7) were recorded on an inventory containing a list of ninety-four events. Events were dated and respondents recorded the degree of satisfaction or distress occasioned by each event.

The inventory was a modified form of the "List of Recent Experiences" (Henderson *et al.*, 1981). These investigators in turn drew on inventories developed by Holmes and Rahe (1967) and Tennant and Andrews (1976). The main modifications made to the list of recent experiences involved redressing an imbalance in the original inventory by adding favourable events (e.g. "you made lots of new friends"; "you experienced a religious conversion or a great deepening of faith") in order to help explain improvements in subjective well-being. It should be noted that the list of recent experiences, unlike older inventories, includes continuing experiences and "daily hassles" (e.g. "serious problems/arguments with your children") as well as discrete events.

The usual way to score life events inventories has been to calculate total stress and/or change scores for each respondent, based on predetermined stress or change weights for events. Given our focus on the relationship between psychic income and subjective well-being, it was more appropriate to distinguish between favourable/satisfying events (e.g. got married; promoted at work) and adverse/distressing events (e.g. spouse died; became unemployed). We used two scoring methods. First we used unit weights, having found, like previous researchers, that simple frequency counts enabled us to account for as much variance in outcome measures as more elaborate scoring systems based on predetermined weights (Dawes and Corrigan, 1974; Rahe and Arthur, 1978; Schroeder and Costa, 1984). This method required us to determine, somewhat arbitrarily, which events were favourable and which adverse. The second method (not adopted until the 1985 survey) involved asking panel members to rate each event which happened to them on a 0–10 scale ranging from "extremely distressing" to "extremely satisfying". By summing these scores we obtained a measure of subjective reaction to events—psychic income—in each time period. The correlations between events scored on the unit weighting system and the satisfaction-distress scores were high, ranging between 0.70 and 0.85. In view of these correlations we shall sometimes, in the following analysis, treat the former scores as if they were measures of psychic income, although strictly speaking only the satisfaction-distress scores measure subjective response.

Results of the Victorian Quality of Life Panel Study

The results are set out in a series of propositions which, taken together, constitute a preliminary theory of well-being. Before considering the results, however, Figure 4.1 shows the stocks and flows framework for analysing subjective well-being.

Proposition 1.1   Some people experience persistently higher levels of subjective well-being than others.

Proposition 1.2   Nevertheless considerable change can occur in individual levels of subjective well-being. So it is more appropriate to regard subjective well-being as a fluctuating state rather than a stable trait.

Some people tend to be persistently happier than others. Table 4.1 gives two-, four- and six-year correlations for life satisfaction, positive affect and negative affect.

TABLE 4.1. *Over time correlations of life satisfaction, positive affect and negative affect*

Measure	Years				
	1981–3	1981–5	1981–7	Reliability[a]	Est. stability 1981–7[b]
Life satisfaction	.64	.51	.52	.92	.57
Positive affect	.39	.31	.35	.64	.55
Negative affect	.42	.36	.40	.65	.65

[a] Cronbach alpha.
[b] Correlation divided by Cronbach alpha.

These correlations may be interpreted as showing a moderate degree of stability over time. We should note, however, that the over time correlations are well below the reliabilities (Cronbach alphas) of the measures; an indication that some change in levels of subjective well-being does occur. Table 4.2 confirms this by showing the percentage of respondents whose subjective well-being changed by more than one standard deviation in the same two-, four- and six-year periods.

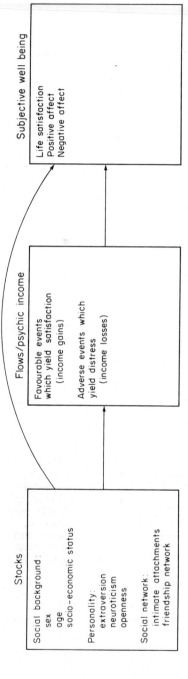

FIG. 4.1. A stocks and flows framework for analysing subjective well-being.

TABLE 4.2. *Per cent of members whose subjective well-being scores changed by more than one standard deviation (N = 649)*

Measure	Years			X^a	Standard Deviation
	1981–3	1981–5	1981–7		
Life satisfaction	18.1%	21.1%	25.1%	6.8	1.1
Positive affect	28.3%	31.8%	31.1%	3.4	1.4
Negative affect	27.7%	25.4%	27.3%	1.3	1.3

[a] In 1981. There were negligible shifts in means and standard deviations in later years.

Plainly there are many people whose lives take a sharp turn for the better or worse in any given time period. To highlight just one set of figures: the life satisfaction scores of 25.1 per cent of respondents shifted by over one standard deviation between 1981 and 1987, while the equivalent shifts for positive affect and negative affect were 31.1 per cent and 27.3 per cent.

The moderate degree of change in subjective well-being scores indicates that it is reasonable to regard subjective well-being measures as measures of fluctuating states rather than stable traits. The scales were originally designed as state measures but some observers have implied that they might be better regarded as trait measures (e.g. Costa and McCrae, 1980; Diener, 1984). In this regard it is worth noting that, while the subjective well-being measures show over time correlations well below their reliabilities (see Table 4.1), the trait measures of personality included in the Victorian Quality of Life survey show six year correlations which are close enough to their reliabilities to suggest that very little "true" change occurs.[2]

Proposition 2.1 Persistent differences in subjective well-being are due to stable stocks (stable personal characteristics). As a result of stable stocks each person has a level of subjective well-being which represents his/her own "normal" *equilibrium* level.

Proposition 2.2 The most important of those stocks are (a) *social background*: sex, age and socio-economic status (b) *personality*: extraversion, neuroticism and openness to experience and (c) *social networks*: intimate attachments and friendship networks.

Proposition 2.3 People who experience higher levels of life satisfaction than others tend to be extraverted, low in neuroticism, open to experience and have good social support networks.

Proposition 2.4 People who score high on positive affect tend to be young, high socio-economic status, extraverted, open to experience and have good social networks.

Proposition 2.5 People who score high on negative affect tend to be young, low socio-economic status, neurotic and open to experience.

Proposition 2.1 says that each person may be thought of as having their own "normal" or equilibrium level of subjective well-being, depending on stable personal characteristics or stocks. The stocks which seem to matter most are the social background variables of sex, age and socio-economic status, the personality traits of extraversion, neuroticism and openness to experience and the social support variables of "availability of intimate attachments" and "availability of friendships".

Stocks both contribute directly to subjective well-being and can be drawn on to generate and deal with specific life experiences (flows), so that the satisfaction obtainable from potentially favourable experiences is enhanced and the distress arising from potentially adverse experiences is diminished. We address the relationship between stocks and flows later. Table 4.3 displays the direct relationship between stocks measured in 1983 and subjective well-being in 1985. The choice of these time points is to illustrate that current stock levels influence future (as well as present) levels of subjective well-being.

TABLE 4.3. *Effect of stocks on subjective well-being (N = 727)*[a] (see Appendix 1)

Stocks 1983	Dependent variables		
	Life satisfaction 1985	Positive affect 1985	Negative affect 1985
Social background			
Sex (m = 1, f = 2)	.08	.02[ns]	−.02[ns]
Age	−.02[ns]	−.15	−.09
Socio-economic status	.04[ns]	.17	−.10
Personality			
Extraversion	.12	.14	.07[ns]
Neuroticism	−.24	−.03[ns]	.42
Openness[b]	.16	.12	.09
Social networks			
Intimate attachments	.20	.20	−.11
Friendship network	.13	.02[ns]	−.10
Variance explained by all stocks (R^2)	(20%)	(16%)	(26%)

[a] Standardized regression coefficients (Betas).
[b] Openness 1987 serves as a proxy for openness 1983.
[ns] Not significant at the 5 per cent level.

It should be noted that results in Table 4.3 (and Tables 4.5–4.7) are based on regression analyses. A regression coefficient shows the net effect of a particular antecedent variable on a dependent variable, controlling for other antecedent variables. Regression analyses also enable us to assess the combined effects of a set of antecedent variables on a dependent variable (the variance accounted for: R^2). In this paper, standardized coefficients (coefficients expressed in standard deviation units) are used to facilitate direct comparisons between the effect of antecendent variables. Means, standard deviations and correlations among variables are given in Appendix 2.

The main interest of Table 4.3 lies in finding that different stocks contribute to life satisfaction, positive affect and negative affect. Social background variables are unrelated to life satisfaction, but age and socio-economic status are related to positive affect and negative affect. Younger people experience both more positive affect *and* more negative affect (they are more up and down), while higher status people experience more positive affect and less negative affect. The finding that life satisfaction is not related (or, at most, very weakly related) to social background has been made in many countries (Andrews, 1981; Argyle, 1987; Diener, 1984; Veenhoven, 1984) and suggests that people in all walks of life adjust their expectations and aspirations so that these have a close fit with their current situation. The reason for claiming this is that cognitive judgments of life satisfaction are known to depend heavily on the fit between expectations and aspirations and one's current level of achievement (Campbell, Converse and Rodgers, 1976; Michalos, 1985). By contrast, it is interesting that higher status people more frequently experience positive feelings and less frequently suffer negative feelings.

All three personality traits contribute to life satisfaction; more satisfied people tend to be more extraverted, less neurotic and more open to feelings. However, extraversion contributes to positive affect but not negative affect, while neuroticism is unrelated to positive affect but is a major determinant of negative affect.[3] The role of openness to feelings is particularly interesting. Openness is positively related to both positive affect and negative affect; it has its bright side and dark side (Costa and McCrae, 1985).

Finally, Table 4.3 suggests that the net effect of social networks on subjective well-being is also significant. As one would expect, intimate attachments contribute more to well-being than more casual friendships.

Proposition 3 Levels of psychic income are also fairly persistent over time. People who experience favourable/satisfying life events in one time period are likely to experience favourable/satisfying events in subsequent periods. People who experience adverse/distressing events in one period are likely to experience continuing adversity/distress.

History apparently repeats itself in people's lives. The extent to which both favourable and adverse events are correlated over time is quite remarkable; perhaps the most unexpected finding to emerge from the Victorian Quality of Life panel surveys.

Correlations between favourable events scores from one time period to the next are around 0.5 and the same is true for adverse events scores. Perhaps even more surprising are the positive correlations between favourable and adverse events scores. Apparently people who experience many favourable events are more rather than less likely to experience many adverse events. These results suggest the possibility that stable personal characteristics (or stocks) may partly account for the incidence of events, and that not all events should be regarded as unpredictable exogenous shocks. It also seems possible that certain characteristics predispose people to experience both many favourable and many adverse events.

Before considering these possibilities we need to consider the validity of events reports. It could be that the observed correlations in Table 4.4 are not due to any tendency for similar events actually to be repeated but are due to biased reporting. As noted in the introduction, reports of events can be biased by both personality and mood. Indeed, the issue is not whether these factors affect reports to some degree but whether results such as those in Table 4.4 could be largely or wholly due to bias or selective perception.

TABLE 4.4. *Over time correlations among aggregate life events scores: all events and objective events only (in parentheses)*[a]

Events	1	2	3	4	5	6
Favourable						
1. 1981–3	—					
2. 1983–5	.52(.37)	—				
3. 1985–7	.43(.32)	.50(.35)	—			
Adverse						
4. 1981–3	.15(.10)	.18(.05)[b]	.20(.04)[b]	—		
5. 1983–5	.21(.11)	.28(.10)	.32(.07)	.49(.34)	—	
6. 1985–7	.24(.14)	.31(.13)	.44(.07)	.33(.18)	.49(.33)	—

[a] Observed Pearson correlations between events occurring in different time intervals.
[b] Not significant at the .05 level.

A method of addressing this issue is to divide events into those which are relatively "objective" and those which are relatively "subjective". Objective events are those which it is difficult to believe anyone could forget or mis-perceive (e.g. "got married"; "child died"). Recording of subjective events (e.g. "made lots of new friends"; "serious arguments with children"), on the other hand, could readily be affected by mood or personality. In the events inventory used for this research it appeared that six favourable events could be classified as objective, together with twenty adverse events.[4] Table 4.4 also gives over time correlations for objective events only (in parentheses).

It can be seen that although correlations are lower for objective than for all events, the pattern of results is unaffected. Objective favourable and objective adverse events are correlated over time, and correlations between favourable and objective events scores remain positive, although not all coefficients are significant at the 5 per cent level. We infer that the results in Table 4.4 have a solid basis in "objective reality", although we do not doubt that event reporting is to some degree affected by mood and personality.

Proposition 4.1 Favourable events and high levels of psychic income are due to high stock levels. Adverse events and low levels of psychic income are due to low stock levels. As a result of stable stocks each person has a level of psychic income which represents his/her own "normal" *equilibrium* level.

Proposition 4.2 People who are young, extraverted and open to experience enjoy many favourable/satisfying events, particularly in the friendship and work domains. People who are young, neurotic and open to experience suffer many adverse/distressing events, particularly in the financial and work domains.

People who are young, extraverted, neurotic and open to experience have⸱ many favourable and many adverse events. People who are older, introverted, stable (non-neurotic) and closed to experience have few events of either kind.

The stocks-flows framework would lead us to expect that persisting patterns of events might be due to differences in individuals' stocks. Table 4.5 shows the impact of stocks measured in 1983 on events in the 1983–5 period. Results are shown for both methods of scoring life events. Columns 1 and 2 show relationships between stocks and the frequencies of favourable and

TABLE 4.5. *Effect of stocks on psychic income* ($N = 734$)[a] (see Appendix 1)

Stocks 1983	Dependent variables		
	Favourable events 1983–5[c]	Adverse events 1983–5[c]	Satisfaction/distress from events 1983–5[c] (0–10 scale)
Social background:			
Sex (m = 1, f = 2)	.01[ns]	−.07[ns]	.08[ns]
Age	−.24	−.22	−.18
SES	.16	−.02[ns]	.09
Personality:			
Extraversion	−.16	−.03[ns]	.15
Neuroticism	.07[ns]	.16	−.10
Openness[b]	.17	.14	.09
Social support:			
Intimate attachments	.02[ns]	−.09	.11
Friendship network	.01[ns]	−.02[ns]	.01[ns]
Variance explained by all stocks (R^2)	(21%)	(13%)	(13%)

[a] Standardized regression coefficients (Betas).
[b] Openness 1987 serves as a proxy for Openness 1983.
[c] Frequency count.
[ns] Not significant at the 5 per cent level.

adverse events, while column 3 shows the relationship between stocks and the more direct measure of psychic income (satisfaction/distress arising from events).

The results indicate that, just as stocks produce a "normal" or equilibrium level of subjective well-being, they also contribute to each individual having his/her own equilibrium pattern of life events and psychic income. In practice five stocks seem mainly to influence life events. If we know a person's age, socio-economic status and three personality traits, we can to a modest degree predict the pattern of events which will subsequently happen to him/her and the psychic income which will result. People who are young, extraverted, open to experience and of high social status have many favourable events. People who are young, neurotic and open to experience have many adverse events. It is interesting that extraversion and socio-economic status are associated only with favourable life events and not with adverse, while neuroticism is associated only with adverse events. Age (being young) and openness to feelings, on the other hand, are associated with both favourable and adverse events.

Strictly speaking, Table 4.4 only showed that favourable events of some kind and adverse events of some kind keep happening to the same people. We conjectured, however, that history perhaps repeats itself in a more direct fashion and that particular categories of events or even specific events are repeated in people's lives. Given the evidence in Table 4.5, one plausible hypothesis was that young high status extraverts would be predisposed to experience and report favourable events of an interpersonal kind. Young neurotic people, by contrast, might be expected to keep experiencing adverse events in domains of life (financial affairs, work?) in which their relative youth would make them vulnerable.

Detailed analyses (not shown here) indicated that young high status extraverts were particularly likely to keep experiencing favourable friendships and work related events. Young relatively neurotic people were particularly likely to keep reporting adverse financial and work events. Specific friendship events which tended to be repeated were "a friendship with someone of the same sex became closer", "a friendship with someone of the opposite sex became closer" and "made lots of new friends". The job events were "promoted at work", "your boss praised you for your work" and "your ability to do your job well increased". Similarly, age and neuroticism predict adverse financial and job events, with openness being related only to the former. The specific financial and job events which tended to be repeated were "you had a financial crisis", "continuous financial worry", "unemployed or seeking work", "sacked or laid off", "you found out you were not going to be promoted" and "trouble or arguments with people at work".

The links between personality traits and events (psychic income) are perhaps of greater theoretical interest, but we should recognize that age is the best single predictor. Younger adults are at a stage of their careers and family lives when major events (promotions, unemployment, marriage, divorce, birth of children) are more likely to happen than is the case for older adults, whose lives have attained a more stable pattern.

Proposition 5.1   Recent life events/psychic income influence current levels of subjective well-being over and above the influence of stable personality characteristics/stocks.

Proposition 5.2   However, provided that no change occurs in a person's own "normal" equilibrium pattern of life events and psychic income, subjective well-being remains unchanged. Stocks, psychic income and subjective well-being remain in *dynamic equilibrium.*

Proposition 5.3   Deviations from a person's equilibrium level of subjective well-being occur when he/she deviates from his/her "normal" pattern of events and psychic income. An increase in psychic income enhances subjective well-being, whereas a decrease reduces subjective well-being.

TABLE 4.6. *Combined effect of stocks and flows on subjective well-being (N = 727) (see Appendix 1)*

Stocks 1983, Flows 1983–5	Dependent variables		
	Life satisfaction 1985	Positive affect 1985	Negative affect 1985
Variance accounted for by all stocks[a]	20%	16%	26%
Additional variance accounted for by flows (Betas in parentheses)	8% (B = .29)[b]	7% (B = .30)[c]	4% (B = .22)[d]
Total variance accounted for	28%	23%	30%

[a] Regression coefficients for each stock are given in Table 4.3.
[b] Satisfaction arising from favourable events and distress from adverse events both account for variance in life satisfaction 1985.
[c] Only satisfaction from favourable events accounts for significant variance in positive affects 1985.
[d] Only distress from adverse events accounts for significant variance in negative affect 1985.

Proposition 5.1 requires us to assess the combined effects of stocks and psychic income on subjective well-being. The method used in Table 4.6 is hierarchical regression. Stocks measured in 1983 were entered at the first step of the analysis and psychic income 1983–5 (satisfaction and distress arising from life events) was entered at the second step. The dependent variables were life satisfaction, positive affect and negative affect measured in 1985.

It is clear that both stocks and flows contribute significantly to levels of subjective well-being. This is a point of considerable interest because it has previously been suggested that stocks, and in particular personality traits, account for virtually all the variance in subjective well-being and that life events have no effect (Costa and McCrae, 1980). In fact, in the Australian data, life events (psychic income flows) accounted for an additional 8 per cent of variance in life satisfaction 1985 over and above the variance due to stocks.[5] The satisfaction arising from favourable events accounted for 7 per cent additional variance in positive affect 1985 which, however, was not affected by distress due to adverse events (cf. Block and Zautra, 1981; Headey, Holmstrom and Wearing, 1984). The position was reversed for negative affect 1985 in that only distress arising from adverse events accounted for additional variance (4 per cent), while positive events had no impact.

Proposition 5.1 by no means tells the whole story regarding the effects of life events/psychic income on subjective well-being. In particular, it takes no account of the finding that the same events keep happening to the same people, so that each individual may be said to have an equilibrium pattern of events which is "normal" (typical) for him or her. In this context it is useful to think of recent life events (recent psychic income) which have happened to individuals as consisting of two components:

Equation 1
    recent events = normal events + deviation from normal events.

The next two propositions imply that only the deviation from normal is responsible for the association between events scores and subjective well-being shown in Table 4.6. Proposition 5.2 says that provided an individual exactly maintains his/her own normal pattern of events/psychic income in a given time period, then no change in subjective well-being will occur. Stocks, psychic income and subjective well-being will remain in dynamic equilibrium. Proposition 5.3 states the corollary which is that, if psychic income increases above its normal level, subjective well-being will be enhanced, whereas if psychic income declines, subjective well-being will fall below its equilibrium level.

In seeking to test propositions 5.2 and 5.3, we focus entirely on the relationship between life events/psychic income and subjective well-being. Measures of "normal" life events/psychic income and of "normal" subjective well-being are required. In practice the best available measure of a person's "normal" life events score is the average of his/her scores for the two periods 1981–3 and 1983–5.[6] The same approach is taken with regard to subjective well-being. A person's normal, equilibrium level of subjective well-being is given by the average of their scores in 1981, 1983 and 1985.

The following regression equation provides an appropriate method of testing both propositions 5.2 and 5.3 (Kessler and Greenberg, 1981).

Equation 2

$$\text{SWB}_{1987} = B_1 \underset{\text{Normal}}{\text{SWB}_{1981\text{-}5}} + B_2 \underset{\text{Recent}}{\text{Events}_{1981\text{-}5}} + B_3 \text{Events}_{1985\text{-}7} + e$$

SWB—subjective well-being.

Remember that each regression coefficient can be viewed as showing the net effect of its variable on subjective well-being 1987, controlling for or removing the effects of other variables in the equation. The consequence of including Normal Subjective Well-Being 1981–5 on the right hand side is to remove variance in Subjective Well-Being 1987 which is due to this variable. So the dependent variable in effect becomes the extent to which a person's Subjective Well-Being 1987 score deviated from normal. B_2 can then be interpreted as the effect of Normal Events 1981–5 on deviations from normal in subjective well-being. We now consider B_3, the coefficient of greatest interest. Variance in subjective well-being 1987, which is due to Normal Events 1981–5, is removed, so B_3 can be regarded as showing the effect of the deviation from normal component of Recent Events 1985–7 (see equation 1) on deviations from normal in subjective well-being.

We now test a dynamic equilibrium model for each of three dimensions of subjective well-being. Proposition 5.2 implies that, for each dimension, B_2 should not be significantly different from zero. Proposition 5.3 says that B_3 should be significant and positive. (B_1 is of course expected to be a large positive since, for most individuals, Recent Events 1985–1987 will be similar to Normal Events 1981–1985.

Results for all three dimensions of subjective well-being are consistent with our hypotheses. All three B_2s are not significantly different from zero,

TABLE 4.7. *A dynamic equilibrium model: empirical results (N = 649)[a] (see Appendix 1)*

Antecedent variables	Dependent variables		
	Life satisfaction 1987	Positive affect 1987[b]	Negative affect 1987[c]
Normal (average) SWB 1981–5 (B1)	.69	.41	.70
Normal (average) Events 1981–5 (B2)	−.05[ns]	−.06[ns]	0.04[ns]
Recent events 1985–7 (B3)	.18	.29	.16

[a] See Table 4.3.
[b] Only favourable/satisfying events are significantly related to change in positive affect.
[c] Only adverse/distressing events are significantly related to change in negative affect.
[ns] Not significant at the 5 per cent level.

indicating that normal events (or a repetition of one's own equilibrium pattern) have no effect in changing subjective well-being away from its normal equilibrium level. By contrast, all three B_3s are significant and positive. That is, deviations from a person's equilibrium pattern of events shift subjective well-being away from its equilibrium level. In the case of life satisfaction, both deviations in favourable events and deviations in adverse events make a difference. In the case of positive affect only deviations in favourable events matter, whereas for negative affect only adverse events matter. The dynamic equilibrium model is broadly confirmed.

Discussion

In this section we discuss alternatives to the dynamic equilibrium model and reasons for rejecting them. Secondly, we consider objections to the view that history repeats itself in people's lives and that events are partly determined by personal characteristics. Finally, we outline some directions for future research suggested by the stocks and flows model of subjective well-being.

Before considering alternatives to the dynamic equilibrium model, one of its limitations should be explicitly stated. The model is only supposed to account for stability and change in subjective well-being in the medium term; say, five to ten years. In the longer term, stock levels, which play a crucial equilibrating function in the model, may well change. This would have important consequences for psychic income and subjective well-being. We now consider three alternatives to our (medium term) model. Brickman, Coates and Janoff–Bulman (1978) proposed an *adaptation level model* in which people adapt so rapidly even to cataclysmic life events that virtually no effect on subjective well-being can be detected. Their evidence related to lottery winners and paraplegics. However, their sample sizes were small and many researchers have shown that adverse events have significant effects not only on subjective well-being but also on mental and physical health (e.g. Abbey and Andrews, 1985; Block and Zautra, 1981; Headey, Glowacki, Holmstrom and Wearing, 1985; Henderson, Byrne and Duncan-Jones, 1981; Reich and Zautra, 1983). Other researchers besides ourselves have also found that favourable events affect subjective well-being (Block and Zautra, 1981; Reich and Zautra, 1983). We do not doubt that some adaptation occurs, so that in the face of major events people adjust their expectations for the future, but the evidence runs counter to the conclusion that adaptation is so rapid and so complete that the impact of events is undetectable.

A second alternative model, proposed by Costa and McCrae (1980, 1984) is that subjective well-being depends almost entirely on stable personality traits. Clearly personality matters, but if that were the whole story, people's levels of subjective well-being would remain virtually unchanged over their entire lifetimes. Stable personality would produce stable well-being. In fact, as we have seen (Tables 4.1 and 4.2), levels of subjective well-being are correlated over time, but many individuals nevertheless record substantial changes.

A third set of alternatives may be described as static equilibrium models. In these models it is recognized that life events can change levels of subjective well-being (see Chapter 5). However, life events are treated as exogenous shocks which disturb an equilibrium level of subjective well-being. The implicit assumption—a static equilibrium assumption—is that if no events happened subjective well-being would remain unchanged. We have challenged this assumption by indicating that the "normal" condition is not for no events to happen but for the same kinds of events to keep happening to the same people, largely because of their stable "stock" levels. Stocks, events (psychic income) and subjective well-being are in dynamic equilibrium.[7]

A serious objection to the view that history actually repeats itself in people's lives is that reports of events could be so biased by personality and mood-at-interview as to be almost worthless (see previous references). No student of personality would doubt that personality and mood have some effect on event recall and, perhaps, on designation of events as more or less satisfying or distressing (but see Cohen, Towbes and Flocco, 1988). The issue is not whether event reports contain *some* bias but whether the degree of bias totally invalidates the reports. Maddi, Bartone and Puccetti (1987) have investigated this issue by restricting analysis to those events which appeared so "objective" that it is difficult to believe reports could be biased (see also Rowlison and Felner, 1988). They found that there were still significant relationships between events scores and outcome measures. In the same vein, we have re-run all analyses reported in this chapter using "objective" events only. This greatly reduced the "sample" of events, but even so all relationships had the same sign, although some were clearly weaker.

If it be provisionally accepted that the same or similar events actually tend to be repeated in people's lives, then further implications of the dynamic equilibrium need to be considered. It will be important in future research to investigate psychological mechanisms underlying the link between events and subjective well-being. Clearly, in suggesting that changes from a person's normal pattern of events play a key role in changing levels of subjective well-being, we are implying that people in some way contrast recent events with their own normal, equilibrium pattern. In this paper we have treated a person's mean (average) events score for previous periods as a measure of normal. It is recognized, however, that other possibilities exist. In particular, range-frequency theory predicts that in evaluating a recent event people use a baseline half-way between the mean and the median of previous events (Emmons and Diener, 1985; Michalos, 1985; Parducci, 1984).[8]

Much further work is required on the factors which induce repetition of events. In this paper the focus has been on personal characteristics. It seems likely, however, that environmental factors are involved. Some events (e.g. difficulties with one's boss) may happen repeatedly in part because of the actions of other people in one's environment. Event stability may also be due to geographical environment. One is more likely to be unemployed living in a high unemployment region, and more likely to be assaulted in a low socio-economic status than a high socio-economic status area. Finally, events may come in predictable sets. Promotions are accompanied by increases in standard of living and often by house moves. Unemployment often leads to divorce and health problems (Argyle, 1987).

It is important to translate a theory which says that events are by no means entirely exogenous into appropriate statistical models. Some previous researchers, following Dohrenwend and Dohrenwend (1974), have recognized that certain events are "controllable", but have retained the convention of treating them as exogenous in statistical models. It would be preferable to relax this convention and to try and classify events according to whether they are, practically speaking, exogenous, or whether they are driven by personal characteristics or by environmental factors. Events in the later two categories should be treated as endogenous in statistical models.

The stocks and flows accounting framework offers one way of modelling endogenous events (but was admittedly imposed on our data post hoc). The ideal way to implement the framework would be for the "accountant" to record stock levels and subjective well-being on 1 January and 31 December each year (the beginning and end of the accounting period). Psychic income flows for the year would also be recorded and their effects on stock levels and subjective well-being calculated.

The framework suggests interesting hypotheses and questions which would come "naturally" to an economist accustomed to thinking in an accounting framework, but which are quite novel in subjective well-being research. An economist naturally thinks of conducting longitudinal research covering changes in stocks, flows and well-being in a given accounting period (e.g. one year, five years). An economist investigates hypotheses about the interest or rates of return obtainable from different stocks (e.g. rates of return in satisfaction from work and leisure obtainable for individuals with differing personalities, skills, equipment and social networks). An obvious hypothesis, partly tested in this paper, concerns inequality of subjective well-being. People with higher stock levels are likely to generate continuously higher levels of psychic income and hence maintain higher levels of subjective well-being. In general, an economist is geared to asking questions about the relative contributions of stocks and flows to current well-being, and about the feedback effects of transactions in the current account on stocks (e.g. the effect of life events on social networks).

An economic framework, more than frameworks in social psychology, is designed to clarify choice, to assist with decisions. How can an individual or household improve stock management . . . improve the social networks and, conceivably, personalities of its members? How can higher rates of return on stock be achieved, so that increased psychic income flows are obtained? Which particular events and experiences most affect subjective well-being? Could a better balance be struck between obtaining immediate psychic income and augmenting stocks in order to enhance future income? These questions leap to mind if one thinks about subjective well-being in an accounting framework, but represent somewhat new lines of inquiry and would require novel research instruments, particularly in regard to stock management (investment and disinvestment). We hope to pursue some of these inquiries in future waves of the Victorian Quality of Life survey.

Notes

1. We shall therefore treat the four waves as equivalent and include all available cases in data analyses. Analyses are *not* restricted to the 649 people interviewed on all four occasions.
2. Sex is of course 100 per cent stable. Relative ages do not change at all among Victorian Quality of Life panel members. Socio-economic status was estimated to have a six-year stability (1981–7) in the Victorian Quality of Life data of over 0.9, as were extraversion and neuroticism. Costa and McCrae (1988) have given similar results for openness to experience. The two social support measures have estimated "true" reliabilities of almost 0.85 (Henderson, Byrne and Duncan-Jones, 1981).
3. There is some suspicion of "contamination" or overlap beween the antecedent and dependent variables. Neuroticism is thought of as a stable trait, while negative affect is a fluctuating state. However, in practice, items measuring the trait and the state are not as distinct as one would wish.
4. The favourable events classified as "objective" were: you were promoted; you passed an important exam; you became engaged; you got married; husband and wife got together again after separation; you experienced a religious conversion.
   The "objective" adverse events were: you were unemployed; sacked or laid off; you had a major financial crisis; your own business failed; you failed an important exam; you had a serious illness or injury; you had a serious accident; you broke off an engagement; you separated from your spouse; you divorced; your spouse died; a child of yours died; a close family member (not including spouse or own child) died; you (your wife) had a miscarriage, abortion or stillbirth; a close friend died; you were robbed; you were physically assaulted; problems with the police leading to a court appearance; prison sentence; you had a civil suit (e.g. divorce, custody, debt).
5. It should be noted that results are virtually identical if the unit weighting method of scoring events is used and, indeed, if analysis is restricted to the list of "objective" events in note 4.
6. The unit weighting method of scoring events had to be used for calculating "normal" events/psychic income because satisfaction-distress scores were not obtained for 1981–3 life events. To calculate a net events/net psychic income score for each period the frequency count for adverse events was subtracted from the favourable events count.
7. Another possible model, which we reject, is that people to whom mainly favourable events happen become steadily happier, while people to whom mainly adverse events happen become steadily more distressed. This could be termed a "dynamic feedback" model. The Victorian Quality of Life data do not support this model.
8. Unfortunately, the Australian panel study does not yield sufficiently detailed events data to differentiate between predictions based on different judgment theories. For an excellent review of these theories see Diener (1984).

References

ABBEY, A. and ANDREWS, F.M. Modelling the psychological determinants of life quality. *Social Indicators Research*, 1985; **16**, 1–16.

ANDREWS, F.M. Subjective social indicators, objective social indicators and social accounting systems. In F.T. Juster and K.C. Land (eds.), *Social Accounting Systems*, New York: Academic Press, 1981.

ANDREWS, F.M. Construct validity and error components of survey measures: a structural modelling approach. *Public Opinion Quarterly*, 1984; **48**, 409–42.

ANDREWS, F.M. and McKENNELL, A.C. Measures of self-reported well-being. *Social Indicators Research*, 1980; **8**, 127–56.

ANDREWS, F.M. and WITHEY, S.B. *Social indicators of well-being.* New York: Plenum Press, 1976.

ARGYLE, M. *The psychology of happiness.* London: Methuen, 1987.

BLOCK, J. Some enduring and consequential structures of personality. In A. I. Rabin (ed.), *Further explorations in personality.* New York: Wiley, 1981.

BLOCK, J. and ZAUTRA, A. Satisfaction and distress in a community: A test of the effect of life events. *American Journal of Community Psychology*, 1981; **9**, 165–180.

BOWER, G.H. Mood and memory. *American Psychologist*, 1969; **36**, 129–148.

BRADBURN, N.M. *The structure of psychological well-being.* Chicago: Aldine, 1969.

BRICKMAN, P., COATES, D. and JANOFF-BULMAN, R. Lottery winners and accident victims: is happiness relative? *Journal of Personality and Social Psychology*, 1978; **36**, 917–927.

CAMPBELL, A., CONVERSE, P.E., and RODGERS, W.R. *The quality of American life.* New York: Russell Sage Foundation, 1976.

COAN, R.W. *The optimal personality.* New York: Columbia University Press, 1974.

COHEN, L.H., TOWBES, L.C. and FLOCCO, R. Effect of induced mood on self-reported life events and perceived and received social support. *Journal of Personality and Social Psychology*, 1988; **55**, 669–674.

COSTA, P.T. and McCRAE, R.R. Influence of extraversion and neuroticism on subjective well-being. *Journal of Personality and Social Psychology*, 1980; **338**, 668–678.

COSTA, P.T. and McCRAE, R.R. Personality as a lifelong determinant of well-being. In C. Malatesta and C. Izard (eds.), *Affective processes in adult development and aging.* Beverly Hills: Sage, 1984.

COSTA, P.T.and McCRAE, R.R. *The NEO Personality Inventory.* Odessa, Florida: Psychological Assessment Resources Inc., 1985.

COSTA, P.T. and McCRAE, R.R. Personality in adulthood: A six-year longitudinal study of self-reports and spouse ratings on the NEO Personality Inventory. *Journal of Personality and Social Psychology*, 1988; **54**, 853–863.

DAWES, R.M. and CORRIGAN, B. Linear models in decision-making. *Psychological Bulletin*, 1974; **81**, 95–106.

DIENER, E. Subjective well-being. *Psychological Bulletin*, 1984, **45**, 542–575.

DIENER, E., EMMONS, R.A. LARSEN, R.J. and GRIFFEN, S. The satisfaction with life scale. *Journal of Personality Assessment*, 1985; **49**, 71–75.

DIENER, E., LARSEN, R.J. and EMMONS, R.A. Bias in mood recall in happy and unhappy persons. *American Psychological Association Conference*, Toronto, 1984.

DOHRENWEND, B.S. and DOHRENWEND, B.P. *Stressful life events.* New York: Wiley, 1974.

EMMONS, R.A. and DIENER, E. Factors predicting satisfaction judgments: a comparative examination. *Social Indicators Research*, 1985; **16**, 157–167.

EYSENCK, H.J. and EYSENCK, S.B.G. Manual of the Eysenck Personality Inventory. London: University Press, 1964.

FORDYCE, M.W. The Psychap Inventory: a multi-scale test to measure happiness and its concomitants. *Social Indicators Research*, 1986; **18**, 1–34.

HEADEY, B.W., HOLMSTROM, E.L. and WEARING, A.J. The impact of life events and changes in domain satisfactions on well-being. *Social Indicators Research*, 1984; **15**, 203–227.

HEADEY, B.W. HOLMSTROM, E.L. and WEARING, A.J. Models of well-being and ill-being. *Social Indicators Research*, 1985; **17**, 211–234.

HEADEY, B.W., GLOWACKI, T., HOLMSTROM, E.L. and WEARING, A.J. Modelling change in perceived quality of life. *Social Indicators Research*, 1985; **17**, 276–298.

HEADEY, B.W., KELLEY, J. and WEARING, A.J. Dimensions of mental health. *Social Indicators Research*, 1990 (unpublished).

HELSON, H. *Adaptation level theory: an experimental and systematic approach to behaviour.* New York: Harper & Row, 1964.

HENDERSON, A.S., BYRNE, D.G. and DUNCAN-JONES, P. *Neurosis and the social environment.* New York: Academic Press, 1981.

HOLMES, R.H. and RAHE, R.H. The social readjustment rating scale. *Journal of Psychosomatic Research*, 1967; **11**, 213–218.

KAMMAN, R., CHRISTIE, D., IRWIN, R. and DIXON, G. Properties of an inventory to measure happiness. *New Zealand Psychologist*, 1979; **8**, 1–9.

KESSLER, R.C. and GREENBERG, D.F. *Linear panel analysis.* New York: Academic Press, 1981.

KISH, L., *Survey sampling.* New York: Wiley, 1965.

LARSEN, R.J., DIENER, E. and EMMONS, R.A. An evaluation of subjective well-being measures. *Social Indicators Research*, 1985; **17**, 1–18.

MADDI, S.R., BARTONE, P.T. and PUCCETTI, M.C. Stressful events are indeed a factor in physical illness: reply to Schroeder and Costa (1984). *Journal of Personality and Social Psychology*, 1987; **52**, 833–843.

MICHALOS, A.C. Multiple discrepancies theory. *Social Indicators Research*, 1985; **16**, 347–414.

NORMAN, W.T. Towards an adequate taxonomy of personality attributes. *Journal of Abnormal and Social Psychology*, 1963; **66**, 574–583.

PARDUCCI, A. Value judgments: toward a relational theory of happiness. In J.R. Eiser (ed.), *Attitudinal judgement.* New York: Springer Verlag, 1984.

RAHE, R.H. and ARTHUR, R.H. Life change and illness studies. *Journal of Human Stress*, 1978; **4**, 3–15.

REICH, J.W. and ZAUTRA, A.J. Life events and perceptions of life quality: developments in a two factor approach. *Journal of Community Psychology*, 1983; **11**, 121–132.

ROWLISON, R.T. and FELNER, R.D. Major life events, hassles and adaptation in adolescence: confounding in the conceptualization and measurement of life stress and adjustment revisited. *Journal of Personality and Social Psychology*, 1988; **55**, 432–444.

SCHROEDER, D.H. and COSTA, P.T. Influence of life event stress on physical illness: substantive effects or methodological flaws? *Journal of Personality and Social Psychology*, 1984: **46**, 853–863.

STONES, M.J. and KOZMA, A. Structural relationships among happiness scales: a second order factorial study. *Social Indicators Research*, 1985; **17**, 19–28.

TEASDALE, J. and FOGARTY, S. Differential effects of induced mood on retrieval of pleasant and unpleasant events from episodic memory. *Journal of Abnormal Psychology*, 1979; **88**, 248–257.

TENNANT, C. and ANDREWS, G. A scale to measure the stress of life events. *Australian and New Zealand Journal of Psychiatry*, 1976; **10**, 27–32.

VEENHOVEN, R. *Conditions of happiness.* Dordrecht: Reidel, 1984.

WARR, P.B. A study of psychological well-being. *British Journal of Psychology*, 1978; **69**, 111–121.

WARR, P.B., BARTER, J. and BROWNBRIDGE, G. On the independence of positive and negative affect. *Journal of Personality and Social Psychology*, 1983; **44**, 644–651.

WATSON, D. and TELLEGEN, A. Towards a consensual structure of mood, *Psychological Bulletin*, 1984; **98**, 219–235.

Appendix 1: Corrections for measurement error

In Tables 4.3, 4.5, 4.6 and 4.7 results are based on correlations which have been "corrected" (disattenuated) for measurement error. In the case of regression analyses a disattenuated correlation matrix provided the input into the analyses. The Betas and R^2s may thus be regarded as disattenuated estimates.

"Correction" for measurement error was undertaken in the usual way (e.g. Andrews, 1984) by dividing each observed correlation (rAB) by the product of the square roots of the reliabilities of the two variables. This yielded an estimated true correlation (rAB^1)

$$rAB^1 = \frac{rAB}{\sqrt{Rel.A \times Rel.B}}$$

The estimated reliabilities of the variables used in this paper were given by the Cronbach alphas for variables measured by multiple indicators. Reliabilities were (conservatively) estimated by the authors for variables measured by single indicators. The imputed reliabilities were as follows: life satisfaction = 0.92, positive affect = 0.64, negative affect = 0.65, sex = 1.0, age = 1.0, socio-economic status = 0.7, extraversion = 0.62, neuroticism = 0.82, openness = 0.76, availability of intimate attachments = 0.60, availability of friendships = 0.68, favourable events = 0.9, adverse events = 0.9, satisfaction-distress from events = 0.9. The measures of "normal" subjective well-being and "normal" events/psychic income used in Table 4.7 were assumed to have reliabilities of 1.0. These assumptions, like the other reliability estimates employed, had the conservative effect of *minimizing* the degree of "correction" (disattenuation) for error.

APPENDIX 2

Over time observed correlations, means and standard deviations[a]

	(1)	(2)	(3)	(4)	(5)	(6)	(7)	(8)	(9)	(10)	(11)	(12)	(13)	(14)	x	sd
Life satisfaction (1)	1.00														71.39	13.01
Positive affect (2)	.39	1.00													68.07	28.35
Negative affect (3)	-.40	-.16	1.00												23.64	26.81
Sex (m = 1) (f = 2) (4)	-.01	.01	.01	1.00											1.5	0.5
Age (5)	-.02	-.17	-.16	.00	1.00										42.35	12.95
Socio-economic status (6)	.10	.19	-.06	-.13	-.24	1.00									58.93	22.64
Extraversion (7)	.26	.22	-.12	-.07	-.16	.05	1.00								59.92	14.40
Neuroticism (8)	-.32	-.12	.42	.21	-.13	-.17	-.19	1.00							42.76	20.16
Openness (9)	.14	.18	.05	.22	-.19	.13	.09	.09	1.00						69.05	12.75
Intimate attachments (10)	.29	.14	-.17	.05	.05	.15	.11	-.12	.05	1.00					81.97	27.89
Friendship network (11)	.20	.15	-.10	-.16	-.05	.10	.29	.10	.04	.06	1.00				58.84	19.96
Favourable events (12)	.08	.32	.10	.10	-.24	.14	.19	.10	.23	.03	.11	1.00			7.76	5.12
Adverse events (13)	-.20	.05	.31	.01	-.22	.07	.04	.21	.21	-.13	-.04	.44	1.00		3.40	2.83
Satisfaction/distress from events (14)	.33	.34	-.08	.11	-.16	.09	.25	-.04	.22	.12	.16	.86	.76	1.00	40.10	10.52

[a] 1987 data. Life events scores relate to 1985–7 (data collected in 1987).

The Dynamics of Subjective Well-Being

5

The psychological causes of happiness

MICHAEL ARGYLE and MARYANNE MARTIN

Definition and measurement

If people are asked what they mean by "happiness" they give two kinds of answer. They either describe it as often being in a state of joy, or as a state of satisfaction. The first is an emotion, the second a cognition, the result of reflection. Some measures of happiness emphasize joy, some satisfaction, others a combination. They all involve some kind of self-rating, and people can be asked how they feel now, or today, or over a longer period. There has been controversy about how far happiness is the *opposite* of unhappiness (or depression), that is how far are they negatively correlated, to what extent are they due to different causes. This is of practical importance, since if the two are largely independent the methods used to relieve depression would not necessarily be expected to make normals happier and different methods would be needed to do this. Bradburn (1969) gave subjects scales for experience of positive and negative affect, and found evidence for complete independence of the two, but if subjects are asked *how much* of the time they felt happy or unhappy over a period of time, a correlation of −.58 has been obtained (Warr *et al.*, 1983). Diener and Emmons (1984) found that the correlation between positive and negative affect was more strongly negative the shorter the time period. Diener *et al.* (1985), found that the negative correlation between average positive and negative emotion was quite low, but with intensity of emotion partialled out this became as high as −.86; the reason is that the intensities of positive and negative affect are positively correlated at .70, thus concealing the true negative correlation between the two kinds of affect. Further evidence of the partial independence of positive and negative affect comes from examination of their sources, which are rather different; for example women are more likely to be depressed, but are on average just as happy as men (Argyle, 1987).

It seems useful to suppose that happiness may have three, partly independent components: (1) the frequency and degree of positive affect, or joy, (see Chapter 7), (2) the average level of satisfaction over a period, (see Chapter 4) and (3) the absence of negative feelings, such as depression (see Chapter 8) and anxiety.

However, no one measure of happiness has so far found general favour and come into general use, though a number of scales have been found to have reasonable validity (Larsen *et al.*, 1985). Measurement of depression is quite different, since the Beck Depression Inventory has come to be generally accepted (Beck *et al.*, 1961). We decided to develop a new measure of happiness along similar lines (Martin, Argyle and Crossland, in preparation). After discussion with Beck we drafted twenty-one items by reversing the Beck Depression Inventory items. However, since positive and negative affect are not quite the opposite of each other, we added eleven further items, to cover aspects of subjective well-being not so far included.

Following (in reverse) the design of the Beck Depression Inventory, the new items were designed with four incremental steps:
e.g. item 1

0 ☐ I do not feel happy (i.e. unhappy, mildly depressed).
1 ☐ I feel fairly happy (i.e. a low level of happiness).
2 ☐ I am very happy (i.e. a high level of happiness).
3 ☐ I am incredibly happy (i.e. manic).

This thirty-two item scale was then presented to eight graduate students in psychology, who were asked to rank the four choices for each item and also to comment on the face validity of each item. This resulted in extensive detailed revision, and the dropping of three items. The remaining items correlate well with the total score. We shall refer to this twenty-nine item scale as the Oxford Happiness Inventory.

Reliability. A seven week follow-up study found test-retest reliability of .78. A five month follow-up with ninety-six new subjects found a test-retest reliability of .67.

Validity. The twenty-nine item scale was then given by members of a psychology practical class to 147 people they know. An attempt was made to find people high, medium and low in subjective well-being, and the students also rated the happiness of the subjects on a 10-point scale. Oxford Happiness Inventory scores correlated with friends' ratings of happiness at .43.

Construct validity. Cronbach's alpha was computed on the twenty-nine item Oxford Happiness Inventory, yielding alpha = .90. Subscales composed of sub-sets of the twenty-nine item inventory yielded alpha coefficients ranging from alpha = .64 to .84, N = 347.

How well does this scale measure the three dimensions of happiness described above:

Positive affect:	current mood: happy	.54
	Bradburn, positive affect	.32
Satisfaction:	Life satisfaction index	.57
	Life events questionnaire	.60
Negative affect:	Beck depression inventory	−.52
	Current mood: depressed	−.40
	Bradburn, negative affect	−.32
	Neuroticism	−.47

It is clear that the Oxford Happiness Inventory correlates at .40—.60 with each of three postulated components of happiness.

The causes of joy

Anger is caused by frustration, insults and attacks, depression by the loss of social attachments and failure. What causes joy? Scherer and colleagues (1986) find that the most common reported cause is social relationships, followed by success. We shall examine the effects of social relationships in more detail later. MacPhillamy and Lewinsohn (1976) published a list af 320 different pleasant events and activities, of which forty-nine were powerful enough to cheer many people up for the whole day.

From these and other studies it may be suggested that there are seven main causes of joy, as follows:

1. Social contacts with friends, or others in close relationships.
2. Sexual activity.
3. Success, achievement.
4. Physical activity, exercise, sport.
5. Nature, reading, music.
6. Food and drink.
7. Alcohol.

Another source which may need to be added is the use of skills, the completion of valued tasks, especially in a group, as at work (see below), though this is perhaps more a cause of satisfaction. Some experiences of joy have a dimension of depth, intensity, "absorption" or "flow", for example when tackling a demanding task (Csikszentmihalyi, 1975). We found that some social activities had this property (e.g. "getting on well with loved ones"), as did some non-social activities (e.g. "listening to a beautiful piece of music") (Argyle and Crossland, 1987).

It is not entirely clear why there should be an emotion of joy at all, since it occurs in situations where there is no need to energize the organism to fight, flight or other action. Perhaps it is really the opposite of pain, an amplified biological signal, in this case to stay in the situation, or repeat the action. The list of seven sources of joy is a most interesting and rather curious one, from this point of view. It is obvious why eating, drinking and sex are biologically rewarded by joy. We shall see why social activity is beneficial later. Nature, reading and music are, so far at least, much more mysterious, though we will offer some speculations about reading later.

Presumably each source of joy leads in some way to the pleasure centres. The discovery of these was one of the most exciting developments in recent research on the brain. It was found that if an electrode was inserted in this part of a rat's brain, electrical impulses were so rewarding that animals would press a bar as much as 10,000 times per hour for up to twenty-six hours. While we do not really know that rats experience "pleasure", stimulation of these areas is evidently highly rewarding (Olds and Milner, 1954; Rolls, 1979). Research on electrical stimulation of the human brain in patients has found that pleasurable experiences, sometimes with sexual overtones, are produced from parts of the Medial Forebrain Bundle, in the Septum and Amygdala (Buck, 1988).

The passage of messages in the brain is facilitated by various neuro-transmitters, and this applies to the activation of the pleasure centre. These include *dopamine* and *nor-adrenaline*: experiments have shown that they are released by amphetamine. Higher levels of them increase the rate of self-stimulation, showing that greater reward is being received. This may be why amphetamine is able to act as an anti-depressant and produce more positive moods. Another set of neurotransmitters are the *endorphins*, which are released by vigorous exercise. It can be assumed that while some activities, like eating, drinking, and sex are innately linked to the pleasure centres, others like achievement, become linked by learning.

The causes of satisfaction

The most likely source of satisfaction is objective satisfaction. It would be expected that a person would be more satisfied with his income if he had a large income, for example. However, this effect has been found to be small or non-significant. Korman et al. (unpublished) reviewed nineteen American studies, and found that in twelve studies all relationships between income and measures of well-being were non-significant, while they were mostly non-significant in four others. If comparisons are made between countries, there is very little relationship between satisfaction with income, housing, etc., and actual conditions. In the USA the standard of living has increased more or less continuously since 1957, but repeated surveys have found a generally falling level of satisfaction (Easterlin, 1974). Similar lack of correlation is found for satisfaction with education, sports facilities, crime prevention and housing (Argyle, 1987).

However, there are certain aspects of life which are much more strongly linked to satisfaction—marriage and other social relationships, the conditions of work, and leisure activities. These will be discussed later.

The failure of some direct measures of satisfaction to explain satisfaction has led to a number of cognitive theories. The first of these was the theory that satisfaction is based mainly on comparisons with other people. In some spheres of judgment this is a logical necessity: "tall" means taller than other people, for example. Runciman (1966) found that British manual workers, in the top third of all incomes, were more satisfied with their pay than non-manual workers paid the same amount—because the manual workers were comparing themselves with other less well-paid manual workers. American studies have found that comparisons with "typical Americans" gave better predictions of satisfaction than the objective level of pay, or of other variables (Carp and Carp, 1982). In a study in Wisconsin it was found that the most powerful predictors of satisfaction with pay were equity considerations—though actual living standards and intrinsic satisfaction were also important (Berkowitz et al., 1987). There are limits to the importance of comparisons—as we have seen, certain objective conditions do have some effect, and as Diener (1984) said, it is not the case that "if everyone has a pain, then mine doesn't hurt".

An elaboration of comparison theory is the "Michigan model". According to this theory, satisfaction is greater when achievements are close to aspirations, lower when they fall short. Aspirations in turn are based on

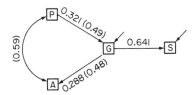

Fig. 5.1. Michalos (1980): Satisfaction with life as a whole: the goal-achievement gap model.

comparisons with other people and own past experience. To test this theory it is necessary to ask about the gap between aspirations and achievements. In a later paper Michalos (1986) reviewed forty-one tests of the hypothesis and found that the model was confirmed in thirty-seven cases, often accounting for a substantial amount of variance. An example is shown in Figure 5.1. It can be seen that the goal-achievement gap gives a good prediction of satisfaction ($r = .64$), and this in turn is predictable from comparisons with best previous experience (P) and with "average people" (A). It is also found that P and A do not in themselves give good predictions of satisfaction. They have to be combined with achievements for the model to work.

The theory also provides an explanation of an interesting age difference—satisfaction increases continuously with age. The reason is that as people become older their achievements increase and their aspirations decline, until eventually the gap closes (Campbell et al., 1976). The falling satisfaction of Americans during the last twenty-five years may be because aspirations are rising faster than economic achievement can realize. The same process could explain the greater decline in the satisfaction of educated blacks over this period.

While there is some evidence that this theory applies to achievement, money, etc., it probably does not apply to more basic forms of satisfaction, like sex (Freedman, 1978). Also, we should not expect it to apply to intrinsic forms of satisfaction based, for example, on satisfying work or leisure. Aspirations may be very high, and tend to be revised upwards once a certain level has been achieved. High aspirations are a threat to happiness (Diener, 1984), and happiness therapy sometimes includes persuading clients to lower their aspirations.

A final model is adaptation level theory. This asserts that we become adapted to any particular level of stimuli, so that satisfaction is dependent on increases, dissatisfaction on decreases, of sources of satisfaction. Impressive evidence for this theory comes from studies of people who have had very serious accidents and become paraplegic or quadriplegic: after a time they become nearly as satisfied again as the general population, though never quite as much (Brickman *et al.*, 1978). Similar results have been found for people who win football pools and lotteries, though here the findings are more complex.

The adaptation-level theory can explain the curious effects of the weather. Between countries (and climates) there appears to be very little effect of climate—presumably because people get used to their weather. However, within a country people are happier on sunny days compared with rainy days. Schwarz and Clore (1983) telephoned German subjects on sunny and rainy days to ask about immediate mood and about well-being; some subjects were told that the study was to find out how the weather influences mood. On sunny days subjects reported high levels both of momentary happiness and of well-being, whether they had been primed or not; on rainy days mood was lower under both conditions, but well-being was less only for subjects who had not been primed. It was concluded that affect is directly influenced by the weather, but that well-being, a more cognitive state, is also influenced by seeking explanations for negative states.

However, there is one rather obvious exception to the effects of adaptation: some people are depressed, and for them adaptation has evidently failed. As we shall see later, some other people are above average in happiness: fortunately for them adaptation has failed again.

The effects of social relations

Campbell *et al.* (1976) in their classic study *The Quality of American Life* found that certain "domains" of satisfaction were very important for satisfaction with life-as-a-whole. The most important domains were family life and marriage, with friendship not far behind. In fact social relationships affect all of the three components of happiness which we distinguished earlier—positive affect, satisfaction, and prevention of distress, and we will consider the three separately.

Joy. Many studies have shown the effects of friendship, love, parent-child and other close relationships of joy. As Scherer *et al*. (1986) showed, this is the most common cause of joy. The finding is not in doubt; what is not agreed is its explanation.

The answer may be found in the things which friends, for example, do together, Argyle and Furnham (1982) found the activities which were most characteristic of a number of relationships, by finding the frequency of carrying out each activity, divided by the average frequency for all relationships. The results for friends, spouses and work colleagues are shown in Table 5.1.

TABLE 5.1. *Situations and activities most chosen for certain relationships*
(ratios to mean frequency for all relationships)

Friend, similar age mean ratio 1.26		Spouse mean ratio 1.64		Work colleagues, liked, same status mean ratio 1.11	
Situations above this ratio		Situations above this ratio		Situations above this ratio	
Dancing	2.00	Watch TV	2.61	Attend lecture	2.11
Tennis	1.67	Do domestic tasks together	2.48	Work together on joint task	1.56
Sherry party	1.63	Play chess or other indoor game	2.31	Together in a committee	1.55
Joint Leisure	1.63	Go for a walk	2.28	Morning coffee, tea	1.50
Pub	1.60	Go shopping	2.15	Casual chat, telling jokes	1.35
Intimate conversation	1.52	Play tennis, squash	2.03	One helps the other	1.31
Walk	1.50	Informal meal	1.93		
		Intimate conversation	1.91		
		Have argument, disagreement	1.84		

It can be seen that friends, in this Oxford adult sample at least, spend their time together eating, drinking, talking, and playing games—a collection of pleasant activities.

A second explanation is in terms of non-verbal communication. People who love or like each other smile, look and generally send positive non-verbal signs of liking to one another. Kraut and Johnston (1979) found that players at a bowling alley smiled at each other a lot, but rarely smiled at the skittles: smiling is a directed social signal rather than simply a pleasure response. If A smiles at B, B is pleased and reciprocates, thus rewarding A. In addition, for many, when A smiles his own mood will be enhanced via facial feedback (Laird, 1984).

A third explanation comes from the hypothesis that close social interaction is a basic source both of positive affect and bonding (Argyle, 1988).

For example babies are happy to interact with their mothers over closed circuit television, but not to watch a recording of her made previously (Murray and Trevarthen, 1985). Adult subjects like a confederate who copies their bodily movements and gestures (Dabbs, 1969). Friends and others in close relationships are likely to develop such closely synchronized and responsive interaction patterns.

Satisfaction. The effects of social relationships on satisfaction are a lot more straightforward. Again the facts are not in dispute. The most striking positive effect is that of marriage, as found for example by Veroff *et al.* (1981, Table 4.3) in an American national sample survey (Table 5.2).

TABLE 5.2. *Veroff et al. (1981): Happiness of the married, single and divorced*

	Percentage "very happy"	
	Men	Women
Married	35.0	41.5
Single	18.5	25.5
Divorced	18.5	15.5

In our study, with a smaller British sample, of the estimated satisfaction

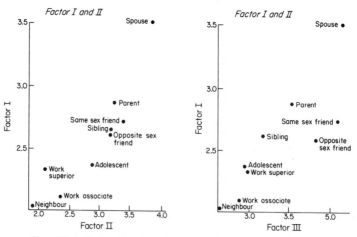

FIG. 5.2. Relationships plotted on the satisfaction dimensions.

from different relationships we obtained the results shown in Figure 5.2. The scores are the ratings on 1–5 scales of satisfaction for each relationship, averaged across the scales correlating most highly with each factor. We found *three* dimensions of satisfaction: material; tangible help; emotional support and shared interests. It can be seen that the spouse is by far the greatest source of satisfaction, close relatives and friends next, and work-mates and neighbours last. Our second dimension, emotional support, includes degrees of trust and disclosure, use of others as a confidant. The third factor is extent of shared interests and activities. Here, in a nutshell, is the explanation for the effects of social relationships on satisfaction—they give material help, social support and shared activities.

Prevention of distress. Social relationships have a powerful effect on the prevention of ill-health, mental disorder and other forms of distress. In a famous study in California (Berkman and Syme, 1979), 7,000 people were interviewed to ascertain the strength of their supportive social networks. Nine years later they were interviewed again—to see which interviewees were still alive. As Figure 5.3 shows, those with strong networks fared better, even after being matched for initial health, health practices, obesity, smoking, drinking and social class: for men in their fifties, for example, 30.8 per cent of those with the weakest networks had died, compared with only 9.6 per cent of those with the strongest networks. The effects were greater for marriage than for friends and relatives, which in turn were greater than those due to belonging to churches or other organizations.

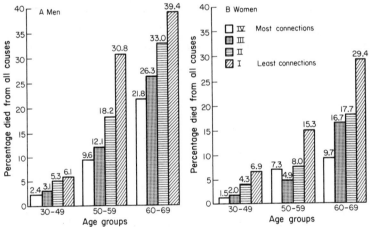

Fig. 5.3. Berkman and Syme (1979): Social networks and mortality.

In a number of studies it has been found that marriage has a greater positive effect on the mental health of men than of women (Argyle, 1987). This is probably because wives provide more social support, act as better confidants, than husbands (Vanfossen, 1981).

The way in which social support sustains good health is fairly well understood: stress disturbs the immune system, making people more liable to become ill; but social support restores it, perhaps by replacing negative emotions by positive ones (Jemmott and Locke, 1984). Social support also enables people to cope with stress by methods more constructive and less harmful than drinking, smoking, and risky behaviour like dangerous driving (Badura, 1984).

The effects on mental health are similar. Simply being married puts people much less at risk, as Cochrane (1988) showed for England (Table 5.3). Interestingly it also appears that if the marriage ends due to divorce or death, the person becomes more at risk of mental illness or death than those who have remained single.

TABLE 5.3. *Cochrane (1988): Mental hospital admissions and marital status (England, 1981)*

Marital status	Mental hospital admissions per 100,000
Single	770
Married	260
Widowed	980
Divorced	1,437

It is not just being married, but the quality of the relationship that counts. In a famous study in South London (Brown and Harris, 1978) it was found that women who had experienced a lot of stressful life events were less likely to be depressed if they had a spouse who acted as confidant—"someone to whom you can talk about yourself and your problems" (Table 5.4).

TABLE 5.4. *Brown and Harris (1978): Depression, stress and social support (% depressed)*

	Support		
	High	Mid	Low
Women who had stressful life event	10	26	41
Women with no such events	1	3	4

This shows the way in which social support buffers the effects of stressful life events, which has been confirmed in many later studies (Cohen and Wills, 1985).

Table 5.4 shows that 41 per cent of women had experienced stressful life events and who did not have a supportive husband became depressed, compared with only 10 per cent of those who had strong support. These results are at least partly due to reverse causation, i.e., some people may not get married because they are mentally disturbed. However, the explanation of the effect of social support on mental health is probably that it enables people to cope with stress, and to replace negative emotions, like depression and anxiety, and low self-esteem, with positive emotions and thoughts.

Negative effects of relationships. Everyone knows that relationships have a negative side, too. Argyle and Furnham (1983) found two factors of conflict in relationships—a general factor, and a second factor of conflict due to mutual criticism. It is interesting that a spouse is the greatest source of conflict as well as of satisfaction. Work superior is the next greatest source of conflict—but is a rather low source of satisfaction.

Children are a great source of joy and satisfaction. They can also be a

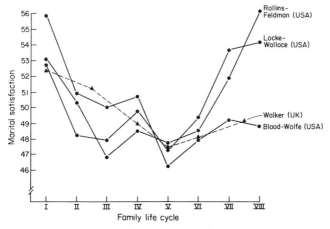

FIG. 5.4. Mean scores on marital satisfaction by stage of family life cycle.

source of trouble. Figure 5.4 shows a number of British and American studies of marital satisfaction at different points in the family cycle. The vertical variable is marital satisfaction. It can be seen that marital satisfaction is depressed when there are children in the home, especially adolescent children.

Job satisfaction

Work is a major component of overall satisfaction with life (see Chapter 12). Job satisfaction can be measured by single questions, such as "How well do you like your job", from "I love it", to "I hate it", or by asking people if they would work if it was not financially necessary, or if they would do the same job again. If more detailed questions are asked, job satisfaction divides into a number of factors, such as satisfaction with the work itself ("intrinsic satisfaction"), and satisfaction with the pay, promotion prospects, supervision and co-workers (Smith *et al.*, 1969). Of these, intrinsic satisfaction, and satisfaction with co-workers are particularly important.

Intrinsic satisfaction is satisfaction derived from the work itself. Hackman (1977) suggested that five features of jobs produce satisfaction. Many studies have investigated this issue, and the latest meta-analysis found the following average correlations with job satisfaction:

task identity—completing a clear and identifiable piece of work   .32
task significance—the degree to which the job has an impact on
    lives of others   .38
skill variety   .41
autonomy—the degree to which the job provides freedom,
    independence and discretion   .46
feedback—the extent to which information about effectiveness
    is available   .41

(Loher *et al.*, 1985)

It may be objected that subjective ratings by workers of these job characteristics are almost another measure of job satisfaction. However, such ratings
do correlate with ratings by supervisors while objective job changes related
to these characteristics, e.g. job enrichment, lead to increased job satisfaction (Argyle, 1989).

Job satisfaction varies a great deal between different jobs. Generally
speaking the more highly skilled and highly paid jobs are associated with
the greatest job satisfaction. For example 91 per cent of mathematicians
said that they would do the same job again, compared with 16 per cent of
unskilled steel workers. It is not the most highly paid jobs which give the
most satisfaction, but those which would be expected to give the highest
intrinsic satisfaction in Hackman's terms—university teachers, scientists,
social workers and clergymen (Sales and House, 1971). It is important for
people to be in jobs which "fit" their personalities, in terms of task difficulty,
stressfulness, and in other ways. When the fit is poor, job satisfaction is low
and depression is high (Caplan *et al.*, 1975; Furnham and Schaeffer, 1984).

Satisfaction with co-workers is also very important, job satisfaction is
greater and absenteeism and labour turnover is less, when people belong to
small work groups where the others like them, and it is possible to talk. This
is partly because other people at work cooperate and help with the work.
In addition workers enjoy the informal social life of gossip, games, jokes,
and general fooling about. The fooling about may be partly to relieve tension—this is one source of industrial sabotage—and partly to relieve boredom. In a group of workers on a repetitive task "banana time" was when
one man would steal and eat another's banana at a certain hour; later
another would open a window, creating a row about the draught, and so
on. They said "If it weren't for the talking and fooling you'd go nuts" (Roy,
1959). Social support from the group is a major source of defence against
outside threats, from the supervisor or elsewhere, and reduces the effect of
such stresses on anxiety and depression (Caplan *et al.*, 1975).

We suggested that people at work can be considered in four categories:

A. Those who become normal friends, and are also seen outside work,
    e.g. at home.

B. Those who are seen at coffee-breaks or at lunch, but not outside work.
C. Those with whom work encounters are pleasant, but who are not seen at coffee breaks.
D. Those who are avoided as far as possible.

We found that there was more activity of the following kinds with co-workers in the closer categories (Henderson and Argyle, 1985):

1. Joking with the other person.
2. Chatting casually.
3. Discussing work.
4. Having coffee, drinks or meal together.
5. Teasing him/her.
6. Helping each other with work.
7. Asking or giving personal advice.
8. Discussing your feelings or emotions.
9. Discussing your personal life.
10. Teaching or showing the other person something about work.

Research on unemployment has thrown further light on the benefits of work. Fryer and Payne (1984) found a number of individuals who had become unemployed, but who were more satisfied than when they were at work. Their jobs had been unsatisfying, but they took up more satisfying activities: one started a small nature reserve; one was the leader of a community project. In addition, workers who had apparently unsatisfying jobs are often even more depressed when they lose them. It seems likely that work conveys a number of benefits even to those who are unaware of them. Jahoda (1982) listed five such benefits, and Warr (1987) later expanded this to nine "vitamins", which he thinks must be above a certain level to avoid distress:

1. Opportunity for control.
2. Opportunity for skill use.
3. Externally generated goals (i.e. demands for purposeful activity, and structuring of time).
4. Variety.
5. Environmental clarity (e.g. certainty about the future).
6. Availability of money.
7. Physical security (i.e. safety).
8. Opportunity for interpersonal contact.
9. Valued social position.

Like vitamins, it is suggested, these factors have non-linear effects. Thus vitamins C and E improve health up to a point and then have no further effect; pay, physical conditions and interpersonal contact may be like this.

Vitamins A and D produce an increase in health up to a point, but too much is bad for health; control, variety, clarity and workload may be like this.

Retirement makes an interesting comparison with unemployment, since the retired are a lot more satisfied, on average more so than those still at work. The explanation for this difference is no doubt that while the unemployed see their situation in terms of rejection and failure, the retired see themselves as enjoying their due rewards. However, 25–30 per cent of workers have difficulty in adjusting to retirement, and wish they had carried on working. What they miss most is the money and the work associates, rather than the work itself (Parkes, 1980). More highly skilled people do miss the work, though some of them are able to keep it up during retirement.

Leisure satisfaction

Leisure means what people do in their free time, because they want to, for its own sake, for fun, entertainment, or for goals of their own choosing, but not for material gain. Even among those in full-time work, for 19 per cent leisure is more important than work, and for another 32 per cent it is equally important (Veroff *et al.*, 1981). For men at work, there are 4 hours of leisure on week-days and 11.4 hours at week-ends (General Household Survey, 1977).

Some leisure activities, the more serious and demanding ones, provide intrinsic satisfaction similar to intrinsic job satisfaction. Some provide more than this—a feeling of "absorption", i.e. intensity of experience (Csikszentmihalyi, 1975). Intrinsic satisfaction is provided by (1) sport, which can be more or less serious or competitive, and which is also a source of joy through the release of endorphins, (2) hobbies, from amateur archeology, to writing books, often involving some group activity, (3) clubs and classes—Scottish country dancing, church, politics, evening classes, (4) voluntary work, which gives the added satisfaction of service to others, (5) home-based leisure—gardening, needlework, do-it-yourself, and looking after the children.

There is a major social component to most leisure. Most leisure is done in the company of others. Social satisfaction is a good predictor of overall leisure satisfaction. Some of the serious forms of leisure listed above have a social element—sport and clubs for example. A lot of leisure is primarily social—seeing friends and relations, going to the pub, going out to eat and dancing.

Leisure provides another source of satisfaction, which appeared as one of the hidden benefits of work—giving a sense of identity, and sometimes status. Leisure activities can do this in several ways, such as:

1. Dressing up (for sport, dancing, etc.);
2. acquiring status by holding offices in clubs, or informal status in sporting or other groups;

3. acquiring new skills and competencies (in sport, music, dancing, pottery, etc.);
4. special styles of performance (e.g. dancing, art);
5. expressing distance from common styles, showing individuality;
6. acquiring membership of a special social group; and
7. talking about the activity to outsiders.

These aspects of identity can be tried out in leisure situations, with little commitment or risk, but they may become central life concerns.

Finally we come to an important aspect of leisure satisfaction which did *not* arise with job satisfaction—relaxation. An Australian study of leisure needs found that the need to relax and take it easy was rated as one of the most important needs (Kabanoff, 1982). Holidays are especially motivated by the need to relax. A survey in the USA of readers of *Psychology Today* (a very large but rather odd sample) found this was the most common motivation, and was agreed by 37 per cent of the sample. However, most went with family or friends (hence social needs), women wanted to indulge themselves, as did some men. The workaholics wanted to go home and get back to work (Rubenstein, 1980). The benefits of these holidays are shown in Table 5.5.

TABLE 5.5. *Rubenstein (1980): Percentages reporting symptoms while on vacation, and during the past year*

	Vacation	During past year
Tired	12	34
Irritable	8	30
Constipation, worry, anxiety	7	27
Loss of interest in sex	6	12
Digestive problems	6	16
Insomnia	4	11
Headaches	3	21

However, the leisure activity on which most time is spent in the modern world is watching TV: in the UK women watch on average 4½ hours a day, men 3¾ hours. The explanation of this devotion to TV is far from clear, especially as it provides quite low levels of satisfaction. While watching programmes in general people are found to be relaxed, cheerful and sociable; but they are more drowsy, weak and passive after watching TV than for reading, work, other leisure, eating, or talking (Csikszentmihalyi and Kubey, 1981). In an American survey, Robinson found that only 17 per cent reported "great" satisfaction from watching TV—even less than for housework (25 per cent), less than reading (32 per cent), and much less than from their children (79 per cent) (Robinson, 1977).

Part of the explanation may be that TV is indeed "relaxing", i.e., it is an opportunity for rest, and achieving a lower level of mental and bodily arousal.

It has been found that if different moods are aroused experimentally, subjects who are stressed will choose relaxing TV programmes, while those who are bored choose exciting ones (Bryant and Zillmann, 1984). TV watching can also provide social satisfaction, though at secondhand. Livingstone (1987) found that regular watchers of Coronation Street in Britain felt they knew the characters in much the same way as their real friends. Finally TV has the great advantage over real sport, hobbies or social life—it is relatively cheap, takes no effort, needs no skill, or good weather, and involves no risk.

Happy people

Are there individuals who are consistently happier than others, across a range of situations? There are certainly people who are depressed, and person-situation interaction researchers have found a substantial amount of person variance in happiness (Diener and Larsen, 1984).

One of the best predictors of individual happiness is extraversion. We find a correlation of .48 between the Oxford Happiness Inventory and the Eysenck Personality Questionnaire measure of extraversion (Martin, Argyle and Crossland, in preparation). Costa *et al.* (1981) found that extraversion predicted happiness seventeen years later at .24 to .35 for different measures. It is the social component of extraversion which predicts best, and positive affect which is best predicted.

Headey *et al.* (1985) (see Chapter 4) carried out a repeated panel study of 600 Australians, in 1981, 1983 and 1985. They found that extraversion predisposed people—especially young people—to have favourable life events, especially in the domains of friendship and work; these in turn led to a high level of positive well-being, and to increases in extraversion.

However, the explanation of the correlation with extraversion is in as much doubt as the explanation of the benefits from social relationships. Following the rival explanations offered for that, the effect of extraversion could be due to:

(a) choice of more enjoyable activities. Furnham (1981) found that extraverts choose more social activities and physical pursuits when they have a free choice—both are sources of joy. Headey and Wearing (op.cit.) found that extraverts experienced more positive events with friends and at work.

(b) Extraverts emit more positive non-verbal signals than introverts—they smile more, look more, stand a little closer, and are more expressive.

(c) Extraverts also emit different verbal behaviour. They ask more questions, agree, compliment, try to find things they have in common, talk about pleasant things, joke and laugh more (Thorne, 1987; Argyle, unpublished). However, it is not clear whether extraverts are trying to form relationships, have fun, or simply expect that social relations will be positive and enjoyable.

(d) Gray (1972) put forward a neurological theory, part of which postulates that extraverts magnify rewards while introverts magnify punishments, because of differences in brain structure. It would be expected that this would be reflected in levels of neurotransmitters in such a way that extraverts would have higher levels of non-epinephrine, introverts higher levels of serotonin. This was not found by Ballenger (1983), though experiments on sensitivity to rewards and punishments have frequently obtained the predicted results.

Another source of individual differences in happiness is attributional style. Depressives interpret bad events as internal (i.e. due to themselves), global (i.e. will happen in other spheres) and stable (i.e. will continue to occur) (Martin and Clark, 1985). We find that happy people (on the Oxford Happiness Inventory) do not make these attributions for bad events, while they do make internal, global and stable attributions for good events (Martin, Argyle and Crossland, 1988).

Happy people tend to "look on the bright side"; this has been described as the "Pollyanna principle". In support of this idea it has been found that some individuals score high on happiness and optimism, rate events as pleasanter, have a more positive view of others, recall more positive events and have pleasanter free associations (Matlin and Gawron, 1979). Martin, Argyle and Crossland (in preparation) find that happy people ruminate about good events in the past and can't stop thinking about them. If they think about bad things it is to see how they could be put right. Unhappy people on the other hand ruminate about bad events. If they think about good ones it is to wonder how they might go wrong. Happy people are higher on internal control—they believe that events are under their own control rather than that of other people of chance.

Taylor and Brown (1988) conclude that happy people and those in good mental health engage in three kinds of distortion of reality—they have an unrealistically positive view of the self, exaggerated beliefs of control over events, and unrealistic optimism. Depressed people, and those with low self-esteem see things more accurately. On the other hand, happy people really do have more "resources", e.g. intelligence, education, physical attractiveness, social skills and better jobs (Campbell et al., 1976), which are likely to give greater control and other grounds for optimism.

Experimental mood induction

It has been found possible to induce positive emotions in the laboratory. Velten (1968) asked subjects to read silently, then aloud, sixty statements such as "this is great", "I really do feel good", "I *am* elated about things", trying to put themselves in the mood suggested. Later versions of this procedure have asked people to spend twenty seconds each on twelve statements taking about seven minutes in all, and to try to put themselves in the mood suggested (Teasdale and Russell, 1983). There is no doubt that the Velten method does produce a more positive mood for many people. However, the effects are short-lived, and disappear after ten or fifteen minutes (Frost and Green, 1982). Furthermore, between 30 and 50 per cent of subjects are not affected at all (Clark, 1983).

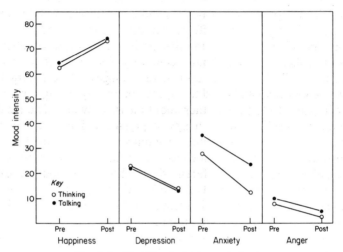

Fɪɢ. 5.5a. Mood levels for happy induction.

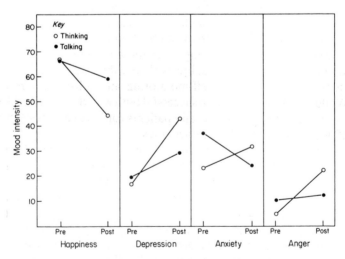

Fɪɢ. 5.5b. Mood levels for depressed induction.

Listening to cheerful music, again asking subjects to try to get into the mood suggested, has also been studied. It has been found to be rather more effective than Velten's methods (Sutherland, Newman and Rachman, 1982), and it affects nearly all the subjects tested, not just some of them (Clark, 1983).

Showing films has often been used as an experimental procedure for positive mood induction (e.g. Buck, 1984; Marston, Hart, Hileman and Faunce, 1984; Martin, 1985). We have used this technique to study the effect of mood on facial expression, and to avoid any imitation effects we have used films of puppies at play. Isen and Gorgoglione (1983) found that funny films had longer-lasting effects than the Velten method.

Schwarz and Clore (1983) found that positive mood can be enhanced if subjects are asked to think about recent very pleasant events for twenty minutes, in detail, and calling up concrete images. Martin, Argyle and Crossland (under review) hoped to improve on this by asking subjects, put together in pairs, to tell each other about pleasant events. The result was that the effect on self-ratings of happy, depressed and anxious mood were the same as for other subjects thinking about such events alone (see Figure 5.5a). However, if they were asked to talk or think about recent unhappy events the effects were quite different: those who talked about these events became less unhappy, depressed and anxious than those who thought about them alone—"a trouble shared is a trouble halved" (see Figure 5.5b).

The Velten technique has been used in a number of happiness training courses, as a twice-a-day exercise, although it appears as if a number of alternative techniques would be better for this purpose.

A more powerful method of enhancing happiness has been devised by Lewinsohn *et al.* (1982). Clients are asked to keep daily records for a month of pleasant events, and daily mood. Computer analysis then reveals which events and activities have the greatest effect on mood for each individual, and he or she is encouraged to engage in these activities more often. This procedure is more successful if subjects choose the activities freely, though techniques like goal-setting, self-monitoring and self-reward have been used. While the method has been successful both with depressed and normal subjects, it doesn't always work, and patients can recover from depression without any increases in pleasant activities.

Happiness training courses and courses for depressed patients have some-times included assertiveness training, and this has been found to be success-ful. Social skills training of other kinds is widely used for people who have difficulty with relationships—friendship, marriage, work etc. The findings which we have reported on the happiness of extraverts suggest that training might well be given in the social interaction style of extraverts—sending positive non-verbal signals, and reaching for similarity and asking questions, etc., in the verbal sphere (Argyle, 1987).

Cognitive therapy has been found to be successful as treatment for depression, and can also improve the happiness of normals, using the methods devised by Ellis (1962) and Beck (1967, 1976). The research which we have reviewed here suggests some other possible directions for cognitive therapy—persuading people to make different attributions for good and bad events, trying to change the content of ruminations, and increasing optimism and self-esteem.

A happiness training course in New Zealand for normal people was mainly based on improving insight and understanding, and correcting irrational beliefs, in eight two-hour sessions over four weeks. This was very

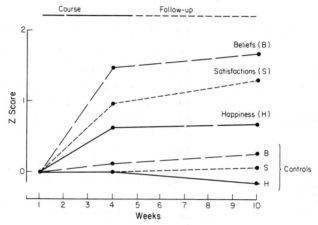

FIG. 5.6. Lichter, Haye and Kammann (1980): Effects of a happiness training course.

successful: see Figure 5.6, which shows standardized scores over the period of the course and its follow-up (Lichter, Haye and Kammann, 1980).

However, the research we have discussed suggests that for many people no training or therapy is necessary. What they need to do to increase their happiness is to improve (and enjoy) their social relationships, find work which is intrinsically (and socially) satisfying, and leisure which is sometimes active as well as sometimes relaxing. What is not clear is whether people should try to change their thinking patterns consciously in the first instance, so that these improvements in their relationships, work and leisure become a natural consequence of their more positive thinking, or whether behavioural changes should be made, even if the person does not feel much like making the effort, in the confidence that the cognitive benefits will follow. The solution may lie in the conjunction of approaches, by analogy with cognitive therapy, which despite its name combines a cognitive approach with a behavioural one. It may be that neither approach on its own is as likely to be sustained—in a similar way that drastic diets which cannot be maintained in the long term are not of much value. It could be argued that the combination of cognitive and behavioural is more than the sum of the parts.

References

ARGYLE. M. *The psychology of happiness*. London: Methuen, 1987.
ARGYLE. M. Social cognition and social interaction. *The Psychologist*, 1988; **1**, 177–83.
ARGYLE. M. *The social psychology of work*. Second edition. Harmondsworth: Penguin, 1989.
ARGYLE, M. and CROSSLAND, J. Dimensions of positive emotions. *British Journal of Social Psychology*, 1987; **26**, 127–37.
ARGYLE, M. and FURNHAM, A. The ecology of relationships: choice of situation as a function of relationship. *British Journal of Social Psychology*, 1982; **21**, 259–62.
ARGYLE, M. and FURNHAM A. Sources of satisfaction and conflict in long-term relationships. *Journal of Marriage and the Family*, 1983; **45**, 481–93.
BADURA, B. Life-style and health: some remarks on different view points. *Social Science and Medicine*, 1984; **19**, 341–7.
BALLENGER, J. C. Biochemical correlates of personality traits in normals: an exploratory study. *Personality and Individual Differences*, 1983; **6**, 615–25.
BECK, A. T. *Depression: clinical, experimental, and theoretical aspects*. New York: Hoeber, 1967.
BECK, A. T. *Cognitive therapy and the emotional disorders*. New York: International Universities Press, 1976.
BECK, A. T., WARD, C. H., MENDELSON, M., HOCK, J. and ERBAUGH, J. An inventory for measuring depression. *Archives of General Psychiatry*, 1961: **7**, 158–216.
BERKOWITZ, L., FRASER, C., TREASURE, F. P. and COCHRAN, S. Pay, equity, job qualifications, and comparison in pay satisfaction. *Journal of Applied Psychology*, 1987; **72**, 544–51.
BERKMAN, L. F. and SYME, S. L. Social networks, host resistance, and mortality: a nine-year follow-up study of Alameda county residents. *American Journal of Epidemiology*, 1979; **109**, 186–204.
BRADBURN, N. M. *The structure of psychological well-being*. Chicago: Aldine, 1969.
BRICKMAN, P., COATES, D. and JANOFF-BULMAN, R. Lottery winners and accident victims: is happiness relative? *Journal of Personality and Social Psychology*, 1978; **36**, 917–27.
BROWN, G. W. and HARRIS, T. *Social origins of depression*. London: Tavistock, 1978.
BRYANT, J. and ZILLMANN, D. Using television to alleviate boredom and stress: selective exposure as a function of induced excitational states. *Journal of Broadcasting*, 1984; **28**, 1–20.
BUCK, R. *The communication of emotion*. New York: Guilford, 1984.
BUCK, R. *Human motivation and emotion*. New York: Wiley, 1988.
CAMPBELL, A., CONVERSE, P. E. and RODGERS, W. L. *The quality of american life*. New York: Sage, 1976.
CAPLAN, R. D., COBB, S., FRENCH, J. R. P., HARRISON, R. V. and PINNEAN, S. R. *Job demands and worker health*. US Department of Health, Education and Welfare, 1975.
CARP, F. M. and CARP, A. Test of a model of domain satisfaction and well-being. *Research on Aging*, 1982; **4**, 503–22.
CLARK, D. M. On the induction of depressed mood in the laboratory: evaluation and comparison of the Velten and musical procedures. *Advances in Behavior Research and Therapy*, 1983; **5**, 24–49.
COCHRANE, R. Marriage, separation and divorce. In S. Fisher and J. Reason (eds.) *Handbook of life stress, cognition and health*. Chichester: Wiley, 1988.
COHEN, S. and WILLS, T. A. Stress, social support, and the buffering hypothesis. *Psychological Bulletin*, 1985; **98**, 310–57.
COSTA, P. T., McRAE, R. R. and NORRIS, A. H. Personal adjustment to ageing: longitudinal prediction from neuroticism and extraversion. *Journal of Gerontology*, 1981; **36**, 78–85.
CSIKSZENTMIHALYI, M. *Beyond boredom and anxiety*. San Francisco: Jossey-Bass, 1975.
CSIKSZENTMIHALYI, M. and KUBEY, R. Television and the rest of life: a systematic comparison of subjective experiences. *Public Opinion Quarterly*, 1981; **45**, 317–28.
DABBS, J. M. Similarity of gestures and the structure of the nonverbal communication of emotion. *Journal of Personality*, 1969; **45**, 564–84.
DIENER, E. Subjective well-being. *Psychological Bulletin*, 1984; **95**, 542–75.
DIENER, E. and EMMONS, R. A. The independence of positive and negative affect. *Journal of Personality and Social Psychology*, 1984; **47**, 1105–17.

DIENER, E. and LARSEN, R. J. Temporal stability and cross-situational consistency of positive and negative affect. *Journal of Personality and Social Psychology*, 1984; **47**, 871–83.

DIENER, E., LARSEN, R. J., LEVINE, S. and EMMONS, R. A. Intensity and frequency: dimensions underlying positive and negative affect. *Journal of Personality and Social Psychology*, 1985, **48**, 1253–65.

EASTERLIN, R. A. Does economic growth improve the human lot? Some empirical evidence. In P. A. David and M. Abramovitz (eds.), *Nations and households in economic growth*. New York: Academic Press, 1974.

ELLIS, A. *Children of the Great Depression*. Chicago: Chicago University Press, 1962.

FREEDMAN, J. L. *Happy people*. New York: Harcourt Brace Jovanovich, 1978.

FROST, R. O. and GREEN, M. L. Duration and post-experimental removal of Velten mood induction procedure effects. *Personality and Social Psychology Bulletin*, 1982: **8**, 341–7.

FRYER, D. and PAYNE, R. Proactive behaviour in unemployment: findings and implications. *Leisure Studies*, 1984; **3**, 273–95.

FURNHAM, A. Personality and activity preference. *British Journal of Social Psychology*, 1981; **20**, 57–68.

FURNHAM, A. and SCHAEFFER, R. Person-environment fit, job satisfaction and mental health. *Journal of Occupational Psychology*, 1984; **57**, 295–307.

General Household Survey (1977) Nos **11** and **12**. London: H.M.S.O.

GRAY, J. A. The psychophysiological nature of introversion-extraversion: a modification of Eysenck's theory. In V. D. Neblitsyn and J. A. Gray (eds.), *Biological bases of individual behavior*. New York: Academic Press, 1972.

HACKMAN, J. R. Work design. In J. R. Hackman and J. L. Suttle (eds.), *Improving life at work*. Santa Monica: Goodyear, 1977.

HEADEY, B., GLOWACKI, T., HOLMSTROM, E. L. and WEARING, A. J. Modelling change in perceived quality of life. *Social Indicators Research*, 1985; **17**, 276–98.

HENDERSON, M. and ARGYLE, M. Social support by four categories of work colleagues: relationships between activities, stress and satisfaction. *Journal of Occupational Behaviour*, 1985; **6**, 229–39.

ISEN, A. M. and GORGOGLIONE, J. M. Some specific effects of four affect-induction procedures. *Personality and Social Psychology Bulletin*, 1983; **9**, 136–43.

JAHODA, M. Employment and unemployment: a social-psychological analysis. Cambridge: Cambridge University Press, 1982.

JEMMOTT, J. B. and LOCKE, S. E. Psychosocial factors, immunology mediation, and human susceptibility to infectious diseases: how much do we know? *Psychological Bulletin*, 1984; **95**, 78–108.

KABANOFF, B. Occupational and sex differences in leisure needs and leisure satisfaction. *Journal of Occupational Behaviour*, 1982; **3**, 233–45.

KORMAN, A. K. *et al.* Income and well-being. Department of Management, Barush College, C.U.N.Y., unpublished manuscript.

KRAUT, R. E. and JOHNSTON, R. E. Social and emotional messages of smiling: an ethological approach. *Journal of Personality and Social Psychology*, 1979; **37**, 1539–53.

LAIRD, J. D. The real role of facial response in the experience of emotion: a reply to Tourangeau and Ellsworth, and others. *Journal of Personality and Social Psychology*, 1984; **47**, 909–17.

LARSEN, R. J., DIENER, E. and EMMONS, R. A. An evaluation of subjective well-being measures. *Social Indicators Research*, 1985; **17**, 1–18.

LEWINSOHN, P. M., SULLIVAN, J. M. and GROSSCUP, S. J. Behavioural therapy: clinical applications. In A. J. Rush (ed.), *Short-term therapies for depression*. New York: Guilford, 1982.

LICHTER, S., HAYE, K. and KAMMANN, R. Increasing happiness through cognitive training. *New Zealand Psychologist*, 1980; **9**, 57–64.

LIVINGSTONE, S. M. *Social knowledge and programme structure in representations of television characters*. Unpublished doctoral thesis, Oxford University, 1987.

LOHER, B. T., NOE, R. A., MOELLER, N. L. and FITZGERALD, M. P. A meta-analysis of the relation of job characteristics to job satisfaction. *Journal of Applied Psychology*, 1985; **70**, 280–9.

MacPHILLAMY, D. J. and LEWINSOHN, P. M. Manual for the *Pleasant Events Schedule*. University of Oregon, 1976.

MARSTON, A., HART, J., HILEMAN, C. and FAUNCE, W. Toward the laboratory study of sadness and crying. *American Journal of Psychology*, 1984; **97**, 127–31.

MARTIN, M. Induction of depressed mood in the laboratory. *American Journal of Psychology*, 1985; **98**, 635–39.

MARTIN, M., ARGYLE, M and CROSSLAND, J. On the measurement of happiness. *The Psychologist*, 1988; **1** (8), 33.

MARTIN, M., ARGYLE, M. and CROSSLAND, J. *A trouble shared is a trouble halved: Social and solitary, positive and negative mood induction.* Manuscript under review.

MARTIN, M., ARGYLE, M. and CROSSLAND, J. The Oxford Happiness Inventory. Manuscript in preparation.

MARTIN, M. and CLARK, D. M. Cognitive mediation of depressed mood and neuroticism. I.R.C.S. *Medical Science*, 1985; **13**, 252–3.

MATLIN, M. W. and GAWRON, V. J. Individual differences in Pollyannaism. *Journal of Personality Assessment*, 1979; **43**, 411–12.

MICHALOS, A. C. Satisfaction and happiness. *Social Indicators Research*, 1980; **8**, 385–422.

MICHALOS, A. C. Job satisfaction, marital satisfaction and the quality of life: A review and a preview. In F. M. Andrews (ed.), *Research on the quality of life*. Ann Arbor: University of Michigan, Survey Research Center, 1986.

MURRAY, L. and TREVARTHEN, C. Emotional regulation of interactions between two-month-olds and their mothers. In T. M. Field and N. A. Fox (eds.), *Social perception in infants*. Norwood, N. J.: Ablex, 1985.

OLDS, J. and MILNER, O. Positive reinforcement produced by electrical stimulation of septal areas and other regions of the rat brain. *Journal of Comparative and Physiological Psychology*, 1954; **47**, 419–27.

PARKES, S. *Work and retirement*. London: Allen and Unwin, 1982.

ROBINSON, J. P. *How americans use time*. New York and London: Praeger, 1977.

ROLLS, E. T. Effects of electrical stimulation of the brain on behaviour. *Psychological Surveys*, 1979; **2**, 151–69.

ROY, D. Banana Time: job satisfaction and informal interaction. *Human Organization*, 1959; **18**, 158–68.

RUBENSTEIN, C. Vacations. *Psychology Today*, 1980; 13, 62–76.

RUNCIMAN, W. G. *Relative deprivation and social justice*. London: Routledge & Kegan Paul, 1966.

SALES, S. M. and HOUSE, J. Job dissatisfaction as a possible risk factor in coronary heart disease. *Journal of Chronic Disease*, 1971; **23**, 861–73.

SCHERER, K. R., WALBOTT, H. S. and SUMMERFIELD, A. B. *Experiencing emotion*. Cambridge: Cambridge University Press, 1986.

SCHWARZ, N. and CLORE, G. L. Mood, misattribution and judgments of well-being: information and directive functions of affective states. *Journal of Personality and Social Psychology*, 1983; **45**, 513–23.

SMITH, P. C., KENDALL, L. M. and HULIN, C. L. *The measurement of satisfaction in work and retirement*. Chicago: Rand McNally, 1969.

SUTHERLAND, G., NEWMAN, B. and RACHMAN, S. Experimental investigation of the relation between mood and intrusive unwarranted conditions. *British Journal of Medical Psychology*. 1982; **55**, 127–38.

TAYLOR, S. E. and BROWN, J. D. Illusion and well-being: a social psychological perspective on mental health. *Psychological Bulletin*, 1988; **103**, 193–210.

TEASDALE, J. D. and RUSSELL, M. L. Differential effect of induced mood on the recall of positive, negative, and neutral words. *British Journal of Clinical Psychology*, 1983; **22**, 163–71.

THORNE, A. The press of personality: a study of conversations between introverts and extraverts. *Journal of Personality and Social Psychology*, 1987; **53**, 718–26.

VANFOSSEN, B. E. Sex differences in the mental health effects of spouse support and equity. *Journal of Health and Social Behavior*, 1981; **22**, 130–43.

VELTEN, E. A laboratory task for induction of mood states. *Behaviour Research and Therapy*, 1968; **6**, 473–82.

VEROFF, J., DOUVAN, E. and KULKA, R. A. *The inner american*. New York: Basic Books, 1981.

WALKER, C. Some variations in marital satisfaction. In R. Chester and J. Peel (eds.) *Equalities and inequalities in family life*. London: Academic Press, 1977.

WARR, P. *Work, unemployment, and mental health*. Oxford: Clarendon Press, 1987.

WARR, P., BARTER, J. and BROWNBRIDGE, G. On the independence of positive and negative affect. *Journal of Personality and Social Psychology*, 1983; **44**, 644–51.

6

Endowment and contrast in judgments of well-being

AMOS TVERSKY and DALE GRIFFIN

Introduction

In a recent educational television programme, an amnesic patient was asked about his childhood and high-school experiences. Verbally fluent, he was able to converse about daily events, but could not remember any details about his past. Finally, the interviewer asked him how happy he was. The patient pondered this question for a few seconds before answering, "I don't know."

Clearly, memory plays a crucial role in the assessment of well-being. The present evidently does not provide enough information to define happiness without reference to the past. Yet memories have a complex effect on our current sense of well-being. They represent a direct source of happiness or unhappiness, and they also affect the criteria by which current events are evaluated. In other words, a salient hedonic event (positive or negative) influences later evaluations of well-being in two ways: through an *endowment* effect and a *contrast* effect. The endowment effect of an event represents its direct contribution to one's happiness or satisfaction. Good news and positive experiences enrich our lives and make us happier; bad news and hard times diminish our well-being. Events also exercise an indirect contrast effect on the evaluation of subsequent events. A positive experience makes us happy, but it also renders similar experiences less exciting. A negative experience makes us unhappy, but it also helps us appreciate subsequent experiences that are less bad. The hedonic impact of an event, we suggest, reflects a balance of its endowment[1] and contrast effects. The present chapter explores some descriptive and prescriptive implications of this notion.

A few examples illustrate the point. Consider a professor from a small midwestern town who attends a conference in New York and enjoys having dinner at an outstanding French restaurant. This memorable event contributes to her endowment—she is happier for having had that experience—but it also gives rise to a contrast effect. A later meal in the local French restaurant becomes somewhat less satisfying by comparison with the great meal she had in New York. Similarly, exposure to great theatre is enriching, but makes it harder to enjoy the local repertory company. The same principle applies to accomplishments. A successful first novel contributes a great deal to the author's endowment and self-esteem, but it also reduces the satisfaction derived from future novels if they are less good.

The effects of endowment and contrast also apply to negative events. Some people, dominated by a negative endowment, become depressed and unable to enjoy life in the aftermath of a bad experience; others are elated by the contrast between the present and the bleak past. People may vary in the degree to which their reactions are dominated by endowment or by contrast. Note that the endowment-contrast dimension of individual differences is orthogonal to the more familiar dimension of optimism-pessimism. Both endowment and contrast, of course, are memory based. The stronger the memory of the past, the greater its impact on present well-being. With no memory, there can be no endowment and no contrast, just immediate pleasures and pains.

There is little novelty in suggesting that well-being depends both on the nature of the experience that is being evaluated and on the standard of evaluation. Furthermore, many authors have observed that satisfaction is directly related to the quality of the experience, or its endowment, and inversely related to the evaluation standard, which serves as a contrast. What is perhaps less obvious is the observation that the same (past) event makes a dual contribution to well-being—a direct contribution as endowment and an inverse contribution as contrast. Although these effects have been discussed in the well-being literature (under various names), we know of no explicit attempt to integrate them.

The distinction between endowment and contrast has nothing to do with the character of the event itself; any hedonic experience affects our well-being both through the endowment it generates and through the contrast to which it gives rise. The endowment depends primarily on the quality and the intensity of the event, whereas the contrast depends primarily on its similarity or relevance to subsequent events. A great meal at a French restaurant in New York will probably not reduce your ability to enjoy a Chinese meal back home; similarly, while a great theatre performance may spoil your taste for the local repertory company, you will probably continue to take pleasure in concerts or even high-school plays.

Because the contrast effect depends on similarity or perceived relevance, it is susceptible to framing and other cognitive manipulations. The same sequence of events can produce varying degrees of satisfaction depending on whether an early event is viewed as similar or relevant to the evaluation of later events. Thus, happiness should be maximized by treating positive experiences as endowments and negative experiences as contrasts. To achieve this goal, one should find ways to treat the positive experiences of the past as different from the present (to avoid comparisons with the glorious past). By the same token, one should compare present conditions to worse situations in the past (to enjoy the benefits of a positive contrast). This prescription raises some intriguing questions that lie beyond the scope of this chapter. Are people who emphasize the endowment of positive events and the contrast of negative events generally happier than those who do not? And how much freedom do people have in the framing of hedonic events?

The present chapter reports some preliminary explorations based on experimental manipulations of endowment and contrast. In the next section we vary the quality and the relevance of past events and investigate their effects on judgments of well-being. We develop a simple method for assessing the relative contributions of endowment and contrast in these studies, and we apply this analysis to some experiments of Schwarz, Strack and their colleagues (see Chapter 3), and to the study of expectation effects. In the last section of the chapter, we discuss the use of choice and of judgment for the assessment of well-being, illustrate the discrepancy between the two procedures, and relate it to the relative contribution of endowment and contrast.

Studies of endowment and contrast

The following two experiments employ the same design to study the impact of a past event on present judgments of happiness. In the first study, we use fictitious scripts to investigate the role of endowment and contrast in judgments regarding the well-being of another person. In the second study, subjects rated their own satisfaction following an actual experience.

In our first study, subjects were given a "story"—a description of two events, allegedly taken from an interview with a student—and were asked to rate the happiness of that student. In each case, the earlier event was either positive or negative, and the later event was neutral. Four types of events were used in the study: a date, a term paper, a party, and a movie. The two events presented to the subject could be of the same type (e.g. two term papers or two parties) or of different types (e.g. a date followed by a party or vice versa). This arrangement gives rise to a 2×2 (between subjects) design in which a neutral event is preceded by either a positive or a negative event that could be of the same type or of a different type.

Because the second event is always neutral, we can focus on the endowment and the contrast effects produced by the first event. For events of different types, we expect an endowment effect, with little or no contrast. Judged happiness, therefore, should be high when the first event is positive and low when the first event is negative. For events of the same type, however, both contrast and endowment effects are expected. As a consequence, a related positive event should produce less happiness than an unrelated positive event, whereas a related negative event should produce greater happiness than an unrelated negative event. For example, an excellent paper followed by an average paper should produce less satisfaction than an excellent paper followed by an average party because the original paper makes a subsequent paper (but not a subsequent party) somewhat disappointing by contrast. On the other hand, a bad paper followed by an average paper should produce more satisfaction than a bad paper followed by an average party.

Sixty-four students participated in our first experiment, which was administered in a class setting in four groups of approximately sixteen students each. All subjects received the following instructions:

> On the next few pages you will find several descriptions of life events experienced by high-school students. These are everyday sorts of events that you or your friends have probably experienced some time in your high-school career.
>
> Your task will be to read these stories carefully and try to understand how the person felt during these episodes. Each individual narrator will present two vignettes from his or her own high-school experience. The vignettes were all gathered during the narrator's junior year in high school. After each pair of stories, you will be asked to rate the feelings of the narrator.
>
> Each storyteller was asked to recount two experiences. First, they were asked to describe an experience from the week before, and then they were asked to describe something that had happened that very day. These narratives were given orally, so the grammar and prose are not perfect.
>
> Each story is very short, so please take your time and try to imagine what the scene looked like and felt like to the narrator. Especially try to imagine how the narrator was feeling as he or she recounted the story.

The stories refer to four domains: a date with a young woman, performance in a course, the planning of a party, and the reaction to an Australian movie. Three events were constructed for each domain: positive, neutral, and negative. Recall that for each pair of events, the present event was always neutral and it was preceded either by a positive or a negative event that was either related or unrelated. Each respondent evaluated four stories, one in each quality/relation condition (i.e. positive/related, positive/unrelated, negative/related, and negative/unrelated). The following story describes a negative event regarding class performance followed by a related neutral event; an unrelated neutral event is also given for comparison.

Tim's Story

(Past, Negative)

What happened last week? Last week, let's see. I had a bad day. A really, really bad day. In the morning, I had a quiz in French. I was so tired and I just couldn't keep my mind on the problems. And then with about 10 minutes to go in the period, I sort of woke up and realized that I was in bad trouble. I had sort of puttered on the first page of a three-page quiz and there was no way I was going to finish. I almost broke out in a cold sweat; the quiz wasn't very important or anything, but it was like a dream where I was racing against time and my heart was pounding and there was no way I was going to get finished. So I felt bad about that all morning, not to mention embarrassed at blowing the quiz, and then in the afternoon I got a test back in Chemistry. I had almost failed it; it was a pretty hard test and everything, but it just made me want to give up. I was just stunned, not to mention tired. Good grades in Chemistry are important to me because I want to take sciences in college. So I skipped track practice that day and just went home. I didn't want to deal with anything else bad that could happen to me.

(Present, Related)

What happened today? I had three classes this morning, but since one of them is Civics, it wasn't too bad. In Civics, we discussed political issues that have been in the news. That was o.k., mostly a break from taking notes in other classes. First period I had Geometry, and we had a substitute teacher so we just did our homework in class. Before lunch I had French, which I am taking instead of Spanish this year. We practiced our conversations, which we have to present next week. That's pretty much it, I think.

Story 2 (Present, Unrelated)

What happened today? Well, I had another lunch with Susan. We had a pretty good time. We talked most of the time, about classes and some people we both know. Mostly we talked about the English class, though, and the way that exams were given. We argued some about whether the professor was fair, but we both agreed that the exams were aimed more at trivial detail than were the lectures. We ate pretty slowly, but both made it to our one o'clock classes. It was hard to get a feeling for what was going on, but I think she liked me well enough.

The dependent variable was a rating of happiness on a scale ranging from one (very unhappy) to ten (very happy). Subjects were asked "On the day that Tim answered these questions: how happy do you think he was with his life overall?" Because there were no significant differences between the responses to the stories, the results were pooled. Figure 6.1 displays the average rating of happiness in each of the four conditions, averaged across subjects and stories. The results confirmed our predictions. There was a significant interaction between the quality of the past event (positive or negative) and its relation (related, unrelated) to the present event, $F(1,60) = 6.71, p<.02$. As expected, we observed a significant endowment effect: in both the related and unrelated conditions, judged satisfaction was higher for the positive than for the negative prior event. Furthermore, there was a significant contrast effect: for the positive event, satisfaction was higher in the unrelated ($M = 7.1$) than in the related condition ($M = 6.8$), whereas for the negative event, the pattern was reversed ($M = 4.9$ for the unrelated condition, and $M = 5.5$ for the related condition). For example, the memory of a good date last week diminished the satisfaction with a neutral date this week, but it enhanced the satisfaction with a neutral movie

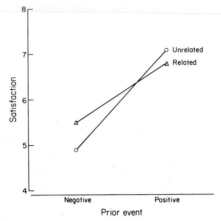

FIG. 6.1. The effect of prior events.

this week. The memory of a painful date, on the other hand, enhanced the satisfaction with a neutral date this week, while it diminished the satisfaction with a neutral movie this week.

To aid in the interpretation of experimental data, we find it useful to express judgments of satisfaction as an additive combination of endowment and contrast effects. We assume that the endowment effect E_{12} is given by the sum of the endowments of the first and second events denoted E_1 and E_2, respectively, and that the contrast effect C_{12} is expressible as the signed hedonic discrepancy between the two events d_{12}, weighted by their degree of relatedness r_{12}. Thus, we obtain the form

$$
\begin{aligned}
\text{Satisfaction} &= \text{Endowment} + \text{Contrast} \\
&= E_{12} + C_{12} \\
&= E_1 + E_2 + r_{12}d_{12}.
\end{aligned}
$$

To apply this scheme to the results of our first study, let S denote the rating of satisfaction. For simplicity, we suppose that the grand mean has been substracted from all observations, so S is expressed as a deviation score. Let S^+ and S^- be respectively the responses in a condition where the first event was positive or negative, and let S_r and S_u denote the responses in a condition where the two events were related or unrelated. Let E^+ and E^- denote the endowment associated with a positive or negative event, and let C^+ and C^- denote the contrast associated with a positive or negative event, respectively. Because the second event in this study was always neutral we can neglect its endowment, and set $E_2 = 0$. Naturally, the contrast associated with a prior positive event is negative, $C^+ < 0$, and the contrast associated with a prior negative event is positive, $C^- > 0$. We also assume that, for unrelated events, $r_{12} = 0$, hence the contrast term vanishes in that case. Judgments of satisfaction in the present design can be represented as:

	Negative	Positive
Unrelated	$S_u^- = E^-$	$S_u^+ = E^+$
Related	$S_r^- = E^- + C^-$	$S_r^+ = E^+ + C^+$

We use this model to estimate the effect of contrast and endowment. The total endowment effect is:

$$E = E^+ - E^- = S_u^+ - S_u^- = 7.1 - 4.9 = 2.2$$

As we assume the unrelated events involve no contrast, the overall endowment effect is simply the difference between mean satisfaction in the cells representing positive versus negative unrelated events. The contrast associated with the positive first event is:

$$C^+ = S_r^+ - S_u^+ = 6.8 - 7.1 = -.3.$$

Similarly, the contrast associated with the negative first event is:
$$C^- = S_r^- - S_u^- = 5.5 - 4.9 = .6.$$

Thus, the total contrast effect in this experiment is $C^- - C^+ = .9$, which is considerably smaller than the endowment effect, as can be seen in Figure 6.1.

In our second study, subjects rated their own satisfaction with actual experiences. Seventy-two subjects took part in a computer-controlled stock-market game played for real money. Subjects were given information about different stocks and were instructed to construct a portfolio from these stocks. They were told that the computer would simulate the market and that their actual payoffs would depend on the performance of their port-folios. Each session included an initial game (with a payoff of $2 or $6) and a later game (with a payoff of $4) separated by a filler task involving no gains or losses. As in the first study, we manipulated two variables: (a) the payoff in the first game and (b) the similarity or relatedness between the first and the second games. In the related condition, subjects played essentially the same game with different stocks. In the unrelated condition, the games involved different markets (stocks versus commodities) and used different procedures for portfolio construction. After subjects played both games, they were asked to rate their overall satisfaction with the experience, using a 10-point scale.

This design allows us to test the following hypotheses regarding judged satisfaction. First, the difference between the low ($2) and the high ($6) payoffs will be greater in the unrelated than in the related condition. This prediction follows from the assumption that for the unrelated games, the difference reflects a pure endowment effect. In the related games, however, the positive endowment will be reduced by the negative contrast, whereas the negative endowment will be reduced by the positive contrast. Second, the negative contrast effect following the high payoff (when $d_{12} > 0$) will be larger than the positive contrast effect following the low payoff (when $d_{12} < 0$), as suggested by the notion of loss aversion in prospect theory (Kahneman and Tversky, 1979).

The pattern of results displayed in Figure 6.2 supported the endowment-contrast analysis. In the unrelated condition, where there is pure endowment and no contrast, those who received the larger payoff in the first game were generally more satisfied ($M = 8.7$) than those who received the smaller payoff in the first game ($M = 6.4$), $t(33) = 1.95, p < .05$, one-tailed. However, in the related condition, where contrast and endowment worked in the opposite directions, there was essentially no difference between the satisfaction of those who received the larger reward in the first game ($M = 7.5$) and those who received the smaller reward in the first game ($M = 7.3$).

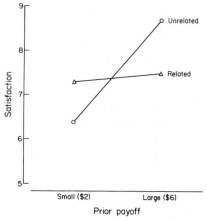

FIG. 6.2. The effect of prior payoffs.

The decomposition scheme introduced in the first study is applicable to the results of the present study. In this study too, E_2 is a constant, and hence can be ignored in the analysis. To simplify matters, we also assume that the difference between the satisfaction derived from the high prior payoff and the low prior payoff in the unrelated games yields an estimate of the total endowment effect:

$$E = S_u^+ - S_u^- = 8.7 - 6.4 = 2.3.$$

The positive contrast (the increase in satisfaction caused by a low expectation) was:

$$C^- = S_r^- - S_u^- = 7.3 - 6.4 = .9;$$

and the negative contrast (the decrease in satisfaction caused by a large expectation) was:

$$C^+ = S_r^+ - S_u^+ = 7.5 - 8.7 = -1.2.$$

Note that the overall endowment effect was about the same in the two experiments, but the overall contrast effect, $C = C^- - C^+ = 2.1$ was doubled in the present study. As implied by loss aversion, people's disappointment with a "loss" of $2 was greater than their satisfaction with a "gain" of $2.

Applications of the endowment-contrast scheme

Our conceptual scheme for the integration of endowment and contrast effects, described above, can be applied to two studies conducted by Schwarz, Strack and their colleagues (see Chapter 3). In one experiment, Strack, Schwarz and Gschneidinger (1985) instructed subjects in one group to recall and write down a very negative event in their lives; subjects in another group were instructed to recall and write down a very positive event in their lives. Within each group, half of the subjects were asked to recall a present event, and half were asked to recall a past event. Subjects were then asked to rate their well-being on a 10-point scale. This procedure yields a 2 × 2 (between-subjects) design in which the recalled event was either positive or negative, in the present or in the past. For the events in the present, the results were hardly surprising. Recalling a positive present event made people feel good, whereas thinking about a negative present event made people feel less happy. The results for past events were more surprising: ratings of well-being were higher for those who recalled a past negative

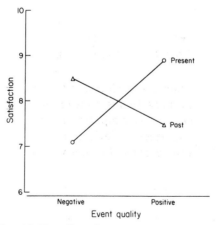

FIG. 6.3. The effect of past versus present events.

event than for those who recalled a past positive event (see Figure 6.3). We have replicated this result at Stanford.

The endowment-contrast scheme provides a natural account of these findings. For the events in the present, there is no room for contrast, hence we get a positive endowment effect for the positive event and a negative endowment effect for the negative event. The recall of past events, however, introduces a contrast with the present, which is positive for negative events and negative for positive ones. Because present events are more salient than past events, the endowment effect is greater for present than past events. Thus, for past events, the contrast component offsets the endowment component and produces the observed reversal.

Again, let S^+ and S^- refer to judged satisfaction when a positive or negative event, respectively, has been brought to mind. (As before, we first subtract the grand mean from each observation and operate on deviation scores). Let S_c and S_p refer to the judgments associated with a current and a past event, respectively. We can represent the average judgment in each cell as follows:

	Negative	Positive
Current	$S_c^- = E^-$	$S_c^+ = E^+$
Past	$S_p^- = E^- + C^-$	$S_p^+ = E^+ + C^+$

The total endowment effect is:
$$E = E^+ - E^- = S_c^+ - S_c^- = 8.9 - 7.1 = 1.8.$$

The contrast associated with the positive first event is:
$$C^+ = S_p^+ - S_c^+ = 7.5 - 8.9 = -1.4.$$

The contrast associated with the negative first event is:
$$C^- = S_p^- - S_c^- = 8.5 - 7.1 = 1.4.$$

The total contrast effect in this experiment is thus $C = C^- - C^+ = 2.8$. In this study, therefore, the contrast effect is considerably greater than the endowment effect.

More generally, thinking about positive events in the past (e.g. a tour of the Greek islands, or a happy time at summer camp) calls attention to the less exciting present. This is the stuff of which nostalgia is made. On the other hand, recalling some bad times in the past (e.g. failing a test or being lonely) reminds us that the present, although imperfect, could be a great deal worse. While Strack et al., (1985) see mood as the carrier of endowment, we do not regard mood as a necessary condition for an endowment effect. We shall address this difference in emphasis at the conclusion of this section.

In another study, Schwarz, Strack, Kommer and Wagner (1987) required subjects to spend an hour either in an extremely pleasant room (spacious, nicely furnished and decorated with posters and flowers) or in an extremely unpleasant room (small, dirty, smelly, noisy and overheated). After the session, subjects were asked to assess general satisfaction as well as satisfaction with regard to their current housing situation. The room influenced the rating of overall satisfaction; subjects who were placed in the pleasant room reported higher overall life satisfaction than those in the unpleasant room. However, subjects' rating of their normal living conditions exhibited the

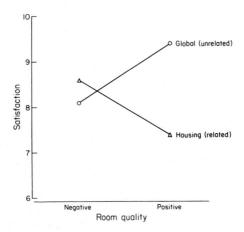

Fıɢ. 6.4. The effect of room quality.

opposite pattern (see Figure 6.4). Those placed in the unpleasant room reported higher satisfaction with their housing than those who had been in the pleasant room. This pattern is naturally interpreted as a contrast effect. One's own room appears less attractive when compared with the pleasant room than when compared with the unpleasant room. Because contrast depends on the relevance or the similarity of the standard to the target, the contrast effect of the experimental room was confined to the evaluation of housing, and did not extend to the rating of life satisfaction. A specific event, therefore, is likely to have a significant contrast effect in the domain to which it belongs, and little or no contrast effect in others.

Using the notation introduced earlier, let S^+ and S^- denote, respectively, judgments of satisfaction for the pleasant and unpleasant rooms, and let S_r and S_u denote, respectively, judgments of satisfaction for the related (housing) and unrelated (life satisfaction) domains. The analysis of these results is then identical to the analysis of Study 1. In particular, the total endowment effect is:

$$E = S_u^+ - S_u^- = E^+ - E^- = 9.4 – 8.1 = 1.3.$$

The contrast effect associated with the positive first event is:

$$C^+ = S_r^+ - S_u^+ = 7.4 – 9.4 = -2.0.$$

The contrast effect associated with the negative first event is:

$$C^- = S_r^- - S_u^- = 8.6 – 8.1 = .5.$$

As one might expect, the contrast effect produced by the room is considerably larger ($C = C^- - C^+ = 2.5$) than its endowment effect.

Although different in focus, our analysis is generally compatible with that offered by Schwarz and Strack (see Chapter 3). They assume the operation of contrast effects and focus on the role of emotion or mood in generating endowment. Our account assumes the existence of endowment effects, produced through either mood or other processes, and focuses on the factors that control the relative strength of endowment and contrast.

Expectations as contrast and endowment

Much psychological research on the assessment of well-being has focused on the role of expectations. It has been shown in many contexts that the same event can be perceived as more or less satisfying, depending on whether a positive or negative expectation has been induced (Feather, 1966; Shrauger, 1975). Whether a given test score is pleasing or disappointing will depend on whether the student was led to expect a low or a high score (Schul, 1989). Expectation effects are generally interpreted as contrast. Indeed, people are commonly advised to lower their expectations in order to avoid disappointment. In line with our previous analysis, we propose that expectations produce endowment as well as contrast. We are relieved when a dreaded event does not happen, but the memory of anxiety and fear still haunts us long afterward. Imagine that you have been living two weeks with the possibility that your child has leukemia. Further tests now prove your worries unfounded. Despite your elation at this news, we suspect that you are worse off for the experience. In such circumstances, the endowment effect of a negative expectation has a strong impact on your well-being long after the specific worry has been relieved.

Much as unrealized fears can generate negative endowment, unrealized hopes can give rise to positive endowment. Consider the experience of someone who owns a lottery ticket. Because the probability of winning is very small, the failure to win does not cause much disappointment. However, the dream of becoming an overnight millionaire could produce enough pleasure to offset the mild disappointment of not winning the lottery. Indeed, it appears that many people enjoy playing the lottery even when they do not win. Probability plays here a critical role. As the probability of winning increases, the costs of disappointment seem to increase faster than the benefits of hope. Holding expected value constant, therefore, playing long odds should be more pleasurable than playing short odds. Losers on long odds had sweeter dreams than losers on short odds; and their disappointment was also less bitter. This analysis suggests another reason for the attractiveness of long shots, in addition to the overweighting of small probabilities (Kahneman and Tversky, 1979).

The present treatment adopts a symbolic rather than a consummatory conception of well-being. We derive pleasure and pain not merely from the positive and the negative events we experience, but also from the memory of past events and the anticipation of future events (Schelling, 1984). Like the memories of past events, expectations of future events, we suggest, serve both as endowment and as contrast. Expectations not only control the evaluation of future events, they have a hedonic impact of their own— whether or not the event they refer to actually comes to pass. Our hedonic portfolio encompasses memories and expectations; successes and failures of the past, hopes and fears of the future.

The assessment of well-being: choice versus judgment

The preceding studies were concerned, like most of the empirical work discussed in this volume, with judgments of satisfaction or happiness, which have served as a major source of data for students of well-being (Argyle, 1987; Diener, 1984). Another paradigm for the study of welfare, dominant in economics, focuses on choice rather than on judgment. In this paradigm, a person is said to be better off in State A than in State B if he or she chooses State A over State B. Indeed, the concept of utility has been used in economics and decision theory in two different senses: (a) experience value, the degree of pleasure or pain associated with the actual experience of an outcome, and (b) decision value, the contribution of an anticipated outcome to the overall attractiveness of an option (Kahneman and Tversky, 1984). Experience values are generally measured by judgmental methods (e.g. self-reports or judgments by observers), although physiological measures (e.g. blood pressure or heart rate) are occasionally used. Decision values are inferred from choices using an appropriate model such as expected utility theory or the theory of revealed preference. The distinction between experience and decision values is rarely made explicit because, with a few notable exceptions (e.g. March, 1978; Schelling, 1984; Sen, 1982), it is commonly assumed that judgment and choice yield the same ordering. In many situations, however, experience values, as expressed in self-ratings, appear to diverge from decision values, as inferred from choice.

First, choice and judgment may yield different results because of moral considerations and problems of self-control. We commonly avoid certain pleasurable experiences because they are immoral, illegal, or fattening. On the other hand, there are times we cannot resist experiences that will ultimately make us unhapppy, because of a lack of self-control. Choice, therefore, could conceal rather than reveal one's "true preferences". Second, a choice-judgment discrepancy is likely to arise if the decision maker's prediction of the consequences of choice is inaccurate or biased. A common bias in the prediction of utility is a tendency to overweight one's present state or mood. Some perceptive consumers have learned to avoid doing their weekly grocery shopping either when they are very hungry (because they would buy too much) or after a very large meal (because they would not buy enough). A related source of error is the failure to anticipate our remarkable ability to adapt to new states. People tend to overestimate the long-term impact of both positive events, such as winning a lottery or receiving tenure, and negative events, such as injury or personal loss (Brickman, Coates and Janoff-Bulman, 1978). The ability to predict future well-being depends largely on the nature of the experience. People generally have a reasonable idea of what it is like to lose money or to have a bad cold, but they probably do not have a clear notion of what it means to go bankrupt, or to lose a limb. For illuminating discussions of the role of adaptation and the problems of predicting one's own future satisfaction, see Kahneman and Snell (in press), and Kahneman and Varey (in press).

But even if the judgment, like the choice, precedes the experience of the consequence, the two tasks can give rise to different answers because they highlight different aspects of the problem. When people are asked to assess the hedonic value of some future states (e.g. job offers) they try to imagine what it would feel like to experience those states. But when asked to choose among these states, they tend to search for reasons or arguments to justify their choice. Consequently, the two procedures could lead to different results. For example, Tversky, Sattath and Slovic (1988) have shown that the most important attribute of a multi-dimensional decision problem is weighted more heavily in choice than in judgment, presumably because it provides a convenient rationale for choice. Recall the stock-market study, presented in the first section of this chapter. Given a choice, subjects would surely elect to participate in the negative contrast condition, where they earn $10, rather than in the positive contrast condition, where they earn $6. Yet subjects who had a lower total endowment ($6) and a positive contrast were just as satisfied as subjects who had a higher total endowment ($10) and a negative contrast. It appears that the choice depends primarily on the payoffs whereas judgments of satisfaction are more sensitive to the contrast.

To explore the choice-judgment discrepancy, we presented the following information to some sixty-six undergraduate students.

> Imagine that you have just completed a graduate degree in Communications and you are considering one-year jobs at two different magazines.
>
> (A) At Magazine A, you are offered a job paying $35,000. However, the other workers who have the same training and experience as you do are making $38,000.
>
> (B) At Magazine B, you are offered a job paying $33,000. However, the other workers who have the same training and experience as you do are making $30,000.

Approximately half the subjects were asked "Which job would you choose to take?" while the other half were asked "At which job would you be happier?" The results confirmed our prediction that the comparison with others would loom larger in judgment, and that the salary would dominate the choice. Eighty-four per cent of the subjects (twenty-seven out of thirty-two) preferred the job with the higher absolute salary and lower relative position, while sixty-two per cent (twenty-one out of thirty-four) of the subjects anticipated higher satisfaction in the job with the lower absolute salary and higher relative position ($\chi^2(1) = 14.70$, p < .01).

We further explored the relation between choice and judgment in the assessment of an actual experience using a within-subjects design. Thirty-eight undergraduate students participated in a study of "verbal creativity" involving two different tasks. One was described as a test of "cognitive production": the ability to come up with many words that fit a sentence. The other task was described as a test of "grammatical production": the ability to produce many words of a particular grammatical type. Subjects were told that their payoffs would depend on their performance in these tasks.

All subjects performed both tasks, each of which consisted of a practice trial followed by a payoff trial. In one task, subjects were told that their performance was below average on the practice trial, and about average on the payoff trial. In the other task, subjects were told that they performed above average on the practice trial, and about average on the payoff trial. Thus, the performance of each subject "improved" on one task and "declined" on the other task. The order and type of task were counterbalanced. The payoff in the declining condition ($3) was higher than the payoff in the improving condition ($1). Thus, one task paired a larger payoff with an unfavourable comparison. The other task paired a smaller payoff with a favourable comparison. After each task, subjects were asked to rate their satisfaction with their performance on a 10-point scale. Following the completion of both tasks, subjects were asked "If you could do just one task, which would you choose to do?"

As predicted, the payoffs loomed larger in choice than in judgment, or (equivalently) the contrast was weighted more heavily in judgment than in choice. Of the twenty-eight subjects whose ratings were not identical on the two tasks, 75 per cent chose the high-payoff task while 54 per cent expressed greater satisfaction with the low-payoff task. This reversal pattern is significant (p < .05 by a McNemar test of symmetry).

These studies show that judgments of satisfaction and choice can yield systematically different orderings. Furthermore, it appears that choice is determined primarily by the payoffs, which reflect the endowment effect, whereas the judgment is more sensitive to comparison or contrast. The salary or payoff one receives provides a more compelling reason for choice than the contrast between one's own salary and the salary of others. This contrast, however, is a very salient feature of the anticipated experience, as reflected in the judgment task. Note that the present use of *contrast* is consistent with, but considerably broader than, the concept invoked in the first part of the chapter. There the term refers to the indirect contribution of a past event to current well-being, whereas here it refers to the standard of reference by which the relevant outcomes are evaluated, which may be determined by prior experience or by other factors, such as the salary of colleagues.

The choice-judgment discrepancy raises an intriguing question: which is the correct or more appropriate measure of well-being? This question cannot be readily answered, and perhaps it cannot be answered at all, because we lack a gold standard for the measurement of happiness. We believe that both choice and judgment provide relevant data for the assessment of well-being, although neither one is entirely satisfactory. Since, as we argue below, the two methods seem to be biased in opposite directions, a compromise between them may have some merit.

Perhaps the most basic principle of welfare economics is Pareto optimality: an allocation of resources is acceptable if it improves everybody's lot. Viewed as a choice criterion, this principle is irresistible. It is hard to object to a policy that improves your lot just because it improves the lot of someone else even more. This is a pure endowment argument that neglects contrast altogether. Policies that ignore contrast effects can create widespread unhappiness. Consider, for example, a policy that doubles the salary of a few people in an organization and increases all other salaries by 5 per cent. Even though all salaries rise, it is doubtful that this change will make most people happier. There is a great deal of evidence (e.g. Brickman, 1975; Brickman and Campbell, 1971; Crosby, 1976) that people's reported satisfaction depends largely on their relative position, not only on their objective situation.

Both experimental and survey research on happiness have shown that judgments of well-being are highly sensitive to comparison or contrast and relatively insensitive to endowment effects. Perhaps the most dramatic illustration of this phenomenon concerns the effect of windfall gains and tragedies. Judged by their ratings, lottery winners are no happier than normal controls, and quadriplegics are only slightly less happy than healthy people and no less happy than paraplegics (Brickman *et al.*, 1978). Surveys indicate that wealther people are slightly happier than people with less money, but substantial increases in everyone's income and standard of living do not raise the reported level of happiness (Easterlin, 1974).

Do these data reflect rapid adaptation that negates the immediate impact of any endowment—as implied by the treadmill theory of happiness (Brickman & Campbell, 1971)? Or do they reflect a normalization of the response scale that makes the ratings of ordinary people and paraplegics essentially incomparable? (As if the paraplegic answers the question: how do I feel relative to other paraplegics?) There are no simple answers to these questions. Obviously, everyone would choose to be healthy rather than paraplegic, and rich rather than poor. But it is not obvious how to demonstrate that the rich are actually happier than the poor if both groups report the same level of well-being. At the same time, it is clear that an adequate measure of well-being must distinguish between rich and poor, and between paraplegic and quadriplegic.

It seems that judgments of well-being are insufficiently sensitive to endowment, whereas choice is insufficiently sensitive to contrast. The exclusive reliance on either method can lead to unreasonable conclusions and unsound recommendations. Welfare policy derived from Pareto optimality could result in allocations that make most people less happy because it ignores the effect of social comparison. On the other hand, a preoccupation with judgment has led some psychologists to the view that "persons with a few ecstatic moments in their lives may be doomed to unhappiness" (Diener, 1984, p. 568), hence, "if the best can come only rarely, it is better not to include it in the range of experiences at all" (Parducci, 1968, p. 90). These conclusions are justified only if endowment effects are essentially ignored. A few glorious moments could sustain a lifetime of happy memories for those who can cherish the past without discounting the present.

References

ARGYLE, M. *The psychology of happiness.* London: Methuen, 1987.

BRICKMAN, P. Adaptation level determinants of satisfaction with equal and unequal outcome distributions in skill and chance situations. *Journal of Personality and Social Psychology,* 1975; **32**, 191–198.

BRICKMAN, P. and CAMPBELL, D. T. Hedonic relativism and planning the good society. In M. H. Appley (ed.), *Adaptation level theory: A symposium* (pp. 287–302). New York; Academic Press, 1971.

BRICKMAN, P., COATES, D. and JANOFF-BULMAN, R. Lottery winners and accident victims: Is happiness relative? *Journal of Personality and Social Psychology,* 1978; **36**, 917–927.

CROSBY, F. A model of egoistical relative deprivation. *Psychological Review,* 1976; **83**, 85–113.

DIENER, E. Subjective well-being. *Psychological Bulletin,* 1984; **95**(3), 542–575.

EASTERLIN, R. A. Does economic growth improve the human lot? Some empirical evidence. In P. A. David and M. W. Reder (eds.), *Nations and households in economic growth* (pp. 89–125). New York; Academic Press, 1974.

FEATHER, N. T. Effects of prior success and failure on expectations of success and failure. *Journal of Personality and Social Psychology,* 1966; **3**, 287–298.

KAHNEMAN, D. and SNELL, J. Predicting utility. In R. Hogarth (ed.), *Insights in decision making.* Chicago, IL: University of Chicago Press, in press.

KAHNEMAN, D. and TVERSKY, A. Prospect theory: An analysis of decision under risk. *Econometrica,* 1979; **47**, 263–291.

KAHNEMAN, D. and TVERSKY, A. Choices, values and frames. *American Psychologist,* 1984; **39**, 341–350.

KAHNEMAN, D. and VAREY, C. Notes on the psychology of utility. In J. Roemer, & J. Elster (eds.), *Interpersonal comparisons of well-being.* Chicago, IL: University of Chicago Press, in press.

MARCH, J. G. Bounded rationality, ambiguity, and the engineering of choice. *The Bell Journal of Economics,* 1978; **9**(2), 587–608.

PARDUCCI, A. The relativism of absolute judgments. *Scientific American,* 1968; **219**, 84–90.

SCHELLING, T. A. *Choice and consequence.* Cambridge, MA: Harvard University Press, 1984.

SCHUL, Y. *Expectations, performance, and satisfaction.* Unpublished manuscript, The Hebrew University of Jerusalem, 1989.

SCHWARZ, N., STRACK, F., KOMMER, D. and WAGNER, D. Soccer, rooms, and the quality of your life: Mood effects on judgments of satisfaction with life in general and with specific domains. *European Journal of Social Psychology,* 1987; **17**, 69–79.

SEN, A. *Choice, welfare and measurement.* Cambridge, MA: MIT Press, 1982.

SHRAUGER, J. S. Responses to evaluation as a function of initial self-perception. *Psychological Bulletin*, 1975; **82**, 581–596.

STRACK, F., SCHWARZ, N. and GSCHNEIDINGER, E. Happiness and reminiscing: The role of time perspective, affect, and mode of thinking. *Journal of Personality and Social Psychology*, 1985; **49***(6)*, 1460–1469.

THALER, R. Toward a positive theory of consumer choice. *Journal of Economic Behavior and Organization*, 1980; **1**, 39–60.

TVERSKY, A., SATTATH, S. and SLOVIC, P. Contingent weighting in judgment and choice. *Psychological Review*, 1988; **95***(3)*, 371–384.

Notes

1. Our use of this term to denote a component of hedonic experience should be distinguished from the endowment effect demonstrated by Thaler (1980), which refers to the impact of acquiring material goods on subsequent choices.

Acknowledgement

This work was supported by a grant from the Alfred P. Sloan Foundation. It has benefited from discussions with Daniel Kahneman and Lee Ross.

7

Happiness is the frequency, not the intensity, of positive versus negative affect

ED DIENER, ED SANDVIK and WILLIAM PAVOT

Introduction

When people seek happiness, some desire to be happy most of the time, even if only mildly so, whereas others appear to live and plan for rare but intense moments of ecstasy. The question addressed here is whether frequent positive affect, intense positive affect, or both are necessary and sufficient for happiness. One common sense view suggests that happiness is greatest when one has the maximum of both frequent positive affect *and* intense positive affect and only minimal amounts of non-intense, negative affect. But many people would suggest that either frequent (but mild) or intense (but infrequent) experiences of positive affect are necessary or sufficient to produce a happy life (see Chapters 2, 3, 5 and 10 for related discussions).

We will argue that happiness researchers should assess primarily the relative frequency of positive versus negative emotional experience. The first reason for this contention is that the relative frequency of positive emotions can be more accurately and validly measured, a consideration that is fundamental to scientific work on the concept of happiness. A second reason that researchers should focus on the relative frequency of positive versus negative affect is that frequent positive affect is both necessary and sufficient to produce the state we call happiness, whereas intense positive experience is not. Thus, what we call happiness seems to actually be comprised of frequent positive affect and infrequent negative affect.

The final reason to emphasize the relative frequency of positive affect in the study of happiness is that intense positive experiences can, surprisingly, have undesirable features. These features tend to offset the benefit of intense positive emotions, making it questionable whether intense experiences in the long run are more valuable to the individual than less intense ones. Thus, although intense positive experiences are individually desirable at the time they are experienced, they may be less related to long-term well-being or happiness because of unattractive side effects, as well as because of their rarity.

In sum, there are several strong justifications for defining and studying happiness as the relative frequency of positive experiences rather than the intensity of positive affect. Although intense positive emotions are an interesting phenomenon in their own right, it is doubtful that they are closely related to the longer-term state we refer to as "happiness" or "subjective well-being".

In this paper we will refer to the "frequency of positive affect," which is a shorthand way of referring to the relative per cent of time individuals are happy versus unhappy. Although we call the per cent of time experiencing predominantly positive affect the "relative frequency of positive affect" (Diener, 1984; Diener, Larsen, Levine and Emmons, 1985), it should be noted that we mean frequency in terms of time sampling, and it is therefore the overall percentage of time the person is in a predominantly positive (as opposed to negative) emotional state. When the intensity of positive emotions is discussed, we mean the average intensity of affect when a person is experiencing positive emotions.

Measurement

One important reason for scientists to focus their attention on the frequency of positive affect in understanding happiness is that frequency of affect is more easily and accurately measured than affect intensity. Scientific research, in contrast to other approaches to knowledge, relies heavily on accurate measurement of the concepts which are studied. There are reasons to believe that frequency of positive affect measures are accurate, and perhaps approximate an interval or even ratio level of measurement. Frequency information can be encoded in memory, accurately recalled from memory, and can be reported in a way that is comparable across persons. Evidence has shown that people are more able to accurately estimate frequency of affect and are less biased in its recall than they assess the intensity of emotional experiences. This is perhaps one reason that most measures of happiness do in fact reflect the frequency of positive experiences to a much greater degree than they reflect intense positive emotions.

Brandstätter (1987; also see Chapter 9) has argued that persons can clearly tell whether or not they are happy or unhappy at a particular time. In his terms, there is a natural "point of indifference" in emotion, above which people feel positive and below which they feel negative.

The judgment of happiness versus unhappiness is facilitated by the fact that when one type of affect is dominant, the other type exists, if at all, at low levels (Diener and Iran-Nejad, 1986). Therefore, because individuals can tell when they are experiencing positive and/or negative affect and can usually judge which is stronger, it is possible for them to store frequency of affect information in memory.

In contrast to frequency information, the intensity of affect is likely to be more difficult to encode because there is no natural system by which to define or label emotional intensity. As one becomes more intensely joyful, it is difficult to calibrate this experience, and therefore, difficult to encode the intensity accurately. How can one clearly distinguish levels of emotional intensity and encode them in comparable ways from one occasion to the next? Frequency information can be encoded because people know whether they are happy or unhappy, joyful or fearful, whereas for intensity, there is no such discrete event. At best, individuals might be able to encode the intensity of their own emotional experiences in an ordinal way.

There is empirical evidence that frequency information can be more accurately recalled than intensity information. Hasher and Zacks (1979, 1984) have shown that people are particularly accurate at recalling frequency information in general. These researchers even hypothesize that humans may be biologically prepared to store such information, and review data which show that people can be accurate in retrieving the frequency of events and objects in their experience.

In the domain of internal experiences such as affect, people may also be much more accurate at recalling frequency information than intensity information. We have collected evidence which shows that people are less accurate in recalling intensity information, and that their intensity estimates are biased by the actual frequency of their emotions. In our laboratory Thomas (1987; Thomas and Diener, 1988) has examined the accuracy of memory for one's own moods. Across a series of studies he found that people are accurate at estimating the per cent of time they are happy. For example, in one study subjects estimated that they were happy 72 per cent of the time on average and later mood recording indicated that they were happy 78 per cent of the time. The estimates correlated substantially across subjects with their later experiences.

In contrast, subjects were much less accurate at recalling the intensity of their emotions. Their estimates were almost twice the actual daily values in an absolute sense and showed little correlation across subjects with the daily intensity figures. Because people's most emotional times are most salient in memory, they tend to greatly overestimate in an absolute sense their emotional intensity. Furthermore, subjects' intensity estimates correlated with how frequently they were actually happy more highly than they correlated with their emotional intensity as sampled over time. In other words, subjects seem to retrieve frequency information when they are trying to estimate intensity.

It is also likely that emotion reports are more comparable across people when they report frequency rather than intensity information. How can we ever know if mood intensity reports have similar meanings across respondents? A person can tell us if she is experiencing positive or negative affect and this appears to have very similar meaning across people because basic emotional experiences are largely universal. Reports of frequency are thus probably comparable across persons because they are the summation of positive and negative emotions which have cross-person meaning. But when a person tells us that she is *moderately* or *very* happy, what does this mean? There is simply no cross-person metric to make such judgments. Because the experiences are internal, it is hard to reach a consensual definition of response alternatives in the emotional intensity domain. Thus, it appears that frequency of positive affect should be easier to measure because it represents the summation over time of a discrete state variable, whereas intensity is very problematical to assess because it is a continuously distributed unobservable which can be scaled idiosyncratically by subjects. Furthermore, it should be noted that to some extent affect frequency reports are themselves unreliable because subjects label their emotions differently, the intensity of these emotions will thus be even more problematical to assess.

One other benefit in measuring the frequency of positive affect is that, in considering levels of measurement, frequency information has both interval and ratio properties. A person who is happy 40 per cent of the time can legitimately be said to be happy 10 per cent more of the time than a person who is happy only 30 per cent of the time. Furthermore, it is meaningful to say that a person who is happy 80 per cent of the time is twice as happy as a person who is happy only 40 per cent of the time. In contrast, we cannot be sure that mood intensity information given by different subjects is even ordinal. For example, can one be sure that individuals who describe their positive moods as "quite strong" are really experiencing more intense affect than persons who describe their moods as "moderate"? Certainly we cannot be certain what response would be twice as strong as another because it is not even clear what this might mean. Thus, mood intensity measures are more likely to have nominal or perhaps ordinal properties rather than the more sophisticated measurement properties which characterize mood frequency measures.

Finally, response artifacts or biases appear to be a greater potential problem in measuring intensity than in assessing frequency of affect. For example, number-use response sets such as extremity bias (a subject's tendency to use very high or low numbers regardless of a question's content) are more likely to influence the reporting of intensity information. Frequency measures with concrete anchors such as the percentage of time the person is happy are less likely to be influenced by such response sets. When one uses time sampling methods of recording mood at particular moments, number use response sets are still a major potential problem for intensity reports, but seem to be unproblematical for reports of whether the person is happy or unhappy. When one "beeps" persons at random moments, their mood intensity report is still quite vulnerable to response artifacts such as extreme number use. But an indication of whether one was predominantly happy or unhappy when the pager sounded is much less susceptible to such artifacts. Social desirability is the tendency of some individuals to give responses which are desirable in that culture. In terms of social desirability, we (Diener, Sandvik, Gallagher and Pavot, 1988) have found that the correlation between this variable and frequency of happiness reports reflects a substantive individual difference characteristic which actually enhances well-being. In other words, individuals who tend to respond in socially desirable ways are truly happier individuals (even when measured by nonself-report measures). Individual differences in social desirability are, therefore, not damaging response artifacts in the case of frequency of happiness reports.

In conclusion, there are both theoretical and empirical reasons for believing that frequency measures are more accurate, more comparable across subjects, and can be measured with scales ⁓which have more sophisticated properties. Therefore, it appears that the typical measurement of positive affect with a single self-report is much more likely to be veridical if it assesses frequency rather than intensity information because people can store and recall this information more accurately. In the next section evidence will be reviewed which shows that frequency of affect information is strongly reflected in subjects' questionnaire reports of happiness, again indicating that such frequency information must be stored in memory. The next question to be addressed relates to the validity of equating the frequency of positive affect with happiness. Although frequency of positive versus negative affect can be measured with some accuracy, is it really what we mean by happiness?

The composition of happiness

In this section it will be shown that frequent positive and infrequent negative affect correlate much more strongly with happiness measures than does the intensity of positive affect. Even more noteworthy, it will be demonstrated that relatively frequent positive affect is both *necessary and sufficient* to produce high scores on a variety of happiness measures. In contrast, those with intense positive emotions are sometimes happy, but are not always so. Thus, we maintain that happiness should be defined as relatively frequent positive affect and infrequent negative affect because this is the common ingredient reflected in widely varying measures of well-being. In other words, measures of subjective well-being all reflect an underlying unitary phenomenon (frequency of positive versus negative affect), and this state is separate from other phenomena such as intense positive affect. Subjective well-being measures all converge on the property of frequent positive affect, indicating that this experience is the essence of a phenomenon which can be labelled "happiness."

We have examined three major self-report measures of happiness as they relate to the frequency and intensity of positive affect in several samples. In the studies reported here we administered the Fordyce (1977) global happiness scale, along with two other widely used scales—Bradburn's (1969) Affect Balance Scale and the 7-point Delighted-Terrible scale of Andrews and Withey (1976). We then assessed the moods of our subjects over a period of six to eight weeks. During this time we measured both the frequency and intensity of positive affect (e.g. see Diener and Emmons, 1984; Diener, Larsen, Levine and Emmons, 1985). We have assessed these variables both at end of the day measurement times, as well as at random moments throughout each day, with parallel results. Frequency of positive affect was defined in our studies as the percentage of time individuals were experiencing positive affect at levels which exceeded their level of negative affect. Intensity of positive affect was the average intensity of positive affect when the person was happy (experiencing more positive than negative affect). Table 7.1 shows how well the daily frequency and intensity of positive affect correlate with the happiness measures across the three groups. As can be seen, the results of the three studies are quite similar, as are the results across the three measures of happiness. The regression analyses shown in the top of the table reveal that frequency of positive affect is always a much stronger predictor of happiness reports than positive emotional intensity. The bottom half of Table 7.1 presents the partial correlations between the happiness reports and the frequency and intensity of positive affect. Because frequent and intense positive affect correlated in one of our samples, the partial correlations are given to show the amount of unique variance in the happiness reports associated with frequency and with intensity. Once again, it can be seen that traditional happiness measures are much more strongly related to the frequency of positive affect than to its intensity. These results are particularly striking when it is considered that these three happiness scales mention nothing about the frequency of positive or negative affect. Indeed, the wording in some of the measures reflects intensity content.

TABLE 7.1. *Predicting happiness scale scores from frequency and intensity of positive affect*

| | Regression betas | | | | | |
| | N = 42 | | N = 62 | | N = 107 | |
	Freq	PI	Freq	PI	Freq	PI
Fordyce	.58***	.23	.58***	.22*	.53***	.29***
Bradburn	.41**	.22	.39**	.06	.39***	.21
Andrews and						
Withey[1]	.42***	.24	.37***	.23	.49***	.25**

	Partial correlations		

Freq with PI controlled

| | Partial | Partial | Partial |
	r	r	r
Fordyce	.60***	.57***	.56***
Bradburn	.42**	.38***	.38***
Andrews and			
Withey[1]	.43**	.38***	.48***

	PI with freq controlled		
Fordyce	.28*	.26*	.34***
Bradburn	.24	.07	.20*
Andrews and			
Withey[1]	.27*	.25*	.25**

[1] Reflected
* $p < .05$, ** $p < .01$, *** $p < .001$

Further light can be shed on the question of the importance of frequency and intensity of positive affect for happiness by turning to the combined results of several of our studies. We were able to identify a number of individuals who were high in frequency (above 80 per cent) and very low in intensity ("slightly" or "somewhat" intense positive affect). *All* seven of these individuals reported very happy scores on the Fordyce Scale ($M = 7.86$). In contrast, *none* of the three individuals who were very high in positive emotional intensity ("much" or "very" intense positive affect), but below 50 per cent in frequency of positive affect, reported scores in the happy range on the Fordyce Scale ($M = 3.00$).

We have also examined affect balance scores derived from our daily mood recordings. Affect balance is computed by subtracting the average negative affect level for a day from the average positive affect level for a day. Subjects' frequency of positive affect scores correlated a very strong .86 with this affect balance score, whereas the positive intensity score correlated a more modest .28 with daily affect balance ($N = 62$). Thus, happiness measures sampled over time also reflect primarily the influence of frequency of positive versus negative affect rather than the intensity of positive affect.

What of the common sense idea that those who are happiest are actually those who have frequent and intense positive affect and infrequently experience only low intense negative affect? Certainly such a formula for happiness seems intuitively appealing, but we have thus far found little empirical support for it. For a sample of 107 subjects, we correlated happiness self-reports with the relative frequency of positive affect. We also correlated the happiness measures with the following formula: frequency of positive affect times positive affect intensity, minus frequency of negative affect times negative affect intensity. This formula score correlated $r = .95$ with the relative frequency of positive versus negative affect, suggesting that intensity information normally adds little to the prediction of happiness. Furthermore, this formula score correlated less well than the relative frequency of positive affect with the Fordyce Happiness score (r's of .67 versus .69), the Bradburn Affect Balance score (.51 versus .53), and the Delighted-Terrible Scale (.70 versus. 72).

In addition to the above analysis, we correlated daily *average* positive affect and negative affect with the happiness scales. We also correlated the frequency that positive and negative emotions were each felt with the happiness scales. These frequencies correlated with the happiness scale scores as well as the daily affect averages. This is noteworthy because the averages reflect the intensity of one's emotions as well as the frequency. When average positive and average negative affect were used to predict the Fordyce happiness scale score, for example, a multiple correlation of .60 resulted. When the frequencies of positive and negative affect were used to predict the Fordyce score the multiple R was higher—.63. Clearly, weighting the frequency of positive affect by its intensity seems to aid little in the prediction of happiness. Thus, the relative frequency of positive versus negative affect is the factor which appears to comprise affective well-being.

The above data indicate that self-reports of happiness reflect frequency of positive affect to a greater degree than the intensity of positive affect. Furthermore, these results generalize to nonself-report measures of well-being, suggesting that frequency of positive affect is not merely what subjects report on happiness scales. In one study we obtained several nonself-report measures of happiness: an expert rating of well-being based on a structured written interview; peer reports of happiness; and a memory based affect balance measure of well-being comprised of the number of happy versus unhappy life events subjects could recall in a timed period. Each of these well-being measures was predicted by the daily relative frequency and intensity of positive affect of subjects. As can be seen in Table 7.2, both predictors can predict significantly when entered first in the prediction equation. Only frequency, however, predicts when entered second, and it does so for all three measures. The results indicate that frequency and intensity share common variance in this sample which predicts the nonself-report happiness scales. In addition, frequency has unique variance which predicts the measures, but intensity does not. Self, peer, and expert ratings, as well as a memory based assessment of happiness, all seem to depend more heavily on the frequency of positive affect. This finding again suggests that the frequency of positive versus negative affect is at the core of a construct we can label happiness or affective well-being.

TABLE 7.2. *Multiple R's squared predicting nonself-report scales of happiness*

	Memdiff[1]	Expert[2]	Peer[3]
Entering frequency first as predictor			
Frequency of positive affect	.21***	.30***	.57***
Intensity of positive affect	.23*	.30	.57
Entering positive affect intensity first as predictor			
Intensity of positive affect	.14***	.13***	.22***
Frequency of positive affect	.23***	.30***	.57***

[1] Memory difference measure of happiness
[2] Expert rating of happiness based on structured interview
[3] Peer-reported measure of happiness
* $p < .05$, ** $p < .01$, *** $p < .001$

We turn now to the questions of whether frequency of positive affect is necessary and sufficient for happiness, and whether intense positive emotions are necessary or sufficient for happiness. Necessity and sufficiency are strong conditions which, if met, suggest that frequency or intensity are not merely influences on happiness, but may be the defining characteristics of happiness. Table 7.3 shows several happiness scores for individuals differing in their frequency of positive affect. In order to determine whether frequent positive affect is necessary or sufficient for happiness, individual data must be examined rather than group averages. This is because single individuals can invalidate the propositions that frequent positive affect or intense positive affect are necessary or sufficient for happiness by providing a single contradictory instance. The high frequency group is comprised of those thirteen individuals (out of 107 subjects) with complete data who showed predominantly positive affect on all forty-two days in which they were queried. The eight low frequency individuals were those who reported predominantly positive affect on fewer than one-half of these days. Because there were few individuals in this sample who were infrequently happy, a less stringent cutoff was mandated for the low group, a division which is not optimal for the present argument. Nonetheless, the results are quite revealing.

The Memdiff score shown in Table 7.3 refers to the number of positive events the subjects could recall and list from their life and last year in a five minute period, minus the number of negative events in his or her life and

TABLE 7.3. *Happiness scores of individuals differing in frequency of positive affect*

Subject number	Sex	High frequency			
		Memdiff	Expert	Fordyce	PI
9	F	1	4	8	15.7
19	F	22	4	8	19.0
22	M	4	4	8	15.2
39	M	4	5	7	8.2
63	M	15	4	8	15.0
70	F	5	3	8	12.2
75	M	4	4	8	17.3
76	F	9	4	8	8.9
8	M	4	5	8	17.1
117	F	16	4	8	16.0
118	F	20	6	10	19.7
123	F	10	4	8	18.7
125	F	1	4	8	12.0
		Low frequency			
16	M	−4	2	6	6.5
69	M	−4	1	2	5.8
84	M	−13	1	2	5.3
86	M	7	2	5	8.4
96	F	−9	2	7	11.8
97	F	−1	2	4	9.1
132	M	−2	2	4	14.3
134	M	−7	1	2	10.2

past year recalled in a separate five minute period. As can be seen in Table 7.3, only one infrequently happy subject (number eighty-six) remembered more positive than negative events, whereas all of the frequent positive affect group did so. Similarly, the expert rating clearly discriminated between the two groups: in fact, virtually perfectly. The expert rating varied from zero (extremely unhappy) to six (extremely happy), with three being the neutral point. These ratings were made blind as to the subjects' identities, yet only one neutral rating (for subject number seventy) failed to perfectly place the individuals into happy versus unhappy groups. Finally, the subjects' Fordyce scores (varying from zero to ten, with five being the neutral point) properly classified individuals in almost every case. Peer reports were also collected but are not presented in Table 7.3. There was little overlap between the two frequency groups in the peer happiness ratings. Peers erred, however, in the direction of believing that the low frequency subjects were happier than the other happiness measures revealed them to be.

Given that some low frequency subjects were not that extreme in terms of frequency, and that some normally happy individuals may have been unhappy during the six week sampling period used to measure frequency, the discrimination among the groups is remarkable. Although a definitive case cannot be made for the idea that frequent positive affect is necessary and sufficient for happiness, these data indicate that this is a strong possibility. Every individual who experienced frequent positive affect was happy on virtually every measure. And every individual who experienced infrequent positive affect was unhappy on virtually all of the measures. From this pattern it appears that frequent positive affect is sufficient for happiness. Because no individual with infrequent positive affect scored in the happy range on more than one of the three scales reviewed above, it also seems likely that frequent positive affect is necessary for happiness. We suggest that if a more extreme infrequent positive affect group was examined (e.g. predominant positive affect 20 per cent or less of the time), the case for the necessary and sufficient connection between happiness and frequency could be made without reservation.

In reference to intensity, there are several noteworthy findings in Table 7.3. Firstly, it can be seen that in this sample there is a tendency for the intensity and frequency of positive affect to be related, although we have not found this to be true in other samples. Secondly, it appears that intense positive affect is neither necessary nor sufficient for happiness. Low frequency subject number 132 experienced intense positive affect, yet was unhappy on every measure. In contrast, high frequency subject numbers thirty-nine and seventy-six had low intensity positive affect, yet were happy on every measure. It appears that frequent positive affect is sufficient for happiness regardless of its level of intensity, but that intense positive affect is neither necessary nor sufficient for happiness (see also Chapter 6).

Intense positive affect

In this section it will be argued that intense positive experiences are less related to long-term well-being not simply because of measurement considerations. In other words, frequency of positive experiences are reflected to a greater degree in well-being measures not only because they can be accurately recalled or more validly measured across subjects. There are also even more substantive psychological reasons related to affective dynamics that intense positive emotions are only weakly related to the state of long-term happiness. In the first place, extremely positive experiences are quite rare and are therefore less likely to be important to global well-being. In the second place, there are both empirical and theoretical reasons to believe that intense positive experiences often carry emotional costs in terms of being accompanied by increased negative affect and lowered positivity of other good experiences. Thus, intense positive experiences may be counterbalanced by opposing forces in such a way that they do not greatly enhance long term well-being and are therefore not strongly reflected in happiness measures.

Rareness of intense positive affect

It is unlikely that intense positive emotional experiences form the core of well-being because these experiences are so uncommon. In contrast, the frequent experience of mild levels of positive affect seems to occur quite often. Sigmund Freud recognized the difficulty in maintaining intense happiness when he wrote that the experience of intense positive affect is limited by our biological constitutions. Flugel (1925) found that the half life of extremely positive moods is very short—the more intense the mood, the shorter it lasted.

In our research based on time sampling, we have found that the extremely intense moods are quite unusual. For example, a sample of 133 subjects reported on their daily moods for forty-two days. Of the total 5586 days assessed, extremely positive affect was reported on only 2.6 per cent of the days. We also signalled the subjects at random moments at which time they completed mood reports. Of the 3639 moment reports, 1.2 per cent were marked as extremely intense on the positive mood adjectives. In another study of forty-two subjects, the respondents were asked to indicate their maximum mood for each day. Of the 1756 reports, 266 or 15 per cent showed a maximum mood sometime during the day of "extremely" happy. It is clear that extremely intense positive moods are quite rare. This is even more dramatic because the subjects were in general quite happy and in a youthful age group which more frequently experiences intense emotions than most adults (Diener, Sandvik and Larsen, 1985). Because these subjects reached an extremely happy state about once a week and for about one per cent of their waking time, we would expect intensely happy moods very infrequently in older samples.

Finally, we have found that extremely positive events are relatively uncommon. In one study we asked subjects to write down the best thing which happened to them each day. We then had coders rate the events in terms of how good the events were on a 5-point scale ranging from neutral to extremely good. Only one of the 3214 events was rated as extremely good and only thirty-seven or 1.2 per cent were rated as very good. The vast majority of events were rated as slightly or moderately good. Again, we can see that intense positivity is a very scarce commodity. Indeed, if an event occurred frequently it would probably lose its intense character. It seems unlikely that subjective well-being is built on experiences which occur so seldom (see also Chapter 10).

The prevalence of frequent positive affect

When we turn from intense positive emotions to positive affect in general, a very different picture emerges; positive moods at less intense levels occur

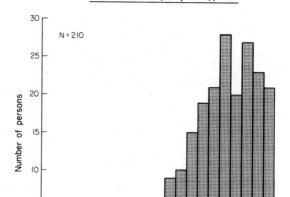

FIG. 7.1. Amount of time individuals experience positive versus negative affect

most of the time for the majority of our subjects. This fact squares nicely with the finding in all large-scale surveys that the majority of respondents claim to be happy. In a sample of 210 subjects, our respondents reported a preponderance of positive over negative affect on 75 per cent of their days. Only 8 per cent of the subjects were happy less than half of the time. Figure 7.1 shows the distribution of the per cent of days these subjects were predominantly happy. As can be seen, the distribution is highly skewed, with a plurality of subjects reporting a high percentage of happy days. At the same time, the average intensity of the happy days was only 3.2 on a zero to six scale, a response anchored by "moderate" in reference to how intensely the positive mood adjectives were being felt. Thus, it appears that our subjects experience weak levels of positive affect most of the time.

Costs of positive intensity

In addition to their rarity, there appear to be affective costs related to intense positive emotional experiences and these may counterbalance the good effects of these experiences in terms of long-term subjective well-being (see Chapters 2 and 6). Early thinkers recognized that intense positive emotions can involve a price. For example, the Epicureans counselled that happiness lies in quiet of the mind and not desiring things too strongly. Similarly, the Stoics believed that individuals should avoid extreme "highs."

In *The Discourses*, Epictetus (1952) suggested that when we are delighted with a thing, we should temper this delight by thinking of its loss. Thus, if we lose the thing, we will be less disappointed. Epictetus recommends that we not allow our pleasures to go too far; we should check or curb them. Implicit in both Epicureanism and Stoicism is the idea that very intense positive affect can lead to more intense negative affect, a price that can be high. Similarly, Freud (1930) in *Civilization and Its Discontents* wrote that wild, untamed craving can lead to more intense satisfactions than curbed desires. On the other hand, he recognized that such unbridled desires also cause greater displeasure when they are not satisfied. Furthermore, he believed that we are so constituted that we can only intensely enjoy contrasts. It is impossible to attain uninterrupted intense positive affect. We will review theoretical and empirical works which indicate that one does indeed at times pay affectively for experiences of intense positive affect. Intense positive affect is not entirely a blessing and is therefore less related to long term emotional well-being.

In our studies on the temperament of emotional intensity, we have repeatedly found that those people who experience the most intense positive affect are likely to be those who will experience the most intense negative affect when unhappy (Larsen and Diener, 1987). For example, when we asked subjects to complete mood reports when they felt quite emotional, the relationship across persons between their intensity of positive feelings when they were happy and their intensity of negative feelings when feeling unhappy was strong $r = .80$. Thus, one reason that happiness reports do not correlate more strongly with positive intensity is that the same individuals who are experiencing positive emotions intensely are also likely to be experiencing negative emotions more intensely.

If we examine factors which intuitively lead to intense positive affect, we find that most of these inputs can also heighten the intensity of negative affect. For instance, if a person works hard and long to gain some goal (high effort), intense positive affect will be experienced if the person is successful in reaching the goal. If the person fails to reach the goal, however, intense negative affect will ensue. One reason that subjects who experience positive events in an intense way are likely to experience negative events in an intense way also is that these individuals think of specific outcomes as quite important. For example, if a person thinks that the local team's winning of the next ball game is quite important because he identifies with the team, a win will produce more intense positive affect. But a loss will produce more intense negative affect. Similarly, if persons have their heart set on getting a particular job because it fulfils certain personal motives, receiving an employment call will make them quite happy. But they will also be more disappointed if they do not receive the offer. This phenomenon is what Freud meant by unbridled desires leading to more intense pleasure *or* to more intense displeasure. Thus, persons can achieve intense positive emotions by giving their goals a high subjective valence. If most of persons' goals are considered by them to be enormously important, they are likely to experience more intense positive emotions when the goals are reached. But in magnifying the importance of their goals, the persons will increase the intensity of their negative emotions whenever a goal is not attained.

Another related reason some people feel emotions intensely is because of certain cognitive styles. For example, the Freudian mechanism of repression would be likely to dampen the intensity of a person's negative affect. Interestingly, Davis and Schwartz (1987) found that repressors experienced both negative and positive affect less intensely. In other words, not only might repression lead to less intense negative affect, but the dynamics involved also seem to take the edge off positive emotions. Similarly, Gorman and Wessman (1974) found that repressive subjects reported less intense negative emotions, but were also less capable of hitting high peaks. The repressive subjects showed more shallow affect and less mood variability. Although repression has usually been studied in terms of negative affect, it may be that it blunts all types of emotions.

We have recently examined how cognitions can be used by individuals to blunt or dampen emotions. We asked subjects to list the best and worst event which happened to them each day for four days. We also requested that they write down each day their thoughts when these events occurred. Coders rated these thoughts for their emotional amplifying and emotional dampening qualities. It is noteworthy that those who showed the most amplifying thoughts for positive events also amplified their negative emotions the most, and a similar pattern occurred for dampening thoughts. What this and other laboratory studies (Colvin, Pavot and Diener, 1988; Diener, Smith, Allman and Pavot, 1988; Larsen, Diener and Cropanzano, 1987) show is that when persons increase their use of either a dampening or an amplifying strategy in relation to positive stimuli, this is likely to carry over to negative stimuli as well. Thus, cognitions which allow high peaks or intense positive emotions will also lead to more extreme lows when one encounters a negative event.

Another reason that people are intense in their emotions is because of greater arousal or physiological reactivity. For example, Larsen and Scheffer (1987) showed that skin conductance was higher for emotionally intense subjects when they were exposed to either positive *or* emotional slides. Some individuals may have greater arousability and therefore experience intense positive affect in less extreme circumstances than others. These persons, however, are also likely to experience more intense negative emotions in unpleasant situations.

Our work and that of others suggests that a number of interrelated factors which influence the intensity of positive emotions also influence the intensity of negative emotions for the individual: high assessment of the importance of events; repression; cognitive amplifying and dampening strategies; and physiological reactivity. The end result of these mechanisms is the same: to amplify or dampen both positive and negative affective responses. Thus, it seems that in the long run in people's lives, many high peaks will be paid for to some extent by lower lows when the person becomes unhappy. There appear to be long-term individual differences in several of the factors which heighten emotional intensity. Therefore, some individuals will consistently show more intense positive reactions to the world, and also more intense negative reactions. In addition, an individual may show a more intense reaction to a particular event or situation. But factors such as being aroused or greatly wanting a particular outcome can heighten either the positive or negative response intensity in specific situations.

Opponent process theory

There are formal theories which maintain that there are costs related to intense positive emotions. Solomon's (1980) opponent process model predicts that intense emotional peaks often come at the cost of negative affect. According to this theory, novel positive events can produce high peaks. But these novel events are quickly habituated to and thereafter lead to only mild positive reactions. The other course to very positive emotional reactions is to have first suffered negative events. If a negative event occurs over time (e.g. being in prison) so that the person adapts to it, its withdrawal can then produce intense positive affect.

It can be predicted from the theory that extremely positive events will inevitably be quite rare. They must either be based on novelty (which is rare) or on habituation to a negative event which necessarily means that the person has suffered for a period of time in order to experience the intense positive event. Solomon also maintains that positive experiences can plant the seeds for unhappiness because the loss of the positive things will cause withdrawal or negative affect. The theory supports the current argument in suggesting that there are often emotional costs to intense positive experiences, especially those which are repeated.

Parducci's range-frequency theory

Another theory which maintains that there are emotional costs to extremely good events is the range-frequency model of human judgments and happiness (Parducci, 1968, 1984; Smith, Wedell and Diener, 1989). This theory is built on the presumption that all judgments are relative—events are judged in relation to other events. How good or bad an event is judged to be depends on the other events against which it is compared. For an event to produce happiness, it must be judged positively in the context of relevant events. What is noteworthy for the present argument is that extremely bad events create a context in which later good events can produce more intense happiness. Similarly, extremely good events can make future negative events even more negative. Parducci's theory predicts that the intensity of positive and negative experiences influence one another.

Richard Smith conducted a study in our laboratory to demonstrate how the relational property of judgments is affected by intensely good events. He showed subjects grade distributions they might receive in a difficult class. They were shown their scores on fifteen weekly quizzes on which the possible number of points was fifty per quiz. It was stressed that this was a very difficult class with a low grading distribution. The subjects were asked how happy they would feel when earning various grades. One group of subjects received a normal distribution of grades centering around twenty. Another group received the same distribution, but they had one score of

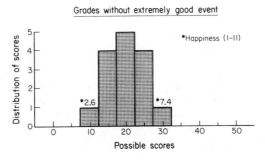

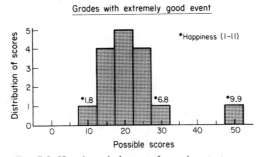

FIG. 7.2. Happiness judgments for various test scores

fifty. The average happiness various scores would produce is shown in Figure 7.2. Not surprisingly, the score of fifty would make people "extremely happy"—a 9.9 on the 11-point scale. But notice what happened to the other happiness values when an extremely high score was received. The lowest score (ten) is seen as more negative if the person had received a score of fifty. Even an otherwise high score (thirty) became less desirable if they had received a score of fifty. The extremely high score is very pleasing in itself, but it lowers the happiness one gains from other good events. Perhaps even worse, it makes the low scores even more painful. The above study is an empirical demonstration of the pleasure-pain connection about which Freud and the Stoics were concerned. The same effect was shown by Brickman, Coates and Janoff-Bulman (1978) who found that those who won large lotteries were thereafter less happy when small positive everyday events occurred (see also Chapter 3). To quote Parducci (1984):

> One type of "high" that can work against subsequent happiness comes from experiencing a new event better than any that had previously been experienced in the same domain. This new event extends the range upward so that lesser events become less satisfying. Although this makes an immediate positive contribution to the balance of happiness, its long-term effects are harmful unless the new upper endpoint can be experienced with high relative frequency . . ." (p. 14)

Thus, it is clear that intense positive moments may lower the intensity of future positive moments, and that intense positive moments are often purchased at the price of past unhappy moments. It is unsurprising, therefore, that intense positive affect is not closely related to long-term happiness.

Conclusions

The basic tenet of this paper is that happiness or affective well-being can be equated with the relative amount of time a person experiences positive versus negative affect. Frequent positive affect is both necessary and sufficient for the experience of happiness and for high scores on happiness measures. Further study should certainly be devoted to examining the implications of this idea. This paper, however, advances a number of additional hypotheses which are researchable:

(a) Intense positive affect is neither necessary nor sufficient for happiness, although intense positive experiences might sometimes heighten happiness among those who frequently experience positive affect.

(b) The frequency of positive versus negative emotions can be measured across persons with accuracy and with a sophisticated level of measurement, whereas this is probably not true of the intensity of people's feelings.

(c) Intense positive experiences often follow after a period of deprivation or suffering. In addition, intense positive experiences can cause later events and situations to be evaluated less positively. Thus, intense positive affect tends to be rare and to come with a price.

The above hypotheses are quite important to the field of subjective well-being because they are related to the most basic question of what comprises emotional well-being. Furthermore, these hypotheses are related to the fundamental issues about measuring well-being. Finally, the hypotheses raise interesting general questions about the causes of subjective well-being. The hypotheses we advance are of primary importance to the field, and yet are admittedly speculative. We have collected some data which support them but they have not yet received broad confirmation.

The above arguments raise a number of interesting researchable questions. When are the negative costs of positive emotional intensity exacted and when can they be avoided? That is, are there predictable times that a person will or will not suffer more negative emotions because of intense positive experiences? What factors increase positive emotional intensity and which of these generalize to negative emotional intensity? If seeking or obtaining intense positive experiences can have negative consequences for the individual, it seems imperative that we understand how this occurs because a large number of individuals in our culture are seeking such experiences. Theory should be developed which explains what personality and situational variables will effect the frequency of positive affect, its intensity, or both. A related set of questions has to do with the degree to which people seek and desire experiences which are intense versus those which produce mild happiness spread over time.

Another interesting question has to do with the independence of positive and negative affect (e.g. Bradburn, 1969; Diener and Emmons, 1984; Watson, Clark and Tellegen, 1984). If these two types of emotions show some degree of independence across persons, it could be that looking separately at their frequencies would give even greater power in understanding happiness. In a sample of 100 college subjects, we found that the relative frequency of positive versus negative affect correlated with the Fordyce happiness scale, $r = .57$. When a regression was computed in which the Fordyce score was predicted by the frequency of positive affect and the frequency of negative affect, a multiple R of .59 was achieved. It appears that some small increment in knowledge can be gained by separately examining the frequencies of positive and negative affect, but further work on this issue is clearly required.

The arguments presented in this paper also have important applied implications. It appears that people who are successful at attaining frequent positive affect will be happy. Thus, interventions which aim at increasing happiness should centre on increasing the frequency and duration of happy experiences. The above arguments suggest that interventions or events which lead to intense but relatively infrequent positive experiences are unlikely to enhance long-term happiness to a substantial degree. It could be, however, that expectations about future intense events and the recall of past intense events may in some cases enhance long-term happiness. Therefore, the role of intense positive experiences to happiness needs to be explored in more depth.

References

ANDREWS, F.M. and WITHEY, S.B. *Social indicators of well-being: America's perception of life quality*. New York: Plenum Press, 1976.

BRADBURN, N.M. *The structure of psychological well-being*. Chicago: Aldine, 1969.

BRANDSTÄTTER, H. Emotional responses to everyday life situations: An individual difference approach. *Paper delivered at the Colloquium on Subjective Well-Being*. Bad Homburg, Germany, 1987.

BRICKMAN, P., COATES, D. and JANOFF-BULMAN, R. Lottery winners and accident victims: Is happiness relative? *Journal of Personality and Social Psychology*, 1978; **36**, 917–927.

COLVIN, C.R., PAVOT, W. and DIENER, E. *Emotional regulation: Affective amping and damping carryover*. In preparation, University of Illinois, 1988.

DAVIS, P.J. and SCHWARTZ, G.E. Repression and the inaccessibility of affective memories. *Journal of Personality and Social Psychology*, 1987; **52**, 155–162.

DIENER, E. Subjective well-being. *Psychological Bulletin*, 1984; **95**, 542–575.

DIENER, E. and EMMONS, R.A. The independence of positive and negative affect. *Journal of Personality and Social Psychology*, 1984; **47**, 1105–1117.

DIENER, E. and IRAN–NEJAD, A. The relationship in experience between various types of affect. *Journal of Personality and Social Psychology*, 1986; **50**, 1031–1038.

DIENER, E., LARSEN, R.J., LEVINE, S. and EMMONS, R.A. Intensity and frequency: Dimensions underlying positive and negative affect. *Journal of Personality and Social Psychology*, 1985; **48**, 1253–1265.

DIENER, E., SANDVIK, E. and LARSEN, R.J. Age and sex effects for emotional intensity. *Developmental Psychology*, 1985; **21**, 542–546.

DIENER, E., SANDVIK, E., GALLAGHER, D. and PAVOT, W. *The effects of response artifacts on measures of subjective well-being*. In preparation, University of Illinois, 1988.

DIENER, E., SMITH, R.H., ALLMAN, A. and PAVOT, W. *The costs of intense positive emotions*. In preparation, University of Illinois, 1988.

EPICTETUS. *The discourses*. Chicago: Encyclopaedia Brittanica, 1952.

FLUGEL, J.C. A quantitative study of feeling and emotion in everyday life. *British Journal of Psychology*, 1925; **15**, 318–355.

FORDYCE, M.W. *The happiness measures: A sixty-second index of emotional well-being and mental health*. Unpublished manuscript. Edison Community College, St. Meyers, Florida, 1977.

FREUD, S. *Civilization and its discontents*. London: The Hogarth Press, 1930.

GORMAN, B.S. and WESSMAN, A.E. The relationship of cognitive style and moods. *Journal of Clinical Psychology*, 1974; **30**, 18–25.

HASHER, L. and ZACKS, R.T. Automatic and effortful processes in memory. *Journal of Experimental Psychology: General*, 1979; **108**, 356–388.

HASHER, L,. and ZACKS, R.T. Automatic processing of fundamental information: The case of frequency of occurrence. *American Psychologist*, 1984; **39**, 1372–1388.

LARSEN, R.J. and DIENER, E. Emotional response intensity as an individual difference characteristic. *Journal of Research in Personality*, 1987; **21**, 1–39.

LARSEN, R.J., DIENER, E. and CROPANZANO, R.S. Cognitive operations associated with the characteristic of intense emotional responsiveness. *Journal of Personality and Social Psychology*, 1987; **53**, 767–774.

LARSEN, R.J. and SCHEFFER, S. *The influence of cognitive operations on physiological response to emotion-provoking stimuli*. Unpublished study, Purdue University, 1987.

PARDUCCI, A. The relativism of absolute judgments. *Scientific American*, 1968; **219**, 84–90.

PARDUCCI, A. Value judgments: Toward a relational theory of happiness. In J.R. Eiser (ed.) *Attitudinal judgment*. New York: Springer-Verlag, 1984.

SMITH, R.H., WEDELL, D. and DIENER, E. Interpersonal and social comparison determinants of happiness. *Journal of Personality and Social Psychology*, 1989; **56**, 317–325.

SOLOMON, R.L. The opponent-process theory of acquired motivation: The costs of pleasure and the benefits of pain. *American Psychologist*, 1980; **35**, 691–712.

THOMAS, D. *Memory bias in the recall of emotions*. Unpublished master's thesis, University of Illinois, 1987.

THOMAS, D. and DIENER, E. *Memory accuracy in the recall of emotions.* Paper submitted for publication, 1988.

WATSON, D., CLARK, L.A. and TELLEGEN, A. Cross-cultural convergence in the structure of mood: A Japanese replication and a comparison with US findings. *Journal of Personality and Social Psychology*, 1984; **47**, 127–144.

8

The relationship between life satisfaction and psychosocial variables: new perspectives

PETER M. LEWINSOHN, JULIE E. REDNER and JOHN R. SEELEY

Introduction

Life satisfaction

Subjective well-being is a construct which has been studied by a large number of disciplines extending over many centuries, and has been defined in ethical, theological, political, economic, and psychological terms (see Chapter 2). Considering this paradigmatic diversity, it is not surprising that a number of names have been used to label it, including happiness, objective and subjective well-being, quality of life, and life satisfaction. While each of these terms has a somewhat different meaning, each is derived from a similar point of origin.

At the most general level, "happiness" describes a very broad characteristic of the human condition. At the other end of the spectrum, it involves concern with an individual's feelings of satisfaction within clearly circumscribed domains including work (see Chapter 12), leisure activities, neighbourhood, family life, marriage and competence (Campbell, Converse and Rodgers, 1976 (see Chapter 5)). While each of these specific areas is important in its own right, it is also true that satisfaction with each domain is substantially correlated with the others as well as with overall life satisfaction (Campbell *et al.*, 1976). It thus appears that overall measures of satisfaction reflect an aggregate which is integrally related to each of the specific satisfaction sub-measures.

Another aspect recognized as important by researchers in this area is the distinction between happiness and life satisfaction. In general, happiness is seen as an emotion or feeling state, whereas life satisfaction refers to a more cognitive, judgmental process. Our study focused on the latter in that we used a measure derived from Andrews and Withey (1976) and Campbell *et al.* (1976). These measures, as well as ours, are very similar to Diener's more recently developed Satisfaction With Life Scale (Diener, Emmons, Larsen and Griffin, 1985). In that paper, Diener reports moderate to high correlations between his scale and those of others measuring subjective well-being, including those of Andrews and Withey (1976) and Campbell *et al.* (1976).

Pervasiveness of depression

Over the past twenty years, first at the University of Oregon and more recently at the Oregon Research Institute, our research group has focused on the study and treatment of individuals of various ages suffering from clinical depression. During this time, theoretical, laboratory, and clinical research has helped us to expand our understanding of this emotional disorder. Depression is a much more pervasive human problem than has previously been thought. It is estimated that at least 4 per cent of the adult population meets rigorous diagnostic criteria for depression at any given time (Lehman, 1971; Weissman and Myers, 1978; Myers *et al.*, 1984), that approximately 10 per cent of the population will develop an episode of depression within a one year period (Amenson and Lewinsohn, 1981), and that at least 25 per cent of the general population becomes clinically depressed at some point in their lives (Lewinsohn, Zeiss and Duncan, 1988). In the course of investigating why so many individuals become depressed, we have also been impressed by the opposite of sadness and despair—why some people tend to be either temporarily or enduringly happy, while others may tend towards either temporary or enduring depression.

Why are some depressed and others satisfied?

Factors associated with depression

Factors associated with depression have been studied by a number of researchers, and have been summarized by Becker (1974), Beckham and Leber (1985), Carson and Carson (1984), Mendels (1975), Paykel (1982) and Whybrow, Akiskal and McKinney (1984). Depressed individuals have been shown to have difficulties in interpersonal interactions (e.g. Coyne, 1976; Weissman and Paykel, 1974; Lewinsohn and Libet, 1972), show reduced participation in and enjoyment of pleasant activities (Lewinsohn, Youngren and Grosscup, 1979; MacPhillamy and Lewinsohn, 1974), report a greater number of stressors (e.g. Brown and Harris, 1978; Lewinsohn and Talkington, 1979); and have a range of negative cognitive patterns (e.g. Beck, 1967; Rozensky, Rehm, Fry and Roth, 1977; Seligman, Abramson, Semmel and von Baeyer, 1979). Variables predictive of an episode of depression include being young, female, having had a previous episode of depression, and having experienced an elevated level of stress (Lewinsohn, Hoberman and Rosenbaum, 1988).

Factors associated with satisfaction

Similarly, through previous research, many variables have been shown to be related to subjective well-being or its correlates, life satisfaction and happiness. In terms of personality characteristics, for example, people who are happy tend to have an internal locus of control (Diener, 1984), and have a relative absence of inner conflicts (Wilson, 1967). Good social relationships (Argyle, 1987) and involvement with goal-directed work (see Chapter 12) and leisure activities (Campbell *et al.*, 1976) also show a positive relationship with happiness. As one might suspect, health is an important determinant of overall well-being, with healthier people reporting greater happiness (Palmore and Luikart, 1972; Kozma and Stones, 1983; Campbell *et al.*, 1976).

Other factors that have been shown to be related to happiness include having friends, being satisfied with one's family life, and being married (Argyle, 1987). In general, married persons are happier than those who are single. This is particularly true for males. Weaker, though positive associations have been found with education, wealth, and physical attractiveness (Argyle, 1987). Age appears to be related to satisfaction but not to happiness. This apparent discrepancy between the emotion of happiness and the cognitive evaluation of satisfaction may be related to the finding that older people experience emotions—both positive and negative ones—less intensely than younger people (Argyle, 1987; Diener, Sandvik and Larsen, 1985).

Relationship of satisfaction and depression

Depression and other measures of psychopathology have been shown to be related to indicators of subjective quality of life (Mechanic, 1979; Reich and Zautra, 1981; Tanaka and Huba, 1984). In fact, a central component of the phenomenology of depression is a pervasive sense of dissatisfaction. This centrality is recognized in Beck's cognitive triad (Beck, 1967) in which depressed persons are hypothesized to experience a pervasive sense of pessimism about their lives, their world, and their future.

Removing the effects of current depression

Given that depression and satisfaction are related, the inquisitive reader might wonder about the relationship between life satisfaction, depression, and the aforementioned psychosocial variables. As we have seen, both depression and life satisfaction are related to a large number of psychosocial variables. Is it possible that these two are different terms which refer to the same process? In other words, if we control for the variance due to one, is there any variance left over?

Researchers have investigated a similar question about the relationships between positive affect, negative affect, and life satisfaction. The conclusion that has emerged from these studies supports the view that negative and positive affect are two relatively independent and additive determinants of satisfaction (e.g. Bradburn, 1969; Bradburn and Caplovitz, 1965; Emmons and Diener, 1985; Harding, 1982; Perry and Warr, 1980; Warr, 1978; Watson and Tellegen, 1985). In other words, the presence of positive affect and the absence of negative affect conjointly determine a person's level of life satisfaction. From these results, we would thus expect to have variance left over in the relationship between life satisfaction and the psychosocial variables after controlling for current depression level. We would also expect this leftover variance to be uniquely related to positive affect or happiness.

Nature of the relationships

Given that life satisfaction and the psychosocial variables are related, we were also interested in the *nature* of those relationships. In particular, we wanted to investigate whether scores on the relevant psychosocial variables correlated with the person's current, and often fluctuating level of satisfaction (i.e. state-dependent), or whether they are more stable characteristics of more and less satisfied people (i.e. trait-dependent).

The importance of the distinction between personality characteristics which are state-dependent and those which represent traits has been emphasized by personality theorists such as Allport and Odbert (1936), Cattell (1963), Norman (1967), Spielberger (1972), and Chaplin, John and Goldberg (1988). Differences between these two types of relationships include temporal stability, locus of attributed causality, and cross-situational consistency. Pure state-dependent variables are temporary characteristics of the person which last only while the person is in the state, are usually perceived as externally induced, and are less stable across situations. A purely trait-dependent variable, on the other hand, represents an enduring personality characteristic which is expected to exhibit temporal stability, is usually attributed to sources within the person, and tends to show cross-situational consistency (Chaplin *et al.*, 1988). For the purposes of this study, the term "trait" is used to represent either a stable aspect of the person, a stable aspect of the person's environment (e.g. caring for a sick relative), or a stable aspect of the person-environment interaction (e.g. marital discord).

Data available for analysis

As a result of our earlier research, we had a great deal of data that could be employed to investigate subjective well-being. The data to be presented in this chapter originated from two longitudinal prospective studies aimed at identifying risk factors for depression in a general community sample (Amenson and Lewinsohn, 1981; Lewinsohn *et al.*, 1988). Both studies began with a large number of people from the general community, most of whom were not depressed at the beginning of the study (T1). These individuals were then followed over time and those who became depressed were identified at a later assessment (T2). In both studies, measures of many psychosocial variables including subjective well-being were included at T1 and T2.

Hypotheses to be tested

Given this large, longitudinal data set, there were several issues we were able to address:

(1) Are our life satisfaction items measures of a single underlying dimension? We predicted that they would be.

(2) Can we replicate previous findings concerning the relationships of life satisfaction and psychosocial variables? We assumed that we would.

(3) What is the relationship between life satisfaction and current depression? We predicted that the two would vary inversely.

(4) Is low life satisfaction a risk factor for future depression? We thought it would be.

(5) Are people who have been depressed more dissatisfied even when they are not depressed? We hypothesized that they would be.

(6) What is the effect of partialling out the effects of depression? Assuming that our data replicated previous findings regarding the relationships between various psychosocial variables and subjective well-being, and given the strong negative correlation between life satisfaction and depression and other measures of psychopathology, our next emphasis was on whether life satisfaction would continue to correlate with these psychosocial variables, even with dysphoria (which we assume to be the key subjective phenomenon of clinical depression) partialled out. This would enable us to pinpoint variables having a unique relationship with life satisfaction as well as those whose apparent relationship with life satisfaction was explainable because of a high correlation with dysphoria. Such correlates might shed light on the nature and phenomenology of life satisfaction, as well as on the construct validity of the life satisfaction measure.

(7) What is the nature of the relationship between life satisfaction and the psychosocial variables? We were interested in clarifying the temporal

stability of the relationships between life satisfaction and various psychosocial and personality factors. Specifically, for those psychosocial variables found to be associated with life satisfaction, we wanted to determine whether they are state-dependent (i.e. co-varying with the currently experienced level of satisfaction) or whether they represent relatively stable characteristics (i.e. traits) of persons who are either high or low on life satisfaction.

In the present study we wanted to examine our data in light of this state-trait distinction, that is, to examine whether the relationships between life satisfaction and specific social and psychological variables is more congruent with a state or a trait.

The longitudinal design of our study allowed us to divide subjects into four mutually exclusive groups according to their levels of life satisfaction at T1 and T2: (a) those reporting high satisfaction both at T1 and T2 (high-high); (b) those reporting low satisfaction at T1 and T2 (low-low); (c) those reporting they were satisfied at T1, but became dissatisfied by T2 (high-low); and (d) those reporting they were dissatisfied at T1, but satisfied by T2 (low-high). This division of subjects allowed us to test whether status on the psychosocial variables changes as a function of the current level of life satisfaction (state-dependent). It also allowed us to determine whether the variable represents a relatively stable characteristic of individuals (or their environments) who are high or low on that dimension (trait-dependent). The division of subjects into high-low and low-high groups additionally allowed us to examine whether any of the included variables had prognostic value or whether they functioned as a risk factor. Specifically, a variable may be said to have positive prognostic value (predict improvement) if, among those who are initially dissatisfied, it predicts those whose satisfaction will improve (i.e. the low-highs are different from low-lows at T1). A variable would be said to constitute a risk factor (or antecedent) if it identifies which people among those who are initially satisfied will become less satisfied (i.e. high-highs are different from high-lows at T1).

Method

Participants

The population for this study consisted of a subset of individuals who had participated in one of two large longitudinal, prospective epidemiological studies of depression in community residing persons in Eugene and Springfield, Oregon. The goals and demand characteristics for the two studies were similar; extensive methodological details are described elsewhere (Amenson and Lewinsohn, 1981; Lewinsohn et al., 1988). Both samples were self-selected, and cannot be considered to be random or representative samples of the population of Eugene and Springfield.

Sample 1

The subjects for Sample 1 were recruited in March 1978 through an announcement mailed to 20,000 individuals randomly selected from the county voter registration list. Of this original sample, 998 subjects eventually participated through to the end of the study in June 1979. Inspection of the demographic characteristics of this sample revealed that they differed somewhat from the larger population from which they were drawn: the majority were female (69 per cent), the ages of twenty-five to thirty-four were over-represented (40 per cent), more were divorced (17 per cent), fewer were never married (20 per cent), more were employed (64 per cent), more had gone to or completed college (64 per cent), and there was an excess, of middle class income and few high income subjects. The mean age of the sample at T1 was 39.0 (SD 15.9). Depression, other psychopathology, and psychosocial variables (including life satisfaction) were assessed at two times: on the first, extensive questionnaire (T1), and at the diagnostic interview (T2). Subjects were selected to be interviewed at T2 on the basis of high scores (≥ 18) on the Center for Epidemiologic Studies-Depression Scale (CES-D; Radloff, 1977), which was mailed to subjects on a trimonthly basis. A random sample of 100 subjects with low scores on the CES-D as well as subjects selected on the basis of certain nondepression-related symptom ratings were also interviewed.

Through these procedures, 115 subjects were identified who had a history of depression but were not depressed during the study, sixty-three were depressed at T1, eighty-five were not depressed at T1 but developed a diagnosable episode of depression with onset after T1, and 154 were never depressed controls (never depressed, currently or in the past). The average time between T1 and T2 was 8.3 months (range = 3 to 11 months).

Sample 2

Subjects for Sample 2 were identified through a list of licensed drivers over the age of fifty. Letters were sent to 4133 potential subjects randomly selected and stratified by age and gender between May 1982 and November 1983. Of this original sample, 749 eventually participated in both the T1 and T2 phases of the study. In contrast to the larger population from which they were drawn, participants were better educated, and females were over-represented (57 per cent). Mean ages were 63.9 (SD 8.0) for the T1 sample, and 65.9 (SD 7.5) for the T2 sample.

The T1 assessment consisted of an extensive self-report questionnaire and a diagnostic interview (SADS-L; Endicott and Spitzer, 1978). Following this assessment, subjects were sent the Center for Epidemiologic Studies-Depression Scale (CES-D; Radloff, 1977) every two months. Any subject who was not depressed at the T1 interview and who scored twelve or above on any subsequent CES-D was a candidate for a post-T1 follow-up interview; subjects with the highest CES-D scores were given first priority.

At T2 (between November 1984 and March 1986), 749 of the original 1008 subjects (74 per cent) were re-assessed with the T1 measures and interview. Resource limitations prevented the follow-up of the complete original sample; those who were depressed at T1, those who became depressed during the post-T1 case finding period, and those who reported depressive symptoms on the final post-T1 questionnaire received the highest priority. A random selection of subjects with no evidence of depressive disorder before or after T1 were also re-interviewed.

These procedures yielded 284 individuals with a history of depression but who were not depressed at any time between T1 and T2, ninety-six individuals who were depressed at T1, 139 who were not depressed at T1 but who became diagnosably depressed between T1 and T2, and 274 who were never depressed controls.

Measures of psychopathology

CES-D

The Center for Epidemiologic Studies-Depression Scale is a self-report measure of the frequency of twenty symptoms of depression rated for the past week. The CES-D has demonstrated utility as a screening instrument in general community samples (Roberts and Vernon, 1983; Weissman, Sholomskas, Pottenger, Prusoff and Locke, 1977), possesses adequate psychometric properties, and correlates substantially with other self-report measures (Radloff, 1977).

Diagnostic interview

Diagnoses of depression and other psychopathological syndromes were based on information gathered in diagnostic interviews using the Schedule for Affective Disorders and Schizophrenia (Endicott and Spitzer, 1978). The three versions of this interview are similarly formatted semi-structured diagnostic interviews; choice of interview was based on the specific requirements of each study. The Longitudinal Interval Follow-up Evaluation (LIFE; Shapiro and Kellar, 1979) was also employed to gather detailed information about the longitudinal course of RDC-diagnosed mental disorders at post-T1 follow-ups. Interview information was then combined using the Research Diagnostic Criteria (RDC; Spitzer, Endicott and Robins, 1978). In both studies, depression was defined as a diagnosis of major, minor, or intermittent depressive disorder.

Demographic variables

In Sample 1, subjects reported their gender, age, marital status, educational level (Hollingshead and Redlich, 1958), and family income. Subjects in Sample 2 only reported their gender, age, marital status, and educational level.

Psychosocial variables

In order to assess as many variables as possible in questionnaires of manageable size, original inventories were shortened by a two-step procedure. Items shown to be strongly related to depression in previous studies were selected and then the number of items for each measure was reduced using a computer program developed by Serlin and Kaiser (1976). The Serlin and Kaiser procedure selects the subset of the original items maximizing internal consistency as measured by coefficient alpha.

(1) *Life satisfaction*

Items shown to be related to "happiness" and "feelings of satisfaction" were chosen from among those used by Andrews and Withey (1976) and Campbell *et al.* (1976). Fifteen items were selected for Sample 1 and ten for Sample 2. These items assessed the subjects' degree of satisfaction with the quality and frequency of their activities, accomplishments, family life, marital interaction, work, community, and recreational activities. On the basis of inter-item correlations and factor analysis in initial pilot studies, items were grouped into six subscales in Sample 1 and three subscales in Sample 2. A summary score was also computed.

(2) *Social support and social interaction*

In Sample 1, frequency of social contact was estimated by the subject using a 3–point scale (Berkman and Syme, 1979), while the number of close friends were assessed on a 5–point scale. These two items were combined to form a single social support index (test-retest reliability = .41).

In Sample 2, social support was assessed with several scales:

(a) *Social Support Network*. Subjects' social support networks were assessed with a nine-item scale addressing the amount of contact with the members of subjects' social network (coefficient alpha = .60; test-retest reliability = .70, $p < .001$).

(b) *Perceived Social Support—from Family and from Friends*. Abbreviated versions of these two scales from the Perceived Social Support Questionnaire (Procidano and Heller, 1973) were included (coefficients alpha = .87 and .90, respectively; test-retest reliability = .45 and .55, *p* <.001).

(c) *Satisfaction with relationships*. Seven items were designed to ascertain subjects' satisfaction with the quality and the quantity of their inter-actions with relatives and friends (coefficient alpha = .68; test-retest reliability = .60, *p* <.001).

(d) *Availability of help*. Five items were used to assess the potential avail-ability of help from members of the subjects' social network (coef-ficient alpha = .70; test-retest reliability = .46, *p* <.001).

(e) *Brown intimacy scale*. This scale was adapted from Brown and Harris (1978) to rate the presence of a close and confiding relationship on a 4–point scale (test-retest reliability = .47, *p* <.001).

(f) *Self-perceived social skill*. Subjects were asked to rate themselves using a 6–point scale on sixteen adjectives (e.g. "friendly", "popu-lar", "assertive") designed to elicit the subjects' self rated social com-petence (coefficient alpha = .86; test-retest reliability = .80, *p* <.001).

(3) *Pleasant activities*

For Sample 1, twenty items were selected from the mood-related events of the Pleasant Events Schedule (PES) (MacPhillamy and Lewinsohn, 1982). The frequency of occurrence and the enjoyability of the events was rated separately (coefficient alpha = .90 and .93; test-retest reliabilities = .67 and .61). For Sample 2, seven items were selected. Subjects were asked to rate the enjoyability (not the frequency) of each item on a three-point scale (coefficient alpha = .76; test-retest reliability = .67, *p* <.001).

(4) *Cognitions*

Sample 1 measured the following aspects of cognition:

(a) *Irrational beliefs*. The Personal Beliefs Inventory (PBI; Muñoz and Lewinsohn, 1976b) samples irrational beliefs that have been hypo-thesized to be associated with depression. Five items were selected (coefficient alpha = .66; test-retest reliability = .53).

(b) *Expectancies of positive and negative outcomes*. The Subjective Prob-ability Questionnaire (Muñoz and Lewinsohn, 1976a) was designed to operationalize Beck's "cognitive triad" by having subjects rate the probability of occurrence of negative and positive outcomes. Six positive items (alpha = .86) and four negative items (alpha = .75) were selected (coefficient alpha = .86 and .75; test-retest reliability = .62 and .49).

(c) *Locus of control*. Sixteen of the twenty-four items of the locus of control for affiliation scale from the Multidimensional Multi-attributional Causality Scale (Lefcourt, von Baeyer, Ware and Cox, 1979) were chosen for the study. Four scores were computed (alphas and test-retest reliabilities are given in parentheses): Internal-Positive (alpha = .68; test-retest = .46, p <.001), Internal-Negative (alpha = .43; test-retest = .43, p <.001), External-Positive (alpha = .42; test-retest = .42, p <.001), and External-Negative (alpha = .56; test-retest = .46, p <.001).

(d) *Perception of control.* Three items were selected from an original group of seven items (Muñoz and Lewinsohn, 1976b) designed to assess perception of control over one's life (coefficient alpha = .62; test-retest reliability = .39, p <.001).

The following aspects of cognition were measured in Sample 2:

(a) *Social mastery.* Three items were included to assess perceptions of control over social outcomes on a 5–point scale (coefficient alpha = .64; test-retest reliability = .49, p <.001).

(b) *Cognitive dysfunction.* Six items were selected from the Inventory of Psychic and Somatic Complaints-Elderly Scale developed by Raskin (1979) to measure the degree to which subjects felt themselves to be experiencing difficulties with memory, confusion, concentration, and thinking (coefficient alpha = .71; test-retest reliability = .68, p <.001).

(5) *Stress*

Three facets of stress were assessed in Sample 1:

(a) *Unpleasant events (micro-stressors).* Twenty items were selected from the mood-related items scale (Lewinsohn and Amenson, 1978) of the Unpleasant Events Schedule (UES) (Lewinsohn and Talkington, 1979; Lewinsohn, Mermelstein, Alexander and MacPhillamy, 1985). Subjects rated the frequency of occurrence and the aversiveness of the events (coefficient alpha = .84 and .90; test-retest reliability = .46 and .26, p <.001).

(b) Stressful life events (macro-stressors). Twenty-three items were arbitrarily chosen from the Social Readjustment Rating Scale (Holmes and Rahe, 1967). The sum of the life change unit scores was computed (coefficient alpha = .52; test-retest reliability = .13, p <.001).

In Sample 2, similar components of stress were assessed:

(a) *Unpleasant events (micro-stressors).* The forty-four items of the mood-related scale were taken from the Unpleasant Events Schedule (Lewinsohn *et al.*, 1985). Subjects rated these items for their frequency of occurrence during the past thirty days (coefficient alpha = .85; test-retest reliability = .68, p <.001).

(b) *Stressful life events (macro-stressors)*. Eighteen items from the Social Readjustment Rating Scale (Holmes and Rahe, 1967) were selected, and a total stress score computed (coefficient alpha = .68; test-retest reliability = .24, p <.001).

(6) *Personality dimensions*

Sample 1: Five items from a twenty-three item self-esteem scale, similar to the Semantic Differential Inventories constructed by Coyne and Holzman (1966), were included (Flippo and Lewinsohn, 1971), (coefficient alpha = .85). Self-esteem was assessed at T1 only.

Sample 2 assessed the following aspects of personality:

(a) *Interpersonal dependency*. Two scales from the Interpersonal Dependency Questionnaire (Hirshfeld, Klerman, Chodoff, Korchin and Barret, 1976) were included. The Emotional Reliance Scale focuses on the subjects' desire for contact with and emotional support from other persons. Items in the Social Self-Confidence Scale focus on wishes for help in making decisions and in taking the initiative (coefficients alpha = .83 and .79; test-retest reliability = .71 and .80).

(b) *Social desirability*. Ten items from the Crowne-Marlow Social Desirability Scale (Crowne and Marlow, 1960) were summed to assess the degree to which subjects had a social desirability response set. Coefficient alpha was .69 and the test-retest correlation was .74 (p <.001).

(c) *Cognitive and behavioural coping factors*. As a part of a separate study of the dimensionality of coping behaviour (Rohde, Lewinsohn, Tilson and Seeley, in press), factor analytic procedures were applied to items selected from various scales designed to measure cognitive and behavioural coping (Folkman and Lazarus, 1980; Rosenbaum, 1980; Rippere, 1977; Parker and Brown, 1979). A three factor solution was accepted as optimal; the three factors were labelled Cognitive Self-Control, Maladaptive Escapism, and Solace Seeking. Scales based on these three factors had high internal consistency (Kuder-Richardson formula twenty coefficients at T1 for factors 1, 2 and 3 = .87, .83, and .80, respectively; and at T2 = .88, .84, and .83), and good test-retest reliability (.63, .60, and .52, respectively). Details of the factor analytic procedure are described in Rohde, Lewinsohn, Tilson and Seeley, 1988.

(6) *Health*

The following health related data were collected for Sample 2:

(a) *Self-rated health.* A total health score based on ten items was computed (coefficient alpha = .71; test-retest reliability = .69, p <.001).
(b) *Global rating of health.* Interviewers rated each subject for the presence and severity of health problems on a 6–point scale (test-retest reliability = .46, p <.001).

Results

Statistical considerations

Data for this study was analysed sequentially in the following manner. Firstly, the psychometric properties of the life satisfaction items were examined. Secondly, the psychosocial variables predicted to be associated with life satisfaction were investigated via univariate analyses. Thirdly, the relationship of life satisfaction with depression was then investigated; it was expected that depression would be strongly related with life satisfaction. In order to assure that significant univariate correlations between life satisfaction and psychosocial variables were not mediated entirely by the relationship of life satisfaction with depression, we then statistically removed the effects of depression by computing the partial correlations, controlling for CES-D level. In order to evaluate the contribution of all of the psychosocial variables when entered together, the multiple regression of the variables with life satisfaction as the dependent variable was computed. Finally, the nature of the relationships of life satisfaction with the various psychosocial variables was examined as follows.

Firstly, those psychosocial variables which were significantly (p <.05) and consistently (i.e. in the same direction) related to life satisfaction at T1 and T2 were identified. Secondly, subjects were assigned to four groups based on their summary scores on the life satisfaction measure at T1 and T2. Those in the high-high group fell more than .25 standard deviation above the mean life satisfaction score at both T1 and T2 and those in the low-low group fell at least .25 standard deviation below the mean at both T1 and T2. Similarly, those in the high-low group fell higher than .25 standard deviation above the mean at T1 and lower than .25 standard deviation below the mean at T2, and those in the low-high group fell lower than .25 standard deviation below the mean at T1 and higher than .25 standard deviation above the mean at T2. Means, standard deviations, gender, age and number of subjects for the four life satisfaction groups at T1 and T2 appear in Table 8.1.

TABLE 8.1. *Life satisfaction scores and demographic information for the four life satisfaction groups*

Life satisfaction	Sample	N	Life satisfaction summary score				% Female	Age mean	Age SD
			T₁		T₂				
			Mean	SD	Mean	SD			
High-high	1	144	4.33	.31	4.32	.29	66.0	43.7	17.11
	2	225	4.37	.25	4.34	.28	58.7	64.1	7.52
High-low	1	26	4.14	.19	3.34	.28	76.9	36.3	13.27
	2	23	4.24	.15	3.55	.13	60.9	61.6	7.46
Low-high	1	37	3.24	.50	4.14	.21	81.1	39.3	16.19
	2	32	3.57	.19	4.14	.15	71.9	63.5	7.13
Low-low	1	160	3.14	.35	3.18	.33	66.9	37.2	13.14
	2	182	3.23	.39	3.25	.36	58.8	62.9	7.23

Secondly, we subjected the data to a series of ANOVAs focusing on the interaction of measurement time (T1 versus T2) with life satisfaction group using only the labile (High-low versus Low-high) groups. This interaction was important because it looks at the two groups whose life satisfaction level fluctuates and tests whether the psychosocial variable of interest fluctuates in tandem with life satisfaction. For a variable to be considered to be state-dependent, we required that this interaction be significant at the .05 level. All other associated psychosocial variables were automatically considered to represent relatively stable characteristics of people ("traits"), or the environments of people (e.g. a sick relative), with varying levels of life satisfaction.

Thirdly, we performed two planned contrasts to further clarify the nature of the relationship: (1) low-low versus low-high at T1, and (2) high-high versus high-low at T1. For the former, a significant difference would indicate that the variable has positive prognostic value, i.e. it predicts improvement. A significant difference for the latter would indicate that the variable is a risk factor in that it predicts deterioration (becoming less satisfied).

Demographic characteristics associated with life satisfaction

Age and education emerged as consistently related to life satisfaction, with older and more educated people being more satisfied ($p < .01$ for all tests). Income, which was measured only in Sample 1, was also positively correlated with life satisfaction ($p < .001$). Gender and marital status were only weakly and not consistently related.

Does the life satisfaction measure have a single underlying dimension?

In order to examine the dimensionality of the life satisfaction items, the inter-correlations were computed separately for each sample and for the two observation points, and submitted to factor analysis. The magnitude of the inter-correlations were substantial, and the first principal component accounted for a substantial proportion of the variance. In each data set, all items had high loadings on the first principal component. In addition, the latter accounted for 36 per cent and 31 per cent at T1 and T2 for Sample 1, and for 28 per cent and 50 per cent of the common variance at T1 and T2 for Sample 2. The results were thus consistent with the hypothesis that all of the life satisfaction items are to a considerable extent measures of the same underlying dimension. Consequently we decided to use the total score based on a subject's responses to all life satisfaction items to represent life satisfaction. Coefficient alphas for Sample 1 were .87 (T1) and .84 (T2); for Sample 2 they were .88 (T1) and .88 (T2). Test-retest reliabilities were .63 and .76, both $p < .001$, for Samples 1 and 2, respectively.

Relationships of life satisfaction with depression

(a) *Current depression and life satisfaction.* The correlations between life satisfaction ratings and self-reported depression as measured by the CES-D for both samples at T1 and T2 are included in Table 8.2. As can be seen, all of these correlations are substantial and negative. Depression, as measured by the CES-D, emerged as the variable most strongly correlated with life satisfaction in a consistent manner across the study. Similarly, the group that was currently depressed at T1 and the never depressed controls (thus currently not depressed) differed substantially on the life satisfaction measure (Sample 1: $F(1,542)=32.00$, $p < .001$; Sample 2: $F(1,906)=159.52$, $p < .001$).

TABLE 8.2. *Correlation of life satisfaction with current depression as measured by the CES-D*

Variable	Time	r
CES–D$_1$	T$_1$	−.60***
	T$_2$	−.49***
CES–D$_2$	T$_1$	−.48***
	T$_2$	−.53***

Note: CES–D=Center for Epidemiological Studies-Depression Scale (Radloff, 1977). *** $p<0.001$.

(b) *Relationship of life satisfaction with future occurrence of depression.* The results of the ANOVAs for Samples 1 and 2 indicate that the people who were destined to develop an episode of depression between T1 and T2 already differed from the never depressed controls at T1 at which point, of course, they were not depressed (Sample 1: $F(1,802)=4.40$, $p < .05$; Sample 2: $F(1,532)=16.96$, $p < .001$). Our results thus indicate that low life satisfaction is a risk factor for future depression.

(c) *Are people who have been depressed more dissatisfied even when they are not depressed?* Even though the participants with a history of previous depression were not depressed at the time of assessment, their CES-D scores were slightly higher than those of the never depressed controls; this difference attained statistical significance for Sample 2 ($p < .05$). In ANOVA comparisons of these groups, T1 CES-D was consequently entered as a covariate to control for initial depression level. None of the differences between the never depressed and previously depressed groups attained statistical significance after controlling for T1 CES-D.

Psychosocial correlates of life satisfaction

(a) *Univariate correlations.* As expected, most of the psychosocial variables were significantly correlated with life satisfaction; these results are shown in Table 8.3. Individuals with higher life satisfaction levels described themselves as having more extensive, frequent, and reliable social supports; as being more socially skilled; and as feeling more content with their relationships with others. Those who were satisfied reported themselves as engaging in a greater number of pleasant activities. However, the results for the rated enjoyability of the events were inconsistent in that in Sample 2 they were highly significant and in Sample 1 nonsignificant. This may be due to the different sample of items chosen. More satisfied individuals were less likely to endorse items indicating an external locus of control for both failure and success experiences, and felt they had more control over their lives and social outcomes. They reported fewer irrational beliefs, were more optimistic and less pessimistic, and had lower levels of reported cognitive difficulty. Stress also emerged as an important psychosocial correlate of life satisfaction in that individuals who were more satisfied reported fewer microstressors and macrostressors and also rated potential microstressors as less aversive. Life satisfaction was positively correlated with self-esteem and with greater use of coping responses relying on Cognitive Self-control, and negatively correlated with the coping responses of Maladaptive Escapism and Solace Seeking. More satisfied individuals also attained scores indicating less defensiveness, more self-confidence and less reliance on others for support. Health, both self-rated and interviewer-rated, was positively related to higher levels of satisfaction.

TABLE 8.3. *Correlations of life satisfaction with the psychosocial variables*

Variable	Time	Correlations before depression partialled out (Univariate correlations)	Correlations after depression partialled out
Social support and interaction			
Frequency of social contact[1]	T1	.16***	.14***
	T2	.14***	.07
Social support network[2]	T1	.34***	.28***
	T2	.35***	.28***
Perceived social support-family[2]	T1	.30***	.25***
	T2	.30***	.23***
Perceived social support-friends[2]	T1	.20***	.17***
	T2	.15***	.12***
Satisfaction with relationships[2]	T1	.22***	.14***
	T2	.29***	.23***
Availability of help[2]	T1	.14***	.09***
	T2	.18***	.14***
Brown Intimacy Scale	T1	−.30***	−.24***
(Brown and Harris, 1978)	T2	−.26***	−.20***
Self-perceived social skill[2]	T1	.33***	.25***
(Lewinsohn *et al.*, 1980)	T2	.26***	.16***
Pleasant Activities (PES)			
(MacPhillamy and Lewinsohn, 1982)			
PES-Frequency of events[1]	T1	.17***	.06*
	T2	.11**	.01
PES-Enjoyability of events[1]	T1	−.02	−.04
	T2	−.03	−.08*
PES-Enjoyability of events[2]	T1	.26***	.19***
	T2	.30***	.21***
Cognitions			
Personal Beliefs Inventory[1]	T1	−.31***	−.16***
(Muñoz and Lewinsohn, 1976b)	T2	−.30***	−.17***
Subjective Probability Questionnaire			
(Muñoz and Lewinsohn, 1976a)			
Positive events[1]	T1	.16***	−.01
	T2	.13***	.00
Negative events[1]	T1	−.45***	−.22***
	T2	−.41***	−.29***
Multidimensional Multiattributional			
Causality Scale (Lefcourt *et al.*, 1979)			
External locus for success[1]	T1	−.23***	−.14***
	T2	−.36***	−.27***
External locus for failure[1]	T1	−.23***	−.13***
	T2	−.37***	−.28***
Internal locus for success[1]	T1	−.04	−.07**
	T2	−.13**	−.14***
Internal locus for failure[1]	T1	.00	.01
	T2	−.04	−.04
Perception of control	T1	.29***	.13***
(Muñoz and Lewinsohn, 1976b)	T2	.33***	.21***
Social mastery[2]	T1	.11***	.12***
	T2	.13***	.14***
Inventory of Psychic and Somatic			
Complaints—Elderly Scale[2]	T1	.21***	.06*
(cognitive dysfunction) (Raskin, 1979)	T2	.23***	.04

TABLE 8.3 *Correlations of life satisfaction with the psychosocial variables—contd.*

Variable	Time	Correlations before depression partialled out (Univariate correlations)	Correlations after depression partialled out
Stress			
Unpleasant Events Schedule (UES)			
(Lewinsohn and Amenson, 1981)			
UES frequency of events	T1	−.21***	−.07*
(microstressors)[1]	T2	−.50***	−.41***
UES frequency of events	T1	−.21***	−.14***
(microstressors)[2]	T2	−.28***	−.17***
UES aversiveness of events[1]	T1	−.12***	−.05*
	T2	−.39***	−.32***
Social Readjustment Rating Scale			
(SRSS) (Holmes and Rahe, 1967)			
SRSS (macrostressors)[1]	T1	−.06*	.01
	T2	.08*	.18***
SRSS (macrostressors)[2]	T1	−.11***	−.06*
	T2	−.14***	−.08*
Personality Dimensions			
Self-esteem[1]	T1	.52***	.18***
		(not measured at T2)	
Interpersonal Dependency			
Questionnaire[2] (Hirshfield *et al.*,			
1979)			
Self-Confidence Scale[2]	T1	.31***	.16***
	T2	.29***	.16***
Emotional Reliance Scale[2]	T1	−.19***	−.07**
	T2	−.16***	−.03
Crowne-Marlow Social Desirability	T1	−.27***	−.23***
Scale[2] (Crowne and Marlow, 1960)	T2	−.26***	−.22***
Cognitive and Behavioural Coping			
Factors[2] (Rohde, Lewinsohn, Tilson			
and Seeley, 1988)			
Coping Factor 1:	T1	.30***	.17***
Cognitive Self-Control[2]	T2	.35***	.21***
Coping Factor 2:	T1	−.12***	−.13***
Maladaptive Escapism[2]	T2	−.06*	−.07*
Coping Factor 3:	T1	−.10***	−.08**
Solace-Seeking[2]	T2	−.04	−.04
Health			
Self-rated health[2]	T1	.23***	.08***
	T2	.30***	.08*
Interviewer-rated health[2]	T1	.19***	.09**
	T2	.24***	.12***

[1] Variable assessed in Sample 1.
[2] Variable assessed in Sample 2.
*** p <.001.
** p <.01.
* p <.05.

(b) *Multiple Regression Analysis.* A stepwise multiple-regression analysis
was performed for each sample using those variables which had been
shown to be significantly related to life satisfaction in the univariate

analyses, including the demographic variables. For Sample 1, the multiple correlation was .65 after thirteen variables were entered, accounting for 41.6 per cent of the variance in life satisfaction. Self-esteem emerged as the best predictor variable (26.6 per cent of the variance) with expectancies of negative outcomes (5.7 per cent), irrational beliefs (2.6 per cent), microstressors (1.4 per cent), and income (1.2 per cent) contributing incremental (i.e. › 1 per cent) variance.

For Sample 2, eleven variables contributed to a final multiple correlation of .65, accounting for 41.9 per cent of the total variance in life satisfaction. The best predictors (those contributing › 1 per cent of the total variance) were social support (12.1 per cent), coping factor 1 (cognitive self-control, 8.1 per cent), social intimacy (6.9 per cent), general health (4.9 per cent), social self-confidence (3.0 per cent), and microstressors (2.5 per cent).

(c) *Correlation after the effects of depression are partialled out.* As can also be seen in Table 8.3, most psychosocial variables continued to be related to life satisfaction even after the effects of depression are partialled out, although the magnitude (and often the significance level of the correlations) is reduced. In order to further pinpoint which part of the variance of the psychosocial variables was uniquely related to life satisfaction, even after the effects of depression were removed, we performed a multiple regression forcing CES-D in as the first predictor. For Sample 1, this resulted in a final multiple correlation of .69, accounting for 47 per cent of the total variance in life satisfaction with thirteen variables. Although CES-D accounts for a large portion of this variance (35.8 per cent), self-esteem (6.5 per cent) and low expectancies for negative events (1.1 per cent) still continue to make a sizeable contribution to the multiple regression.

Similarly, for Sample 2, a multiple regression forcing CES-D as the first predictor resulted in a final multiple correlation of .69, accounting for 45 per cent of the total variance with ten variables. CES-D accounted for 23.4 per cent of this variance. Other variables continuing to contribute substantial variance include social support network (6.5 per cent), social intimacy (4.0 per cent), social desirability (4.0 per cent), social self-confidence (2.0 per cent) and general health (1.5 per cent).

Nature of the Relationships

The results of the statistical analyses and tests which were performed to evaluate the nature of the relationships of life satisfaction with the psychosocial variables are summarized in Table 8.4 (all significance levels for this

TABLE 8.4. *Nature of the relationship of life satisfaction with the psychosocial variables*

Variable	Nature of the relationship				
	State Related	Trait Related	Unrelated	Risk Factor	Predictor of improvement
Depression					
Center for Epidemiological Studies Depression (CESD) Scale (Radloff, 1977)					
CESD[1]	x			x	
CESD[2]	x				
Social Support and Interaction					
Frequency of social contact[1]	x				x
Social support network[2]	x				
Perceived social support-family[2]	x				
Perceived social support-friends[2]		x			
Satisfaction with relationships[2]		x			
Availability of help[2]		x			
Brown Intimacy Scale (Brown and Harris, 1978)		x			
Self-perceived social skill[2] (Lewinsohn et al., 1980)		x			
Pleasant Activities (PES) (MacPhillamy and Lewinsohn, 1982)					
PES-Frequency of events[1]	x				x
PES-Enjoyability of events[1]			x		
PES-Enjoyability of events[2]		x			
Cognitions					
Personal Beliefs Inventory[1] (Muñoz and Lewinsohn, 1976b)		x			
Subjective Probability Questionnaire (Muñoz and Lewinsohn, 1976a)					
Positive events[1]	x				x
Negative events[1]		x			x
Multidimensional Multi-attributional Causality Scale (Lefcourt et al., 1979)					
External locus for success[1]		x			x
External locus for failure[1]		x			x
Internal locus for success[1]		x			
Internal locus for failure[1]			x		
Perception of control (Muñoz and Lewinsohn, 1976b)		x		x	
Social mastery[2]		x			
Inventory of Psychic and Somatic Complaints—Elderly Scale[2] (cognitive dysfunction) (Raskin, 1979)	x				

Variable	Nature of the relationship				
	State Related	Trait Related	Unrelated	Risk Factor	Predictor of improvement
Stress					
Unpleasant Events Schedule (UES) (Lewinsohn and Amenson, 1981)					
UES frequency of events (microstressors)[1]		x		x	
UES frequency of events (microstressors)[2]		x		x	
UES aversiveness of events[1]	x			x	
Social Readjustment Rating Scale (SRSS) (Holmes and Rahe, 1967)					
SRSS (macrostressors)[1]		x			
SRSS (macrostressors)[2]		x		x	
Personality Dimensions					
Interpersonal Dependency Questionnaire[2] (Hirshfield et al., 1979)					
Self-Confidence Scale[2]		x			
Emotional Reliance Scale[2]		x			
Crowne-Marlow Social Desirability Scale[2] (Crowne and Marlow, 1960)		x			
Cognitive and Behavioural Coping Factors[2] (Rohde, Lewinsohn, Tilson and Seeley, 1988)					
Coping Factor 1: Cognitive Self-Control[2]		x			
Coping Factor 2: Maladaptive Escapism[2]		x			
Coping Factor 3: Solace Seeking[2]			x		
Health					
Self-rated health[2]	x			x	
Interviewer-rated health[2]	x				

[1] Variable assessed in Sample 1.
[2] Variable assessed in Sample 2.

section <.05). The following variables were state-related, i.e. they covaried with life satisfaction levels: depression (CES-D); frequency of social contact; social support network; perceived social support from family; frequency of pleasant events; expectancies for positive events; cognitive dysfunction; rated aversiveness of microstressors; self-rated health and interviewer-rated health. A number of variables were trait dependent in that they did *not* covary with the vicissitudes of life satisfaction. Examples include perceived social support from friends and satisfaction with relationships; a full listing appears in Table 8.4. These trait-dependent variables seem to be stable characteristics of people depending on their general level of life satisfaction.

The following variables acted as risk factors for decreased life satisfaction at T2: CES-D (for Sample 1 but not Sample 2); perceived control over one's life; frequency of microstressors (for both samples); rated aversiveness of microstressors; frequency of macrostressors (for Sample 2 but not Sample 1), and self-rated health. Furthermore, the following variables acted as T1 predictors of improved life satisfaction at T2: CES-D (for Sample 1 but not Sample 2); frequency of social contact; frequency of pleasant events; greater expectancies for positive events and lesser expectancies for negative events; and a lower external locus of control (for both success and failure).

Discussion

In this study, our interest was in life satisfaction. Parallelling previous studies, we measured "life satisfaction" by asking people to indicate their degree of satisfaction with items representing several different and important domains including self, spouse and family life, work or school, neighbourhood and community, friends, and sports and recreational facilities. Consistent with previous studies, we found the ratings of these separate domains to be highly intercorrelated, indicating the presence of a strong underlying unitary dimension. The relative stability over time of this dimension, assumed to represent the persons' overall satisfaction with their lives, also supported its authenticity as a meaningful personality construct. For these reasons, we felt justified in combining the domains into a single score representing an aggregate of a person's satisfaction. Our use of an aggregate was not to negate the potential importance of each of the individual life satisfaction domains; indeed, there may be psychosocial variables which are uniquely related to each domain. Instead, the use of an aggregate measure, which provided a global view of individuals' life satisfaction, was more consistent with the goals of our research.

Our interest in life satisfaction was twofold—firstly, we were interested in the relationships between life satisfaction and depression, and secondly, we wished to explore the relationships between life satisfaction and various psychosocial variables.

Relationships of life satisfaction and depression

Consistent with both expectation and previous research, we found current depression and life satisfaction to be related. The fact that the relationship between life satisfaction and depression was found to be state-dependent serves to clarify the nature of their relationship; the two co-vary in a way which suggests that both are susceptible to transient influences. Nevertheless, our results indicate that when one controls for a person's level of depression, one is still left with significant variance in life satisfaction. For example, if we looked at all of the people who are not depressed, there would still be significant differences between them in life satisfaction and associated variables such as self-esteem, mode of thinking, social support network, social intimacy, self-confidence, and self-perceived and interviewer-rated health. Life satisfaction is related to depression, it co-varies with depression, but it is not reducible to depression. This is consistent with the findings of several studies, including those by Bradburn (1969), Bradburn and Caplovitz (1965), Warr (1978), Costa and McCrae (1980), Perry and Warr (1980), Harding (1982), Warr, Barter and Brownbridge (1983), Watson and Tellegen (1985) and Emmons and Diener (1985) supporting the view that negative and positive affect are two relatively independent and additive determinants of happiness. As is well known, correlation does not prove causation. It could be that being depressed causes people's life satisfaction to decline, and/or that when people are dissatisfied with their lives, they become depressed. Alternately, it is possible that both depression and life satisfaction are affected by a third variable such as environmental stress. For example, when people encounter difficult life conditions, they may tend to become both depressed and to experience reduced life satisfaction.

It is thus intriguing that low life satisfaction tended to precede the onset of depression. In other words, individuals with low life satisfaction ratings were more likely to become depressed than those with higher reported life satisfaction. This is important not only because it provides a potential method of identifying people at risk of impending depression, but also because it may help to generate hypotheses about the etiology of depression.

The finding that individuals with a history of depression did not differ from the never depressed controls is important. This finding is consistent, however, with some of our other recent findings which show that formerly depressed people do not differ from controls on any psychosocial variable with which they have been compared (Zeiss and Lewinsohn, 1988; Rohde *et al.*, in press; Lewinsohn, Steinmetz, Larson and Franklin, 1981; Lewinsohn and Rosenbaum, 1987). In essence, then, our findings indicate that when people are about to become depressed, they have low life satisfaction ratings; when they are depressed, they have very low life satisfaction ratings; but when they recover from depression, they have average or normal life satisfaction ratings. Although there are several possible explanations for this, one way of interpreting these findings is to suggest that decreased life satisfaction may be prodromal, or an early manifestation, of depression's onset.

Relationships between life satisfaction and psychosocial variables

The results of this study replicate earlier findings and demonstrate the wide network of psychosocial variables in which life satisfaction is embedded. Life satisfaction is not an isolated attribute of people, but rather a characteristic with very wide ranging implications for a person's social interactions, activities, thoughts, self-esteem, typical methods of dealing with stress, and evaluation of their health. In our analyses, we focused on distinguishing state-dependent relationships from those which reflect more stable characteristics of people who are either high or low in life satisfaction. Some of the variables were found to be state-dependent, some to possess trait characteristics and yet others were both state- and trait-related. To account for why some of the variables fall into one or another of these categories, we offer the following hypotheses. They are considered to be very tentative. An attentive reader will undoubtedly detect relationships (present or absent) which do not entirely fit our proposed framework; we thus encourage you to formulate your own hypotheses.

Certain variables were found to be state-dependent in the sense that they covaried with intra-individual vicissitudes of life satisfaction. Inspection of those variables which were state-dependent and comparing them with those which were trait-dependent reveals the following contrast: the state-related variables all had to do with either frequency of social or other positive events, in reality or expectation (frequency of social contact, social support network, perceived social support from family, frequency of pleasant events, expectancies for positive outcomes); or physical/psychic complaints (cognitive dysfunction, rated aversiveness of microstressors, self-rated health, interviewer-rated health, CES-D). In other words, a person's life satisfaction changes in a positive direction as a function of the degree to which the person experiences or expects to experience pleasant social interactions and change in a negative direction as a function of experiencing physical and psychological symptoms. It was more difficult to detect common threads in the variables designated as trait-related (i.e. not state-related). From the perspective of the dissatisfied person, those variables appeared more related to frequency of negative and aversive aspects of the environment: more reported microstressors and macrostressors; greater expectancies for negative outcomes; lack of social support from friends; low satisfaction with relationships; little potential availability of help from others; low social intimacy, and low enjoyability of events. Other trait-related characteristics included low self-perceived social skill, depressogenic thinking styles, little perception of control over one's life, low self-rated social mastery, low self-confidence, high emotional reliance, an unwillingness to reveal socially undesirable things about oneself, and poor coping skills in stressful situations. These are similar to the characteristics of a depressed person in the sense that they reflect a very negative perception of oneself and of the world. Inspection of the means of the four groups revealed that when the low-low and the high-high groups were compared with the total population means on the psychosocial variables, generally the low-low group was most discrepant. It is thus likely that the trait relationships that we are reporting are more characteristic of people who are chronically dissatisfied than of those who are chronically satisfied. Finally, the two-panel nature of our data allowed us to look at the antecedents for a decrease and for an increase in life satisfaction. As noted earlier, most people remain stable in their level of life satisfaction, but a few deteriorate and a few improve. Inspection of the variables which predict improvement suggests that an elevated rate of pleasant activities (in reality or expectation), few negative events, and not thinking that one lacks control were predictive of improved satisfaction. Apparently, feeling in control of improving one's life and actually carrying these plans out may be an important step in improving one's life satisfaction.

On the opposite side of the ledger, those psychosocial variables which were antecedents of becoming more dissatisfied have also been identified as predictors for the onset of depression in a previous study (Lewinsohn, Hoberman and Rosenbaum, 1988). These variables were: frequency of stressful life events; rated aversiveness of stressful events; occurrence of mild depression; occurrence of health related problems; and the perception that one has no control over one's life.

In summary, it is clear from our data that life satisfaction is a meaningful and important aspect of personality which is often not given the amount of attention it deserves. Our study began with a large set of psychosocial variables, most of which were found to be related to life satisfaction in the expected direction. Life satisfaction and the clinical syndrome of depression were found to be especially highly related. The vicissitudes of life satisfaction, to the extent to which they exist, seem to be highly associated with the same kinds of things that cause people to be more or less depressed. Furthermore, the two-panel nature of the data allowed us to differentiate those individuals who were more stable in their level of life satisfaction from those who were less stable, and identify differences between these groups. This approach helped us generate a number of hypotheses which we hope will be examined with other data sets. In any case, it is clear that the life satisfaction construct is very important, and that it will continue to generate interesting and useful research in the years to come.

References

ALLPORT, G. W. and ODBERT, H. S. Trait names: A psycho-lexical study. *Psychological Monographs*, 1936, **47**, 1 (Whole No. 211).

AMENSON, C. S. and LEWINSOHN, P. M. An investigation into the observed sex differences in the prevalence of unipolar depression. *Journal of Abnormal Psychology*, 1981; **90**, 1–13.

ANDREWS, F. M. and WITHEY, S. B. *Social indicators of well-being*. New York and London: Plenum Press, 1976.

ARGYLE, M. *The psychology of happiness*. London: Methuen & Co, 1987.

BECK, A. T. *Depression: Clinical, experimental and theoretical aspects*. New York: Harper & Row, 1967.

BECKER, J. *Depression: Theory and research*. New York: Winston & Sons, 1974.

BECKHAM, E. E. and LEBER, W. R. (eds.) *Handbook of depression: Treatment, assessment, and research*. Homewood, IL: Dorsey Press, 1985.

BERKMAN, L. F. and SYME, S. L. Social networks, host resistance, and mortality: a nine year follow-up study of Alameda county residents. *American Journal of Epidemiology*, 1979; **109**, 186–204.

BRADBURN, N. M. *The structure of psychological well-being*. Chicago: Aldine, 1969.

BRADBURN, N. M. and CAPLOVITZ, D. (eds.). *Reports on happiness*. Chicago: Aldine, 1965.

BROWN, G. W and HARRIS, T. *Social origins of depression*. New York: Free press, 1978.

CAMPBELL, A., CONVERSE, P. E. and RODGERS, W. L. *The quality of american life*. New York: Sage, 1976.

CARSON, T. P. and CARSON, R. C. The affective disorders. In H. E. Adams and P. B. Sutker (eds.), *Comprehensive handbook of psychopathology*. New York: Plenum Press, 1984.

CATTELL, R. B. Personality, role, mood, and situation-perception: A unifying theory of modulators. *Psychological Review*, 1963; **70**, 1–18.

CHAPLIN, W. F., JOHN, O. P. and GOLDBERG, L. R. Conceptions of states and traits: Dimensional attributes with ideals as prototypes. *Journal of Personality and Social Psychology*, 1988; **54**, 541–557.

COSTA, P. T. and MCCRAE, R. R. Influence of extraversion and neuroticism on subjective well-being: Happy and unhappy people. *Journal of Personality and Social Psychology*, 1980; **38**(3), 181–203.

COYNE, J. C. Depression and the response of others. *Journal of Abnormal Psychology*, 1976; **85**, 186–193.

COYNE, L. and HOLZMAN, P. Three equivalent forms of a semantic differential inventory. *Educational and Psychological Measurement*, 1966; **2**, 665–674.

CROWNE, D. P. and MARLOW, D. A new scale of social desirability independent of psychopathology. *Journal of Consulting Psychology*, 1960; **24**, 349–354.

DIENER, E. Subjective well-being. *Psychological Bulletin*, 1984; **95**(3), 542–575.

DIENER, E., EMMONS, R. A., LARSEN, R. J. and GRIFFIN, S. The Satisfaction with Life Scale. *Journal of Personality Assessment*, 1985; **49**, 71–76.

DIENER, E., SANDVIK, E. and LARSEN, R. J. Age and sex effects for emotional intensity. *Developmental Psychology*, 1985; **21**, 542–546.

ENDICOTT, J. and SPITZER, R. L. A diagnostic interview: The schedule for affective disorders and schizophrenia. *Archives of General Psychiatry*, 1978; **35**, 837–844.

EMMONS, R. A. and DIENER, E. Personality correlates of subjective well-being. *Personality and Social Psychology Bulletin*, 1985; **11**, 89–97.

FLIPPO, J. and LEWINSOHN, P. M. Effects of failure on the self-esteem of depressed and non-depressed subjects. *Journal of Consulting and Clinical Psychology*, 1971; **36**, 151.

FOLKMAN, S. and LAZARUS, R. S. An analysis of coping in a middle-aged community sample. *Journal of Health and Social Behavior*, 1980; **21**, 219–239.

HARDING, S. D. Psychological well-being in Great Britain: An evaluation of the Bradburn Affect Balance Scale. *Personality and Individual Differences*, 1982; **3**, 167–175.

HIRSHFELD, R. M. A., KLERMAN, G. L., CHODOFF, P., KORCHIN, S. and BARRET, J. Dependency, self-esteem, clinical depression. *Journal of the American Academy of Psychoanalysis*, 1976; **4**, 373–388.

HOLLINGSHEAD, A. B. and REDLICH, F. C. *Social class and mental illness*. New York: Wiley, 1958.

HOLMES, T. H. and RAHE, R. H. The Social Readjustment Rating Scale. *Psychosomatic Medicine*, 1967; **11**, 213–218.

KOZMA, A. and STONES, M. J. Predictors of happiness. *Journal of Gerontology*, 1983; **38**(5), 626–628.

LEFCOURT, H. M., VON BAEYER, C. L., WARE, E. E. and COX, D. J. The multidimensional-multiattributional causality scale: The development of a goal specific locus of control scale. *Canadian Journal of Behavioural Science*, 1979; **11**, 286–304.

LEHMAN, H. E. Epidemiology of depressive disorders. In R. R. Fieve (ed.), *Depression in the 70's: Modern theory and research*. Princeton, NJ: Excerpta Medica, 1971.

LEWINSOHN, P. M. and AMENSON, C. Some relations between pleasant and unpleasant mood related activities and depression. *Journal of Abnormal Psychology*, 1978; **87**, 644–654.

LEWINSOHN, P. M., HOBERMAN, H. S. and ROSENBAUM, M. A prospective study of risk factors for unipolar depression. *Journal of Abnormal Psychology*, 1988; **97**, 251–264.

LEWINSOHN, P. M., LARSON, D. W. and MUÑOZ, R. F. The measurement of expectancies and other cognitions in depressed individuals. *Cognitive Therapy and Research*, 1982; **6**, 437–446.

LEWINSOHN, P. M. and LIBET, J. Pleasant events, activity schedules, and depression. *Journal of Abnormal Psychology*, 1972; **79**, 292–295.

LEWINSOHN, P. M., MERMELSTEIN, R. M., ALEXANDER, C. and MACPHILLAMY, D. J. The unpleasant events schedule: A scale for the measurement of aversive events. *Journal of Clinical Psychology*, 1985; **41**, 483–498.

LEWINSOHN, P. M., MISCHEL, W., CHAPLIN, W. and BARTON, R. Social competence and depression: The role of illusory self-perceptions. *Journal of Abnormal Psychology*, 1980; **89**, 203–212.

LEWINSOHN, P. M. and ROSENBAUM, M. Recall of parental behavior by acute depressives, remitted depressives and nondepressives. *Journal of Personality and Social Psychology*, 1987; **52**, 611–619.

LEWINSOHN, P. M., STEINMETZ, J. L., LARSON, D. W. and FRANKLIN, J. F. Depression related cognitions: Antecedent or consequence? *Journal of Abnormal Psychology*, 1981; **90**, 213–219.

LEWINSOHN, P. M. and TALKINGTON, J. Studies on the measurement of unpleasant events and relations with depression. *Applied Psychological Measurement*, 1979; **3**, 83–101.

LEWINSOHN, P. M., TILSON, M., ROHDE, P. and SEELEY, J. Risk factors for depression in the elderly. Unpublished mimeo.

LEWINSOHN, P. M., YOUNGREN, M. A. and GROSSCUP, S. J. Reinforcement and depression. In R. A. Depue (ed.) *The psychobiology of the depressive disorders: Implications for the effects of stress*. New York: Academic Press, 1979.

LEWINSOHN, P. M., ZEISS, A. and DUNCAN, E. M. Probability for relapse after recovery from an episode of depression. Unpublished mimeo.

MACPHILLAMY, D. J. and LEWINSOHN, P. M. Depression as a function of levels of desires and obtained pleasure. *Journal of Abnormal Psychology*, 1974; **83**, 651–657.

MACPHILLAMY, D. J. and LEWINSOHN, P. M. The Pleasant Events Schedule: Studies on reliability, validity, and scale intercorrelations. *Journal of Consulting and Clinical Psychology*, 1982; **50**, 363–380.

MECHANIC, D. Development of psychological distress among young adults. *Archives of General Psychiatry*, 1979; **36**, 1233–1239.

MENDELS, J. (ed.). *The psychobiology of depression*. New York: Spectrum Publications, 1975.

MUÑOZ, R. F. and LEWINSOHN, P. M. *The Subjective Probability Questionnaire*. Unpublished manuscript, University of Oregon, 1976a.

MUÑOZ, R. F. and LEWINSOHN, P. M. *The Personal Beliefs Inventory*. Unpublished manuscript, University of Oregon, 1976b.

MYERS, J. K., WEISSMAN, M. M., TISCHLER, G. L., HOLZER, C. E., LEAF, P. J., ORVASCHEL, H., ANTHONY, J. C., BOYD, J. H., BURKE, J. D., KRAMER, M. and STOLTZMAR, R. Six-month prevalence of psychiatric disorders in three communities. *Archives of General Psychiatry*, **41**, 959–967.

NORMAN, W. T. *2800 personality trait descriptors: Normative operating characteristics for a university population.* Department of Psychology, University of Michigan, unpublished manuscript, 1967.

PALMORE, E. and LUIKART, C. Health and social factors related to life satisfaction. *Journal of Health and Social Behavior,* 1972; **13**, 68–80.

PARKER, G. and BROWN, L. Repertoires of response to potential precipitant of depression. *Australian and New Zealand Journal of Psychiatry,* 1979; **13**, 327–333.

PAYKEL, E. S. *Handbook of affective disorders.* New York: Guilford Press, 1982.

PERRY, G. and WARR, P. The measurement of mothers' work attitudes. *Journal of Occupational Psychology,* 1980; **53**, 245–252.

PROCIDANO, M. E. and HELLER, K. Measures of perceived social support from friends and from family: Three validations studied. *American Journal of Community Psychology,* 1983; **11**, 1–24.

RADLOFF, L. S. The CES-D scale: A self-report depression scale for research in the general population. *Applied Psychological Measurement,* 1977; **3**, 385–401.

RASKIN, A. Signs and symptoms of psychopathology in the elderly. In A. Raskin and L. Jarvik (eds.), *Psychiatric symptoms and cognitive loss in the elderly.* Washington DC: Hemisphere, 1979.

REICH, J. W. and ZAUTRA, A. Life events and personal causation: Some relationships with satisfaction and distress. *Journal of Personality and Social Psychology,* 1981; **41**, 1002–1012.

RIPPERE, V. Commonsense beliefs about depression and antidepressive behavior: A study of social consensus. *Behavior Research and Therapy,* 1977; **15**, 465–473.

ROBERTS, R. E. and VERNON, S. W. The center for epidemiological studies depression scale: Its uses in a community sample. *American Journal of Psychiatry,* 1983; **140**, 41–46.

ROHDE, P., LEWINSOHN, P. M. and SEELEY, J. *Dimensionality of coping and relationships with depression.* Unpublished mimeo.

ROHDE, P., LEWINSOHN, P. M., TILSON, M. G. and SEELEY, J. The dimensionality of coping and its relation to depression. *Journal of Personality and Social Psychology,* in press.

ROSENBAUM, M. A schedule for assessing self-control behaviors: Preliminary findings. *Behavior Therapy,* 1980; **1**, 109–121.

ROSENSKY, R. H., REHM, L. P., FRY, G. and ROTH, D. Depression and self-reinforcement behavior in hospitalized patients. *Journal of Behavior Therapy and Experimental Psychiatry,* 1977; **8**, 35–38.

SELIGMAN, M. E. P., ABRAMSON, L. Y., SEMMEL, A. and VON BAEYER, C. Depressive attributional style. *Journal of Abnormal Psychology,* 1979; **88**, 242–247.

SERLIN, R. C. and KAISER, H. F. A computer program for item selection based upon maximum internal consistency. *Educational and Psychological Measurement,* 1976; **36**, 757–759.

SHAPIRO, R. and KELLAR, M. *Longitudinal Interval Follow-up Evaluation (LIFE).* Boston: Massachusetts General Hospital, 1979.

SPITZER, R. L., ENDICOTT, J. and ROBINS, E. Research diagnostic criteria: Rationale and reliability. *Archives of General Psychiatry,* 1978; **35**, 773–782.

SPIELBERGER, C. D. Conceptual and methodological issues in research in anxiety. In C. D. Spielberger (ed.). *Anxiety: Current trends in theory and research* (Vol. 2). New York: Academic Press, 1972.

TANAKA, J. S. and HUBA, G. J. Confirmatory hierarchical factor analyses of psychological distress measures. *Journal of Personality and Social Psychology,* 1984; **43**(3), 621–635.

WARR, P. B. A study of psychological well-being. *British Journal of Psychology,* 1978; **69**, 111–121.

WARR, P., BARTER, J. and BROWNBRIDGE, G. On the independence of positive and negative affect. *Journal of Personality and Social Psychology,* 1983; **44**(3), 644–651.

WATSON, D. and TELLEGEN, A. Toward a consensual structure of mood. *Psychological Bulletin,* 1985; **98**(2), 219–235.

WEISSMAN, M. M. and MYERS, J. K. Affective disorders in a U.S. urban community. *Archives of General Psychiatry,* 1978; **35**, 1304–1311.

WEISSMAN, M. M. and PAYKEL, E. S. *The depressed woman*. Chicago: University of Chicago Press, 1974.

WEISSMAN, M. M., SHOLOMSKAS, D., POTTENGER, M., PRUSOFF, B. A. and LOCKE, B. Z. Assessing depressive symptoms in five psychiatric populations: A validation study. *American Journal of Epidemiology*, 1977; **106**, 203–214.

WHYBROW, P. C., AKISKAL, H. S. and McKINNEY, W. T. *Mood disorders: Toward a new psychobiology*. New York: Plenum Press, 1984.

WILSON, W. Correlates of avowed happiness. *Psychological Bulletin*, 1967; **67**, 294–306.

ZEISS, A. M. and LEWINSOHN, P. M. Enduring deficits after remission of depression: A test of the "Scar Hypothesis". *Behavior Therapy and Research*, 1988; **26**, 151–158.

Subjective Well-Being in its Social Context

9

Emotions in everyday life situations. Time sampling of subjective experience

HERMANN BRANDSTÄTTER

Introduction

There are many different ways of defining an emotion as a phenomenon of human experience and in explaining its functioning in human life. To me Philipp Lersch's (1952) concept of emotion as a spontaneous, immediate and intimate ("endothymic") evaluation of situations as providing or preventing need fulfilment is the most convincing and useful one. In his "functional circuit of experience" (Funktionskreis des Erlebens), emotions are closely linked to cognitions and action impulses. Moreover, emotional responses to objects and events are embedded in more enduring states of mood reflecting a person's comprehensive feeling as a living organism and self-conscious individual striving for a meaningful human life.

Obviously, there is a rather close correspondence to more recent phenomenological conceptualizations of emotions; i.e. to descriptions and explanations of emotions based on subjective experience and/or the way people speak about their emotions (cf. Arnold, 1960; Averill, 1980; Lazarus, Kanner and Folkman, 1980; Scherer, 1984; Weiner, 1986). Since Lersch (1952), and other German psychologists with a similar phenomenological orientation like Klages (1943), Krüger (1928), and Vetter (1966) are probably not known to these authors, we may assume that any phenomenological approach to emotions leads to basically similar interpretations.

Emotions and subjective well-being

The present study aims at analysing the internal (personal) and external (environmental) conditions of emotional responses to everyday life situations, based on a reanalysis of seven different studies with the author's time sampling diary (TSD) of subjective experience in everyday life situations.

The random time sampling of subjective experience was first used, independently of each other, by the author (Brandstätter, 1977) and by Csikszentmihalyi, Larson and Prescott (1977). Meanwhile a number of studies and reviews have proved the usefulness of this approach (e.g. Brandstätter 1981, 1983, 1989; Brandstätter and Wagner, 1988; Csikszentmihalyi and Larson, 1987; Diener, 1984; Hormuth, 1986; Kirchler, 1984, 1985, 1989). As the author became aware later, more than half a century ago, Flügel (1925) had used some kind of time sampling in his "study of feeling and emotion in every life". His subjects were to write down in a diary as often as possible, how they felt for the time since the last record. However, the samples were not taken at random, and the emotions were not clearly related to situations.

The more traditional way of measuring subjective well-being is to ask people for global ratings of their satisfaction with various domains of life (e.g. family, neighbourhood, work, leisure) or with life as a whole (Andrews, 1986; Andrews and Withey, 1976; Bradburn, 1969; Bradburn and Caplovitz, 1965; Cantril, 1965; Campbell, Converse and Rodgers, 1976; cf. also the review of Diener, 1984). Although some of the measures seem to be quite sophisticated and well constructed, all of them share some serious shortcomings:

(1) In answering questions about subjective well-being people have to give a summary statement integrating a wide variety of experiences over a long period of time. As yet we know little about how the continuous flow of experience is analysed; i.e. compared with some evaluative standards, weighted, integrated and transformed into a mark on a rating scale by the subjects in answering questions about their subjective well-being (see Chapter 3). An evaluative response to a symbolically (by means of language) represented object may mirror the prior positive or negative experience with the object only if it is visible and easily identifiable as a unit like another person, my house or my car. In such a case the present evaluative response can be conveniently explained as a consequence of emotional conditioning in the past, depending on the number, quality and intensity of emotional experiences with the object (Byrne, 1969). However, entities like "my work" or "my marriage" provide no clear cut stimulus pattern to which the emotional experience could be attached by conditioning. Giving a reasonable answer to the interviewer's question about one's satisfaction with such a complex issue would demand highly complicated conceptual and judgmental processes in remembering, classifying, comparing and weighting the experiences with the various components of life situations. This presumably is too difficult

a task for most persons. Nevertheless, forcing them to answer could easily lead them to rely on rather irrelevant cues, for example on the momentary affective state or on objective living conditions like income, housing, and job characteristics which generally are supposed to be related to happiness.

(2) Even if a person were able to integrate the variety of experiences in a specific area of life over a defined time period into a meaningful comprehensive evaluation, many people would still be tempted to follow social norms in answering questions of subjective well-being rather than to reveal sincerely their intimate feelings.

(3) The categories used in interviews and questionnaires often do not correspond to the way individuals cognitively structure their experiences. This too could lead to invalid responses. At least we may miss a deeper understanding of a person's life space.

(4) Traditional measures of subjective well-being tell us almost nothing about the hidden regularities in the interplay between life circumstances and events on the one hand and personality characteristics on the other hand.

(5) Retrospective reports on the past day's experience (cf. Wessman and Ricks, 1966) are an important step toward a more concrete and better differentiated representation of personal experience, but they still rely too much on reviving emotions by remembering the past day's events.

The time sampling diary was designed to overcome some of the flaws and restrictions inherent in the traditional rating methods.

Conceiving of time sampling of emotional experience and rating life satisfaction as different but possibly complementary ways of measuring subjective well-being poses the question of their theoretical and empirical relationships. In the studies on which the present report is based, the correlations between relative frequencies of positive emotions derived from the diary data and traditional rating measures of life satisfaction vary remarkably from study to study with a range of .10 to .75, a variation which cannot be explained by sampling error alone. This means that it is worthwhile to search more closely for the conditions of both the correspondences and discrepancies of the two ways of measuring subjective well-being.

It is obvious and almost trivial that momentary affective states as well as happiness in the sense of global evaluation of one's life are combined effects of a person's propensity to experience life as joyful (because the person has the appropriate goals, skills, attribution strategies and neurochemistry) and an environment's offerings of rewards. This does not mean that we know much of how personality influences emotional experience and how emotional experience builds up a person's readiness to feel unhappy or happy (see Diener, 1984, to some theoretical concepts for explaining happiness). Thus, much remains to be done in analysing the conceptual and empirical relationship between the two kinds of measures.

Classifying situations, persons and emotions

Relating environmental and personal characteristics to emotions presupposes a theoretically meaningful classification of situations, persons and emotions. Classifying situations or, using a concept of Barker (1968), behaviour settings, is a psychological task which has attracted much attention in recent years (Argyle, Furnham and Graham, 1981; Cantor, Mischel and Schwartz, 1982; Eckes and Six, 1984; Forgas, 1982; Frederiksen, 1972; King and Sorrentino, 1983; Magnusson, 1981; Nascimento-Schulze, 1981; Wakenhut, 1978). Phenomenological ("intuitive") classifications compete with classifications based on some kind of multidimensional scaling. (cf. Eckes and Six, 1984, p. 11). For the present analysis we rely on a rather simple phenomenological a priori classification according to (a) social distance of other persons present (1 = nobody, 2 = partner, 3 = children, 4 = relatives, 5 = friends, 6 = acquaintances, 7 = authority figures, 8 = strangers), (b) unfamiliarity of the place (at home, out of home), (c) restraint of activities (leisure, work). The social distance characterizing a situation will be indicated by the average social distance score of the classes of people present in the situation.

The persons are classified according to their pattern of four 16PF second order factor scores: norm orientation; emotional stability; independence and extraversion (Schneewind, Schröder and Cattell, 1983). Norm oriented people describe themselves as conscientious (G+) and conservative (Q1-); emotionally stable subjects as self-assured (O-), controlled (Q3), emotionally stable (C+), trusting (L-) and relaxed (Q4-); independent subjects see themselves as assertive (E+), venturesome (H+) and suspicious (L+); extraverts as group dependent (Q2-), happy-go-lucky (F+) and outgoing (A+). A median split in each dimension results in $2 \times 2 \times 2 \times 2 = 16$ categories, each category comprising highly similar personality structures.

The 16PF questionnaire was chosen as a personality measure because it seemed to be more comprehensive than any other personality questionnaire in German language designed for use with normal adults. The four second order dimensions are very similar to those reported by Cattell, Eber and Tatsuoka (1970; see also Barton, 1986) for the English version of the 16PF and called conscientiousness (norm orientation), anxiety (lack of emotional stability), independence (independence), and extraversion (extraversion).

The emotional responses are analysed in terms of adjectives freely generated by the subjects in describing their momentary affective states. Since a great number of different adjectives had been used by the subjects, a classification of those emotion words had to be performed first. Because it is the first time that such a classification was based on subjects' descriptions of emotions in random time samples of their daily life experiences, we may expect that the results will be somewhat different from those reported in the literature.

The study looks for preliminary answers to the questions of how emotions (a) depend on behaviour settings characterized by combinations of persons present (alone, partner, relatives/friends, acquaintances/strangers), kind of activity (leisure/work), and place (home/out of home), (b) relate to attributions, (c) are tied to frustrated and satisfied motives, and (d) are dependent on personality structure.

According to the exploratory character of the study, no specific hypotheses will be tested. The general assumption is that different behaviour settings induce different emotions and that the relative frequencies of emotions experienced by persons depend on their personality structure as well as on the motives involved. Person-environment interaction effects are not considered in this report but dealt with elsewhere (Brandstätter, in press, 1989).

Method

Subjects

Altogether 188 subjects participated in seven different studies: (a) a class of twenty-five students of social economics (Brandstätter, 1981), (b) eighteen faculty members (including doctoral students) of a psychology department (Brandstätter and Ott, 1979), (c) twenty-four housewives (Brandstätter, 1983), (d) twenty-seven soldiers of the Italian army (Kirchler, 1984), (e) twenty-eight unemployed men and women (Kirchler, 1985), (f) twenty-four members of a charity organization (Auinger, 1987), and (g) twenty-one men and twenty-one women participating as couples (Kirchler, 1988). Thirty-seven per cent of subjects are women. The age of the subjects varies from eighteen to sixty with a median at twenty-eight. Around 50 per cent have a lower level of education (less than thirteen years, most of them four years primary, four years intermediary school and three years apprenticeship), 40 per cent finished secondary school with maturity (the majority of this group participated in the study as students), and 10 per cent have a University degree. Four groups (students, faculty, soldiers and volunteers) were willing to participate as complete organizational units. The housewives constituted a random sample drawn from the telephone directory of a typical district of Augsburg. The unemployed were contacted at the unemployment registration office (Arbeitsamt) of Linz. The couples were recruited by announcements on the blackboard at the University of Salzburg and via personal acquaintance. Four groups (students, housewives, soldiers and unemployed) were paid for their participation (between DM 100 and DM 300).

Diary format and questionnaire

With only minor modifications and some variations in the additional questionnaires the procedure was virtually the same in all studies.

At the first meeting the subjects were thoroughly informed of the procedure they should follow: the subjects had to make notes in a booklet on their momentary experience about four times a day during a period of thirty days. The random time samples were different for each day and each person. There were seven questions to answer each time: (a) "Is my mood at the moment rather negative, indifferent, or rather positive?"; (b) "How can I describe my momentary mood state using one or two adjectives?"; (c) "Why do I feel as I have indicated?"; (d) "Where am I?"; (e) "What am I doing?"; (f) "Who else is present?"; (g) "To what extent do I feel free to choose to stay in or leave my present activity?". Before leaving the first meeting the subjects answered a German version of Cattell's 16PF questionnaire (Schneewind, Schröder and Cattell, 1983). Afer a few days' experience with the diary the participants met again with the experimenters and discussed their problems with the method. The following day they started with the diary, which had to be kept during thirty consecutive days. Only the unemployed had a different time schedule. They took notes at four periods of ten days each, in the first, second, and third month after job loss. The final period fell in the fourth, fifth or sixth month after job loss. At the end of the recording time span the subjects answered the 16PF questionnaire a second time and a questionnaire on their attitudes toward the study.

Time sampling

The schedule for the time sampling, printed on a sheet of paper and handed out to the subjects, had been generated by a computer program by dividing the twenty-four hours of the day into six segments of four hours each and choosing randomly one point of time within each segment. In the booklet a separate page was provided for each of the 180 scheduled observation times (six per day over thirty days). Since subjects slept eight hours on average, the expected number of records per day was four, resulting in a total expected number of 120 per person over thirty days. The actual number varied between days and persons owing to a variation in hours of sleeping and in frequencies of omissions. Whenever it came into mind that time for diary recording might have come subjects had to take their notes immediately if the prescribed time point was no more than half an hour later. In case a scheduled time point had been forgotten, the subjects had been instructed to take their notes just for the moment they became aware of their omission. In situations where they knew it was time for taking notes but were for some reason not able to do so, they had to memorize their answers to the seven questions immediately in order to write them down as soon as possible. They were not allowed to record remembered situations from the past if they had not explicitly memorized them. Because there were also times for recording scheduled during the night, the subjects had to mark the next morning those that were within their hours of sleep.

Classification of emotion words

Since the subjects were free in choosing any adjective for describing their moment to moment emotional experience, each study came up with great numbers of emotion words. They had to be classified before they could be used in further analyses.

In a pilot study aimed at classifying emotion words Gaug (1985) used the set of 537 adjectives generated by the eighteen men and twelve women participating in the unemployment study (Kirchler, 1985). First, 193 words were eliminated as at least sixteen out of twenty-two judges marked them unacceptable as descriptions of emotions, like amusing, straining, diligent. The remaining 344 words were typed, one by one, on small cards. Individually, each of the forty-four subjects (eighteen male, twenty-six female), mostly students of business administration and economics, divided the whole set of words in as many distinct categories as it seemed appropriate to the subjects in order to achieve high semantic similarity within and clear semantic differences between the categories. The average number of categories used by the judges for classifying the adjectives was thirty-three.

The relative frequency of subjects who had put two adjectives into the same category was used as the similarity measure for each pair of adjectives. Based on this kind of similarity matrix a hierarchical cluster analysis according to the Average Linkage method (Schubö and Vehlinger, 1986, p. 224) was performed in order to arrive at a managable and meaningful number of categories.

Results

Cluster analysis of emotion words

The hierarchical cluster analysis of emotion words according to the relative frequency by which the judges put them into the same category resulted in seventeen classes of emotions. Because some of them were rarely (in less than 1 per cent of the observations) used by our subjects (sentimentality, pride, inebriation, loneliness, abasement, restriction, guilt, surprise and indifference, the last two mostly with a negative connotation), only eight categories and a residual category were kept for the analysis (Table 9.1).

TABLE 9.1. *Categories of Emotion Words*

Residual
Joy
Relaxation (relaxation, sentimentality*)
Activation (activation, optimism, pride*)
Satiation (satiation, inebriation*)
Fatigue (stress, fatigue, exhaustion)
Sadness (sickness, discomfort, frustration, sadness, boredom, indifference*, loneliness*, abasement*, restriction*, guilt*)
Anger (discontent, disgust, anger, surprise*)
Fear (nervousness, fear)

* Categories with low frequencies; they were added to those categories to which they joined at higher hierarchical levels. Emotion words in brackets without asterisks are subclusters of the main categories.

Emotions related to behaviour settings

Sixteen categories of behaviour settings are considered by combining four classes of persons present (according to the average social distance of persons present) with two classes of activities (leisure, work), varying in the degree of restraint, and two classes of localities (at home, out of home), varying on the dimension private-public. As to social distance, being alone was coded with 0; partner, one's children, relatives, friends, acquaintances, authority figures, and strangers were coded with 1 to 7. For determining the social class of persons present, the social distance scores of persons present were averaged and divided into four classes (class 1: average social distance score 0; class 2: 1.00–2.30; class 3: 2.31–4.66; class 4: 4.67 and more). Thus, social distance class 1 is equivalent to being alone, class 2 means being predominantly with family members, class 3 centres around relatives and friends, whereas class 4 is characterized mainly by the presence of acquaintances and strangers.

One should be aware that being alone is a special category which does not fit well into the order of social distance of the other three categories. Actually, being alone may be experienced by many people as a situation where they feel socially most distant from others.

As one can imagine, the TSD-data would allow more refined classifications of persons present, activities and places. However, low cell frequencies restrict the possibilities of differentiating more categories within an aspect (persons, activities, places) and/or adding some other aspects (like time of the day, motives involved, or causal attributions).

With a contingency coefficient of $C = .28$, Table 9.2 clearly shows an association between classes of emotions and behaviour settings. For giving a clearer impression of how emotions are related to the kind of people present, the data of Table 9.2 is condensed to five classes of emotions, four social situations are represented in Table 9.3. Besides the residual category we distinguish "Positive Active" (joy and activation), "Positive Passive"

TABLE 9.2. *Relative frequencies of emotions dependent on behaviour settings (Social Distance × Leisure/Work × Home/Out)*

	(1)	(2)	(3)	(4)	(5)	(6)	(7)	(8)	(9)	(10)	(11)	(12)	(13)	(14)	(15)	(16)	(All) N	(All) %
Persons	Alone				Family				Relatives/Friends				Acquaintances/Strangers				All	
Leisure/Work	L	L	W	W	L	L	W	W	L	L	W	W	L	L	W	W	N	%
Home/Out	H	O	H	O	H	O	H	O	H	O	H	O	H	O	H	O		
Residual	17.2	17.1	20.0	24.3⁺	15.2⁻	15.5	15.0	14.4	11.8	17.0	12.9	18.2	15.2	18.2	15.7	23.5⁺	3461	17.8
Joy	11.6⁻	19.8	13.0⁻	12.9⁻	20.6	29.3⁺	18.2	20.6	27.8⁺	34.8⁺	22.3	23.2	18.5	25.4⁺	31.3	13.9⁻	4181	21.5
Relaxation	23.9	18.4	22.3	14.4⁻	31.8⁺	24.1	25.2	24.4	25.7⁺	18.1⁻	29.2	12.8⁻	23.9	17.4⁻	18.1	12.9⁻	4096	21.0
Activation	4.2	3.9	5.2	5.0	2.6⁻	3.5	3.7	3.1	3.9	3.7	3.0	4.9	8.7	5.6⁺	7.2	5.0	820	4.2
Satiation	1.8	0.8	0.5⁻	0.4	2.1	2.6	0.4	0.6	3.5⁺	2.2	0.4	0.8	4.3	2.1	1.2	0.7	304	1.6
Fatigue	16.6⁺	12.8	15.0⁺	12.0	12.3	9.9	14.4	16.6	7.8⁻	7.9⁻	8.7	9.6	7.6	9.2⁻	4.8	15.5⁺	2327	12.0
Sadness	14.1⁺	15.9⁺	10.4	15.3⁺	7.2	7.2	7.7	6.3	8.6	8.5	6.8	17.1⁺	7.6	11.3	8.4	11.5	2062	10.6
Anger	4.5	4.4	3.9	5.6	3.3	3.2	8.1⁺	5.6	3.3	2.6	6.8	6.3	5.4	3.9	7.2	5.7⁻	847	4.4
Fear	6.2	6.9	9.7⁺	10.1⁺	4.9⁻	4.8	7.4	8.8	7.5	5.3⁻	9.8	7.1	8.7	6.9	6.0	9.2⁺	1366	7.0
N	2031	904	1429	940	2658	627	1040	160	1114	2966	264	773	92	1966	83	2417	19464	
%	10.4	4.6	7.3	4.8	13.7	3.2	5.3	0.8	5.7	15.2	1.4	4.0	0.5	10.1	0.4	12.4		100.0

Note: Observed column percentages marked with ⁻ or ⁺ are far below or above percentages expected if emotions were independent of behaviour settings ($p < .001$; one-tailed).

(relaxation and satiation), "Negative Active" (anger and fear) and "Negative Passive" (fatigue and sadness).[1] We see that highly activating emotions, both positive and negative ones, are more prominent with Relatives/Friends and Strangers than with Family or when the person is alone. The ratios of Positive Active to Positive Passive are .83, .79, 1.59, and 1.54 for Alone, Family, Relatives/Friends, and Strangers, respectively. For the negative emotions the ratios are .44, .51, .55 and .55, respectively.

TABLE 9.3. *Relative frequencies of five classes of emotions dependent on four social situations*

	Alone	Family	Relatives/ Friends	Acquaintances/ Strangers	All N	All %
Residual	19.3	15.2⁻	16.0⁻	20.9⁺	3505	17.8
Joy + Activation	18.1⁻	24.2	34.6⁺	25.7	5038	25.6
Relaxation + Satiation	21.9	30.6⁺	21.8	16.7⁻	4459	22.7
Anger + Fear	12.4	10.1	9.8⁻	13.0⁺	2228	11.3
Fatigue + Sadness	28.3⁺	19.9⁻	17.8⁻	23.7	4428	22.5
N	5364	4563	5173	4576	19658	
%	27.2	23.2	26.3	23.2		100.0

Note: Observed percentages marked with ⁻ or ⁺ are far below or above percentages expected if emotions were independent of social situations ($p < 0.001$; one-tailed).

From Table 9.4, another summing of Table 9.2, we see Joy is predominantly connected with Leisure Out, Relaxation with Home, Fatigue, Anger and Fear come up most often at Work. The contingency coefficient for Table 9.4 is $C = .21$.

TABLE 9.4. *Relative frequencies of emotions dependent on combinations of leisure/work with home/out.*

	Leisure Home	Leisure Out	Work Home	Work Out	All N	All %
Residual	15.2⁻	17.2	17.4	22.4⁺	3461	17.8
Joy	18.8⁻	29.3⁺	16.3⁻	16.7⁻	4181	21.5
Relaxation	27.8⁺	18.5⁻	23.9⁺	13.7⁻	4096	21.0
Activation	3.5	4.3	4.5	4.9	820	4.2
Satiation	2.3⁺	2.0	0.5⁻	0.6⁻	304	1.6
Fatigue	12.8	9.1⁻	13.8⁺	13.7⁺	2327	12.0
Sadness	9.9	10.2	9.0	13.2⁺	2062	10.6
Anger	3.8	3.3⁻	5.8⁺	5.8⁺	847	4.4
Fear	5.9⁻	6.0⁻	8.7⁺	9.0⁺	1366	7.0
N	5895	6463	2816	4290	19464	
%	30.3	33.2	14.5	22.0		100.0

Note: Observed percentages marked with ⁻ or ⁺ are far below or above percentages expected if emotions were independent of behaviour settings ($p < 0.001$; one-tailed).

Emotions related to attributions

When the subjects explicitly mention Self, Partner, etc. as causes of their emotions (Table 9.5), we see that Self is connected less often with Joy and more often with Relaxation, Fatigue and Sadness than Partner and Other Persons. Children seem quite often to provoke Anger. The rather low contingency coefficient of $C = .19$ may be due to the fact that there is a very broad and heterogeneous category Other Sources. Focusing on social attributions all non-social attributions have been lumped together.

TABLE 9.5. *Relative frequencies of emotions dependent on attributions*

Attributions to:	Self	Partner	Children	Other persons	Other sources	All N	%
Residual	18.6	15.4	8.9⁻	16.4	18.8	3495	17.8
Joy	11.7⁻	25.4⁺	24.6	30.1⁺	20.1	4210	21.4
Relaxation	24.9⁺	26.2⁺	27.1	15.9⁻	20.9	4154	21.2
Activation	3.8	3.8	2.2	4.2	4.5	824	4.2
Satiation	1.2	0.7	0.0	1.4	1.9	303	1.5
Fatigue	16.0⁻	7.5⁻	7.7	7.6⁻	13.2⁺	2340	11.9
Sadness	12.4⁺	9.8	8.6	11.3	9.9	2080	10.6
Anger	4.4	5.1	14.5⁺	5.1	3.6⁻	853	4.3
Fear	6.1	6.1	6.5	8.0	7.1	1370	7.0
N	3308	1846	325	3969	10181	19629	
%	16.9	9.4	1.7	20.2	51.9		100.0

Note: Observed percentages marked with ⁻ or ⁺ are far below or above percentages expected if emotions were independent of attributions ($p < 0.001$; one-tailed).

Emotions related to satisfied and frustrated motives

That there is a rather close correspondence between motives and emotions, as among others Lersch (1952) postulates, can be seen from Table 9.6. For motive frustration $C = .29$, for motive satisfaction $C = .25$.

Naturally, negative emotions appear predominantly with frustrated motives, while positive emotions are tied to satisfied motives. Only rarely do positive emotions appear with motive frustration and negative emotions with motive satisfaction.

People feel sad when the Affiliation motive is frustrated; Anger is the emotional quality of frustrated Power motives. Fear is related to failure in striving for Achievement. On the side of satisfied motives, Joy goes with Affiliation, Relaxation and Satiation with Physical Comfort, Activation with Activity. After simple calculations Table 9.6 tells us the satisfaction ratios of motives (frequency of satisfaction divided by the combined frequencies of frustration and satisfaction). This ratio is for example 86.7 per cent (3206 out of 3696) for Affiliation and 43.8 per cent (1361 out of 3109) for Power.

TABLE 9.6. *Relative frequencies of emotions dependent on frustrated and satisfied motives.*

	Frustrated Motives								Satisfied Motives							
	Activity	Achiev.	Phys. comfort	Affil.	Power	Higher Motives	All N	%	Activity	Achiev.	Phys. comfort	Affil.	Power	Higher Motives	All N	%
Residual	21.7	21.5	22.7	15.5	17.5	19.0	1238	19.9	18.0	21.4$^+$	16.6	13.9$^-$	15.9	17.0	2111	16.7
Joy	1.9	2.7	1.3	3.7	1.5	1.8	119	1.9	27.2$^-$	25.5$^-$	29.1	39.4$^+$	36.1$^+$	27.9	4040	31.9
Relaxation	3.3	3.1	3.1	3.5	1.6	1.8	163	2.6	28.0	32.1	36.4$^+$	28.8	29.6	28.9	3881	30.7
Activation	1.1	1.6	0.5	0.6	0.5	1.7	55	0.9	9.7$^+$	6.5	2.4$^-$	5.3	5.4	7.5	742	5.9
Satiation	1.4	0.5	1.1	0.6	1.2	0.2	60	1.0	0.7	0.6$^-$	5.5$^+$	1.2	0.9$^-$	1.2	230	1.8
Fatigue	20.7	20.8	34.3$^+$	14.3$^-$	15.3$^-$	16.7	1305	21.0	7.4	9.2$^+$	6.6	5.5	5.2	8.4	855	6.8
Sadness	27.8	20.6$^-$	25.2	41.6$^+$	31.1	31.2	1782	28.7	1.9	1.1	1.4	1.3	1.8	3.1$^+$	210	1.7
Anger	12.5	13.2	4.6$^-$	8.8	17.6$^+$	13.2	759	12.2	0.5	0.6	0.4	0.5	0.8	0.9	72	0.6
Fear	9.7	16.0$^+$	7.2$^-$	11.4	13.7	14.4	733	11.8	6.7	3.2	1.6	4.1	4.3	5.1	514	4.1
N	1236	838	1249	490	1748	653	6214		2069	1610	2396	3206	2013	1361	12655	
%	19.9	13.5	20.1	7.9	28.1	10.5	100.0		16.3	12.7	18.9	25.3	15.9	10.8	100.0	

Note: Observed percentages marked with $^-$ or $^+$ are far below or above percentages expected if emotions were independent of motives ($p<0.001$; one-tailed).

TABLE 9.7. *Relative frequencies of emotions dependent on personality structures (norm orientation × emotional stability × independence × extraversion).*

	(1)	(2)	(3)	(4)	(5)	(6)	(7)	(8)	(9)	(10)	(11)	(12)	(13)	(14)	(15)	(16)	N	All %
Norm Orient.	1	1	1	1	1	1	1	1	2	2	2	2	2	2	2	2		
Em. Stabil.	1	1	1	1	2	2	2	2	1	1	1	1	2	2	2	2		
Independence	1	1	2	2	1	1	2	2	1	1	2	2	1	1	2	2		
Extraversion	1	2	1	2	1	2	1	2	1	2	1	2	1	2	1	2		
Residual	14.6^-	17.9	18.0	17.7	29.6^+	18.4	23.2^+	14.9^-	17.6	17.8	16.9	20.2	20.4	11.1	10.0	17.5	3460	17.8
Joy	14.3^-	18.1	17.9	23.0	25.0	17.3	15.1^-	23.1	21.2	22.7	20.3	20.6	21.2	33.0^+	32.8^+	22.8	4173	21.5
Relaxation	20.5	17.4	21.8	17.3	8.7	25.2	19.9	24.9^+	23.3	17.8	20.1	19.8	22.3	22.5	29.6^+	20.3	4098	21.1
Activation	4.2	2.9	5.5	7.3^+	3.1	5.3	4.0	3.3	4.3	4.2	5.5	1.6^-	4.6	2.4	2.9	4.5	798	4.1
Satiation	1.9	2.0	1.7	1.4	1.8	0.5	2.4	2.8^+	0.6^-	1.9	0.9	2.3	0.4^-	0.7	1.6	1.5	300	1.5
Fatigue	17.6^+	11.9	11.3	11.9	10.9	11.3	9.2	11.4	9.3^-	14.7	10.6	10.1	13.2	14.3	7.4^-	11.9	2327	12.0
Sadness	12.8	13.3	11.7	9.4	10.4	7.6	11.0	10.0	10.2	12.2	11.3	10.2	8.6	10.2	8.9	9.6	2055	10.6
Anger	4.2	5.1	4.9	4.6	3.4	6.4	7.5^+	3.0	4.9	4.5	6.8^+	2.3^-	4.6	2.4^-	4.4	2.9	849	4.4
Fear	9.9^+	11.3^+	7.2	7.4	7.2	7.9	7.7	6.7	8.4	4.4^-	7.6	3.9^-	4.6^-	3.4^-	2.5^-	8.9^+	1351	7.0
N of Observations	1771	1050	1451	716	680	825	1173	1818	1649	1390	870	928	1208	1347	869	1657	19402	
%	9.1	5.4	7.5	3.7	3.5	4.3	6.0	9.4	8.5	7.2	4.5	4.8	6.2	6.9	4.5	8.5		100.0

Note: Separately for each study a median split (1 = low; 2 = high) was applied to each distribution on the four personality dimensions. Observed percentages marked with $^-$ or $^+$ are far below or above percentages expected if emotions were independent of personality structure ($p < .001$; one-tailed).

Emotions related to personality structure

Table 9.7 presents the relationship beween emotions and personality structures. The contingency coefficient is $C = .23$ for this table. As in Table 9.2, there are again too many figures to find one's way through all the main and interaction effects hidden in the table. Testing a great number of log-linear models (Langeheine, 1980) would not be very useful either. Instead, we look at more comprehensible two-way interactions of Emotional Stability and Extraversion.

These dimensions are supposed to be based on specific neurophysiological structures (Eysenck, 1967). This makes them particularly relevant for explaining individual differences in frequencies of emotions which also seem to be rather closely tied to neurophysiology (Plutchik, 1980; Plutchik and Kellerman, 1986).

Table 9.8 shows that Joy is abundant with Stable Extraverts and often missing with Unstable Introverts, whereas Fear is characteristic for Unstable Introverts, but not for Unstable Extraverts. The contingency coefficient for Table 9.8 is $C = .11$. Other effects may be tested with the data of Table 9.7, for example the main effect of Norm Orientation on Joy. Its relative frequency is 18.7 per cent for low Norm Orientation (weighted mean of relative frequencies of Joy across columns 1 to 8) versus 24.2 per cent for higher Norm Orientation (weighted mean of relative frequencies of Joy across columns 9 to 16).

TABLE 9.8. *Emotions related to personality structure (emotional stability × extraversion)*

Emotional Stability Extraversion	unstable introvert	extravert	stable introvert	extravert	All N	%
Residual	16.7	20.5$^+$	20.4$^+$	15.3$^-$	3460	17.8
Joy	18.1$^-$	22.6	21.1	24.5$^+$	4173	21.5
Relaxation	21.6	20.8	18.1$^-$	23.0$^+$	4098	21.1
Activation	4.8	3.8	3.8	3.8	789	4.1
Satiation	1.3	1.5	1.9	1.6	300	1.5
Fatigue	12.6	10.3$^-$	12.4	12.2	2327	12.0
Sadness	11.5	9.7	11.6	9.6	2055	10.6
Anger	5.0	5.2	4.2	3.3$^-$	849	4.4
Fear	8.4$^+$	5.5$^-$	6.6	6.7	1351	7.0
N	5741	3930	4084	5647	19402	
%	29.6	20.3	21.0	29.1		100.0

Note: Observed percentages marked with $^-$ or $^+$ are far below or above percentage expected if emotions were independent of personality ($p < 0.001$, one-tailed).

Discussion

Categorization of emotions

It is probably the first time that a classification of emotions has been tried with adjectives generated by the subjects for describing their momentary emotional responses and mood states in really representative samples of everyday life situations. As yet, classifications of emotion words were based on semantic similarity ratings of emotion words selected by the experimenter as prototypical (e.g. Ekman, 1954) or collected from samples of subjects who had to write down all emotion words they could remember (e.g. Marx, 1982) or collected from dictionaries or already existing lists of emotion words and rated by samples of subjects with respect to their appropriateness for describing emotions (Schmidt-Atzert, 1981).

Since there will be a special report on the methods and results of our approach to the classification of emotion words, only a few points should be made here. The time sampling diaries of emotional responses to life situations reveal some clusters of words which are missing from most if not all other categorizations; i.e. Satiation and Inebriation. The subjects using these words as descriptions of mood and emotions, as well as the judges rating the words as verbal expressions of emotions, were convinced that these words dealt with emotions. Therefore, one should seriously think about adding these categories to the list of basic emotions although they seem to be on the borderline of body sensations and feelings. "Restriction" seems to be another unique category represented by words like restricted, feeling confined, constrained.

The categories Joy, Relaxation, Activation, Fatigue, Sadness, and Anger to which in our study the most frequently used words belong are also the main (and only) categories reported by Hampel (1977). He had collected answers to a comprehensive list of emotion words from a highly hetero- geneous sample of more than 800 people. Although each person had answered the mood questionnaire only once, there was a high between person variation of real life situations in which the data were collected. This may explain the rather close correspondence of Hampel's categorization and that of the present study. However, Fear (Nervousness, Anxiety) which is clearly separated from Sadness in the present study, seems to be collapsed in Hampel's list.

Surprise (a low frequency cluster in the present study) and disgust (together with discontent and anger a sub-category of anger in the present study), for which clear differential patterns of facial expressions could be found (cf. Ekman and Friesen, 1975), are rarely mentioned in our verbal reports. Of course, surprise has to be a rare emotion, because following the rules of semantics we speak of surprise only when an event is unexpected and at the same time highly relevant to us, and unexpected events are generally also rare events. As to disgust, one would like to know whether this emotion is really so rare as the TSD reports suggest. The best way to verify the relative frequencies of emotions derived from TSD data would be to collect time sampling data of facial expressions.

Emotions and behaviour settings

The classification of behaviour settings according to social distance of persons present (alone, family members, relatives/friends, strangers), restriction of freedom (leisure, work), and lack of privacy (at home, out of home) is a first approach in imposing some structure on the bewildering variety of situations reported by the subjects of the different samples. Since the frequencies of being in those situations varies between groups (e.g. housewives, students, and professors work alone at home more often than people employed in industrial organizations or soldiers) we have to keep in mind that the results of Tables 9.2 to 9.4 concerning the dependence of emotions on behaviour settings may be somewhat confounded with differences in age, sex, and occupational status of the subjects.

Another problem is the residual category of emotion words which relates to about 18 per cent of observations and comprises all words not contained in the cluster analysis of Gaug (1985) which was based on the vocabulary of people who were unemployed. Therefore, we have to assume that students and professors whose vocabulary is richer (they use a greater number of words and less familiar ones) have contributed more to the residual category than the other groups. However, although the between samples variation of behaviour settings and the shortcomings of the preliminary cluster analysis of emotion words may have some effects, it is extremely unlikely that the most clear cut results could be an artefact.

The most prominent among these results is the predominance of high arousal emotions (Joy and Activation on the positive side, Anger and Fear on the negative side) in encounters with relatives/friends and strangers compared to low arousal emotions characteristic for being alone or with family members. Comparing the relevant figures of Tables 9.4 suggests that both the familiarity of places and the familiarity of persons present (which is often connected) contribute to the frequency of low arousal emotions, in addition to perhaps exciting activities performed more often at unfamiliar places and/or with less familiar persons. One may speculate how this result fits into the arousal theory of social facilitation (cf. Zajonc, 1980). Arousing may be not the presence of other people *per se*, but the presence of people one is unfamiliar with.

Emotions and attributions

The rather high rate of anger responses towards children (14.5 per cent of emotional responses in situations where the subjects perceived their children as causes of their mood states) mirrors the difficulties of being a parent (Table 9.5).

Comparing Table 9.3 to Table 9.5 gives an idea of the degree of correspondence between emotional responses related to the presence of other people and emotional responses related to explicit attributions to other people. Generally, the correspondence seems to be quite good. This means that people feel in a rather consistent way in specific social situations whether they are aware of who makes them feel happy/unhappy or not. It would be of special interest to look closely at the data on an individual level (not just on the aggregation level of people sharing the same personality structure) in order to learn more about a person's consistency in his/her emotional responses to a certain person or a specific category of persons (e.g. friends, authority figures etc.).

Emotions and motives

Table 9.6 impresses by the clear correspondence between negative emotions and motive frustration. Fear (not Sadness) belongs to Achievement, Fatigue (not Anger or Fear) to Physical Comfort, Sadness (not Fatigue) to Affiliation, and Anger (not Fatigue) to Power. There is no prominent emotion with Activity and Higher Motives. On the side of motive satisfaction, Joy is underrepresented in Activity and Achievement, overrepresented in Affiliation and Power, suggesting that Joy is predominantly a social emotion.

Fatigue and Fear are those negative emotions which relatively often (6.8 per cent and 4.1 per cent) come together with motive satisfaction. Taking a closer look at the words contained in the Fatigue cluster, we find by far the highest frequency for "tired" which in some contexts may have a positive connotation. The Fear cluster also comprises a few words which could have a positive meaning like boisterous (aufgekratzt), fidgety (kribbelig), and aroused (erregt).

Emotions and personality structure

The balance of positive versus negative emotions is clearly shifted to the negative side when Norm Orientation, Emotional Stability and Independence are simultaneously low. In this case almost half of the observed situations are negatively tuned. When both Norm Orientation and Emotional Stability are high, positive emotions outweigh negative emotions by about 2 to 1.

That Emotional Stability would be related to positivity of affect had been expected. The influence of Norm Orientation (Conscientiousness according to Cattell, Eber and Tatsuoka, 1970) on positivity of emotions comes as a surprise. We could suspect that norm oriented people are denying their negative emotions by following a social desirability bias even in the completely private situations of taking TSD-records. However, being conscientious may also imply being honest to oneself. Therefore, a better explanation may be that norm oriented people run less often into troubles, thus often feeling better than their counterparts on the other side of the scale.

Statistically speaking, there seem to be some two-way and three-way interactions in the data of Table 9.7. However, since no hypotheses had been formulated in advance, *post hoc* testing by log-linear models of higher order interactions can hardly be justified. Thus, the data may be used for generating hypotheses to be tested with new TSD-data.

Conclusion

Exploring the relationships between emotions (as quasi dependent variables) and behaviour settings, social attributions, and frustrated/satisfied motives (a kind of independent variable) we have seen that emotions experienced in everyday life situations are really sensitive to the ever changing characteristics of the behaviour settings. On the other hand, the probabilities of experiencing various emotions are dependent on personality structure. In part, the contingencies between personality characteristics and emotions are due to the fact that people, depending on their personality characteristics, approach or avoid certain settings which in turn tend to provoke certain emotions. However, often a person has no choice in moving into or leaving an attractive or repulsive behaviour setting. In such a case personality differences bear on the way the situation (i.e. a certain person in a certain environment) is perceived and emotionally evaluated. It will be an important task for future research to study systematically the dynamics of interaction between personal and environmental structures. Since a special report on the correspondence between personal and environmental structures as a prerequisite of subjective well-being will appear elsewhere, this aspect of the TSD-data has not been presented here.

References

ANDREWS, F.M. (ed.), *Research on the quality of life.* Ann Arbor, MI: The Institute of Social Research, University of Michigan, 1986.

ANDREWS, F.M. and WITHEY, S.B. *Social indicators of well-being.* New York: Plenum Press, 1976.

ARGYLE, M., FURNHAM, A. and GRAHAM, J.A. *Social situations.* Cambridge: Cambridge University Press, 1981.

ARNOLD, M.B. *Emotion and personality.* New York: Columbus University Press, 1960.

AUINGER, F. *Subjektives Wohlbefinden als Klimabarometer in Organisationen.* Unpublished master's thesis, University of Linz, Austria, 1987.

AVERILL, J.R. A constructivist view of emotion. In R. Plutchik and H. Kellerman (eds.), *Emotion. Vol. 1. Theories of emotion* (pp. 305–339). New York: Academic Press, 1980.

BARKER, R.G. *Ecological psychology.* Stanford, CA.: Stanford University Press, 1968.

BARTON, K. Personality assessment by questionnaire. In R.B. Cattell and R.C. Johnson (eds.), *Functional psychological testing. Principles and instruments* (pp. 237–259). New York: Brunner/Mazel, 1986.

BRADBURN, N.M. *The structure of psychological well-being.* Chicago: Aldine, 1969.

BRADBURN, N.M. and CAPLOVITZ, D. *Reports on happiness*. Chicago: Aldine, 1965.

BRANDSTÄTTER, H. Wohlbefinden und Unbehagen. Entwurf eines Verfahrens zur Messung situationsabhängiger Stimmungen. In W.H. Tack, *Bericht über den 30. Kongreß der DGfPs in Regensburg 1976*. Göttingen: Hogrefe, 1977.

BRANDSTÄTTER, H. Time sampling of subjective well-being. In H. Hartmann, W. Molt and H. Stringer (eds.), *Advances in economic psychology* (pp. 63–76). Heidelberg: Meyn, 1981.

BRANDSTÄTTER, H. Emotional responses to other persons in everyday life situations. *Journal of Personality and Social Psychology*, 1983; **45**, 871–883.

BRANDSTÄTTER, H. *Motivational person-environment fit in everyday life situations: A time sampling diary approach*. Paper presented at the 4th Meeting of the International Society for Research on Emotions (ISRE), Paris, March, 1989.

BRANDSTÄTTER, H. Motives in everyday life situations. An individual difference approach. In F. Halisch and J. van den Bercken (eds. in collaboration with S. Hazlett), *International Perspectives on Achievement and Task Motivation*. Lisse: Swets & Zeitlinger, 1990.

BRANDSTÄTTER, H. and OTT, H. *Zeitstichproben des Befindens. Ergebnisse und Probleme erster Auswertungen*. Unpublished manuscript. University of Augsburg, 1979.

BRANDSTÄTTER, H. and WAGNER, W. *Alltagserfahrung berufstätiger Ehepaare*. Forschungsbericht. University of Linz, Austria, 1988.

BYRNE, D. Attitudes and attraction. In L. Berkowitz (ed.), *Advances in experimental social psychology, Vol. 4* (pp. 36–89). New York: Academic Press, 1969.

CAMPBELL, A., CONVERSE, P.E. and RODGERS, W.L. *The quality of American life*. New York: Russel Sage Foundation, 1976.

CANTOR, N., MISCHEL, W. and SCHWARTZ, J.C. A prototype analysis of psychological situations. *Cognitive Psychology*, 1982; **14**, 45–77.

CANTRIL, H. *The pattern of human concerns*. New Brunswick, NJ: Rutgers University Press, 1965.

CATTELL, R.B., EBER, H.W. and TATSUOKA, M. *Handbook for the Sixteen Personality Factor Questionnaire*. Champaign, IL.: IPAT, 1970.

CSIKSZENTMIHALYI, M. and LARSON, P. Validity and reliability of the experience-sampling method. *The Journal of Nervous and Mental Disease*, 1987; **175**, 526–536.

CSIKSZENTMIHALYI, M., LARSEN R. and PRESCOTT, S. The ecology of adolescent activity and experience. *Journal of Youth and Adolescence*, 1977; **6**, 281–294.

DIENER, E. Subjective well-being. *Psychological Bulletin*, 1984; **95**, 542–575.

ECKES, T. and SIX, B. Prototypenforschung: Ein integrativer Ansatz zur Analyse der alltagssprachlichen Kategorisierung von Objekten, Personen und Situationen. *Zeitschrift für Sozialpsychologie*, 1984; **15**, 2–17.

EKMAN, P. and FRIESEN, W.V. *Unmasking the face*. Palo Alto, CA: Consulting Psychologists Press, 1975.

EKMAN, W. Eine neue Methode zur Erlebnisanalyse. *Zeitschrift für experimentelle und angewandte Psychologie*, 1954; **2**, 167–174.

EYSENCK, H.J. *The biological basis of personality*. Springfield, IL.: Thomas, 1967.

FLÜGEL, J.C. A quantitative study of feeling and emotion in everyday life. *British Journal of Psychology*, 1925; **15**, 318–355.

FORGAS, J.D. Episode cognition: Internal representations of action routines. In L. Berkowitz (ed.), *Advances in experimental social psychology, Vol. 15* (pp. 59–101). New York: Academic Press, 1982.

FREDERIKSEN, N. Toward a taxonomy of situations. *American Psychologist*, 1972; **27**, 114–123.

GAUG, B. *Klassifikation von Emotionen*. Unpublished Master's thesis. University of Linz, Austria, 1985.

HAMPEL, R. Adjectiv-Skalen zur Einschätzung der Stimmung (SES). *Diagnostica*, **23**, 1977; 43–60.

HORMUTH, S.E. The sampling of experiences in situ. *Journal of Personality*, 1986; **54**, 262–293.

KING, G.A. and SORRENTINO, R.M. Psychological dimensions of goal-oriented interpersonal situations. *Journal of Personality and Social Psychology*, 1983; **44**, 140–162.

KIRCHLER, E. Befinden von Wehrpflichtigen in Abhängigkeit von personellen und situativen Gegebenheiten. Psychologie und Praxis. *Zeitschrift für Arbeits- und Organisationspsychologie*, 1984; **28**(2), 16–25.

KIRCHLER, E. Job loss and mood. *Journal of Economic Psychology*, 1985; **6**, 9–25.

KIRCHLER, E. Marital happiness and interaction in everyday surroundings: A time sample diary approach for couples. *Journal of Social and Personal Relationships*, 1988; **5**, 375–382.

KIRCHLER, E. Everyday life experiences at home: An interaction diary approach to assess marital relationships. *Journal of Family Psychology*, 1989; **2**, 311–336.

KLAGES, L., *Die Grundlegung der Wissenschaft vom Ausdruck*. Leipzig: Barth, 1943.

KRÜGER, F. *Das Wesen der Gefühle*. Leipzig: Akademische Verlagsantalt, 1928.

LANGEHEINE, R. *Log-lineare Modelle zur multivariaten Analyse qualitativer Daten*. Munich: Oldenbourgh, 1980.

LAZARUS, R.S., KANNER, A.D. and FOLKMAN, S. Emotions. A cognitive-phenomenological analysis. In R. Plutchik and H. Kellerman (eds.), *Theories of emotion* (pp. 189–217). New York: Academic Press, 1980.

LERSCH, P. *Der Aufbau der Person. 5th ed*. Munich: Barth, 1952.

MAGNUSSON, D. (ed.), *Toward a psychology of situations. An interactional perspective*. Hillsdale, NJ: Erlbaum, 1981.

MARX, W. Das Wortfeld der Gefühlsbegriffe. *Zeitschrift für experimentelle und angewandte Psychologie*, 1982; **29**, 137–146.

NASCIMENTO-SCHULZE, C.M. Towards situational classification. *European Journal of Social Psychology*, 1981; **11**, 149–159.

PLUTCHIK, R. A general psychoevolutionary theory of emotion. In R. Plutchik and H. Kellerman (eds.), *Theories of emotion* (pp. 3–33). New York: Academic Press, 1980.

PLUTCHIK, R. and KELLERMAN, H. (eds.). *Biological foundations of emotions*. New York: Academic Press, 1986.

SCHERER, K.R. On the nature and function of emotion: A component process approach. In K.R. Scherer and P. Ekman (eds.), *Approaches to emotion* (pp. 293–317). Hillsdale NJ.: Lawrence Erlbaum, 1984.

Schmidt-Atzert, L. *Emotionspsychologie*. Stuttgart: Kohlhammer, 1981.

SCHNEEWIND, K.A., SCHRÖDER, G. and CATTELL, R.B. *Der 16-Persönlichkeits-Faktoren-Test-16PF*. Bern: Huber, 1983.

SCHUBÖ, W. and VEHLINGER, H.M. SPSSX. Handbuch der Programmversion 2.2. Stuttgart: Fischer, 1986.

VETTER, A. *Personale Anthropologie*. Freiburg: Alber, 1966.

WAKENHUT, R. Über die Einbeziehung von Situationen in psychologische Messungen. Frankfurt/Main: Lang, 1978.

WATSON, D. and TELLEGEN, A. Toward a consensual structure of mood. *Psychological Bulletin*, 1985; **98**, 219–235.

WEINER, B. *An attributional theory of motivation and emotion*. New York: Springer, 1986.

WESSMAN, A.E. and RICKS, D.F. *Mood and personality*. New York: Holt, Rinehart & Winston, 1966.

ZAJONC, R.B. Compresence. In P.B. Paulus (ed.), *Psychology of group influence*. Hillsdale; NY.: Lawrence Erlbaum, 1980.

Notes

1. This categorization corresponds to the two-dimensional structure of mood (pleasantness and arousal) often found in empirical studies (cf. Watson and Tellegen, 1985).

Acknowledgement

I want to thank Gernot Filipp for his patient assistance in organizing and analysing highly complex and heterogeneous data sets. To Franz Auinger and Erich Kirchler I am indebted for the permission to include their TSD-data into the present analysis.

10

The situational and personal correlates of happiness: a cross-national comparison

MIHALY CSIKSZENTMIHALYI and MARIA MEI-HA WONG

Introduction

In this paper, we shall compare a group of high school students from the US and from Italy, when answering the following questions bearing on the issue of happiness. First, does happiness have the same phenomenological meaning in the two cultures? Second, are external conditions—the kind of activities pursued, the type of companions present—related in the same way to moment-by-moment fluctuations of happiness in the two groups? Third, does the perception of the ratio of challenges and skills have the same effect on happiness in the two groups? Fourth, are there differences between happy and less happy individuals in the choice of situations (i.e. types of activities and companions) and in subjective interpretatons of experience (i.e. degree of perceived choice, and perception of the challenges and personal skills in daily activities)?

The measurement of happiness

There are two main ways to conceive of happiness. The first one is as a personal **trait**, or relatively permanent disposition to experience well-being regardless of external conditions. The second is to consider it a **state**, or a transitory subjective experience responsive to momentary events or conditions in the environment (cf. Diener *et. al.*, Chapter 7; Schwarz and Strack, Chapter 3; Veenhoven, Chapter 2 for related discussions). Presumably these two aspects are related. One would expect, for instance, that the frequency or intensity of momentary experiences of happiness would add over time to a global trait-like tendency; or conversely, that a happy person will have more frequent and intense momentary experiences of happiness.

Our way of operationalizing happiness attempts to capture both the trait-like and the state-like dimensions of the concept. The measure is based on repeated self-reports of happiness that each respondent provides eight times each day, whenever signalled by an electronic pager, for one week. Thus each respondent provides a record of about forty moments in which experience could vary from "very sad" to "very happy" on a 7–point Likert scale. This has been known as the Experience Sampling Method, or ESM (Csikszentmihalyi, Larson and Prescott, 1977; Csikszentmihalyi and Larson, 1987), and will be discussed again in another section.

In order to measure happiness as a state, individual differences in response style can be eliminated by standardizing responses according to individual means. Thus, "0" represents the average level of happiness for each person throughout the week, "1" represents a score one standard deviation above that average, and "—1" a score one standard deviation below. Factors that lead to deviations above or below the mean level of happiness can then be examined.

In addition, the weekly record for each person can be added up and these raw scores can be averaged, thus providing a trait-like measure of happiness. The person whose average score is higher than another's will be considered to be generally more happy.

Happiness and subjective well-being

No matter how one is to measure subjective well-being, happiness is sure to be an important component of it (Argyle, 1987; Csikszentmihalyi and Csikszentmihalyi, 1988). In previous studies with US respondents, a subjective attribution of happiness is always at the centre of a positive affect factor which includes such other variables as cheerful, sociable, and friendly. The intercorrelation of these dimensions in thousands of self-reports varies between .5 and .7. Another factor included in the concept of optimal experience or subjective well-being is potency, which consists of the variables active, alert, strong, and excited; these typically correlate with happiness in the range of .3 to .5. Finally we also include in our measures of subjective well-being positive motivation and cognitive efficiency; variables measuring these dimensions correlate with happiness in the range between .1 and .4 (Csikszentmihalyi and Larson, 1984, 1987; Larson and Csikszentmihalyi, 1983; Csikszentmihalyi et. al., 1977).

Previous ESM studies have shown that of all the dimensions of subjective well-being the affective one is most trait-like, and least influenced by variations in environmental conditions, or the kind of activities people engage in. Typically, one finds that for potency about 20 per cent of the variance in responses is explained by the person, and 10 per cent by the activity; for motivation the proportion of variance explained by the person is about 15 per cent, and 10 per cent by the activity, for cognitive efficiency the respective proportions are in the order of 30 and 5. For such affect variables as friendly, cheerful, and happy, however, the person accounts for 30 per cent, and the activity only between 2 and 8 per cent of the variance. The interaction between persons and situations generally explains an additional 10 to 20 per cent of the variance in these subjective well-being responses (Graef, 1978).

If one were to choose a single measure of subjective well-being, happiness would be a likely candidate, both because everyone seems to understand what the concept means, and because conceptually as well as empirically it perhaps represents the broader concept best.

The conditions of happiness

A great number of situational factors have been identified as either elevating or depressing happiness. For example, most investigators find a modest positive relationship between happiness on the one hand, and financial affluence and political stability on the other (Argyle, 1987). Several investigators have stressed that happiness depends on how small a gap there is between what a person hopes to achieve, and what he or she is actually achieving (e.g. Michalos, 1985). Being with other people typically improves the quality of experience, while being alone makes most people sad (Argyle, 1987; Csikszentmihalyi and Larson, 1984; Lewinsohn, Sullivan and Grosscup, 1982). Schwarz and Clore (1983) found that the overall quality of subjective well-being can be elevated by such ephemeral means as noticing that the weather is pleasant, or that one's favourite sports team has won a game (Schwarz, Strack, Kommer and Wagner, 1987; cf. Schwarz and Strack, Chapter 3).

In the present paper, we shall look at the relationship between happiness and two conditions of everyday life. The first concerns what the person is doing at the moment of the signal. Whether a person is watching TV, or playing with a friend, or studying for school, is expected to have a strong relationship with the level of happiness. The other condition is companionship: whether a person is alone, with friends, or with family should affect the level of happiness.

It is our belief that external events do not improve happiness directly, but only if they are mediated through an interpretive framework that assigns positive value to the event. However, it is still very important to know whether certain conditions are typically interpreted as conducive to happiness, and whether there is consensus across cultures about what these conditions are.

Happiness and flow

Aristotle believed that happiness was the result of the "virtuous activity of the soul". We agree with this aetiology to the extent that the proximal cause of happiness must also be a psychological state. External conditions like health, wealth, love or good fortune can help bring it about, but only if they are mediated by an appropriate subjective evaluation that labels the external conditions as conducive to happiness.

In our work we have come to the conclusion that a very important dimension of evaluation that contributes to the experience of happiness is the persons' preception of the extent to which their capacities to act (or skills) correspond to the available opportunities for action (or challenges). When skills are perceived to be greater than challenges, people tend to feel bored. When challenges are seen as being higher than skills, they tend to feel anxious. When both challenges and skills are low, the person tends to feel apathetic. It is when high challenges are perceived to be matched with high skills—a subjective condition we have come to call flow—that a person experiences the highest levels of well-being (Csikszentmihalyi, 1975, 1982; Csikszentmihalyi and Csikszentmihalyi, 1988; Csikszentmihalyi and Nakamura, 1989; Massimini, Csikszentmihalyi and Carli, 1987; Massimini and Inghilleri, 1986).

Some critics have objected that this view of well-being mediated by high challenges and skills reveals a typically "American" bias founded on pragmatic, competitive cultural values. According to these critics, in other cultures one would not find happiness associated with high challenges and high skills. Recent studies with samples from Asian and European cultures (Carli, 1986; Massimini *et. al.*, 1987; Massimini, Csikszentmihalyi and Delle Fave, 1988), however, support the notion that flow is a universally prized subjective state.

Differences between happy and less happy individuals: external events and subjective interpretation

Do happy people do things differently when compared to less happy individuals? People may consistently have a positive mood either because they choose certain kinds of situations that make them happy or because they interpret situations in a way that induce happiness (Argyle, 1987). It has been shown that individuals seek to get involved in situations that are consistent with their personality traits. For instance, extraverts are more likely than introverts to seek social situations in their free time and people who are high in need for order spend less time in novel situations than those who are not (Diener, Larsen and Emmons, 1984). A question that follows is: do happy people choose certain activities and companions that make them happy, avoid those that make them sad? Previous studies found that happy people are also sociable (Costa, McRae and Norris, 1981; Headey and Wearing, 1986) and have better relationships with others when compared to unhappy people (Wessman and Ricks, 1966). However, it is still unclear whether happy people actually spend more time with friends and in socializing activities. Or conversely, whether they spend less time alone and in solitary activities such as reading and thinking. We shall address these questions in this paper.

On the other hand, there is some evidence that happy people perceive life experiences in a way that sustains their positive mood. For instance, happy individuals also score high on measures of internality, i.e. a tendency to attribute outcomes to oneself rather than to external causes (Baker, 1977; Brandt, 1980; Sundre, 1978). Happy people perceive a high degree of control and tend to believe that they have choice in their activities (Eisenberg, 1981; Knippa, 1979; Morganti, Nehrke and Hulicka, 1980; Reid and Ziegler, 1980). But as Diener (1984) has pointed out, the direction of causality between happiness and these perceptions is not clear. It is possible that people with external locus of control have to confront unfortunate life events that also make them unhappy. In this report we would examine whether it is more likely for happy individuals to perceive their activities as voluntary and if it is, whether the relationship is the same in both the US and Italian samples.

Earlier we discussed the relationship between happiness and flow. If the perceptions of high challenge and high skill are indeed conducive to happiness, a question that follows is whether it is more probable for happy individuals to interpret their activities and personal skills that way. Specifically, we would examine whether happy individuals have different perceptions of the relationship between challenges and skills in their daily activities, for instance, do they have more flow experience and spend less time being apathetic, worried and bored?

Method

Subjects

The US sample was selected from two large suburban high schools in Chicago. Teachers were asked to nominate freshmen and sophomore students (mostly between fourteen and sixteen years old) who were talented in one or more of the following areas: mathematics, science, music, sports and art. 395 students were nominated and invited to participate. 208 students (92 males, 116 females) completed the study.

The Italian sample was collected by Professor Fausto Massimini and Dr Antonella Delle Fave at the University of Milan (Massimini and Inghilleri, 1986), and consisted of forty-seven students (14 males, 33 females), between sixteen and eighteen years of age, from a classical lyceum in Milan, Italy.

Students from both samples had similar, mostly middle class backgrounds. There were two main differences between the samples other than cultural background. First, the Italian sample was almost two years older on the average than the US counterpart. Second, the Italian lyceum is more academically oriented and selective compared to typical American high schools. However, the US students came from a very good school and were nominated for outstanding achievement, and thus were as comparable to the Italians as possible.

Data

The data were collected with the ESM (Csikszentmihalyi, *et. al.*, 1977; Larson and Csikszentimihalyi, 1983; Csikszentmihalyi and Larson, 1987), which allows repeated measurement of activities, thoughts, and feelings in natural environments. Respondents were asked to carry an electronic pager for one week. Whenever they were signalled, they filled out one of the Experience Sampling Forms (ESF). Each respondent received seven to eight random signals daily, in two-hour intervals. Signals were sent between 7 a.m. and 10 a.m. on weekdays, 9 a.m. and 12 noon at the weekend. The US teenagers filled out a total of 7672 valid responses (or an average of thirty-seven); the Italians gave a total of 1729 responses, for an average of thirty-seven each.

The ESF consists of openended questions about what the person was thinking of when the pager signalled, where he or she was, what he or she was doing, and of a number of Likert scales measuring different dimensions of subjective experience: affect (happy, cheerful, sociable), potency (alert, strong, active, excited), cognitive efficiency (concentration, ease of concentration, self-consciousness, clear), and motivation (wish to do the activity, control, feeling involved). The openended questions were coded with an inter-rater reliability of 90–95 per cent.

Procedure

Respondents in both samples participated on a voluntary basis. Before beginning the experience sampling procedure, they received instructions on the use of the electronic pager. Questions in the ESF were explained. They were asked to fill out a sample page of the ESF so that they could discuss their questions with the research staff. The ESF, which were bound in small daily pads (5.5 inches × 8.5 inches; each pad had about fifteen self-report forms) were then given to the respondents. They were encouraged to carry the pager and booklets with them whenever possible for one week and to fill out the ESF immediately after receiving the signals. A phone number was given where staff members could be reached to answer questions and discuss possible complications. Subjects were "debriefed" after one week and the ESF booklets were collected.

Coding

Happiness

The experience sampling method provided repeated self-reports of happiness from each respondent in different situations. Happiness was rated on a 7–point Likert scale ("sad" to "happy" for the US sample, "triste" to "contento" for the Italians). In this paper, happiness is treated both as a state and a trait. To examine happiness as a state, ratings of each respondent were standardized by his or her mean level of happiness. This procedure eliminated individual differences (e.g. response style, personality) and made it possible to compare fluctuations from the individual's mean across persons and groups.

To study happiness as a trait, the weekly record for each person was added up and the raw scores were averaged. We divided the respondents into two groups based on a median split. (Different medians were used to categorize the US and the Italian groups.) Those individuals with an average score higher than the median were considered more happy than those with an average score below the median.

Activity and companionship

What the person was doing at the moment of the signal was indicated by the response ot the question, "what was the main thing you were doing?" Activities were first coded in 154 detailed codes that were collapsed into fourteen major activity categories. These included four major types of activities: productive (class and studying), structured leisure (sports and games, art and hobbies, reading, and thinking), unstructured leisure (socializing, watching TV, listening to music), and maintenance (eating, personal care, transportation, chores and errands, resting and napping).

Social context was indicated by the question, "who were you with?" The choices given in the ESF included: alone, mother, father, sister(s), brother(s), male/female friend(s), strangers and others. For the purpose of this paper, only three types of companions were analysed: alone, family, and friends.

Flow and the eight channels of experience

On each experience sampling form, subjects were asked to indicate the challenges of the activity and their skills in it at the moment they were signalled. These responses were then standardized by individual means of challenge and skill. Thus each standardized z scores of challenge and skill would have a mean "0" and a standard deviation of "1". Eight combinations representing eight different ratios of the standardized challenge and skill scores can be obtained:

Channel one: arousal	High challenges and average skills
Channel two: flow	High challenges and high skills
Channel three: control	Average challenges and high skills
Channel four: boredom	Low challenges and high skills
Channel five: relaxation	Low challenges and average skills
Channel six: apathy	Low challenges and low skills
Channel seven: worry	Average challenges and low skills
Channel eight: anxiety	High challenges and low skills

Quality of experience

Several other experiential variables were measured by 7–point Likert scale items: alert-drowsy, active-passive, strong-weak, excited-bored, involved-detached, and clear-confused. Other variables such as concentration ("how well were you concentrating?"), unselfconsciousness ("how self-conscious were you?"; responses were recorded so that a high value implied not at all self-conscious), not wishing to do the activity ("do you wish you had been doing something else?"; responses were recorded so that a high value indicated a positive motivation), control ("were you in control of the situation?"), satisfaction about performance ("were you satisfied with how you were doing?") were measured by a 10–point scale ranging from "not at all" to "very much".

Perceived choice

Whether the respondent perceived the activity as an obligation, a voluntary decision, or something done in order to "kill time", was indicated by the question "why were you doing the particular activity? " Three choices were given: "I had to", "I wanted to do it", "I had nothing else to do". Respondents could select more than one choice if relevant.

Results

The correlations of happiness and other dimensions of experience

Despite linguistic differences which are bound to change slightly the meaning of the terms denoting the various dimensions of experience, the correlations of happiness and other quality of experience variables were very similar for both the US and Italian respondents (see Table 10.1). These

TABLE 10.1. *Correlation of "happy-sad" (contento-triste) and other variables*[a]

	N	Americans	N	Italians
Cheerful-irritable	7069	.69***	1722	.72***
(Allegro-irritabile)				
Sociable-lonely	7047	.50***	1722	.50***
(Socievole-Isolato)				
Alert-drowsy	7091	.47***	1729	.26***
(Ben sveglio-sonnolento)				
Active-passive	7047	.42***	1728	.40***
(Attivo-passivo)				
Strong-weak	7050	.46***	1723	.45***
(Forte-debole)				
Excited-bored	7042	.52***	1729	.48***
(Eccitato-annoiato)				
Concentration	7072	.11***	1726	.06*
(Eri ben concentrato?)				
Ease of concentration	7068	.16***	1634	.14***
(Era difficile concentrarsi?)				
Un-selfconsciousness	7035	.07***	1719	.14***
(Ti sentivi imbarazzato?)				
Clear-confused	7003	.42***	1727	.45***
(Con le idee chiare-confuso)				
Wishing to do something else	6989	.29***	1727	.24***
(Avresti preferito far qualcosa d'altro?)				
Involved-detached	7028	.43***	1721	.33***
(Coinvolto-distaccato)				
Control	7018	.28***	1721	.31***
(Ti sentivi in controllo?)				
Satisfied about performance	6918	.28***	1721	.55***
(Ti sentivi soddisfatto di te stesso?)				
Open-closed	7019	.47***	1718	.56***
(Aperto-chiuso)				
Tense-relaxed	7055	−.28***	1729	−.41***
(Ansioso/teso-rilassato)				

Significance of correlation coefficients (2-tailed): * $p < .05$. ** $p < .01$. *** $p < .001$.
[a] The coefficients represent correlations between the positive ends of each item (i.e. happy with cheerful etc.). On the ESF, positive and negative ends alternated (i.e. cheerful, lonely, alert, passive etc.).

results were also extremely similar to a previous study on US adolescents conducted about a decade earlier (Csikszentmihalyi and Larson, 1984). Happiness was very highly correlated (.50 to .72) with two other affect variables: cheerfulness and sociability. Potency and activation variables such as alertness, activeness, strength and excitement were also highly correlated (.26 to .52) with happiness for both groups. When they felt happy, respondents also related actively to themselves or the environment, feeling alert, strong and excited about what they were thinking or doing. There was a moderate correlation (.24 to .43) between happiness and motivation variables: not wishing to do something else, feeling involved and in control of the situation. When one strongly wishes to do something else and feels detached from the situation at hand, mood is bound to be negatively affected.

Happiness was least related (.07 to .16) to cognitive efficiency variables such as level of concentration, ease of concentration, and lack of self-consciousness. In other words, teenagers in this study did not necessarily feel happy when their attention was highly focused and under their control. Activities that usually require high concentration are mainly productive work (Csikszentmihalyi and Larson, 1984). Studying and attending classes are something that the adolescents have to do rather than something they freely choose. So they are often not happy even though they are able to utilize their mental energy efficiently.

Although the pattern of correlations was extremely similar, the US and Italian groups differed significantly from each other in the strength of the correlations on five variables. When compared to Italian respondents, happiness correlated more with alertness (Fisher $z=7.77$, $p<.001$), and involvement (Fisher $z=3.77$, $p<.001$) among US teenagers. On the other hand, the correlation between happiness and satisfaction with performance (Fisher $z=$—8.52, $p<.001$), open (Fisher $z=-3.33$, $p<.001$), and tense (Fisher $z=4.82$, $p<.001$), was stronger for the Italian students.

The general level of happiness

In general, US (mean=4.85, $N=7672$) respondents rated themselves happier than their Italian (mean=4.55, $N=1729$) counterparts. The absolute difference, though small, was statistically very significant ($t(9399)=8.20$, $p<.0001$). This finding is consistent with past studies assessing subjective ratings of happiness in different countries. For instance, Italians reported the lowest ratings of happiness and satisfaction when compared to seven other European countries (Euro-Barometre, 1983). In another study (Easterlin, 1974), data from fourteen countries showed that Americans reported the highest personal happiness scores.

It is impossible to tell whether these differences reflect a real difference in the quality of experience, in its evaluation, or in its reporting. Italians and Americans may feel equally happy, but cultural values favouring optimism in self-expression may have inflated the US students' self-reports. In any case, as we have seen in the previous section, happiness has an almost identical meaning in the two groups, as shown by the pattern of correlations, despite semantic and other cultural differences.

How much is happiness influenced by what people are doing, and is the relationship between activity and happiness different in the two cultures? These are the next set of questions to which we shall now turn.

Activities and happiness

Different types of activity have a significant effect on happiness for both the US ($F(13,6586)=18.81$, $p<.001$) and Italian groups ($F(13,1639)=6.20$, $p<.001$). The comparison of happiness in different activities, as shown in

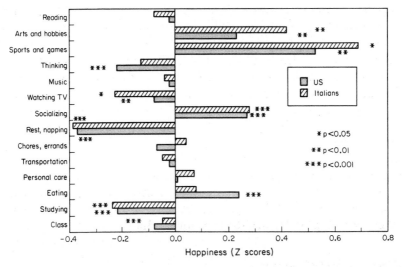

Fig. 10.1. Happiness levels of US and Italian teenagers in major activities.
Note: p values refer to differences from the mean of 0

Figure 10.1, indicated that the relationship between types of activities and happiness was very similar in the two samples. For both groups, the highest levels of happiness were reported when respondents were involved in "sports and games", "socializing", "eating", and "art and hobbies". Three of these activities involve freely chosen leisure, and one concerns homeostatic maintenance. Socializing and eating are similar to the extent that they both require very little mental effort but provide immediate satisfaction, whether emotional or physiological. Sports and art, on the other hand, require active participation. Like productive activities, they have clear rules and goals. To fully enjoy them, one needs to invest time and energy to develop relevant skills. It is comforting to know that young people do not feel happy only when involved in "mindless" and unstructured activities.

The activities with the lowest scores of happiness were again very similar for both US and Italian teenagers. Both groups reported feeling most unhappy when they were "resting or napping", "studying", "thinking" and "watching TV". US students were also as unhappy when involved in classroom activities as when they were watching TV; whereas this was not true for the Italians. It is important to notice that leisure activities do not necessarily elevate happiness. People usually watch television when they have nothing better to do (Csikszentmihalyi and Kubey, 1981) and they are also likely to feel apathetic during the process (Kubey and Csikszentmihalyi, in press).

Studying was not a happy experience for either group. This is not surprising, given that students have to forgo immediate pleasure in order to get long term rewards, e.g. passing a test or answering teachers' questions in class. Studying is seldom a self-initiated activity but is usually imposed by some external demands. In this sense, it is very different from structured leisure activities such as sports and art.

Thinking was a negative experience for both groups, although much more for the Americans than the Italians. Previous studies (Csikszentmihalyi and Larson, 1984) found that adolescents reported "thinking" as a primary activity when they were struggling with personal problems or concerns. Seeking solutions to problematic issues involves uncertainty and often produces tension and anxiety. Resting or napping had the lowest scores of happiness. These responses probably indicate that respondents were annoyed when the electronic pager disturbed them while they were resting.

The activities that did not either elevate or depress happiness were mainly maintenance activities: personal care, transportation, chores and errands. Listening to music and reading, though typically self-initiated, did not elevate happiness probably because teenagers do them primarily to "kill" time (Csikszentmihalyi et. al., 1977; Csikszentmihalyi and Larson, 1984).

Companions and happiness

Is happiness influenced by who one is with? The pattern of happiness as a function of companionship is again very similar in the two cultures (US: $F(2, 4791)=93.38$, $p<.0001$; Italians: $F(2,1281)=30.59$, $p<.0001$, also see Figure 10.2). Respondents felt happiest while with friends and worst being alone. When they were with family members, level of happiness was close to the average.

Adolescence is a time when teenagers begin to explore the world outside the family and establish new relationships. They enjoy being with friends and spend a great deal of time with them (e.g. Jersild, Brook and Brook, 1978). With friends even daily routine activities become enjoyable (Csikszentmihalyi and Larson, 1984). Friends provide material as well as emotional support, which alleviate unnecessary stress and suppress negative emotions. They increase self-esteem by giving positive feedback or simply by expressing similar beliefs. They can also serve as companions in enjoyable activities because friends usually share common interests (Argyle, 1987).

On the other hand, being alone is usually quite difficult for adolescents. Without the stimulation of companions, attention is "forced" to focus on one's feelings, needs, and goals. Instead of responding to the environment and getting feedback, one has to decide what to do. This is a potentially

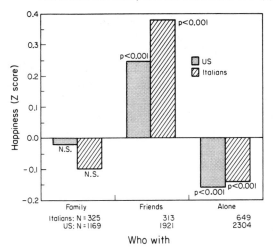

Fig. 10.2. Average happiness of US and Italian teenagers in three different social contexts.

anxiety provoking situation. It is therefore not surprising that all respondents reported the lowest happiness scores in solitude. In fact, being alone is a negative experience also for adults. Lonely people are more likely to be emotionally disturbed (Argyle, 1987), and loneliness is one of the most threatening conditions throughout life (Peplau and Perlman, 1982).

Being with family did not seem to have a significant effect on happiness. Previous studies have shown that interactions with family members can be as enjoyable as that of friends (Csikszentmihalyi and Larson, 1984). However, living under the same roof also brings along conflict. Fights with parents or siblings can be a source of anger and distress. These factors may level off the average ratings of happiness with the family. Besides, home is the place where most of the maintenance activities (e.g. doing the dishes, cutting grass, helping parents to clean the car) and passive leisure activities (e.g. watching TV, listening to music) are carried out. As mentioned before, these activities are not conducive to happiness.

Flow experience and happiness

The flow model (Csikszentmihalyi, 1975; Csikszentmihalyi and Csikszentmihalyi, 1988) suggests that the level of perceived challenge and personal skills lead to optimal experience. Table 10.2 shows mean z scores of happiness in the different channels, defined by the ratio of challenge and skills. These channels have a significant relation to happiness for both groups (US: $F(7,6717)=14.96$, $p<.001$; Italians: $F(7,1698)=15.29$, $p<.001$). All respondents experienced the highest level of happiness while in flow (Channel 2), i.e. when the opportunities for actions in the environment matched personal abilities and both were above the respondents' average for the week. An *a priori* contrast testing happiness scores in channel two versus all other channels combined was significant for both groups (US: $t(6717)=5.80$, $p<.001$; Italians: $t(1698)=6.78$, $p<.001$). American students were least happy when they were anxious, while Italian students reported being least happy when they were worried. In other words, respondents felt most sad when challenges were relatively high with respect to personal skills.

TABLE 10.2. *Z-scores of happiness in different channels*

	N	Americans	N	Italians
Channel 1: Arousal	938	—.05*	205	.14
Channel 2: Flow	904	.16***	348	.33*
Channel 3: Control	457	.08*	118	.15
Channel 4: Boredom	1671	.10***	278	.04
Channel 5: Relaxation	516	.00	155	—.01
Channel 6: Apathy	973	—.10***	336	.31*
Channel 7: Worry	542	—.14***	145	—.36**
Channel 8: Anxiety	724	—.21***	121	—.11

Significance of difference from zero: *$p<.05$. **$p<.01$. *** $p<.001$.

Joint effects of channels and activities on happiness

Considering these results together, one wonders whether the opportunity to match actions and personal abilities affects subjective ratings of happiness regardless of what one does and who one is with? Or do the challenge/skill channels interact with types of activities and companions? Analyses of variance with activities and channels as factors were performed separately for the Americans and Italians to answer these questions. To simplify the analysis, activities were grouped into five categories: productive, structured leisure, unstructured leisure, maintenance, and other.

The results showed that types of activity, as well as channels, were both important factors that affect one's happiness. For the American group, the main effects of activity ($F(4,6685)=15.35$, $p<.001$), channel ($F(7,6685)=12.99$, $p<.001$), and their interaction effect ($F(28,6685)=5.89$, $p<.001$) all reached significance. Happiness was highest in structured leisure, followed by unstructured leisure, maintenance and productive activities. Except in productive activities, happiness was highest in the flow channel. A priori contrasts testing the difference between this channel and the rest were significant in structured leisure ($t(577)=3.70$, $p<.001$) and unstructured leisure ($t(1922)=3.30$, $p<.001$), but not in maintenance. When involved in productive work, US teenagers reported the highest happiness in the boredom channel, followed by the flow channel. A posteriori contrasts testing the two channels versus all others showed that scores in these channels were significantly different from others ($t(2188)=5.77$, $p<.001$); differ- ences between the two also reached statistical significance ($t(2188)=2.77$, $p<.01$). This suggests that when involved in productive work, American students were quite happy in high challenge/high skill situations, but were even happier when skills exceeded challenges by a wide margin. A strong achievement orientation in the US may have led teenagers to enjoy such situations, because they ensure academic success.

Similar results were found in the Italian group. Again, the main effects of activity ($F(4,1666)=5.76$, $p<.001$), and channel ($F(7,1666)=15.2$, $p<.001$) were significant. However, their interaction ($F(28,1666)=1.03$, n.s.) was not. Students were happiest while doing structured leisure, followed by unstructured leisure, maintenance and productive activities. A priori con- trasts showed that happiness in the flow channel was highest and significantly different from others in all types of activities (unstructured leisure: $t(574)=5.60$, $p<.001$; maintenance: $t(367)=3.69$, $p<.001$; productive: $t(521)=2.96$, $p<.01$) except in structured leisure, where the relaxation chan- nel had the highest scores, followed by the flow channel. A posteriori con- trasts showed that happiness ratings in these two channels were not significantly different from one another.

Joint effect of companions and channels on happiness

Types of companions and channel also jointly affect happiness. For the US students, the main effects of companion ($F(3,6693)=63.51$, $p<.001$), and channel ($F(7,6693)=16.04$, $p<.001$) were highly significant. No interaction effect was found. Happiness was highest in the flow channel both when students were with friends and when they were alone. A priori contrasts found that scores of happiness in this channel were significantly higher than the rest (friends: $t(1653)=2.54$, $p<.05$; alone: $t(1819)=3.47$, $p<.001$). When teenagers were with family, happiness ratings were highest in the relaxation channel and positive also in the flow, control, and boredom chan- nels. The ratings in these channels were very similar to one another and a posteriori contrasts showed that they were significantly different from the rest ($t(1086)=4.61$, $p<.001$).

Similar results were observed in the Italian group. The main effects of companions ($F(3,1674)=19.34$, $p<.001$) and channel ($F(7,1674)=14.65$, $p<.001$) were significant while their interaction was not. A priori contrasts again suggested that happiness ratings in the flow channel were significantly higher than the rest when students were with friends ($t(304)=2.34$, $p<.05$) and when they were alone ($t(632)=4.73$, $p<.001$). When they were with family, students were also most happy in the flow channel. However, there is no significant difference in the *a priori* contrast comparing this channel with others. Except for the apathy and worry channels, happiness ratings in all other channels were very similar to the flow channel.

These results suggest that level of challenge and skill did not have an important effect on happiness when students were with their family. As mentioned before, this is probably due to the routine activities and inter-actions (e.g. passive leisure such as watching TV, maintenance activities such as having dinner together and doing the chores, etc.) that are usually carried out with family members. The functions of most of these activities are primarily relaxation and homeostatic maintenance, which are something that the teenagers do to satisfy physiological needs. They may be enjoyable but not at all challenging.

On the other hand, all respondents reported feeling most happy in the flow channel when they were with friends and when they were alone. Hap-piness ratings in this channel were more distinctly different from others when teenagers were alone than when they were with friends. The oppor-tunity to be involved in situations when challenge and skills are both high seem to be particularly salient in solitude. When there is a lack of stimulation from the external environment, the possibility of obtaining satisfaction from the task one is engaged in becomes more important.

Differences between happy and less happy teenagers

All of the analyses we discussed above treated happiness as a state. In this section, happiness is considered as a trait and a different set of questions is addressed. As the ESM made possible the repeated measurement of an individual's happiness for one week, the ratings were averaged to obtain a trait-like measure of happiness. Respondents were regarded as more happy if their scores were above the median, less happy if their scores were equal or below (US median = 4.83; Italian median = 4.46). The following ques-tions were examined here: do happy students and less happy students engage in different activities, spend their time with different companions, and have different perceptions of challenge and personal skills?

For the US group, there was no significant difference between the low and high happy group in the percentage of time spent doing different activit-ies. A similar pattern was found in the Italian group, except for one compari-son—happier Italian students spent less time studying $(t)45)=2.35, p<.05)$. Again, no significant difference was observed for either the US or the Italian students in terms of the proportion of time spent with different companions. In other words, happy students spent similar amounts of time in different activities and with different companions when compared with their less happy counterparts. This does not contradict the findings in previous sec-tions, namely, types of activities and companions had a substantial effect on happiness ratings for all respondents. Happy students were happier than others probably not because they chose or avoided certain situations, but simply because they were happier in every situation. What factors may account for this difference?

Table 10.3 shows differences in the percentage of time spent in different channels. Happy US students spent more time in the arousal channel when compared with their less happy counterparts ($t(187.39)=-2.65$, $p<.01$). Happy Italian students, on the other hand, reported more time in the flow channel when compared to less happy ones ($t(45)=-3.61$, $p<.001$) but less time in the arousal channel ($t(45)=3.28$, $p<.01$). In other words, happy individuals appeared to enjoy situations in which perceived challenge was relatively high, and personal skills were at least, moderately high.

When students were asked to indicate whether they perceived an activity as an obligation, a voluntary decision or something done because they had nothing to do, happy students perceived more choice in their actions than others. Happy US teenagers reported feeling that they wanted to do a particular activity 37.65 per cent of their time. The figure for less happy US students was 32.03 per cent ($t(206)=2.70$, $p<.01$). Happy Italian students reported feeling that their actions were voluntary 54.24 per cent of their time. The figure for less happy Italians was 44.91 per cent ($t(45)=1.95$, $p=.058$).

TABLE 10.3. *Percentage of time in different channels*

Happy N	Americans		Italians	
	Low (104)	High (104)	Low (24)	High (23)
Productive				
Channel One	11.98%	14.64%**	14.99%	9.24%**
Channel Two	13.46%	13.95%	15.12%	25.83%***
Channel Three	7.38%	5.66%	7.20%	6.06%
Channel Four	22.59%	24.44%	19.16%	13.92%
Channel Five	7.75%	7.23%	8.67%	9.48%
Channel Six	14.28%	14.16%	20.05%	19.18%
Channel Seven	8.15%	7.51%	9.03%	8.14%
Channel Eight	11.13%	9.89%	5.78%	8.17%

Significance of difference between the low and high groups within each sample: * $p<.05$. **$p<.01$. *** $p<.001$.

In general, there was not much difference in daily activities between happy and less happy individuals in either the US or the Italian groups. The main difference concerned the way they perceived their environment— happy students were more likely to feel they made voluntary decisions, and that the tasks they engaged in were challenging and their skills were ample enough or just a little below the requirement of those tasks.

Conclusion

The objectives of this paper were to find out the cross-national differences in the meaning of happiness, the external conditions that lead to happiness, the perception of challenges and skills that affect happiness, and the characteristics that differentiate happy and less happy individuals. The comparisons of the US and Italian teenagers regarding these issues have shown more similarities than differences. Happiness relates to other dimensions of experience similarly for both groups. Despite semantic differences, happiness was strongly correlated with other affect and potency variables, moderately correlated with motivation variables and least correlated with cognitive efficiency variables. This may reveal, as some people believe, the "transcultural characteristics of a generic human mind" (Spiro, 1984, p. 334). However, it is also possible that the relationships between different dimensions of experience simply reflect, as some argue, social practices and forms of understanding in these two cultures (e.g. Rosaldo, 1984).

The types of activities and companions that elevate or depress happiness are also the same for both US and Italian teenagers. They felt most happy in structured leisure such as "sports and games" and least happy in productive activities such as "studying for an exam". They enjoyed being with friends most and did not like to be alone. A precise understanding of how the environment affects happiness can allow parents and educators to plan better and predict teenagers' involvement with different facets of their lives. For instance, it may be possible to make better use of time spent with friends for productive ends. If the environment of the school were to utilize the enjoyment of friendship for the purpose of learning, the educational process might become much more happy and intrinsically motivated. Another possibility may be to emphasize the similarities between productive work and structured leisure (both being structured activities with clear rules and goals, and both requiring discipline to develop necessary skills), and to structure school work in a more enjoyable way.

The perception of high challenge and high skill was conducive to happiness for both US and Italian teenagers. This confirms the results of previous studies (Carli, 1986; Delle Fave and Massimini, 1988; Massimini *et. al.*, 1987) showing that flow is a universally valued subjective state.

In both the US and the Italian groups, happy individuals did not spend their time differently when compared to less happy ones. However, they perceived activities as highly challenging and their skills as relatively high. They also seemed to experience more choice in their actions. What accounts for these differences in perception is less clear. Are happy adolescents more capable of detecting certain characteristics of the environment that elevate happiness or are they ignoring certain characteristics that depress happiness? Is it possible that they integrate new experience more quickly with their goals, thus enabling them to perceive activities as more meaningful, challenging, and voluntary? How do they develop such perception? Is it something inborn or is it something that can be learned from experience?

Many resources are used nowadays to help people increase happiness. It is believed that people can be made more happy by involving them in certain activities and staying with enjoyable companions. The rationale for such practice has found some support in this paper. However, doing so may only have a short term effect on subjective states. The analysis of differences in perception between happy and less happy individuals suggests that in the long run, seeking high challenges in the environment and developing necessary skills to deal with them may be more important. Continual growth and development is a slow but also a more reliable way to bring about subjective well-being.

References

ARGYLE, M.*The psychology of happiness*. New York: Methuen, 1987.

BAKER, E. K. Relationship of retirement and satisfaction with life events to locus-of-control (Doctoral dissertation, University of Wisconsin-Madison, 1976). *Dissertation Abstracts International*, **37**, 4748B. (University Microfilms No. 76–28900), 1977.

BRANDT, A. S. Relationship of locus of control, environmental constraint, length of time in the institution and twenty-one other variables to morale and life satisfaction in the institutionalized elderly (Doctoral dissertation, Texas Woman's University, 1979). *Dissertation Abstracts International*, **40**, 5802B. (University Microfilms No. 80–12153), 1980.

CARLI, M. Selezione psicologica e qualita dell'esperienza. In F. Massimini and P. Inghilleri (eds.), *L'esperienza quotidiana*. Milan: Franco Angeli, 1986.

COSTA, P.T., McRAE, R.R. and NORRIS, A.H. Personal adjustment to aging: Longitudinal prediction from neuroticism and extraversion. *Journal of Gerontoloy*, 1981; **36**, 78–85.

CSIKSZENTMIHALYI, M. *Beyond boredom and anxiety*. San Franciso: Jossey-Bass, 1975.

CSIKSZENTMIHALYI, M.Towards a psychology of optimal experience. In L. Wheeler (ed.), *Review of personality and social psychology* (Vol. 2). Beverly Hills, CA.: Sage, 1982.

CSIKSZENTMIHALYI, M. and CSIKSZENTMIHALYI, I. S. *Optimal experience: Psychological studies of flow in consciousness*. New York: Cambridge University Press, 1988.

CSIKSZENTMIHALYI, M. and KUBEY, R. Television and the rest of life. *Public Opinion Quarterly*, 1981; **45**, 317–328.

CSIKSZENTMIHALYI, M. and LARSON, R. *Being adolescent: Conflict and growth in the teenage year*. New York: Basic Books, 1984.

CSIKSZENTMIHALYI, M. and LARSON, R. Validity and reliability of the Experience Sampling Method. *The Journal of Nervous and Mental Diseases*, 1987; **175**(9), 526–536.

CSIKSZENTMIHALYI, M., LARSON, R. and PRESCOTT, S. The ecology of adolescent activity and experience. *The Journal of Youth and Adolescence*, 1977; **6**, 281–294.

CSIKSZENTMIHALYI, M. and NAKAMURA, J. The dynamics of intrinsic motivation. In R. Ames and C. Ames (eds.), *Handbook of motivation theory and research* (Vol. 3): *Goals and cognition*. New York: Academic Press, 1989.

DELLE FAVE, A. and MASSIMINI, F. Modernization and the changing contexts of flow in work and leisure. In M. Csikszentmihalyi and I. S. Csikszentmihalyi (eds.), *Optimal experience: Psychological studies of flow in consciousness*. New York: Cambridge University Press, 1988.

DIENER, E. Subjective well-being. *Psychological Bulletin*, 1984; **95**, 542–575.

DIENER, E., LARSEN, R.J. and EMMONS, R.A. Person x situation interactions: Choice of situations and congruence response models. *Journal of Personality and Social Psychology*, 1984; **47**, 580–592.

EASTERLIN, R.A. Does economic growth improve the human lot?: Some empirical evidence. Irr P.A. David and M. Abramovitz (eds.), *Nations and households in economic growth*. New York: Academic Press, 1974.

EISENBERG, D.M. Autonomy, health and life satisfaction among older persons in a life care community (Doctoral dissertation, Bryn Mawr College, 1980). *Dissertation Abstracts International*, **41**, 3724A. (University Microfilms No. 81–03906), 1981. The mood of Europeans. *Euro-Barometre* 1983; **20**, 1–38.

GRAEF, R. An analysis of the person by situation interaction through repeated measures. Unpublished doctoral dissertation, University of Chicago, 1978.

HEADEY, B. and WEARING, A. Chains of well-being, chains of ill-being. Paper presented at the International Sociological Association conference, New Delhi, 1986.

JERSILD, A.T., BROOK, J.S. and BROOK, D.W. *The psychology of adolescence*. New York: Macmillan, 1978.

KNIPPA, W. B. The relationship of antecedent and personality variables to life satisfaction of retired military officers (Doctoral dissertation, University of Texas at Austin, 1979). *Dissertation Abstracts International*, **40**, 1360A. (University Microfilms No. 79–20, 146), 1979.

KUBEY, R. and CSIKSZENTMIHALYI, M. *Television and the quality of life: How viewing shapes everyday experience*. Hillsdale, NJ: Lawrence Erlbaum, 1990.

LARSON, R. and CSIKSZENTMIHALYI, M. The experience sampling method. In H. T. Reis (ed.), *Naturalistic approaches to studying social interaction (New Direction for Methodology of Social and Behavioral Science, No. 15)*. San Francisco: Jossey-Bass, 1983.

LEWINSOHN, P.M., SULLIVAN, J.A. and GROSSCUP, S.J. Behavioral therapy: Clinical applications. In A. J. Rush (ed.), *Short-term therapies for depression*. New York: Guilford, 1982.

MASSIMINI, F., CSIKSZENTMIHALYI, M. and CARLI, M. The monitoring of optimal experience: a tool for psychiatric rehabilitation. *Journal of Nervous and Mental Diseases*, 1987; **175**(9), 545–549.

MASSIMINI, F. and INGHILLERI, P. *L'esperienza quotidiana: teoria e metodo d'analisi*. Milan: Franco Angeli, 1986.

MASSIMINI, F., CSIKSZENTMIHALYI, M. and DELLE FAVE, A. Flow and biocultural evolution. In M. Csikszentmihalyi and I. Csikszentmihalyi (eds.). *Optimal experience: psychological studies of flow in consciousness*. New York: Cambridge University Press, 1988.

MICHALOS, A.C. Multiple discrepancies theory (MDT). *Social Indicatiors Research*, 1985; **16**, 347–413.

MORGANTI, J.B., NEHRKE, M. F. and HULICKA, I. M. Resident and staff perceptions of latitude of choice in elderly institutionalized men. *Experimental Aging Research*, 1980; **6**, 367–384.

PEPLAU, L.A. and PERLMAN, D. *Loneliness*. New York: Wiley, 1982.

REID, D.W. and ZIEGLER, M. Validity and stability of a new desired control measure pertaining to psychological adjustment of the elderly. *Journal of Gerontology*, 1980; **35**, 395–402.

ROSALDO, M.Z. Toward an anthropology of self and feeling. In R. A. Shweder and R. A. LeVine (eds.), *Essays on mind, self, and emotions*. New York: Cambridge University Press, 1984.

SCHWARZ, N. and CLORE, G.L. Mood, misattribution and judgments of well-being: Information and directive functions of affective states. *Journal of Personality and Social Psychology*, 1983; **45**, 513–523.

SCHWARZ, N., STRACK, F., KOMMER, D. and WAGNER, D. Soccer, rooms and the quality of your life. *European Journal of Social Psychology*, 1987; **17**, 69–79.

SPIRO, M.E. Some reflections on cultural determinism and relativism with special reference to emotion and reason. In R.A. Shweder and R.A. LeVine (eds.), *Essays on mind, self, and emotions*. New York: Cambridge University Press, 1984.

SUNDRE, D.L. The relationship between happiness and internal-external locus of control. Unpublished master's thesis, California State University, 1978.

WESSMAN, A.E. and RICKS, D.F. *Mood and personality*. New York: Holt, Rinehart and Winston, 1966.

11

Subjective well-being in the face of critical life events: the case of successful copers

SIGRUN-HEIDE FILIPP and THOMAS KLAUER

Introduction

Although research on "subjective well-being" and research on "critical life events" represent two fairly independent domains, each concept obviously plays a prominent role in the respective "other" domain. On the one hand, research on subjective well-being has often used life events in order to manipulate levels of well-being, e.g. by making subjects focus selectively on positive or negative events in their lives (see Chapter 3). In addition, it has been demonstrated repeatedly that recall of positive versus negative events in one's life is dependent on momentary levels of well-being, i.e. whether positive or negative moods have been induced by the experimenter (for overviews see Bower, 1982; Blaney, 1986)[1].

In research on life events, on the other hand, an interest in subjective well-being is rather common and less surprising, since the impairment of well-being is often regarded as the crucial element inherent in critical life events (cf. Filipp, 1981). Accordingly, the restoration of well-being in victims of life crises has been equated with "successful coping" in the majority of studies. It has been claimed that human beings seem to possess a unique ability to maintain or regain high levels of well-being even in the face of the most aversive life changes as, for example, the onset of cancer or the sudden death of a child (e.g. Bulman and Wortman, 1977; Meyer and Taylor, 1987; Wortman and Silver, 1987). An excellent illustration of this ability is provided by the well-known study of Brickman, Coates, and Janoff-Bulman (1978), who compared a sample of lottery winners and a sample of paralysed accident victims with regard to levels of subjective well-being. One year after the respective event accident victims were found to be less different from lottery winners as well as from a control group than one might have expected.

However, it is well known that individual differences in adaptation to critical life events are, by no means, negligible, e.g. a "core of distress" symptom seems to persist in some victims of life crises even for years (e.g. Wirtz and Harrell, 1987). These differences, in our view, are to be explained by taking individual modes of coping as well as conditions for successful coping into consideration.

"Successful" coping and its determinants: an overview of explanatory accounts

The question of whether or not a given life event can be coped with success-fully, and under which conditions, has been addressed from different per-spectives (for an overview see, for example, Kessler, Price and Wortman, 1985). Characteristics of the triggering event (in particular predictability, controllability, contextual purity, among other variables) have often been taken into account, and it has been demonstrated that coping with and adapting to adverse life events is shaped by such properties of life events (for an overview, see Reese and Smyer, 1983). In addition, *personal* and *contextual* variables conceived of as "resources" have been investigated with regard to their contribution to "successful" coping which, in turn, may be further subdivided according to their stability or changeability, respec-tively.

When taking the social *context* into consideration, a rather *static* perspec-tive focusing primarily on social integration or network density has often been adopted, whereas the adaptational *dynamics* to be observed within social networks are captured by the term "social support". The latter has been extensively investigated within studies of adaptational processes (for detailed discussions, see Antonucci, 1985; Cohen and Syme, 1985; Turner, 1983). The empirical evidence for "buffering" effects of supportive behav-iours provided by family members, neighbours, or friends appears to be rather convincing (cf. Cohen and Wills, 1985), although the relative effect size often is not overwhelmingly high, as can be concluded from the meta-analyses performed by Schwarzer and Leppin (1989).

When successful coping is related to personal factors, a *static* model is often emphasized as well. While traditional personality measures are some-times regarded as rather unimportant in the description of successful copers (Taylor and Brown, 1988), other constructs reflecting presumably stable personal dispositions have been proposed in this realm as, for example, the concepts of "hardiness" (Kobasa, 1979), "learned resourcefulness" (Rosen-baum, 1983), "dispositional optimism" (Scheier and Carver, 1985), or "vul-nerability" (Rabkin, 1982). Accordingly, individual differences in these dispositions have been related to variations in adaptational outcomes in many studies, yet without paying much attention to coping behaviours or the coping process *per se*.

However, "coping" being of crucial importance here is by no means to be equated with trait-like dispositions to handle stressful situations on *a priori* grounds. Rather, the *dynamics* that are inherent in the coping process itself have to be underlined, and coping has to be conceived of as a changing (and changeable) phenomenon (see also Lazarus and Folkman, 1984). This implies that "success" in coping with life events cannot be explained *a priori* by personality factors and/or social resources, but has to be related to what people *do* in the face of critical life events, i.e. to the "mechanics" of well-being maintenance. In addition, from an applied perspective, it should be easier to change what people do rather than what they *are* like (Roskies and Lazarus, 1980). Although sometimes coping behaviours may be strongly determined by personality dispositions (as well as social contexts, e.g. McCrae and Costa, 1986; Holahan and Moos, 1987; Scheier, Weintraub and Carver, 1986), sufficient evidence (e.g. Parkes, 1986) suggests that one should not primarily think of "successful copers" as personalities having a "bag of virtues" they can rely on in times of life stress.

What does "coping" mean in the study of "successful copers"?

It is rather trivial to state that the description of what "successful" coping looks like is necessarily linked to how modes of coping have been defined and assessed. A brief overview of various approaches (see Braukmann and Filipp, 1984) yields that conceptualizations of coping behaviours vary along a continuum between extremely rough distinctions of coping modes on the one side and rather fine-graded, narrowly circumscribed behavioural categories on the other. For example, emotion-focused versus problem-focused coping modes (Lazarus and Launier, 1978) as well as avoidant versus vigilant behaviours (Janis, 1958; Roth and Cohen, 1986) may serve as examples for attempts to simply dichotomize coping behaviours on rather high levels of abstraction.

In contrast, coping has been described on a rather microanalytic level, e.g. by McCrae and Costa (1986), who distinguish between twenty-seven ways of coping (e.g. rational action, escapist fantasy, self-blame), or by Weisman (1979) who describes thirteen different modes of coping with cancer (e.g. externalization of responsibility, disengagement, confrontation) presumably serving different functions. Due to the obviously low consensual overlap in the conceptualization of coping behaviours, however, general conclusions in the adaptive value of certain coping modes can hardly be drawn from these various studies.

Still another argument has to be restated here briefly: what is considered as "successful coping", may, by implicaton, not be *included in the definition of "coping" itself*, as is the case in Haan's (1977) notion of "coping" as opposed to "defence" and "fragmentation", as well as in qualifying certain *modes* of coping as "mature" by definition (e.g. Vaillant, 1977). Rather, we will, refer here to "coping" in terms of all covert or overt reactions in the face of stressful events, ultimately aimed at arranging a new fit between the individual and his or her world, i.e. individual desires, options, and capabilities, on the one hand, and the opportunities provided and demands imposed by the external world on the other (Braukmann and Filipp, 1984). Since no single coping response can, in our opinion, be regarded "successful" in any respect on purely conceptual grounds, its contribution to such a new person-environment-fit and its power in producing "desired" outcomes, in general, has to be proven in adequately designed studies, in which outcome measures (e.g. subjective well-being) are not to be confounded with measures of coping behaviours themselves.

What does "success" mean in the study of "successful copers"?

The literature on critical life events and their aftermaths seems to be dominated by an ideal that is most commonly reflected in *homeostatic* models of functioning. Thus, the issue of "successful coping", at first glance, seems to be a rather simple one in that victims of life crises are expected to return to a precrisis baseline within an adequate period of time (see Caplan, 1964). Since the life event construct has become increasingly prominent within developmental psychology as well, a rather different perspective has been adopted. The idea has been proffered that personal gains and benefits can equally result from being exposed to critical life events, which means that success is now to be equated with "growth" rather than with homeostasis (cf. Riegel, 1975; see also Lerner and Gignac, 1988, for a similar notion). Yet, to state that "successful copers" should be equated with individuals who have learned and taken benefits from their crisis experiences on one side; to conceptualize and measure "growth" beyond a clearcut, "monolithic" concept of development, especially during adulthood, is another (see Filipp and Olbrich, 1986). In other words, although the question of values is often omitted from empirical research in psychology, it is inevitably intertwined with the study of "successful coping", since we need to define criteria for its evaluation. As the nature of success is elusive, and as the selection of appropriate indicators either represents a highly normative and value-laden enterprise (or is simply based on grounds of plausibility, e.g. return to work after myocardial infarction), the study of "successful coping" may need more than valid measures, or whatever is usually regarded is a prerequisite in empirical research.

It is only recently that the issue of "success" has also been addressed in the realm of "successful aging" (Baltes and Baltes, 1988). According to these authors, "a first step in the direction of an all-encompassing definition of successful aging is to think in terms of multiple criteria" (p. 9), for

example, length of life, biological health, mental health, psychosocial efficacy, personal control, and life satisfaction—a catalogue of criteria which is
easily applicable in the study of successful coping as well. In particular, the
first three criteria are probably most widely used within the so-called stress
and coping paradigm, e.g. in studies of the recently bereaved (cf. Stroebe
and Stroebe, 1987). A quite similar catalogue has been proposed within one
of the most prominent theories of stress and coping (Lazarus and Folkman,
1984): "social functioning", "morale" and "somatic health" are suggested
as criteria for the evaluation of readjustment, to be supplemented by more
specific indicators; other suggestions have been made by Caplan (1964) and
Kasl (1973), among others.

What is meant by "success", however, is of even greater importance
when coping behaviours do reveal *divergent effects* on various criteria under
investigation. In these cases, the assessment of "success or failure" in coping
with stressful events becomes dependent on the value decision about which
indicator has to be considered preferrable to the respective other. This is
partially reflected in the intense discussion on whether measures of "quality
of life" should be preferred to "length of survival time" as indicators of
adaptation in patients suffering from chronic or incurable disease. For
example, dysphoric mood (as measured by the Bradburn Affect Balance
Scale) has been shown to be predictive of 1-year-survival in a sample of
breast cancer patients (Derogatis, Abeloff and Melisaratos, 1979) demon-
strating that even subjective well-being, *per se*, by no means represents an
unanimous outcome measure since other adaptational goals may be attain-
able only at the price of lowered levels of well-being.

While it is often implied in research approaches that coping success
should, or at least can be evaluated "from the outside", i.e. using objective
indicators, an emphasis on subjective indicators is proffered, which reflects
"the value position that the perceiving self ought to be the litmus test for
the quality of life" (Baltes and Baltes, 1988, p. 10). In many studies, such
indicators are derived from self-reports of, for instance, affective states
or perceptions of control. It is, in addition, equally appropriate to have
individuals evaluate their coping behaviours as "helpful" or "successful"
(e.g. in achieving their goals), as has been proposed by introducing the
concept of coping *efficacy* (Aldwin and Revenson, 1987) and by distinguishing it from "coping effectiveness". While the former refers to the perceived
utility of coping responses in attaining one's subjective goals, the latter
simply denotes an empirically detected association between coping behaviours and adjustment indicators. As these authors have shown, perceived
efficacy may be an important moderator of coping effectiveness.

Another, yet by no means less important aspect is addressed in the concept of coping *efficiency*, originally introduced by Moos (1976). It points to
another dilemma in evaluating "success", namely that desired outcomes of
the coping process can often be achieved only at high costs. This dilemma,

already addressed in the notion of the "adaptive cost hypothesis" by Glass and Singer (1972) presumably comes up whenever coping behaviours are judged as being successful or not and when, at the same time, they exert divergent effects on different outcomes, as mentioned above. Seemingly "successful" coping behaviours may have undesired side effects either on the individual or on his or her social environment, often to be observed only over a longer time span (see also Cohen, Evans, Stokols and Krantz, 1986, chapter 1).

Success is relative: modifiers of coping effectiveness

Temporal differences in coping effectiveness

While the issue to select and justify criteria indicating "successful coping" poses one problem, another is raised when taking into account that the nature of "success" in coping may be a "shifting phenomenon" over time (Cameron and Meichenbaum, 1982). Not only may coping behaviours themselves be changing over time, but they may also change in their effectiveness as well, implying that no single coping mode can be considered successful (or maladaptive, respectively) *per se*. To put it differently: ". . . we are far from describing a magic bullet coping strategy that can instantly solve problems and restore emotional equilibrium" (Aldwin and Revenson, 1987, p. 338). Rather, variations in what appears to be "successful coping" are highly likely to be observed across persons, contexts, events, in particular, across *points of time* in adaptational processes—"success" is relative!

The probably best known example to demonstrate the divergence in outcomes depending on whether one adopts a short-term or a long-term perspective is represented by avoidant versus non-avoidant (vigilant) coping strategies. Various meta-analyses of temporal differences in the effectiveness of both strategies (see Mullen and Suls, 1982; Suls and Fletcher, 1985) are highly illustrative here. Their results indicate that avoidant strategies do produce better physical adaptation and exert more "beneficial" effects on health than vigilant coping strategies, yet only in the short run. In contrast, non-avoidant strategies seem to be superior over avoidance in producing desired outcomes when a larger time span had been under investigation. Apparently, we cannot favour either one of the two strategies in terms of which has to be equated with "successful" coping, because they exert their beneficial effects on physical health at different points in time.

A similar conclusion can be drawn from results of some of the few prospective studies. The above mentioned study of Derogatis *et al.* (1979) may serve here as an example as well. At first glance, one would presumably judge those in their sample of breast cancer patients as "unsuccessful copers" who scored high on measures of dysphoric mood (i.e. depression, hostility, anger, and anxiety). However, one year later, exactly these patients were more likely to be in the group of "survivors" rather than in the group of the deceased. Although the external validity of these results has sometimes been questioned because of sample size, a similar pattern of results reported by Edwards, DiClemente and Samuels (1985) from a well controlled study of patients with testicular cancer over a time span of seven years may serve as a valuable replication.

There are many ways to comment on these results, for example, whether high levels of depression are a "prerequisite" for subsequent recovery (for critical comments, see Wortman and Silver, 1987; 1989); we would like to highlight here temporal variations in coping effectiveness: if coping behaviours are seen to be primarily aimed at altering dysphoric mood in the light of stressful life events, one would certainly evaluate patients with high levels of negative affect as coping poorly; if length of survival time serves as the (ultimate) adaptational outcome (which in some cases implies the dilemma of a value-decision, as mentioned above), we would have to argue differently. Although levels of subjective well-being have not been assessed at various times of measurement, thus not allowing for a better insight in their variations across time, we conclude from these results the necessity to adopt a temporally extended frame of reference with regard to a set of multiple criteria when coping effectiveness is to be evaluated: what appears to be detrimental to one's well-being at one point in time is not necessarily corresponded by negative effects in the long run, or—equally important—by negative effects on other measures.

There are other empirical examples to be used in this context, being presumably less ambiguous with regard to the outcome criteria under study. For instance, Hosack (1983, cited after Wortman, 1983) found that mothers who had been extremely upset after the birth of their malformed child were subsequently more likely to provide effective care for the child, as judged by health professionals, than mothers who were not upset when the baby was born and who, at first glance, seemed to deal more successfully with their situation.

Unfortunately, most studies mentioned so far have not assessed coping behaviours directly, but have rather inferred modes of coping from various measures of, for example, affective states. For example, one might infer from self-reports on positive well-being that an individual is denying the threat imposed on him or her which, in turn, may lead to unfavourable outcomes in the long run (e.g. increased risk of mortality; see Janis, 1982). However, why should high levels of well-being be achieved only by means of denial and avoidance? A host of other modes to cope with critical life-events can be considered as well, potentially contributing to well-being maintenance. Thus, instead of speculative reasonings, will rather investigate them empirically and await whatever results should be obtained. In addition, our plea for adopting a larger time perspective in the study of successful coping is supported by developmental psychologists who made us aware of differences between the short-term and long-term impact of life-events (see Montada, 1981), and who have been talking of "sleeper effects" in the aftermath of life experiences which might last even for many years.

The role of person, context, and event characteristics

It is not unlikely that *person variables* are effective not only in the *selection* of coping strategies, but also as *moderators* in the relationship between coping behaviours and outcome variables. Yet, only few variables have been taken into consideration with regard to that issue.

The way in which the *age* variable, for example, may modify effective coping with stressful encounters with regard to emotional well-being has been demonstrated by Folkman and Lazarus (1988): "seeking social support", for example, proved to be effective only in the older group of their community sample, whereas this strategy was observed to be unrelated to changes in level of distress in the younger group. They propose these differences to be based on, for example, improvements in interpersonal coping skills, which in turn, might account for more adequate support by others (see also Felton and Revenson, 1987).

Differences in coping effectiveness related to *personality* variables have been investigated, although rarely. The role of coping dispositions, i.e. preferences for monitoring or blunting as coping modes, was investigated—among others—by Miller and Mangan (1983). In a field experiment, modes of coping with a threatening medical examination had been induced experimentally (i.e. use of information provided about the procedure), and their interactive effects with coping dispositions on level of distress were investigated. When the induced *actual* coping behaviours (i.e. high versus low use of information) were inconsistent with the subjects' disposition, measures of distress proved to be significantly higher than when the induced behaviours were congruent with subjects' coping styles. Since actual coping behaviours had been manipulated experimentally, it would be helpful to additionally investigate under what "natural" conditions individuals are forced to cope with a stressful event inconsistently to how they would "preferably" deal with it. This, supposedly, could be the case when the social environment hinders an individual to cope in a way that is consistent with his or her disposition (for that issue, see Filipp and Aymanns, 1987) or when the nature of the stressful event itself fosters or requires certain modes of coping.

Accordingly, *event characteristics* have been investigated as modifiers of coping effectiveness (e.g. McCrae, 1984). In fact, one has to assume that "coping tasks" (subjectively) inherent in various life events should differ tremendously, hence requiring different modes of coping in order to meet these tasks. Thus, whether or not coping behaviours prove to be successful should also vary across types of event, although the issue of "task speci-ficity" in coping behaviours has often been overlooked (for exceptions, see Perrez, 1988; Wortman, 1983).

A few attempts have been made to investigate this issue. In particular, *controllability* of the event was selected to highlight that "emotion-focused" modes of coping are especially effective in the face of uncontrollable, rather than controllable, events (e.g. Lazarus and Folkman, 1984; Rothbaum, Weisz and Snyder, 1982). "Problem-focused" coping behaviours, on the other hand, should exert beneficial effects primarily in the face of control-lable events, supposedly being ineffective or even maladaptive in the light of objectively uncontrollable events. Despite the plausibility of this assump-tion, empirical results have not always been in accordance with it. For example, in their study on coping with chronic disease, Felton and Revenson (1984) found, quite contrary to their expectations, the adaptational out-comes of "information seeking" (as a mainly problem-centered strategy) and "wish-fulfilling fantasy" (as a primarily emotion-centered strategy) to be unmodified by the objective (i.e. medical) controllability of the disease. However, chronic disease may be very low on the continuum of (perceived) control over life events in itself, thus creating a floor effect, which in turn diminishes moderator effects.

The *life domain* primarily affected by a stressful event has been con-sidered as still another moderator of coping effectiveness, especially from a sociological perspective. Based on various analyses of the Chicago Panel Data (see Menaghan, 1983, for an overview), it was shown that the four modes of coping under study (namely: optimistic comparisons, selective inattention, restricting expectations, direct actions) exert divergent effects on "role distress" and "problem level" as outcome measures depending on the life domain affected (marital, parental, occupational). Thus, adapt-ational outcomes of the "success" of any single coping mode may vary considerably across types of events and their adaptive requirements; they may vary as well across different sociocontextual conditions under which the individual lives. The nature of an individual's "social network" and the quality of support available from it does, of course, contribute to coping behaviour and should heighten our understanding of what happens in the regulation of well-being in times of stress. It has been repeatedly stated (Brickman *et al.*, 1982; Filipp and Aymanns, 1987; Heller and Swindle, 1983; Thoits, 1986) that a focus on coping behaviours on the one hand and on social support on the other cannot be conceived of as two alternative, rather than mutually supplementary perspectives. If, for example, "support mobilization" (Eckenrode, 1983) or "seeking social support" (Dunkel-Schetter, Folkman and Lazarus, 1987) should be expected to be "suc-cessful" modes of coping, their effectiveness is, at the same time, dependent on and shaped by the social environment, e.g. its responsiveness to the individual. Thus, not only are individual coping strategies themselves often highly influenced by the social context; their effectiveness is modified by the social environment as well.

A more systemic view of "successful copers" provides us with a highly complex picture. For example, some coping modes (e.g. expression of negative affect) may limit the availability of social support or, even worse, interact negatively with supportive behaviours from others (Dunkel-Schetter *et. al.*, 1987; Wortman, 1984). Results from various studies may be seen as indicative of "successful" adaptation to require some degree of *coping-support-fit*, i.e. a convergence of coping behaviours preferably exhibited by the victim, and of supportive behaviours, offered by his or her social environment. "Coping-support-fit" being low may represent an example of when social supportive behaviours "fail" or do not meet their intended effects (for overviews, see Coates, Renzaglia and Embree, 1983; Wortman and Lehman, 1985).

Most researchers, in their attempts to study "successful" coping processes, focus solely on the *individual* under stress; accordingly, the assessment of outcome criteria is usually confined to him or her. Only rarely has "success" been investigated within an enlarged frame of reference, i.e. taking into consideration others within the closer personal network. Consequently, what is considered as "good" coping on the individual level may prove to be highly detrimental to the well-being of others, at the same time. Stern and Pasquale (1979), for instance, investigated the effects of denial and avoidant coping behaviours in a sample of heart attack patients on the affective state of the patients themselves as well as of their wives. High scores of denial and avoidance were related to low levels of anxiety and depression in the group of patients, which is not too surprising. Yet, at the same time, high patient scores were also related to higher proneness to depression in their wives. Another, quite different example comes from studies of maternal coping behaviours in the face of severe illness of one of their children (cf. Spinetta and Deasy-Spinetta, 1981). One may also think of mothers having a chronically ill child which they take intensive care of, while at the same time their other children may suffer remarkably from lonesomeness and neglect. One might think of other mothers as counterparts who try to distribute their attention more symmetrically among all members of their family, yet, at the price of a possibly tremendous impairment of well-being and health in themselves in the long run, as has impressively been described by Belle (1982).

In sum, although studies adopting a systemic view in the study of coping with critical life events are still rather rare, a few examples show a differential impact of coping behaviours on the various others in the closer social environment. This may underscore the necessity of applying a "family coping model", as proposed by McCubbin and Patterson (1983), which should account better for the relativity of "success" in coping with critical life events.

In the last part of our chapter we would like to confine ourselves to the issue of coping with a presumably highly critical event of the adult years, namely the onset of chronic disease.

Does coping help to maintain well-being? The sample case of patients suffering from chronic disease

It is probably most widely accepted that the diagnosis of a life-threatening disease, in particular cancer, can be considered as prototypical of critical life events. Almost all attributes commonly used in the literature to describe critical life events have to be assigned to such a life experience. The diagnosis of cancer confronts individuals with an extreme loss of control over their lives, it is most often accompanied by the necessity to disengage from important goals and options in their lives, and is in sum, most threatening to what has been called the individual's "assumptive world" (Janoff-Bulman and Timko, 1987). Yet patients, though of comparable medical status, obviously seem to differ fundamentally in how they deal with their lot and how successfully they are coping with their disease as well as with the various problems imposed on them by treatment procedures, by the loss of social roles, and many other adaptive demands. Hence, the issue of "successful coping" is an especially crucial one in that context.

Within the Trier Longitudinal Study on Coping with Chronic Disease (see Filipp, Aymanns and Klauer, 1983), we are investigating such adaptational endeavours in a sample of $N=332$ cancer patients of both sexes varying in age, time elapsed since diagnosis, tumor site, medical prognosis and treatment, etc. (see Filipp, Ferring, Freudenberg and Klauer, 1988, for a more comprehensive description).

Our research project is centered around three main issues to be briefly described. First, the issue is addressed to what degree coping behaviours are stable over the time span under study or to what degree they undergo considerable intraindividual variations. Second, a set of variables (e.g. measures of personality, social support, and medical variables) is investigated with regard to their relative contribution in predicting coping behaviours as well as their temporal stability. Third, one central aim of our study, of course, is to investigate the effectiveness of different modes of coping with regard to multiple criteria. In particular, affective-motivational outcomes (e.g. subjective well-being, self-esteem, hopelessness), self-perceptions of coping effectiveness, changes in medical status (e.g. course of the disease, recidivism) as well as social-contextual variables (e.g. changes in network size, social participation, and occupational status) are assessed using four times of measurement within one year with an additional follow-up one year later. Hence, subjective as well as objective indicators of successful coping with and adaptation to chronic disease can serve for the assessment of differential coping effects on these various measures.

The assessment of coping behaviours being of crucial importance here is based on an *a priori* model according to which coping reactions can be classified along three basic dimensions, namely (1) attentional focus, i.e. distracted from or focused upon the disease, (2) behavioural level of the response, i.e. overt or intrapsychic, and (3) degree of sociability, i.e. withdrawal from others versus use of social resources. A cross-classification of these dimensions yields eight mutually exclusive classes of coping reactions, which were included in a sixty-four item questionnaire. These items are to be answered on a 6-point-scale with regard to how often within the last weeks the patient exhibited each response (*FEKB*; Klauer and Filipp, 1987).

Exploratory and confirmatory factor analyses yielded a structural pattern of five factors, which then were used as scales for the assessment of five coping modes, respectively. The first scale, labelled as *rumination (RU)*, is comprised of items that describe intrapsychic behaviours focusing on the disease and implying social withdrawal, e.g. causal reasoning and ruminating upon the disease itself; the second scale, *search for affiliation (SA)*, is reflective of highly sociable coping behaviours which imply diversion and attentional distraction from the disease; the third scale, *threat minimization (TM)*, describes intrapsychic, emotion-focused coping reactions like self-instructions towards positive thinking, rationalization, and self-persuading into trust in the medical regimen; *search for information (SI)*, as the fourth scale, describes overt attempts to gain knowledge about the disease and its medical treatment, as well as joining the company of other cancer patients; *search for meaning in religion (SR)*, finally, circumscribes attempts to find meaning in the illness experience, especially with reference to religious issues. Because we used unit weighting instead of factor scores in the calculation of scale values, the scale values for *RU* and *SI* as well as *TM* and *SA* are moderately, though significantly, intercorrelated. Without being exhaustive, of course, these scales cover a wide range of coping reactions that can also be found in other classifications (e.g. Felton, Revenson and Hinrichsen, 1984; Ray, Lindop and Gibson, 1982; Taylor, 1983; Weisman, 1979) and that are expected to allow for the description of individual differences.

With respect to outcome variables, we will confine ourselves here to subjective well-being (see Filipp *et. al.*, 1988, for results on other criteria) as measured by an extensively validated German instrument (*Bf-S*, von Zerssen, 1976). From self-ratings on twenty-eight bipolar scales describing positive versus negative affective states, a single score, reflective of levels of well-being, is computed[2]. Compared with the general population, levels of well-being were significantly lowered in our sample at each of the three points of measurement realized so far. This indicates that the maintenance of well-being following the diagnosis of cancer cannot be attained by our sample in general.

Correlations between coping behaviours and well-being scores, assessed at each of the first three points of measurement yielded a clear-cut pattern (see Table 11.1)

TABLE 11.1. *Coping modes as correlates of subjective well-being in cancer patients*
(174 ≤ N ≤ 305)

Coping scale	Time of measurement		
	1	2	3
Rumination	W.32*	−.28*	−.47*
Search for affiliation	.44*	.38*	.38*
Threat minimization	.41*	.37*	.35*
Search for information	.02	.03	−.03
Search for meaning in religion	.02	.05	.01

*$p<.001$.

Search for information (*SI*) as well as *search for meaning in religion* (*SR*) are both, at all times of measurement, completely unrelated to well-being at an overall level of analysis. Contrary to this, the three other coping modes yield significant relations to measures of well-being: while *rumination* is negatively related, *search for social affiliation* and *threat minimization* are positively related to high levels of subjective well-being. What can we learn from these results for the study of "successful copers"?

A few methodological considerations have to be restated here. Speaking of "coping effectiveness" with regard to well-being (or any other outcome variables), as we have so far, is based on the assumption that coping behaviours and "outcomes" are *causally* related in an unidirectional way, thus allowing for inferences of who is coping well and who is coping poorly. However, as is well known, the testing of coping effectiveness requires more than the proof of a significant correlation. It has to be shown, in addition, that the causality assumption is valid, i.e. that coping behaviours are causally prior to, rather than being determined by, the respective outcome variable. Yet, empirical evidence on the issue of causal directionality in this realm is rather scarce (for a remarkable exception, see Felton and Revenson, 1984).

In order to investigate the plausibility of three hypothetical models which altogether could explain the observed correlational structures, namely (1) coping being causally predominant to well-being, (2) well-being being causally prior to coping, and (3) both interrelating in terms of reciprocal determinism, we performed hierarchical regression analyses, in which pre-test scores for coping modes and well-being, respectively, were controlled (i.e. used as an "autoregressor") and in which post-test coping and well-being scores served as criteria. The amount of variance explained by the additional "change regressor", i.e. coping when well-being residuals and well-being when coping residuals were the dependent variables, indicates the effect of one variable on pre-test–post-test changes in the respective other. Given similar stabilities of the two variables under study, a comparison of the relative effect sizes may yield some insight on the relative causal position of each of the variables (cf. Rogosa, 1980).

These analyses cover two three-month intervals as well as one six-month interval (t1 vs. t2, t2 vs. t3, t1 vs. t3). Accordingly, a "proximal" as well as a "distal" prediction model were calculated, using pre-test and post-test scores as change regressors, respectively. Table 11.2 summarizes the most relevant results from these analyses with respect to the six-month interval and by focusing on those coping modes that proved to be related to well-being, i.e. "rumination", "search for affiliation", and "threat minimization" (for a more detailed description, see Filipp, Klauer, Ferring and Freudenberg, in press) [3].

TABLE 11.2. *Cross-legged regression of coping on well-being and well-being on coping controlling for pre-test scores (time lag: six months; N=174 cancer patients)*

Criterion[a]	Change regressor	Regression statistics[b]			
		beta	RSQC	$F_{(1:171)}$	R^2
Proximal prediction					
WB 3	RU 3	−.34	.10	26.41**	.34
RU 3	WB 3	−.31	.09	39.70**	.62
WB 3	SA 3	.24	.05	12.16**	.29
SA 3	WB 3	.20	.03	11.79**	.50
WB 3	TM 3	.24	.06	13.73**	.29
TM 3	WB 3	.11	.01	3.48	.51
Distal predictions					
WB 3	RU 1	−.12	.01	2.94	.25
RU 3	WB 1	−.16	.02	8.40**	.55
WB 3	SA 1	.15	.02	4.64*	.26
SA 3	WB 1	.13	.02	5.20*	.48
WB 3	TM 1	.22	.04	9.87**	.28
TM 3	WB 1	−.01	.00	0.01	.50

[a] WB, subjective well-being; RU, rumination; SA, search for affiliation; TM, threat minimization; additionally given is the running number of point of measurement.

[b] Specified are regression coefficients (*beta*), the incremental variance explained by the change regressor (*RSQC*) with the corresponding *F*–value, and the total variance of post-test scores accounted for by pre-test score and change regressor (R^2).

**$p<.01$.   *$p<.05$

As can be seen, the relation between subjective well-being and *rumination* is characterized by a seemingly clear-cut causal predominance of well-being over coping in the distal prediction model. While changes in well-being are unrelated to pre-test RU scores, changes in rumination can be predicted significantly from pre-test well-being scores. In the proximal prediction, however, this pattern is blurred. It seems from these findings that low levels of well-being in cancer patients might be a stronger determinant of dealing with the disease in terms of rumination than is true for the reverse; it is not rumination that lowers well-being, it is obviously negative mood that fosters rumination as a coping mode.

An opposite pattern of results can be observed for *"threat minimization"* (TM): in both distal and proximal predictions, causal analyses point to a predominance of *TM* over subjective well-being, i.e. *TM* scores at both times of measurement are predictive of changes in well-being, whereas the effects of well-being on changes in *TM* miss statistical significance. These intrapsychic coping behaviours that presumably serve a palliative, emotion-regulatory function, seem to be successful in altering levels of well-being towards the positive pole over time. Further analyses are needed to investigate whether there are temporal differences in *TM* effectiveness when larger time spans are considered.

A third pattern of results, finally, was obtained for the relationship between subjective well-being and *"search for affiliation"* (*SA*). With regard to both proximal and distal models of prediction, changes in one variable prove to be predictable from the respective other; thus, not causal predominance, but rather mutual causal interdependence is descriptive of the relationship between well-being and *search for affiliation* in the sample of cancer patients. This relationship can probably best be described by the concept of a "positive feedback cycle", in which tendencies to search for affiliation and subjective well-being mutually reinforce each other over time. On the opposite side of the continuum, such a relation may result in a vicious circle (cf. Felton and Revenson, 1984) in that low levels of well-being foster withdrawal from others, which in turn deteriorates well-being.

Our findings, up to this point, only tell part of the whole story. Firstly, since not all points of measurement, so far, have been realized for all patients in our sample, the results will have to await replications for larger and validations for similar time intervals. In particular, we will have to test whether "sleeper effects" of coping behaviours simultaneously unrelated to well-being might be observed in the long run. Secondly, possible moderators of the relationship between coping and well-being have not been taken into consideration; for example, it is not implausible to assume that effects of well-being on rumination are fostered by, for example, low levels of social support. Thirdly, up to now, we can draw some conclusions on "successful" coping behaviours only with regard to subjective well-being; hence, analyses with regard to other outcome criteria (e.g. medical variables, indicators of social functioning) have to be added which may yield different conclusions on the adaptiveness of the five coping modes investigated here and reveal further evidence as to whether "success" is indeed relative. Fourthly, current data analyses will have to be supplemented by explicit tests of different latent variable models of causal directionality between coping and presumed outcome measures.

What we can demonstrate so far, however, is that coping modes differ in terms of their association to subjective well-being, i.e. in how profoundly they can contribute to maintenance as well as enhancement of well-being. Further, our results show that the hypothesis that coping determines well-being cannot be accepted in general since, in case of "rumination", coping seems to be causally postponed to the presumed outcome criterion. Thus, it would be equally incorrect to qualify rumination as being "maladaptive" with regard to well-being, too. Clear-cut evidence for coping effectiveness can be drawn from our data only with regard to "threat minimization", i.e. with regard to those "cognitive manoeuvres" that shift the patient's attentional focus away from the illness, and that proved to be effective in well-being maintenance as well as enhancement.

Taken together, our findings point to the necessity of methodologically careful investigations of the relationship between coping behaviours and outcomes as well as to the necessity of explicitly stating assumptions on the *causal* structure inherent in these relationships.

Conclusions

Researchers, have presumably always been aware of the fact that victims of life crises, in general, represent fairly sensitive subjects to be enrolled into empirical research. To have, for example, cancer patients, parents who recently lost their child, or paralyzed accident victims fill in questionnaires (or participate in whatever type of data collection is applied) can, in our view, only be justified if such research endeavours will, in the long run, result in the accumulation of knowledge potentially useful for counselling, rehabilitation, or other modes of intervention aimed at supporting victims of life crises. The issue that has been addressed throughout our chapter, i.e. the question of who the "successful" copers are and what they do look like, is of crucial importance not only from the perspective of basic research, but from an applied perspective as well.

Unfortunately, the study of coping behaviours and the investigation of their individual variation in terms of quality and effectiveness to date has not yielded overwhelmingly fruitful results. What we have learned from the "stress and coping paradigm" has often been restricted to rather narrowly defined (often experimentally induced) stressful situations. On the other hand, research has often been simply outcome oriented: levels of distress, depression, or other stress-related phenomena have been focused upon without taking individual differences in coping behaviours into consideration that may have brought about variations in outcomes; thus, coping has often been regarded as an epiphenomenon (cf. McCrae and Costa, 1986), rather than as the crucial link in the whole process.

Even those theories that highlight the necessity to study coping behaviours are, in our view, considerably lacking both predictive and explanatory power when individual variations in coping behaviours and coping effectiveness are to be taken into account. When we began to study coping behaviours in our sample of cancer patients, we felt rather unable to derive hypotheses from any one of the prominent theories (Lazarus, to take just one example), with regard to the prediction of which patients will cope in what manner and which behaviours will have to be considered "successful" as opposed to the "unsuccessful" ones. Differential psychology sometimes seems to be too far away from the stress and coping paradigm, at least as for our research aims are concerned.

What follows, then, is that we have to begin with attempts to aggregate various small pieces of evidence stemming from only few studies in the field and to proceed from there by performing adequately designed studies in order to gain better insight into the dynamics of "successful" coping. It was our intention throughout the chapter to show that such an endeavour necessitates the analysis of coping behaviours over a large time span, at various times of measurement, in order to learn more about their temporal variability and to gain a better understanding of the causal relations between various personal and social "resources" and coping behaviours on the one hand and between coping behaviours and their effects on outcome measures on the other.

Yet the problem to be solved here is by no means solely a methodological one; rather, the issue of values is raised whenever we try to describe "successful" copers. The nature of success is elusive in the study of coping as well as in other realms; in particular, we do not see any justification to assign "good" or "poor" to the descriptions of certain coping behaviours on *a priori* grounds—a few examples, like excessive substance use as one mode to deal with critical life events may be an exception. Is the recently bereaved old lady who insists on laying the table for her deceased husband every morning coping less well than a hypothetical other who joins the "grey panthers" and socializes with them regularly? Can we speak of blaming the self for the occurrence of critical events as "neurotic coping", as McCrae and Costa (1986) would propose? Our answer is no. We first need to go beyond the various coping behaviours and try to investigate the functions these behaviours (presumably) serve for the individual under stress and to relate them to a set of multiple outcomes in order to evaluate them on a more solid basis.

However, this does not solve the problem in a general way either, since the selection of outcome criteria represents—as we tried to demonstrate— a by no means less unambiguous endeavour. The widespread use of the concept of "quality of life" in studies with cancer patients, for example, may be seen as indicative of this dilemma. By focusing on a seemingly "content free" criterion researchers apparently hope to prevent the difficulty to define "desired" outcomes more precisely, which they, of course, cannot accomplish, since the concept itself, as we all know, allows for a tremendous variety of (operational) definitions.

Even if one could reach a considerable degree of consensus in the definition of criteria indicating successful coping (as, for example, is presumably true for "subjective well-being"), one would not, simply by implication, know which coping behaviours can be judged as "successful", i.e. leading to these desired outcomes. It is widely acknowledged that various coping behaviours may serve the same function, i.e. are equifinal in producing a particular outcome. On the other hand, it is equally true that the same coping mode may vary considerably with regard to whether it leads to a desired outcome or not.

We tried to show that short-term and long-term effects of a particular coping response need to be differentiated. We further illustrated that what appears to be "successful" coping also depends on the particular life event, thus the "task specificity" of coping behaviours being as important as the possible interaction of coping tasks and characteristics of the individual under stress. Finally, when adopting a systemic view of successful coping the relativism of success becomes clear in still another way: what can be considered "successful" coping for the individual himself or herself may, at the same time, be judged as "poor" coping when looking at his or her social environment. A similar argument holds true for focusing on an even more widely accepted measure like subjective well-being, since behaviours beneficial to subjective well-being may, at the same time, be highly detrimental to other aspects, like physical health and functioning.

To summarize, we are apparently still in need of a solid body of knowledge on which our description of "successful copers" could be based and which could be potentially useful for those who have to cope with severe life events or with life threatening disease. We are hopeful that our study on coping with the onset of cancer may add some pieces of knowledge in the future. Our warnings of the various problems inherent in identifying "successful" copers may seem to be even counterproductive in a sense that more difficulties have been added than solutions could be offered. On the other hand, however, we believe that too much has been written on what should be considered "mature" or "neurotic" coping, and that coping behaviours have been judged in a highly prescriptive way without having a closer look at how they vary in nature and effectiveness across time, individuals, and stressful life situations.

References

ALDWIN, C. M. and REVENSON, T. A. Does coping help? A reexamination of the relation between coping and adjustment. *Journal of Personality and Social Psychology*, 1987; **53**, 337–348.

ANTONUCCI, T. Social support: Theoretical advances, recent findings and pressing issues. In I. G. Sarason and B. R. Sarason (eds.), *Social support: Theory, research and applications*. Dordrecht: Nijhoff, 1985.

BALTES, P. B. and BALTES, M. M. *Psychological perspectives on successful aging: A model of selective optimization with compensation*. Paper presented at the European Science foundation conference on Successful Aging, June 5-8, Schloß Ringberg, Kreuth, FRG, 1988.

BELLE, D. (ed,). *Lives in stress: Women and depression*. Beverly Hills, CA: Sage, 1982.

BLANEY, P. H. Affect and memory: A review. *Psychological Bulletin*, 1986; **99**, 229–246.

BOWER, G. H. Emotional mood and memory. *American Psychologist*, 1982; **36**, 129–148.

BRAUKMANN, W. and FILIPP, S. H. Strategien und Techniken der Lebensbewältigung. In U. Baumann, H. Berbalk and G. Seidenstücker (eds.), *Klinische Psychologie. Trends in Forschung und Praxis* (Vol. 6). Bern: Huber, 1984.

BRICKMAN, P., COATES, D. and JANOFF-BULMAN, R. Lottery winners and accident victims: Is happiness relative? *Journal of Personality and Social Psychology*, 1978; **36**, 917–927.

BRICKMAN, P., RABINOWITZ, V., KARUZA, J., COATES, D., COHN, E. and KIDDER, L. Models of helping and coping. *American Psychologist*, 1982; **37**, 368–384.

BULMAN, R. J. and WORTMAN, C. B. Attributions of blame and coping in the "real world": Severe accident victims react to their lot. *Journal of Personality and Social Psychology*. 1977; **35**, 351–363.

CAMERON, R. and MEICHENBAUM, D. The nature of effective coping and the treatment of stress related problems: A cognitive-behavioral perspective. In L. Goldberger and S. Breznitz (eds.), *Handbook of stress*). New York: Free Press, 1982.

CAPLAN, G. *Principles of preventive psychiatry*. New York: Basic Books, 1964.

COATES, D., RENZAGLIA, G. T. and EMBREE, M. C. When helping backfires: Help and helplessness. In J. D. Fisher, A. Nadler and B. M. DePaulo (eds.), *New directions in helping. Vol. 1: Recipient reactions to aid*. New York: Academic Press, 1983.

COHEN, S., EVANS, G. W., STOKOLS, D. and KRANTZ, D. S. *Behavior, health, and environmental stress*. New York: Plenum Press, 1986.

COHEN, S. and SYME, S. L. (eds.), *Social support and health*. New York: Academic Press, 1985.

COHEN, S. and WILLS, T. A. Stress, social support, and the buffering hypothesis. *Psychological Bulletin*, 1985; **98**, 310–357.

DEROGATIS, L. R., ABELOFF, M. D. and MELISARATOS, N. Psychological coping mechanisms and survival time in metastatic breast cancer. *Journal of the American Medical Association*, 1979; **242**, 1504–1508.

DUNKEL-SCHETTER, C., FOLKMAN, S. and LAZARUS, R. S. Correlates of social support receipt. *Journal of Personality and Social Psychology*, 1987; **53**, 71–80.

ECKENRODE, J. The mobilization of social supports: Some individual constraints. *American Journal of Community Psychology*, 1983; **11**, 509–528.

EDWARDS, J., DICLEMENTE, C. and SAMUELS, M. C. Psychological characteristics: A pretreatment survival marker of patients with testicular cancer. *Journal of Psychosocial Oncology*, 1985; **3**(1), 79–94.

FELTON, B. J. and REVENSON, T. A. Coping with chronic illness: A study of illness controllability and the influence of coping strategies on psychological adjustment. *Journal of Consulting and Clinical Psychology*, 1984; **52**, 343–353.

FELTON, B. J., REVENSON, T. A. and HINRICHSEN, G. A. Stress and coping in the explanation of psychological adjustment among chronically ill adults. *Social Science and Medicine*, 1984; **18**, 889–898.

FELTON, B. J. and REVENSON, T. A. Age differences in coping with chronic illness. *Psychology and Aging*, 1987; **2**, 164–170.

FILIPP, S.-H. Ein allgemeines Modell für die Analyse kritischer Lebensereignisse. In S.-H. Filipp (ed.), *Kritische Lebensereignisse*. Munich: Urban & Schwarzenberg, 1981.

FILIPP, S.-H. and AYMANNS, P. Die Bedeutung sozialer und personaler Ressourcen in der

Auseinandersetzung mit kritischen Lebensereignissen. *Zeitschrift für Klinische Psychologie*, 1987; **16**, 1–14.

FILIPP, S.-H. and OLBRICH, E. Human development across the life span: Overview and highlights of the psychological perspective. In A. B. Sørensen, F. E. Weinert and L. E. Sherrod (eds.), *Human development and the life course: Multidisciplinary perspectives*. Hillsdale, NJ: Erlbaum, 1986.

FILIPP, S.-H., AYMANNS, P. and KLAUER, T. *Formen der Auseinandersetzung mit schweren köperlichen Erkrankungen als Prototypen kritischer Lebensereignisse: Eine Verlaufsstudie* (Berichte aus dem Forschungsprojekt "Psychologie der Krankheitsbewältigung" Nr.1). Trier: University of Trier, Fachereich I—Psychologie, 1983.

FILIPP, S.-H., FERRING, D., FREUDENBERG, E. and KLAUER, T. Affektivmotivationale Korrelate von Formen der Krankheitsbewältigung—Erste Ergebnisse einer Längsschnittstudie mit Krebspatienten. *Psychotherapie, Psychosomatik, Medizinische Psychologie*, 1988; **38**, 37–42.

FILIPP, S.-H., KLAUER, T., FERRING, E. and FREUDENBERG, E. Wohlbefinden durch Krankheitsbewältigung? Untersuchungen zur "Effektivität" von Bewältigungsverhalten bei Krebspatienten. In R. Verres and M. Hasenbring (eds.), *Jahrbuch der Medizinischen Psychologie* (Vol. 3). Berlin: Springer, in press.

FOLKMAN, S. and LAZARUS, R. S. Coping as a mediator of emotion. *Journal of Personality and Social Psychology*, 1988;.**54**, 466–475.

GLASS, D. and SINGER, J. *Urban stress: Experiments in noise and social stressors*. New York: Academic Press, 1972.

HAAN, N. (ed.). *Coping and defending: Processes of self-environment organization*. New York: Academic Press, 1977.

HELLER, K. and SWINDLE, R. Social networks, perceived social support, and coping with stress. In R. D. Felner, L. A. Jason, J. Moritsuru and S. S. Farber (eds.), *Preventive psychology: Theory, research, and practice in community intervention*. New York: Pergamon, 1983.

HOLAHAN, C. J. and MOOS, R. H. Personal and contextual determinants of coping strategies. *Journal of Personality and Social Psychology*, 1987; **53**, 946–955.

HOSAK, A. *A comparison of crises: Mother's early experiences with normal and abnormal firstborn infants*. Unpublished doctoral dissertation, Harvard University, School of Public Health, 1983.

JANIS, I. L. *Psychological stress: Psychoanalytic and behavioral studies of surgical patients*. New York: Wiley, 1958.

JANIS, I. L. Coping patterns among patients with life-threatening diseases. In P. Defares, C. D. Spielberger and I. G. Sarason (eds.), *Stress and anxiety* (Vol. 9). New York: Wiley, 1982.

JENKINS, C. D., HURST, M. W. and ROSE, R. M. Life changes. Do people really remember? *Archives of General Psychiatry*, 1979; **36**, 379–384.

JANOFF-BULMAN, R. and TIMKO, C. Coping with traumatic events: The role of denial in light of people's assumptive worlds. In C. R. Snyder and C. E. Ford (eds.), *Coping with negative life events*. New York: Plenum Press, 1987.

KASL, S. V. Mental health and work environment: An examination of the evidence. *Journal of Occupational Medicine*, 1973; **15**, 809–818.

KESSLER, R. C., PRICE, R. and WORTMAN, C. Social factors in psychopathology: Stress, social support, and coping processes. *Annual Review of Psychology*, 1985; **36**, 531–572.

KLAUER, T. and FILIPP, S.-H. Der "Fragebogen zur Erfassung von Formen der Krankheitsbewältigung" (FEKB): I. Kurzbeschreibung des Verfahrens (Berichte aus dem Forschungsprojekt "Psychologie der Krankheitsbewältigung" Nr. 13). Trier: University of Trier, Fachbereich I—Psychologie, 1987.

KOBASA, S. C. Stressful life events, personality, and health: An inquiry into hardiness. *Journal of Personality and Social Psychology*, 1979; **37**, 1–11.

LAZARUS, R. S. and FOLKMAN. S. *Stress, appraisal, and coping*. New York: Springer, 1984.

LAZARUS, R. S. and LAUNIER, R. Stress-related transactions between person and environment. In L. A. Pervin and M. Lewis (eds.), *Perspectives in interactional psychology*. New York: Plenum Press, 1978.

LERNER, M. J. and GIGNAC, M. *Coping and growth among the elderly*. Paper presented at the Canadian Psychological Association Meetings, June 10, Montreal, Canada, 1988.

McCrae, R. R. Situational determinants of coping responses: Loss, threat, and challenge. *Journal of Personality and Social Psychology*, 1984; **44**, 919–928.

McCrae, R. R. and Costa, P. T. Personality, coping, and coping effectiveness in an adult sample. *Journal of Personality and Social Psychology*, 1986; **54**, 385–405.

McCubbin, H. I. and Patterson, J. M. The family stress process: The double ABCX model of adjustment and adaptation. *Marriage and Family Review*, 1983; **6**, 7–37.

Meyer, C. B. and Taylor, S. E. Adjustment to rape. *Journal of Personality and Social Psychology*, 1987; **50**, 1226–1234.

Menaghan, E. G. Individual coping efforts: Moderators of the relationship between life stress and mental health outcomes. In H. B. Kaplan (ed.), *Psychosocial stress. Trends in theory and research*. New York: Academic Press, 1983.

Miller, S. M. and Mangan, C. E. Interacting effects of information and coping style in adapting to gynaecologic stress: Should the doctor tell all? *Journal of Personality and Social Psychology*, 1983: **45**, 223–236.

Montada, L. Kritische Lebensereignisse im Brennpunkt: Eine Entwicklungsaufgabe für die Entwicklungspsychologie? In S.-H. Filipp (ed.), *Kritische Lebensereignisse*. Munich: Urban & Schwarzenberg, 1981.

Moos, R. H. (ed.). *Human adaptation: Coping with life crises*. Lexington: Heath, 1976.

Mullen, B. and Suls, J. The effectiveness of attention and rejection as coping styles: A meta-analysis of temporal differences. *Journal of Psychosomatic Research*, 1982; **26**, 43–49.

Parkes, K. R. Coping in stressful episodes: The role of individual differences, environmental factors, and situational characteristics. *Journal of Personality and Social Psychology*, 1986; **51**, 1277–1292.

Perrez, M. Bewältigung von Alltagsbelastungen und seelische Gesundheit. *Zeitschrift für Klinische Psychologie*, 1988; **17**, 292–306.

Rabkin, J. G. Stress and psychiatric disorders. In L. Goldberger and S. Breznitz (eds.), *Handbook of stress*. New York: The Free Press, 1982.

Ray, C., Lindop, J. and Gibson, S. The concept of coping. *Psychological Medicine*, 1982; **12**, 385–395.

Reese, H. W. and Smyer, M. A. The dimensionalization of life events. In E. J. Callahan and K. A. McCluskey (eds.), *Life-span developmental psychology. Nonnormative life events*. New York: Academic Press, 1983.

Riegel, K. F. Adult life crises: A dialectic interpretation of development. In N. Datan and L.H. Ginsberg (eds.), *Life-span developmental psychology. Normative life crises*. New York: Academic Press, 1975.

Rogosa, D. A critique of cross-legged correlation. *Psychological Bulletin*, 1980; **88**, 245–258.

Rosenbaum, M. Learned resourcefulness as a behavioural repertoire for the self-regulation of internal events: Issues and speculations. In M. Rosenbaum, C. M. Franks and Y. Jaffe (eds.), *Perspectives on behavior therapy in the eighties*. New York: Springer, 1983.

Roskies, E. and Lazarus, R. S. Coping theory and the teaching of coping skills. In P. O. Davidson and S. M. Davidson (eds.), *Behavioral medicine: Changing health life style*. New York: Brunner/Mazel, 1980.

Roth S. and Cohen, L. J. Approach, avoidance, and coping with stress. *American Psychologist*, 1986; **41**, 813–819.

Rothbaum, F., Weisz, J. R. and Snyder, S. S. Changing the world and changing the self: A two-process model of perceived control. *Journal of Personality and Social Psychology*, 1982; **42**, 5–37.

Scheier, M. F. and Carver, C. S. Optimism, coping, and health: Assessment and implications of generalized outcome expectancies. *Health Psychology*, 1985; **4**, 219–247.

Scheier, M. F., Weintraub, J. K. and Carver, C. S. Coping with stress: Divergent strategies of optimists and pessimists. *Journal of Personality and Social Psychology*, 1986; **51**, 1257–1264.

Schwarzer, R. and Leppin, A. Sozialer Rückhalt und Gesundheit. Göttingen: Hogrefe, 1989.

Spinetta, J. J. and Deasy-Spinetta, P. (eds.). *Living with childhood cancer*. St. Louis: Mosby, 1981.

Stern, M. J. and Pasquale, L. Psychosocial adaptation to postmyocardial infarction: The spouse's dilemma. *Journal of Psychosomatic Research*, 1979; **23**, 83–87.

STROEBE, W. and STROEBE, M. S. *Bereavement and health. The psychological and physical consequences of partner loss.* Cambridge: Cambridge University Press, 1987.

SULS, J. and FLETCHER, B. The relative efficacy of avoidant and nonavoidant coping strategies: A meta-analysis. *Health Psychology*, 1985; **4**, 249–288.

TAYLOR, S. E. Adjustment to threatening events. A theory of cognitive adaptation. *American Psychologist*, 1983; **38**, 1161–1173.

TAYLOR, S. E. and BROWN, J. D. Illusion and well-being: A social psychological perspective on mental health. *Psychological Bulletin*, 1988; **103**, 193–210.

THOITS, P. A. Social support as coping assistance. *Journal of Consulting and Clinical Psychology*, 1986; **54**, 416–423.

TURNER, R. J. Direct, indirect, and moderating effects of social support on psychological distress and associated conditions. In H. B. Kaplan (ed.), *Psychosocial stress. Trends in theory and research*. New York: Academic Press, 1983.

VAILLANT, G. E. *Adaptation to life*. Boston, MS: Little-Brown, 1977.

WEISMAN, A. D. *Coping with cancer*. New York: McGraw-Hill, 1979.

WIRTZ, P. W. and HARRELL, A. V. Effects on postassault exposure to attack-similar stimuli on long-term recovery of victims. *Journal of Consulting and Clinical Psychology*, 1987; **55**, 10–16.

WORTMAN, C. B. Coping with victimization: Conclusions and implications for future research. *Journal of Social Issues*, 1983; **39**(2), 195–221.

WORTMAN, C. B. Social support and the cancer patient. Conceptual and methodological issues. *Cancer*, 1984; **53**, 2339–2360.

WORTMAN, C. B. and LEHMAN, D. R. Reactions to victims of life crises: Support attempts that fail. In I. G. Sarason and B. R. Sarason (eds.), *Social support: Theory, research and applications*. Dordrecht: Martinus Nijhoff, 1985.

WORTMAN, C. B. and SILVER, R. C. Coping with irrevocable loss. In G. R. Vanderbos and B. K. Bryant (eds.), *Cataclysms, crises, catastrophies: Psychology in action* (Master Lecture Series, Vol. 6). Washington, D.C.: APA, 1987.

WORTMAN, C. B. and SILVER, R. C. The myths of coping with loss. *Journal of Consulting and Clinical Psychology*, 1989; **57**, 349–357.

ZERSSEN, D. VON. *Die Befindlichkeitsskala*. Weinheim: Beltz, 1976.

Notes

1. This line of research, by the way, does have immediate, yet largely overlooked relevance for the assessment of life events, since it illustrates that commonly used life event checklists may suffer from severe reliability problems as long as the conditions under which life events are recalled and reported are not controlled (e.g. Jenkins, Hurst and Rose, 1979).
2. Contrary to the original scale, high scores denote high levels of well-being.
3. Because *search for information* and *search for meaning in religion* were simultaneously uncorrelated to well-being, these scales were omitted from further analyses here. However, the possibility of "sleeper effects", i.e. correlational as well as causal relations emerging within a further enlarged time span, remains.

Acknowledgement

The research project referred to in the last part of this chapter was supported by a grant from the Deutsche Forschungsgemeinschaft (Fi 346/1-3).

12

Work and Leisure Satisfaction

ADRIAN FURNHAM

Introduction

To what extent is subjective well-being determined by a person's job and/or leisure satisfaction? What are the major determinants of job satisfaction? What is the relationship between work and leisure? What are the major consequences of work and/or leisure dissatisfaction for subjective well-being? This chapter will attempt to answer a number of these questions which have stimulated a great deal of empirical research.

Both work and leisure are major sources of general satisfaction, as well as dissatisfaction. The importance of these determinants of well-being are seen perhaps most clearly when they go wrong, such as when people lose their job, stop work for reasons associated with age, ill-health or there is a major change in the economic outlook (depression, hyper-inflation) and they are unable to take part in their preferred leisure activity. From these experiences one can see the role, meaning and function of work and leisure in an individual's life.

What is the role of work in a person's life? Fraser (1962) put it thus:

> "Ought [the individual] to find in [work] his principal means of self-expression? Ought it to be the cause of his deepest satisfactions? Should it be the biggest thing in his life? This is to demand a great deal both of the individual and the job, and it is unlikely that more than a small proportion of any community will ever approach such a standard. Nor may it be desirable that they should, for the number of individuals who have this level of motivation to pour into their work is limited, while the number of jobs into which it should be worth pouring it is similarly restricted. On the other hand, ought work to make as few demands as possible on the individual? Ought it to offer only a limited sense of achievement or identification? Ought it to become a means of putting in part of the day quite agreeably while at the same time providing the wherewithal to finance home and leisure pursuits? There are individuals to whom a job like this would make a strong appeal and who might find their real satisfactions in other areas of their life. Between these extremes there will be jobs and individuals with different levels of expectation and satisfaction to offer and receive, and if we were to match up each with the other we might claim to have achieved the ideal industrial community. Those who expected a great deal from their work and were prepared to put a lot into it would be in jobs which utilized all their potentialities

235

to the full and gave them in return a deep sense of personal achievement. Those who neither expected nor were prepared to contribute very much would be in the comfortable, undemanding jobs where they would be reasonably occupied, well paid and contented."

Whilst everybody might not agree with this very psychological approach it raises many important questions which this chapter hopes, in part, to address. The nature, purpose and benefit of work has been debated by all the great modern writers: Freud, Marx, Morris, Ruskin. Sociological thinking about work is highly political and frequently utopian. Various implicit assumptions and personal values appear to determine, in part, writers' ideas on work (Cherrington, 1980; Salaman 1986). There are many famous essays on work time: Bertrand Russell's "In Praise of Idleness", published in *Harpers Magazine* (1932); William Morris's "Useful work versus useless toil", published in the *Socialist Platform* (1885). Anthony (1984) has suggested that the ideology of work has taken two forms—an official view, representing the employer's injunction that work should be well done and a radical view that work should be re-organized to be more fulfilling to workers. This distinction is, of course, crude but represents the extremes on at least one dimension of the debate. Clearly much depends on how one defines work itself.

Hall (1986) offered as his definition of work: "Work is the effort or activity of an individual performed for the purpose of providing goods or services of value to others; it is also considered to be work by the individual performed" (p. 13). Whereas many would be unhappy with this definition because of the omission of any comment about pay, occupational role etc., he does attempt a taxonomy of work by looking at different types of work: professions, managerial and professional occupations, white collar work, skilled blue-collar work, semi-skilled blue-collar work and unskilled work as well as farm work and housework. He does however try to come to terms with the meaning of work to individuals and in doing so holds three assumptions: people vary hourly/daily in their orientation to work; work varies widely in what it provides the individual; there is the hierarchy of needs in terms of how people respond to or are motivated by their work. This seems to imply complete individual and transient phenomenology and yet he identifies various dimensions of work shared by all. This is certainly a problem for the meaning of the work concept—how it is acquired and how idiosyncratic it is.

The meaning and functions of work

A great deal has been written about the meaning and function of work. Fineman (1987) claims that middle class work is portrayed as:

– A key source of identity, self respect and social status.
– The most central life activity, more important than leisure.

– Intrinsically valuable and rewarding.
– Difficult to separate from other aspects of life.
– Providing secure, predictable and increasing rewards for effort.
– Allowing for the development and acquisition of discretion, power, and control over people, things and processes.

Others have attempted to list the most crucial factors contributing to the psychology of work. In summarizing numerous other authors who have written on the topic, Fagin and Little (1984) listed seven major functions of work:

(1) Work as a source of identity—the work people do classifies them in terms of class status and influence and established hierarchies and groupings from which people demand a sense of security, recognition, belonging and understanding. Work identity may be transferred to children or other family members but may be lost on retirement or unemployment.

(2) Work as a source of relationships outside the nuclear family. Work allows emotional outlet in family relationships as well as enriching the scope of interpersonal relationships which in turn has benefits on family life.

(3) Work as a source of obligatory activity—work provides a very useful framework of regular purposeful activity. Despite the fact that this function is largely imposed and often resented, when it is taken away it can cause considerable difficulty and hardship.

(4) Work as an opportunity to develop skills and creativity—although work can satisfy sensual and aggressive instincts, as well as allay fears or anxieties, it can allow for the mastery, control or altering of the environment. There is considerable satisfaction in the integrating and co-ordinating of intellectual and motor functions which lead, over time, to the development of skills.

(5) Work as a factor which structures time—because work structures time into regular, predictable time periods involved with rest, refreshment and actual work it provides a useful temporal framework, within which people can become materially active and happy.

(6) Work as a sense of purpose—at best work prevents classic signs of alienation such as feelings of powerlessness, self-estrangement, isolation and meaninglessness. While at best work ensures interdependence with others which helps in the development and achieving of life goals.

(7) Work is a source of income and control—work means putting oneself in the hands of employers during working hours so long as it provides sufficient money to assure oneself of independence and free choice of leisure and future outside the work place.

Various writers have attempted to identify the major functions and benefits of work (Shepherdson, 1984; Shimmin, 1966). What they have not done, however, in these listing exercises is either to rank order items or discuss how they are empirically or conceptually related. Indeed most of the researchers in this field have studied the effects of unemployment on individuals and by seeing their various deprivations have inferred the possible benefits of work.

Based on her work dating from the 1930s Jahoda (1982) has developed a theory based on the idea that what produces psychological distress in the unemployed is the deprivation of the latent functions of work. These include: the structuring of time, shared experience, source of identity, experience of mastery and source of activity.

This "deprivation theory" has had its critics, Fryer (1986) has offered three kinds of criticism:

(1) Pragmatic—the theory is very difficult to test.
(2) Methodological—one cannot be sure which or how the deprivations are caused by unemployment; people *not* deprived do not necessarily enjoy, appreciate or acknowledge this state.
(3) Empirical—the theory does not take into account change over time or individual differences in reaction.

Fryer (1986) argues that the latent functions theory has not been properly verified and that some of the observed consequences of unemployment need a different theory. They feel that individuals develop towards self-determination and autonomy and that behaviour is determined as much from within as from external demands. That is, some unemployed people take part in creative and autonomous activities and appear to cope with lack of work fairly well.

In a sense Jahoda (1982) argues that people are *deprived* while Fryer (1986) argues that institutions *impose* things on people (like stigma). Whereas the former underplays individual choice and personal control, the latter tends to underplay social identity and inter-dependence of people at work.

An alternative model has been proposed by Warr (1987) called the "vitamin" model which assumes that mental health is influenced by the environment in a manner analogous to the effects of vitamins on physical health.

"The availability of vitamins is important for physical health up to but not beyond a certain level. At low levels of intake, vitamin deficiency gives rise to physiological impairment and ill-health but after attainment of specified levels there is no benefit derived from additional quantities. It is suggested that principal environmental features are important to mental health in a similar manner: their absence tends towards an impairment in mental health, but their presence beyond a required level does not yield further benefit. In addition, however, certain vitamins become harmful in very large quantities. In these infrequent cases the association between increased vitamin intake and health becomes negative after a broad range of moderate quantities" (p. 10).

Thus, for instance, up to a point vitamins C and E improve health but then have no further effect, while A and D in moderation increase health but in excess are bad for people. Thus pay, physical conditions and interpersonal contact may be like vitamins C and E, while control, job variety, clarity and workload might be like vitamins A and D.

For Warr (1987) there are nine basic vitamins, the benefits of work or the principal features of the environment:

(1) Opportunity for intrinsic and extrinsic control.
(2) Opportunity for skill use.
(3) Externally generated goals.
(4) Variety.
(5) Environmental clarity.
(6) Availability of money.
(7) Physical security.
(8) Opportunity for interpersonal contact.
(9) Valued social position.

Warr (1987) is aware of a number of problems with this approach. Firstly, that his list of nine vitamins may be enlarged (subdivided) or reduced (re-classified), but he believes that in the interests of parsimony, inclusiveness and complexity it seems sufficient. Secondly, that when looking at the relationship between these features at work and mental health it becomes progressively more difficult to define the latter, which has itself many different components and conceptualizations. Thirdly, there is a paucity of empirical evidence in favour of certain features of the model and by definition a plethora in others. Fourthly, that the model is exclusively a situation or environment centred model in that it looks at the effects of job characteristics on mental health and not at individual differences.

However, Warr (1987) does offer some insights into personal characteristics and mental health in jobs and unemployment. The model assumes that the subjective well-being, like general health, is due to a balance of various factors and that too much or too little of one could radically upset the system.

The research on the meaning and function of work appears on the one hand to show some consensus in theoretical speculations regarding what intrinsic psychological features work fulfils, but lack of agreement as to what happens when, through unemployment, retirement or illness people are deprived of work and hence the latent functions associated with it. Perhaps one important distinction to bear in mind is the *quality* of work. Not all work provides these functions and can, in fact, be frustrating and unpleasant. Warr has in fact distinguished between "good" and "bad" work (see Table 12.1).

TABLE 12.1. *The characteristics of "good" jobs and "bad" jobs*

	Current work	
	"Good" jobs have	"Bad" jobs have
1. Money (gross income, perks, retirement benefits etc.)	more	less
2. Variety (of tasks in and outside the job determining where, for how long, with whom, on what one works)	more	less
3. Goals/traction (commitment to an interrelated set of tasks and goals)	more	less
4. Decision latitude (scope for freedom in decision making with reference to a wide variety of activities)	more	less
5. Skill use and development (opportunity to practise already possessed skills while developing others)	more	less
6. Psychological threat (associated with failure, loss of job, no promotion etc.)	less	more
7. Security (in terms of the job itself, one's position, income etc.)	more	less
8. Interpersonal contact (with superiors, peers, and subordinates at work)	more	less
9. Valued social position (the status, title and prestige attached to one's job)	more	less

It is only "good" work that provides the benefits noted above. However, this definition may well be tautologous in that "good" work is defined in terms of its benefits *and* vice versa. Nevertheless, the point is worth making that it is not just work itself but particular types of work that lead to satisfaction and well-being.

The relationship between work and leisure

Despite difficulties with both definitions and measurement, researchers are agreed that the concepts of work and leisure are multidimensional, although there is no clear consensus what the dimensions are, nor is there any agreement about the relationship between work and leisure despite the fact that it has been discussed since the time of Plato (O'Leary, 1973). Since Wilensky (1960) it has been customary to divide the relationship between leisure and work into three quite different relationships: (*Spillover*—leisure is an *extension* of work, hence they are similar, there is no demarcation between work and leisure and work is the person's central interest; *Compensation*— leisure is in opposition to work in which leisure is set apart from and counterposed to work; *Neutrality*—leisure and work are somewhat different and while the demarcation is not strong the person is probably more interested in leisure.

Wilensky (1960) describes two of these as follows:

"The *compensatory leisure* hypothesis: . . . the Detroit auto-worker, for eight hours gripped bodily to the main line, doing repetitive, low-skilled, machine-paced work which is wholly ungratifying, comes rushing out of the plant gate, helling down the super-highway at 80 miles an hour in a second-hand Cadillac Eldorado, stops off for a beer and starts a bar-room brawl, goes home and beats his wife, and in his spare time throws a rock at a Negro moving into the neighbourhood. In short, his routine of leisure is an explosive compensation for the deadening rhythms of factory life. The *spillover leisure* hypothesis: Another auto-worker goes quietly home, collapses on the couch, eats and drinks alone, belongs to nothing, reads nothing, knows nothing, votes for no one, hangs around the home and the street, watches the "late-late" show, lets the TV programmes shade into one another, too tired to lift himself off the couch for the act of selection, too bored to switch the dials. In short, he develops a spillover leisure routine in which alienation from work becomes alienation from life; the mental stultification produced by his labour permeates his leisure."

Though the description above is interesting it remains debatable as to whether the description of the "spill-over" thesis is correct.

Parker (1972) has attempted to look at the consequences of these three relationships, which he calls extension, opposition and neutrality, in a range of relationships.

Work-leisure relationship variables	Extension	Opposition	Neutrality
Content of work and leisure	similar	deliberately different	usually different
Demarcation of spheres	weak	strong	average
Central life interest	work	—	non-work
Imprint left by work on leisure	marked	marked	not marked
Work variables			
Autonomy in work situation	high	—	low
Use of abilities (how far extended)	fully ("stretched")	unevenly ("damaged")	not ("bored")
Involvement	moral	alienative	calculative
Work colleagues	include some close friends	—	include no close friends
Work encroachment on leisure	high	low	low
Typical occupations	social workers (especially residential)	"extreme" (mining fishing)	routine clerical and manual
Non-work variables			
Educational level	high	low	medium
Duration of leisure	short	irregular	long
Main function of leisure	continuation of personal development	recuperation	entertainment

FIGURE 12.1 Types of work–leisure relationship and associated variables (individual level)

Each of these possibilities, particularly the former two suggest a wide variety of hypotheses that may be tested—work satisfaction is correlated with leisure satisfaction, types of work activities are correlated with leisure activities; the degree of role involvement in work might be related to the degree of role involvement in leisure. Naturally a clear cut hypotheses testing opportunity such as this has attracted a good deal of research as well as review and conceptual clarification (Wilson, 1980; Staines, 1980). According to Wilson (1980), who reviewed a number of studies in this area, both the *kinds of activities* and the *satisfaction derived* at work tend to spill over into leisure. Staines (1980) concludes similarly:

> "Data from relevant studies support the notions of spillover and compensation under different conditions but, overall, offer more evidence of spillover than compensation. Support for spillover, for example, is reflected in the positive correlations between general types of activities engaged in at work and corresponding types of activities in non work. Support is also shown in the positive correlations between subjective reactions to work and to leisure and family life. The most important exceptions to this pattern of spillover concern physical effort on the job. Workers who expend a relatively great amount of physical effort at work are less involved in non work activities and less likely to be physically active away from their job" (p. 111).

Recent evidence can be found for the spillover hypothesis, for instance, in the leisure patterns of retired workers whose retirement activities look very much like their previous work (Kremer and Harpaz, 1982). However, there is both argument and evidence for the compensation hypothesis. Miller and Weiss (1982) argued that it cannot be assumed that different leisure activities (writing poetry, gardening, motor mechanics) have different significances for the people engaging in them (they are all forms of creativity). Equally it cannot be assumed that the same activity has the same meaning for all individuals. They argued that individuals sometimes compensate for work deficiences through leisure activities. By examining organized league bowling they found individuals in low status jobs stressed the importance of prize winning in leisure more than people with high status jobs to compensate for their lack of achievement at work. Their argument was that since low and high status individuals did not differ in their abilities actually to win prizes, the results are attributed to the desire of low status individuals to compensate for lack of occupational status through leisure achievement.

Whereas a great deal of effort has gone into examining the spillover and compensation hypothesis for the relation between work and leisure there are at least six possible relationships. These are spelt out in Figure 12.2.

Three things need to be said about Figure 12.2 before these variables are described in any detail. The first is that the precise work and leisure features are not specified. Kabanoff (1980), for instance, has come up with five facets or attributes. This therefore implies that it is possible that one facet of work (e.g. job satisfaction) may be related to a specific aspect of leisure (e.g. absolute amount of time spent) but not another. Furthermore, it is not necessarily the case that features common to both leisure and work such as satisfaction are related.

Secondly, these different possible relationships, as spelt out in Figure

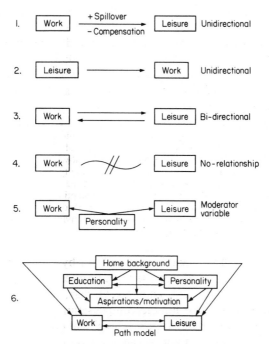

F<small>IG</small>. 12.2. Possible relationships between work and leisure.

12.2 are not mutually exclusive. Indeed the two unidirectional models both operate in the bi-directional model. Similarly the simplistic moderator variable approach could be inducted in a much more complex model. Thirdly, and related to the above two points, it is quite possible that the different models may all apply at the same time but refer to different aspects of, or facets of the relationship.

Furthermore, the examples in Figure 12.2 look at the relationship between work and leisure and not more general features of behaviour. For instance, it does not consider the relationship between job satisfaction and overall life satisfaction or happiness. It may well be that life satisfaction causes job and leisure satisfaction but not vice versa.

Item 1 shows the much debated and intuitive model where work needs, frustrations and attitudes determine (in some sense) leisure such as the choice of leisure, satisfaction in leisure, etc. Item 2 shows the precise opposite where, in some way the experience of leisure (satisfaction, energy level) determines similar or related features at work. Item 3 shows the more realistic bi-directional model of reciprocal causality such that both work and leisure experience have effects on one another. Item 4 shows the possibility of no relationship between the two such that each are independently determined and operative. Items 5 and 6 show the moderator variable approach at different levels of complexity. Item 5 shows personality features (such as extraversion and neuroticism) which have direct effects on both work and leisure so that it may erroneously appear as if the two (work and leisure) are closely directly related, whereas they are moderated through personality. Item 6 shows the fully integrated model which is, in essence, a combination of examples 1, 2, 3 and 5. This suggests that many demographic and psychographic features are related to choice of subjective experience in and attitudes to both work and leisure.

Various attempts to examine the relationship between work and leisure have attempted to break down factors on either side of the equation. The literature on the relationship between work and non-work has been examined in many ways. Shamir (1983) looked at the "conflict" between the two as a function of aspects of a person's *work schedule*. Elizur (1986), on the other hand, used facet analysis to divide work/non-work relations into three different categories: cognitive, affective and instrumental. In this sense the relationship between work and leisure could be compensatory, spillover and extentionary at the same time because each could refer to the relationship in one of the three domains. This of course complicates the picture but probably reflects the somewhat complex nature of reality. Yet another approach has been that of Shaffer (1987) who argued that patterns of work and non-work satisfactions are mediated through individual differences. He found six different profiles including work and non-work compensators materially dissatisfied individuals and dissatisfied isolates.

One additional complication regarding the model for the association between work and leisure is that it is quite possible that different models or theories apply to different work/leisure phenomena. For instance, Parker (1983) considered the relationship between: work and leisure *involvement*; work and leisure *activities*; work and leisure *attitudes*. Thus, it is possible that regarding activities there is evidence of spillover, while involvement shows evidence of compensation, attitudes support the neutrality position. More than others Kabanoff and colleagues (Kabanoff, 1980; Kabanoff and O'Brien, 1980, 1982) have attempted a clear empirical *and* theoretical analysis of the relationship between work and non-work. They proposed a *task attribute* analysis where people described their jobs on five task attributes—autonomy, variety, skill-utilization, pressure and interaction.

Kabanoff (1980) suggests that four distinct work/leisure patterns exist:

(1) Passive generalization—low levels of both the work and leisure attributes (predominantly males with low income, education and intrinsic work motivations).

(2) Supplemental compensation—low levels of an attribute in work, but a high level in leisure (predominantly older, low income, internally controlled, low extrinsic work motivation people).

(3) Active generalization—high levels of an attribute in both work and

leisure (these tended to be better educated, high income, intrinsically, rather than extrinsically, motivated people).

(4) Reactive compensation—high levels of an attribute at work and a low level in leisure (predominantly males, job centred and those with intrinsic motivation).

He concludes:

> "In future we should abandon oversimplified indirectional models of work and leisure that offer little or no account of the processes that underly the interactions among different life spheres. The time for creating *ad hoc* typologies is past, and the future must see a concern with deriving empirical evidence dealing with rather than ignoring the undoubtedly complex in interchange between the individual's work and nonwork life" (p. 94).

Wilson (1980) has also identified major problems in this area of research: "work" is often measured by occupational group rather than what people actually do. In other words, occupational groups or even professionals with similar titles do very different activities at work and it should not be assumed that they are homogeneous. Because it is acknowledged that both work and leisure are multi-dimensional it could be that both compensation and spillover hypothesis are operating at the same time. Hence, similar effects may arise from different causes and vice versa. Intervening variables such as one's position in the life cycle may change the nature of the relationship between work and leisure. It is just as important to demarcate which possible intervening variables are important as defining the nature of the relationship between work and leisure. In examining the relationship between work and leisure one cannot ignore the effect of the occupational milieu. That is, shared, consensually defined and strongly work-related leisure may function to replenish the labour force and legitimate present working arrangements.

Clearly the relationship between work and leisure is crucial for understanding the nature of subjective well-being as a whole, particularly if one presumes to intervene in the process. Certainly current research and thinking has demonstrated that the relationship between work, leisure and general satisfaction is not simple.

The causes of job satisfaction: person, job, fit

There are a number of potential causes of job satisfaction. It may be that some people because of their sex, age, beliefs or personality are more (or less) satisfied in (all) jobs than others and that a select set of specific *person* variables are the best predictors of job satisfaction. On the other hand, it could equally be true that certain jobs, by virtue of their conditions, rewards and opportunities are more satisfying than others. Hence, the best predictors of job satisfaction are certain highly specific and quantifiable job factors associated with all jobs. Alternatively, it may well be that a particular fit or match between specific characteristics of the person and the job are the clearest and most powerful predictors of job satisfaction. That is, it is the "*fit*" between person and job characteristics that best predicts satisfaction and well-being. Presumably a good fit leads to subjective well-being, and a bad fit stress to strain. It may also lead to differences in efficacy. For instance, Furnham (1987) has given the example of a hypothetical relationship between introversion/extraversion and open/closed office design.

It was suggested that extraverts with high needs for arousal and stimulation may perform well in an open-plan office because of the noise, movement and variety but poorly in the comparative deprivation of closed-plan offices, while the opposite will probably be true for introverts. In this sense a fit between types/traits and environment may lead to greater or less efficacy, satisfaction and productivity.

Van Harrison (1978) has suggested that there are two kinds of P-E fit: the extent to which an individual's skills and abilities match the requirements of the job they are doing, and also the extent to which the job environment provides the resources to meet the needs of the individual. Misfit of either kind can threaten the individual's well-being and may result in various adverse effects upon health, job satisfaction and general well-being. The coping strategies that may be employed by an individual to reduce job stress include changes in the objective person or environment in order to improve the fit between the two. The individual may also use defence mechanisms to distort their perception of P-E fit, or to deny the experience of job stress altogether. Use of these coping procedures may reduce strain and overcome the problems involved, but if the measures are unsuccessful the stress effects, which are additive, may lead to long-term problems such as poor health, low self-esteem and job dissatisfaction.

According to Caplan (1983), the theory of person-environment fit distinguishes between two types of fit: the first is between *needs* (such as for achievement) and *values* of the person, with the environmental *supplies* and *opportunities* to meet them, which in the employees' terms may be seen as the needs and supplies fit, or in the employer's terms as the abilities and demands fit. The second type of fit distinguishes between objective and subjective person and environment characteristics. The objective environment refers to the environment as it exists independently of the person's perception of it, while the subjective environment is the person's psychological construction of the world in which he lives. Similarly the objective person refers to the person as he really is, while the subjective person includes the individual's perception of his abilities, needs and values. The correspondence between objective and subjective P is labelled *accuracy of self-assessment* (or self-awareness) while the correspondence between objective and subjective E is labelled *contact with reality* (or environmental awareness). This is illustrated in Figure 12.3.

Furthermore, the exact relationship between *fit* and its opposite, *strain*, are not clear. Caplan (1983) has mentioned three types of relationships:

(1) A U-shape curve: excesses (too much work) or deficits (too little work) in the environment lead to high levels of strain (C).
(2) Asymptotic curve: either an excess of P (but not a deficit) or an excess of E (but not a deficit) can lead to strain (B).
(3) Linear effect: the absolute amount of one PE component (P relative to E) has a linear effect on strain (A).

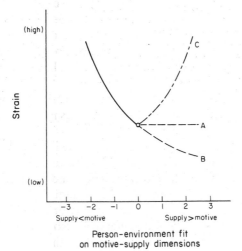

Person–environment fit
on motive–supply dimensions

FIG. 12.3. Three hypothetical shapes of the relationship between person-environment fit, motive-supply dimensions and strain. (Reprinted from van Harrison, 1978, in C. L. Cooper and R. Payne, *Stress at work*, published by John Wiley and Sons Ltd.)

Several examples showing the adverse effects of P-E misfit on health have been reported which highlight the importance of the individual's personality being congruent with their work environment (Brook, 1973; Hinkle, 1973). The need for congruence between a person's interests and abilities, and the factors inherent in their environment forms the basis for a theory of vocational choice proposed by Holland (1973), which has been used as a measure of P-E fit. Holland describes the relationship of P-E fit and stress disorders, low job satisfaction and similar ill-effects in terms of a number of personality and environmental constructs which he has defined. He suggested that one can characterize people by their resemblance to each of the six personality types: realistic, investigative, artistic, social, enterprising and conventional, which are a product of characteristic interaction among a variety of cultural and personal influences. These types form a hexagon where Euclidian distance is a measure of actual difference. As a result of developmental experiences a person learns at first to prefer some activities rather than others; later these activities become strong interests which lead to a particular group of competencies. Finally, when this has occurred, a person's interests and competencies create a particular disposition that leads them to perceive, think and act in ways which are more appropriate to some occupations than others. By comparing a person's attributes to those of each model type one can determine which type they resemble most. The three types which the person most resembles are placed together in descending order to provide what is termed as the person's "personality profile".

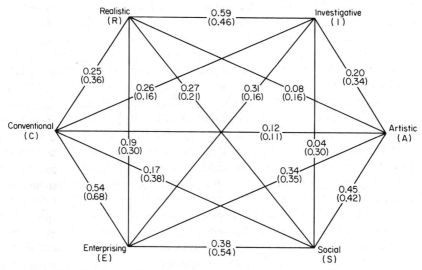

FIG. 12.4. Correlations from the hexagonal model (correlations from Holland in parentheses). Furnham and Schaeffer (1987).

Therefore, following the hexagonal Figure 12.4 it may be concluded that a conventional person in an artistic job (or vice versa) should show maximum signs of dissatisfaction while an investigative person in a realistic or social job would show equal amounts of dissatisfaction, certainly more so than if he or she were in an artistic job. Although the correlations do not always support the thesis the literature tends to offer support for Holland's work.

The environments in which people live and work can also be characterized according to their resemblance to six model environments corresponding to the six personality types above. Because the different types have different interests, competencies and dispositions, they tend to surround themselves with people and situations congruent with their interests, capabilities and outlook on the world. People tend to search for environments that will let them exercise their skills and abilities and express their personality, i.e. social types look for social environments in which to work. It has, however, been suggested that some environments are more satisfying than others irrespective of the personality of the person (Mount and Muchinsky, 1978). Congruent environments provide job satisfaction for people because they are among people with similar tastes and values to their own, and where they can perform tasks which they enjoy and are able to do. Some environments, e.g. the social environment, contain people with whom a wide variety of individuals can get along, and provide tasks which many types of people enjoy and find easy to do. Mount and Muchinsky's results suggest that even if a person's aptitudes were more congruent with a realistic or investigative environment, they find a social environment interesting enough to obtain satisfaction from it.

Studies have been done on people from widely different occupations (Harrison, 1978), in different countries and on different age groups (Kahara, Liang and Fellon, 1980). Furthermore, a large number of dependent variables—career change, labour turnover, performance and motivation—have been shown to be associated with P-E fit (Kasl, 1973). For instance, Caplan *et al.*, (1975) have shown that P-E fit (but not P or E on its own) predicted depression in an occupationally stratified sample of 318 employees from twenty-three occupations. Similarly, Furnham and Schaeffer (1984) showed P-E fit was positively associated with job satisfaction and negatively associated with mental health and vice versa. They note:

"That is, there may be both adaptive and non-adaptive reactions to stress and poor P-E fit. If for whatever reason persons find themselves in a job incongruent with their personality, a number of possible solutions may be found to change this presumably unpleasant state of affairs—the person may leave the job (resign) or try to change it in some way to become more compatible with their needs, or, finally, adapt their needs to fit more closely the contingencies of the job. The latter two approaches may be seen as adaptive while the former is non-adaptive. Another non-adaptive response may be to remain unhappily in the job with no attempt (or a failed attempt) at change and with the result of high job dissatisfaction and the possibility of increased mental and physical illness. Coping with stress is not solely affected by the individual concerned or the P-E fit but may be mediated by outside events, e.g., life-events, financial situation and support from others. Social support factors can act as mediators of stress effects; they can act as buffers against both the psychological and physiological effects of stress caused by P-E fit incongruity. As has been noted above, an increase in minor psychiatric morbidity is only one possible consequence of a person-job incongruence. What is perhaps a more interesting question is what factors lead one person to resign, another to become apathetic or destructive, while yet others become mentally ill" (p. 305).

More recently, Furnham and Walsh (1989) found P-E fit related to absenteeism, work frustration and stress. In the first study P-E fit measures of congruency, consistency and differentiation were correlated with two measures of absenteeism, work frustration and various demographic correlates. Contrary to predictions, two measures of absenteeism were positively correlated with P-E congruence and consistency. However, in accordance with the hypothesis, work frustration was highly negatively correlated with congruence and consistency. In the second study consistency, but not congruence or differentiation was significantly negatively correlated with work stress as predicted.

As Caplan (1983) has concluded: "In general, however, P-E fit has explained only an additional 1 per cent to 5 per cent variance in strain. It has, however, consistently doubled the amount of variance explained" (p. 42). Argyle (1989) has reviewed the Michigan studies and pointed out some of the more important implications of P-E fit. To reduce stress, individuals need to be in the appropriate jobs. This can partly be achieved by better selection in the first place, and then by good supervision and personnel management, sometimes leading if necessary to transfer and retraining. Individuals can change themselves, by training and following a career pattern, to fit the job better. The reason that older workers are more satisfied is probably that they have adjusted more to the job or have managed to alter the job to suit them. Participation in decisions has been found to be one way to improve P-E fit.

There is, then, a wealth of evidence to suggest that a positive fit between persons (their abilities, needs, values, etc.) and their working environment (its demands, output) leads to satisfaction, good performance, higher mental and physical health. However, as has been noted, one of the major problems of the P-E fit literature has been the measurement of P and E. Although researchers have become more and more sophisticated in the identification and measurement of salient, work-related, individual differences, several developments have occurred in the description, measurement and established consequences of work situations. Clearly the implications for well-being are enormous. If work-related difficulties spill over into a persons' private life it may be expected that the nature of their person-job "fit" or "misfit" is fundamentally important to their psychological functioning.

Personality as a predictor of work/leisure satisfaction

Is personality alone a major, sufficient or necessary determinant of work and leisure satisfaction? Are there, quite simply, happy contented people who tend to be happy at work and play irrespective of the extrinsic features of the latter? Are happy, adapted, satisfied people better at choosing or creating more satisfying jobs and leisure activities? If personality is an important determinant of work and leisure satisfaction precisely which dimensions or factors of personality are most or least predictive? How much of the variance in the determinants of leisure, and work satisfaction is accounted for by personality variables?

Despite the obvious interest and importance of the above questions there has been something of a paucity of research (Adler and Weiss, 1988).

However, there has been some work on the relationship between personality and occupational variables. British research on successful businessmen (Eysenck, 1967) and entrepreneurs (Lynn, 1969) has established that they tend to be stable introverts. However, as Wilson (1981) has argued, this may not be true in America where extraversion is a more positively valued characteristic. Also, Henney (1975) has argued that the size of an organization and different management functions (i.e. production, sales, personnel) might moderate the relationship between personality and job aptitude. Bass and Barrett (1981) have noted that those who experience low job satisfaction tend to be poorly socially adjusted, with few personal relationships, and minor psychiatric symptoms. That is, job satisfaction appears to be related to mental health (neuroticism) though the direction of causality is unclear. There are also a number of studies on cognitive or "belief" variables—particularly locus of control—as they relate to different aspects of organizational behaviour (Hammer and Vardi, 1981). Spector (1982) has argued that locus of control is related to job motivation, effort, performance, satisfaction, perception of the job, compliance with authority and supervisory style. Overall people with internal locus of control tend to be more satisfied than those with external locus of control (Organ and Greene, 1974; King, Murray and Atkinson, 1982).

There is also a limited number of studies on personality variables *per se*. For instance, Cooper and Payne (1967), in a study of eighty-one female tobacco packers found that extraverts tended to have higher levels of non-permitted absence and more visits to the sick bay than introverts. Further, a follow-up study a year later found a much greater proportion of the extraverts had left their jobs. Both results are explained in terms of Eysenck's arousal theory and the needs for stimulation by extraverts in boring jobs. Blunt (1978) found personnel managers had higher neuroticism scores than finance or production managers. Further, the sales and marketing managers were most extraverted and the technical and transport group most introverted. Hence, he concluded that the extraversion dimension may be particularly useful in predicting job satisfaction. Skinner (1983) looked at the relationship between machiavellianism, extraversion and toughmindedness in business occupations. As predicted he found business high machiavellians were significantly more extraverted than their non-business counterparts, which confirms the belief that successful entrepreneurs are skilful in public relations. Indeed experimental studies on human performance have demonstrated the importance of personality (particularly arousal-based dimensions) variables (Geen, 1984; Strelau, 1983), many of which are no doubt related to all aspects of work. For instance, Hockey (1972) reviewed the evidence which suggests extraverts prefer and work best in noisy environments while the opposite is true of introverts.

More recently, Furnham and Zacherl (1986) found a set of modest, but consistent, correlations between personality and job satisfaction (see Table 12.2). People scoring highly on the dimensions of neuroticism and psychoticism tended to have lower scores, particularly satisfaction with co-workers, while extraverts and dissimulators tended to be more satisfied. They argued that personality may relate much more closely to job satisfaction when considering the relationship *between*, rather than, *within* occupations.

TABLE 12.2. *Correlations between the four personality measures and the eight job satisfaction factors (N = 88)*

Job satisfaction factors	Personality scale			
	Psychoticism	Extraversion	Neuroticism	Lie
1. Supervision	−0.17*	0.01	−0.12	0.15
2. Nature of the work	−0.21*	−0.11	−0.14	0.32***
3. Amount of work	−0.01	0.10	−0.33***	0.28**
4. Working conditions	−0.05	0.10	−0.08	0.10
5. Co-workers	−0.19*	0.05	−0.31***	0.21*
6. Pay	0.01	0.20*	−0.29**	0.36***
7. Future with the organization	−0.07	0.04	−0.01	0.01
8. Overall job satisfaction	−0.03	0.18*	−0.06	0.10

Note: $*p < 0.05$; $**p < 0.01$; $***p < 0.001$.
A large number of partial correlations were computed partialling out one at a time and then in combination all other personality dimensions when examining the relationship between one dimension (i.e. extraversion) and job satisfaction. *None* of the analyses substantially changed the significance levels of the above results.

Traditional personality traits like extraversion seem modestly but predictably related to work related behaviour including satisfaction. However, it is much more likely that specific work oriented values and attitudes predict a variety of work related behaviours. One such variable that spans nearly all the social sciences is the Protestant Work Ethic. Weber's theory was introduced into psychology by McClelland (1961) who offered a social-psychological explanation for the link between Protestantism and capitalism. The theory is simply that the Protestant Work Ethic ideas and values determine child rearing practices of independence, procrastination of gratifications and mastery training, which in turn leads to the children acquiring strong achievement motivation. These high achievers in turn become successful entrepreneurs and create an expansion of business.

However, it has not been until comparatively recently that psychologists (primarily occupational and social psychologists) have actively pursued research using the Protestant Work Ethic concept. Although psychologists have been interested (and probably ignorant) about the origins of the Protestant Work Ethic and of the criticism of Weber's thesis, they have recognized the behaviour pattern of the typical high Protestant Work Ethic believer. However, it is quite possible that Protestant Work Ethic behaviour, as operationalized by psychologists, is rather different from Protestant Work Ethic beliefs as described by Weber either because they attempt to measure more or different dimensions of the Protestant Work Ethic. Scholars, conversant with Weber's original thesis, may, however, take issue with psychologists for not having read thoroughly or understood the Protestant Work Ethic concept. That is, it may be argued that scales devised to measure the Protestant Work Ethic might measure some aspect of a person's belief system and behavioural patterns but definitely not what Weber himself had in mind. Hence, the use of the term Protestant Work Ethic by psychologists may be challenged.

Most studies using the Protestant Work Ethic concept have not unsurprisingly looked at the relationship between the Protestant Work Ethic and paid employment work. Most of these have looked at the relationship between the Protestant Work Ethic and job satisfaction, but some have looked at the actual work behaviour. For example Blood (1969) using his own scale found that the more workers agreed with the ideals of the Protestant Work Ethic the more they will be satisfied in their paid work and life in general. Aldag and Brief (1975) also looked at the relationship between the Protestant Work Ethic (as measured by the Blood scale) and certain work values (affective response, perceived task dimension, perceived leader behaviour, and higher order need strength). The results confirmed the findings of Blood (1969); the pro-Protestant scale was positively correlated with internal work motivation and growth satisfaction as well as higher order need strength. On the other hand, the non-Protestant scale was negatively correlated with general satisfaction, external work motivation, supervisory satisfaction, growth satisfaction, skill variety, task identity, task significance, autonomy, feedback from job, leader consideration and high order need strength. Certainly the results supported the hypothesis that adherence to the Protestant Work Ethic is associated with strong higher order needs, which are perhaps the main alternatives of work attitudes.

Similarly Kidron (1978) found as predicted a positive relationship between the Protestant Work Ethic and moral and calculative commitment to the work organization. This relationship held over all three organizations tested, an insurance company, a hospital and a personnel department. He concluded that although the Protestant Work Ethic is associated with stronger moral identification with the organization for which one works, it need not necessarily indicate a willingness to remain in a given system.

Other studies have looked at the relationship between the Protestant Work Ethic and actual work behaviour. Merrens and Garrett (1975) suggested that as the Protestant Work Ethic beliefs are, that all had steady work, is in itself worthy, and unwillingness to work is seen as a symptom of absence of grace or as sinful, high Protestant Work Ethic scorers would perform better on tasks designed to provide low motivation and interest levels. As predicted they found high Protestant Work Ethic scorers spent significantly more time participating in a boring repetitive task than low Protestant Work Ethic scorers. Ganster (1981) however, failed to replicate this result and concluded that Merrens and Garrett's task was not representative of real jobs and that their experiment may well have induced apprehension, evaluation and hence blessed the results.

In a recent comprehensive review of the area Furnham (1989) has argued that as an independent, individual difference variable the Protestant Work Ethic may be a very useful predictor of work and leisure belief and behaviour. Furthermore, the Protestant Work Ethic is clearly related to other psychological concepts and demographic variables.

TABLE 12.3. *Hypothetical table indicating the "possible" relationship between some of the variables mentioned in this chapter*

Components of the Protestant Work Ethic	Protestant Work Ethic	Age	Education	Politics	Health	Pathology
Traits						
1. Achievement motivation*	+++	++	++	+	+	+
2. Authoritarianism*	++	+++	+	+++	+	++
3. Beliefs in a just world*	+	++	+	+++	+	+
4. Conservatism*	++	+++	+	+++	+	++
5. Personal Control*	+++	++	++	+	+++	+++
6. Postponement of gratification**	++	+	++	++	++	+
7. Social Values*	++	++	++	++	+	+
8. Type A behaviour pattern*	+	+	+	+	+++	+++
9. Entrepreneurship**	+	+	+	+	+	+
Attitudes						
1. Leisure	+++	+	++	+	++	+
2. Money	++	+	+	++	+	+
3. Time	+++	+	+	+	+	+
4. Success	++	+	+	++	+	+

Note: The + sign indicates the *strength* rather than the *direction* of the relationship.
* Traits and attitudes that represent those on which there is actual data on these relationships.
** Traits and attitudes that are not based on actual available data but hypothesized relationships between the various variables.

Table 12.3 is based partly on speculation and partly on empirical results. It shows how the Protestant Work Ethic is related to nine other psychological variables (themselves inter-related) and attitudes to such things as leisure time and success. Furthermore, the table shows the relationship between psychological health and "pathology" and these variables, though these relationships are complex and frequently moderated by numerous other variables. Nevertheless the table enables one to speculate about the relationship between various "traits" and possible well-being. To some extent, however, this work is tautologous as the traits are themselves conceived of in terms of "good" and "bad" dimensions and it is apparent that the bad or mal-adaptive end (i.e., external locus of control; inability to postpone gratification high A type behaviour) is associated with poor well-being. What would be most impressive, but does not currently exist, is a *theory* about the aetiology of the content and process of a trait that specifies the mechanism by which it leads to well-being. Although this exists to some extent in the clinical literature for traits such as neuroticism it does not seem to be the case for work-related traits. Further work on the Protestant Work Ethic or type A behaviour may, however, yield such a result.

Theories of job satisfaction

Finally, can theories of job satisfaction inform one about general subjective well-being? There is no shortage of theories of job satisfaction. These include:

(1) *Two factor theory* (Herzberg *et al.*, 1957)
 This theory suggests that job satisfaction depends on a certain set of conditions (called motivators, such as recognition and responsibility) while job dissatisfaction depends on an entirely different set of conditions (called hygiene needs, such as salary and physical working conditions). The qualitative and quantitative fulfilment of hygiene needs does not result in job satisfaction, only the elimination of dissatisfaction. Positive motivator factors, however, do lead to satisfaction.

(2) *Need theory* (Maslow, 1970)
 Basic physiological and psychological needs are fulfilled or frustrated at work. Unfulfilled needs of whatever type or level to job satisfaction, while fulfilment relieves tension and is likely to lead to satisfaction. However, because the fulfilment of any one level of needs activates the next level, people at work will, of necessity, always have an active need making long term job satisfaction unlikely.

(3) *Comparison theory* (Locke, 1976)
 Job satisfaction is the result of a comparison between what we want, desire or value in a job and what we actually find in the job. Thus, although outcomes may be the same for different work, and even though these outcomes may provide equivalent levels of need fulfilment, the workers' satisfaction may differ to the extent that the values differ.

(4) *Equity theory* (Adams, 1965)
 Job satisfaction results from the equity in perceptions of inputs and outputs on the job. In other words, there should be parity between what a worker believes he or she should receive, given what he or she brings to the job and actually does and the actual outcomes in terms of benefits.

Above are the major theories of job satisfaction though there are others. How well do they inform the question of the determinants of subjective well-being? To the extent that each theory claims to specify which factors lead to satisfaction *and* dissatisfaction and the process by which these occur, they may be seen to be relevant to subjective well-being. However, there are two things missing. Firstly, the relationship between job satisfaction and well-being itself is not clearly specified and although it seems logical that the two are positively correlated this may not necessarily be the case. This is because a person might easily compensate for work dissatisfaction out of work and have overall moderate to high subjective well-being. Secondly, few of the theories take individual differences seriously. Thus, if one is talking about *subjective* well-being the implication is that subjective—that is, individual difference—factors relate the perceptions of well-being irrespective of the objective, external facets. Most theories appear to assume few or minor individual differences in reactions to the facets or factors each specifies as being the crucial determinants of well-being.

Conclusion

This chapter has focused on the relationship between work and leisure satisfaction and subjective well-being. Despite the fact that these concepts appear to be related and indeed overlapping there appears to be little cross fertilization between the occupational/organization and social/clinical literature.

One way of approaching the issue of the importance of work to well-being is to try to establish the psychological "functions" of work, which may be done by examining the reactions of people who are, for a variety of reasons, unable to work. This research tends to yield a fairly long list of functions though no clear idea of how they relate to each other or subjective well-being *per se*. That is, there is no theory (save Warr's vitamin theory) which enables one to predict subjective well-being or satisfaction itself from a knowledge of the extrinsic or objective features of a person's job.

There is an interesting literature on the relationship between work and leisure though no general agreement as to which of a number of possible relationships is true. Certainly more recent research suggests that because both work and leisure are multi-faceted, various different relationships could exist simultaneously. Why this relationship is important to subjective well-being should be manifestly clear. If a person is able to compensate for job dissatisfaction and the possible poor subjective well-being that is concurrent upon it, they may have much greater overall well-being than someone who is unable to compensate in their leisure or free time. Research suggests that this may be true and that subjective well-being may be dependent on both work *and* leisure satisfaction.

Two rather general approaches have been taken to the causes of job (rather than leisure) satisfaction. The one is that personality traits *per se* relate directly to satisfaction, while the second is that it is the fit between personality characteristics that leads to satisfaction. There is some evidence from both camps which suggests that certain traits, or a congruent fit may account for an important, though somewhat modest amount of variance. Once again, however, there is no powerful theoretical foundation to this work since the application of well-known personality theories such as that of Eysenck (1967). More recent work on specifically work-related individual difference variables, such as the Protestant Work Ethic, seems more promising though there remains much empirical and theoretical work to be done to explain the nature of the relationships between the independent and dependent variables.

Finally various well-known theories of job satisfaction may help to focus on specific factors that relate to well-being in that the different theories focus on quite different aspects of work being the primary determinants of satisfaction, it seems apparent that the determinants of satisfaction are numerous and the relationship complex. Similarly the precise relationship between job and leisure satisfaction/dissatisfaction and well-being also remains unclear.

Continued interest in this field, manifest by books such as this, however, means that these interesting and important issues continue to be addressed.

References

ADAMS, J. Inequality in social exchange. In L. BERKOWITZ (ed.), *Advances in experimental social psychology*, Vol 2. New York: Academic Press, 1965.

ADLER, S. and WEISS, H. Recent developments in the study of personality and organizational behaviour. In C. COOPER and I. ROBERTSON (eds.), *International review of industrial and organizational psychology*. Chichester: Wiley, 1988.

ALDAG, R. and BRIEF, A. Some correlates of work values. *Journal of Applied Psychology*, 1975; **60**, 757–760.

ANTHONY, P. *The ideology of work*. London: Tavistock, 1984.

ARGYLE, M. *The social psychology of work*. Penguin: Harmondsworth, 1989.

BASS, B. and BARRETT, E. *People, work and organization*. Boston: Allyn and Bacon, 1981.

BLOOD, M. Work values and job satisfaction. *Journal of Applied Psychology*, 1969; **53**, 456–459.

BLUNT, P. Personality characteristics of a group of white South African Managers. *International Journal of Psychology*, 1978; **13**, 139–146.

BROOK, A. Mental stress at work. *The Practitioner*, 1973; 210.

CAPLAN, R. Person-environment fit: past, present and future. In C. COOPER (ed.), *Stress research: Issues for the eighties*. Chichester: Wiley, 1983.

CAPLAN, R., COBB, S., FRENCH, J., HARRISON, R. and PINNEAU, S. *Job demands and worker health*. Washington: NIOSH, 1975.

CHERRINGTON, D. *The Work Ethic: Working values and values that work*. New York: AMACOM, 1980.

COOPER, R. and PAYNE, R. Extraversion and some aspects of work behaviour. *Personnel Psychology*, 1967; **20**, 45–57.

ELIZUR, D. Achievement motives and sport performance. *International Review of Applied Psychology*, 1986; **35**, 209–224.

EYSENCK, H. *The biological basis of personality*. Springfield: Thomas, 1967.

FAGIN, L. and LITTLE, M. *The forsaken families*. Harmondsworth: Penguin, 1984.

FINEMAN, S. (ed.). *Unemployment: Personal and social consequences*. London: Tavistock, 1987.

FRASER, J. *Industrial psychology*. Oxford: Pergamon, 1962.

FRYER, D. Employment deprivation and personal agency during unemployment. *Social Behaviour*, 1986; **1**, 3–23.

FURNHAM, A. *The Protestant Work Ethic: The psychology of work related beliefs and behaviour*. London: Methuen, 1989.

FURNHAM, A. and SCHAEFFER, R. Person-environment fit, job satisfaction and mental health. *Journal of Occupational Psychology*, 1984; **57**, 295–307.

FURNHAM, A. and WALSH, D. *The consequences of person-environment incongruence: Absenteeism, frustration and stress*. Unpublished paper, 1989.

FURNHAM, A. and ZACHERL, M. Personality and job satisfaction. *Personality and Individual Differences*, 1986; **1**, 453–459.

GEEN, R. Preferred stimulation levels in introverts and extraverts: effects on arousal and performance. *Journal of Personality and Social Psychology*, 1984; **46**, 1303–1312.

HAMMER, T. and VARDI, J. Locus of control and career self-management among supervisory employees in industrial settings. *Journal of Vocational Behaviour*, 1981; **18**, 13–29.

HARRISON, R. van. Person-environment fit and job stress. In C. COOPER and R. PAYNE (eds), *Stress at work*. New York: Wiley, 1978.

HENNEY, A. Personality characteristics of a group of industrial managers. *Journal of Occupational Psychology*, 1975; **48**, 65–67.

HERZBERG, F., MAUSNER, B., PEDERSON, R. and CAPWELL, D. *Job attitudes: review of research and opinion*. Pittsburgh: Psychological services, 1957.

HINKLE, L. The concept of stress in the biological and social sciences. *Science, Medicine and Man*, 1973; **1**, 31–48.

HOCKEY, G. Effects of noise on human efficiency and some individual differences. *Journal of Sound Vibrations*, 1972; **20**, 299–304.

HOLLAND, J. *Making vocational choices: a theory of careers*. Englewood Cliff: Prentice Hall, 1973.

JAHODA, M. *Employment and unemployment: A social-psychological analysis*. Cambridge: Cambridge University Press, 1982.

KABANOFF, B. Work and non work: A review of models, methods and fittings. *Psychological Bulletin*, 1980; **88**, 60–77.

KABANOFF, B. and O'BRIEN, G. Work and leisure: A task attribute analysis. *Journal of Applied Psychology*, 1980; **65**, 595–609.

KABANOFF, B. and O'BRIEN, G. Relationships between work and leisure attributes across occupational and sex groups in Australia. *Australian Journal of Psychology*, 1982; **34**, 165–182.

KAHARA, E., LIANG, J. and FELLON, B. Alternative models of person-environment for prediction of morale in three homes for the aged. *Journal of Gerontology*, 1986; **35**, 384–395.

KASL, S. Mental health and the work environment: an examination of the evidence. *Journal of Occupational Medicine*, 1973; **15**, 509–518.

KIDRON, A. Work values and organizational commitment. *Academy of Management Journal*, 1978; **21**, 239–247.

KING, M., MURRAY, M. and ATKINSON, T. Background, personality, job characteristics and satisfaction with work in a national sample. *Human Relations*, 1982; **35**, 119–133.

KREMER, Y. and HARPAZ, I. Leisure patterns among retired workers: Spillover or compensatory trends. *Journal of Vocational Behaviour*, 1982; **21**, 183–195.

LOCKE, E. Job satisfaction. In M. GRUNEBERG and T. WALL (eds), *Social psychology and organisational behavior*. New York: Wiley, 1976.

LYNN, R. Personality characteristics of a group of entrepreneurs. *Occupational Psychologist*, 1969; **43**, 151–152.

MASLOW, N. *Motivation and personality*. New York: Harper and Row, 1970.

MCCLELLAND, D. *The achieving society*. New York: Free Press, 1961.

MERRENS, M. and GARRETT, J. The Protestant ethic scale as a predictor of repetitive work performance: A reexamination. *Psychological Reports*, 1975; **48**, 335–338.

MILLER, L. and WEISS, R. The work-leisure relationships; Evidence for the compensatory hypothesis. *Human Relations*, 1982; **35**, 763–771.

MOUNT, M. and MUCHINSKY, P. P-E congruence and employee satisfaction: A test of Holland's theory. *Journal of Vocational Behaviour*, 1978; **13**, 84–100.

O'LEARY, J. Skole and Plato's Work Ethic. *Journal Research*, 1973; **5**, 49–55.

ORGAN, D. and GREENE, C. Role ambiguity, locus of control and work satisfaction. *Journal of Applied Psychology*, 1974; **59**, 101–102.

PARKER, S. *The future of work and leisure*. London: Granada, 1972.

PARKER, S. *Leisure and work*. London: George Allen, 1983.

SALAMAN, G. *Working*. Chichester: Ellis Harwood, 1986.

SHAFFER, G. Patterns of work and nonwork satisfaction. *Journal of Applied Psychology*, 1987; **72**, 115–124.

SHAMIR, B. Some antecedents of work-nonwork conflicts. *Journal of Vocational Behaviour*, 1983; **23**, 98–111.

SHEPHERDSON, K. The meaning of work and employment: Psychological research and psychologists' values. *Australian Psychologist*, 1984; **19**, 311–320.

SHIMMIN, S. Concepts of work. *Occupational Psychology*, **40**, 193–201.

SKINNER, N. Personality correlate of machiavellianism. *Social Behaviour and Personality*, 1983; **11**, 29–32.

SPECTOR, P. Behaviour in organization as a function of employees' locus of control. *Psychological Bulletin*, 1982; **91**, 482–497.

STAINES, G. Spillover versus compensation. *Human Relations*, 1980; **33**, 111–129.

STRELAU, J.A. A regulative theory of temperament. *Australian Journal of Psychology*, 1983; **35**, 305–317.

WARR, P. *Work, unemployment and mental health*. Oxford: Clarendon Press, 1987.

WILENSKY, H. Work, careers and social integration. *International Social Science Journal*, 1960; **12**, 543–560.

WILSON, J. Sociology of leisure. *Annual Review of Sociology*, 1980; **6**, 21–40.

WILSON, G. Personality and Social Behaviour. In H. EYSENCK (ed.), *A Model for Personality*. Berlin: Springer-Verlag, 1981.

13

Quality of life in advanced industrialized countries: the case of West Germany

WOLFGANG GLATZER

Introduction

This chapter consists of two main issues. First, I shall give an impression of the Social Indicators Movement and one of its main goals concerned with the measurement of the quality of life. Secondly, I shall summarize the main findings on the subjective quality of life, illustrating them by empirical evidence from the German Welfare Surveys.

Quality of life and its measurement

Quality of life is the frame of reference of the Social Indicators Movement where the idea of measuring the quality of life was promoted. German Welfare Research and Welfare Surveys followed this line.

The social indicators movement and new types of social survey

The Social Indicators Approach seems to be out of the actual social-scientific debate, but its ideas have sedimented in many fields of the social sciences. This result of disappearance by diffusion seems to be paradoxical only at first glance (Carley, 1981; Rossi and Gilmartin, 1980). Beside general principles of analyzing social phenomena and societies, the social-indicators movement has elaborated, and at least partially established, some new research activities, especially social reporting (Glatzer, 1981). Social reports are assessed as a complement to economic reports and their guiding idea is to measure social welfare or the quality of life of the population. In order to do this adequately, representative surveys are indispensable. Only by such surveys is it possible to investigate the quality of life from the people's point of view and to generalize the results. Related to the objective of measuring the quality of life, the level of living and the individual welfare, special social surveys have been carried out in many countries during the last decade. They were named "quality of life surveys", "welfare surveys" or "comprehensive surveys", and international organizations like the United Nations, the OECD and the European Community supported these activities (Glatzer, 1982). This is the background to the German Welfare Surveys (Zapf, 1987). They are part of a worldwide effort to improve the measurement of state and change of the welfare of people.

Measuring quality of life

"Quality of Life" is a concept of societal goals and objectives which experienced its rise in the early 1970s,[1] gained a prominent place in public discussion and then lost its prominence, being differentiated into a variety of meanings (Glatzer and Mohr, 1987). There is still a basic consensus about the meaning of quality of life which holds that the welfare of society should not be measured in economic terms alone. There is also a consensus that quality of life should be measured precisely, to avoid a bare speculative diagnosis. The concept implies that a variety of life domains such as housing, health or social relations have to be taken into account in order to monitor the quality of life. It has been debated whether there has been adequate measurement of quality of life: Should measurement of the quality of life rely mainly upon objective indicators such as the person-to-room ratio or the number of social contacts a person has, or rather on subjective indicators such as satisfaction with housing or positively evaluated social relations? The unifying position is to study both objective and subjective aspects of welfare in the different life domains. Additionally, the question should be asked how objective and subjective elements of welfare are related to each other. This is the approach taken in German Welfare Research: the quality of life in the Federal Republic of Germany is measured in a selected number of life domains with regard to both the objective and the subjective dimensions, and the question of how these dimensions are related to each other is addressed (Zapf, 1987; see also Chapter 3).

Statistics produced by the national and state statistical offices are the major source of information on the "objective" living conditions in the Federal Republic. These statistics include censuses, microcensuses, economic accounts and specialized surveys, all containing socio-demographic and socio-economic data that contribute to a representative picture of the state of society and its changes in objective terms. Social scientists have often called up this material for secondary analyses (e.g. Zapf, 1977). The limitations of these data have been increasingly cited, however, as the research is restricted to measurements of such "hard" data as numbers of people, amounts of money, size of dwellings, with only few exceptions. Special social surveys are necessary to fill the gap in the traditional official data production.

The German welfare surveys

In this stream of social-scientific activities the plan for a welfare survey in the Federal Republic of Germany was developed at the University of Mannheim and executed by the Research Unit "Microanalytische Grundlagen der Gesellschaftspolitik", with financial aid from the Deutsche Forschungsgemeinschaft. In the meantime three welfare surveys, representative of the Federal Republic of Germany, are available from 1978, 1980 and 1984. The emphasis of the questionnaire is laid on subjective questions: for example, perceptions and evaluations of well-being in different life domains. But there are also questions about objective living conditions because one main intention of the welfare survey project is to analyse the interrelationship between objective living conditions and their subjective perception and evaluation. Of course, the surveys laid emphasis on the replication of questions, but new questions were also introduced to improve the questionnaire and to facilitate the investigation of new problems. The special advantage of the data set consists of the combination of data on different life domains and problem areas with the data on both dimensions, objective living conditions and subjective well-being.

The contributors to the welfare surveys are all people with German citizenship living in the Federal Republic of Germany and West Berlin, having reached the age of 18 at least and living in a private household. The samples were drawn from these contributors according to the standards of the ADM (Arbeitskreis deutscher Marktforschungsinstitute). The welfare surveys consist of valid interviews from 2012 individuals in 1978, 2427 in 1980 and 2067 in 1984. Compared with official statistics from the National Bureau of Census, the distribution of the socio-demográphic variables is quite similar. Young adults are somewhat under-represented, which is typical of all population samples. The original data set was therefore adjusted by the use of weights for individuals and households (Glatzer and Mohr, 1987). In addition to the main samples, special samples were drawn: on the one hand guestworkers, because they are normally excluded from the German polls; and on the other hand couples, in order to include in the investigation people who are sharing their living conditions. A small panel study was also carried out between 1978 and 1980, to allow for the comparison of temporal change for the same individuals. Some methodological studies were designed to prove the reliability and validity of the indicators: for example, in respect to response patterns (Berger-Schmitt, 1988), the comparability of different surveys (Mohr, 1987) and the dimensionality of scales (Berger,

1980). Of course, disturbing influences were found, but never to an extent that would have falsified the results.

Main features of the quality of life

Quality of life in the broad sense is the individual's constellation of objective and subjective components of welfare. In the restricted sense it lays the main emphasis on the perception and evaluation of life; it is concerned with satisfaction with life domains and general well-being (see Chapter 3).

The ambivalence of subjective well-being

One-dimensional satisfaction studies are surprising in their high satisfaction scores. Only the use of broader approaches shows that, despite the high satisfaction reported, many aspects of ill-being exist (Campbell, Converse and Rodgers, 1976, p. 57; Andrews and Withey, 1976, p. 105; Bradburn, 1969, p. 56; Veenhoven, 1988, p. 7; Headey, Holmström and Wearing, 1984, p. 115; Allardt, 1975, p. 17). Some astonishment has been evoked by the fact that the positive and negative aspects of well-being seem to be basically independent of each other (see also Chapter 7).

This is the first important feature of the quality of life, namely its ambivalence. On the one hand, we observe quite a high degree of life satisfaction (Table 13.1). It is situated at a level in the upper area of domain satisfactions (Tables 13.3). General satisfaction is not an arithmetic mean of the domain satisfactions owing to the fact that some domain satisfactions—especially the family and living standard domains—have a higher weight than others (Glatzer, 1984). We also identify a striking dominance of the feeling of happiness in contrast to unhappiness (Table 13.1). But on the other hand, when we observe negative aspects of well-being, we see a fairly broad diffusion of anxiety symptoms (stress, fears, nervousness, depression) and alienation symptoms (work alienation, meaninglessness, loneliness) (Table 13.2). Also on (open) questions about worries and personal problems the Germans report many severe burdens. These burdens have led to resignation, as some people think that they cannot overcome their problems.

Both well-being and ill-being have many components. Different positive components are correlated positively with one another, but in a far from a perfect correlation (Table 13.1). A distinction is made here between more cognitive ("satisfaction") and more affective measures ("happiness") of well-being (Andrews and McKennell, 1978; Michalos, 1980). Positive and negative aspects are correlated negatively with one another, but are also a far from perfect correlation. Positive aspects prevail, but negative aspects exist in many cases simultaneously with positive aspects of well-being (Table 13.2).

Altogether well-being is completely differentiated, with many individuals having ambivalent feelings of satisfaction and deprivation at the same time.

TABLE 13.1. *The relationship between life satisfaction and happiness 1984*

Life satisfaction	Happiness			
	Very happy	Rather happy	Rather and very unhappy	Total
Highly satisfied (10)	9	9	0	18
Satisfied (6–9)	11	55	4	70
Rather dissatisfied (0–5)	0	7	5	12
Total	20	71	9	100

Categories on the satisfaction scale from "0" to "10"
Data Source: Wohlfahrtssurvey, 1984

TABLE 13.2. *Anxiety and life satisfaction*

	Total		Rather dissatisfied[a]		Completely satisfied[b]	
	1978	1984	1978	1984	1978	1984
	in	percent				
Anxiety symptoms[c]						
Frequent spells of complete exhaustion or fatigue	54	47	82	69	46	37
Recurring frightening thoughts	19	21	69	55	11	9
Constantly keyed up and jittery	16	16	51	33	9	10
Usually unhappy or depressed	14	15	64	55	7	6
Often shake or tremble	9	5	31	23	7	6
No symptoms	41	43	8	19	51	58

[a] Range 0 to 4 on Satisfaction Scale.
[b] Point 10 on Satisfaction Scale.
[c] Parts of the Anxiety Scale. See E. Allardt, "About Dimensions of Welfare", Research Report, Vol. 1, Research Group for Comparative Sociology, University of Helsinki, 1973.
Data source: Wohlfahrtssurvey, 1978, 1984.

The satisfaction gap between private and public life domains

In studies that include private and public life domains or public matters a discrepancy seems to emerge between their satisfaction levels (Watts and Free, 1974, p. 205; Campbell, 1981, p. 163; Campbell, Converse and Rodgers, 1976, p. 267; Eurobarometer, 1985, p. 2). This point is not so much elaborated in the literature because most research is restricted to private domains.

Nevertheless, a second main feature of the quality of life can be stated, i.e.that satisfaction is higher in private than in public areas. At the top of the hierarchy of satisfaction levels are to be found the domains of marriage, family and household, and at the bottom the domains of public security and environmental protection (Table 13.3). We do not believe that the individuals gloss over their private sphere, which falls within their own

TABLE 13.3. *Satisfaction[a] with major life domains 1978, 1980, 1984*

		Rather satisfied	Completely satisfied	Rather dissatisfied	
		in percent			Mean
Marriage/partnership[b]	1978	97.4	48.4	0.8	9.0
	1984	95.1	43.7	2.4	8.8
Family life[c]	1978	95.7	38.6	2.0	8.7
	1984	93.4	29.6	1.8	8.4
Household management	1980	93.6	34.8	1.9	8.5
	1984	93.9	38.9	2.8	8.6
Job[d]	1980	89.1	12.0	5.4	7.6
	1984	90.1	22.3	5.4	7.9
Being a housewife[e]	1978	86.9	24.9	5.1	7.9
	1984	85.1	27.0	7.6	7.8
Division of household tasks	1980	85.6	28.4	6.9	7.9
	1984	85.4	29.6	8.4	7.9
Living standard	1978	84.6	14.5	6.6	7.4
	1984	80.8	16.2	9.5	7.4
Housing	1978	83.2	29.2	6.8	7.8
	1984	85.4	35.8	5.6	8.0
Leisure	1978	82.7	25.8	10.4	7.6
	1984	81.5	26.9	9.6	7.7
Household income	1978	82.2	13.3	10.0	7.2
	1980	77.3	14.7	11.0	7.1
	1984	74.1	14.0	14.5	6.9
Health	1978	79.0	16.3	11.6	7.3
	1984	74.1	18.5	14.9	7.1
Social security system	1978	76.6	9.7	13.6	6.9
	1984	74.2	11.2	13.7	6.8
Education	1978	70.9	14.7	17.1	6.7
	1984	72.2	19.0	15.5	7.0
Church	1978	56.8	8.6	24.6	5.9
	1984	54.8	9.2	25.1	5.8
Public safety	1978	43.7	1.9	40.0	5.0
	1984	46.5	2.3	31.4	5.2
Environmental protection	1978	40.4	1.6	38.7	5.0
	1984	22.2	0.9	58.3	3.8

[a] Satisfaction scale: 0–10; "rather satisfied" = 6–10; "completely satisfied" = 10; "rather dissatisfied" = 0–4.
[b] Only respondents having spouse or partner.
[c] Only respondents having partner and children under 18 years.
[d] Full- and part-time employed persons.
[e] Housewives only.
Data source: Wohlfahrtssurvey, 1978, 1980, 1984.

responsibility and we have found that they do not avoid talking about their personal, familiar worries and conflicts, which are present to quite a high degree. The hypothesis is, however, that at the same time, in spite of these burdens, the private domains make important positive contributions to the individual's well-being. And this seems decisive for the high level of satisfaction in private domains; their net balance is assumed to remain positive.

Real danger and diffuse fears are close together in the public domains mentioned above. Public safety and environmental protection are topics very dear to the mass media as well as in the experience of everyday life. But the correlation between dissatisfaction with environmental protection and public safety is quite small and suggests that there is no general negative stereotyping in the domains of public responsibility. We also have to register that public domains such as social security have a higher level of satisfaction than the two subjects mentioned above. Besides, we can see that the domains of living standards (income, housing, leisure) are placed in the middle of the hierarchy of satisfaction levels. It seems that the thesis of private wealth and public poverty finds some expression in this assessment of the German population.

The private domains are obviously much more important for the subjective well-being than are the public domains. The protest potential included in the relatively high dissatisfaction with public matters has therefore presumably not resulted in protest behaviour above the normal present amount.

The level of living and social comparisons as determinants of the perception of quality of life.

One of the really complex questions in the field of quality-of-life research is the explanation of the individual's perception of the quality of life (see Chapters 2 and 3). Nearly every book in our reference list contains at least a preliminary approach to the explanation of how the quality of life is perceived and how subjective well-being is influenced. Since there are many concepts of well-being and quality of life, it is not astonishing that there many different theories. The agreement does not appear to be as strong as in the other features.

On average it is found that people who have good living conditions are more satisfied than people who have poor living conditions. This is shown here for the area of income distribution where, according to rising household income (weighted for family size) the percentage of dissatisfied people declines and the percentage of satisfied people increases (Table 13.4). But the correlation is far from perfect. One idea is that it is not the level of living conditions, but their rate of change, that generates satisfaction. For areas of income it could be shown that a particularly high income satisfaction arises from a disproportionate increase in income (Brachtl and Zapf, 1984,

p. 323). If people think that their household income has increased more than average they have an especially high income satisfaction (Strümpel, 1976). The crucial point is that this can never happen for everyone.

TABLE 13.4. *Satisfaction with household income (by income level)*

	Income level (quintiles)					
	1 Low	2	3	4	5 High	Total
	(%)					
Very high (10)[a]	4	9	11	18	23	17
Medium/high (5–9)	60	70	77	75	69	70
Low (0–4)	37	20	11	7	8	13

[a] Values on satisfaction scale from 0–10.
Data source: Wohlfahrtssurvey, 1984.

TABLE 13.5. *Self-evaluation of own household income in comparison with perceived income of average citizen*[a]

	Income level (quintiles)					
	1 Low	2	3	4	5 High	Total
	(%)					
Own household income compared with average citizen's						
Much higher[a]	1	6	8	12	26	11
Somewhat higher	14	32	36	41	51	35
Equal	28	28	28	29	14	25
Somewhat lower	29	25	24	15	8	20
Much lower	29	9	5	4	1	9
	361	356	365	351	355	1789

[a] Self-Anchoring Striving Scale, developed by Cantril. See H. Cantril 1965: "The Pattern of Human Concerns" (Rutgers, New Brunswick), pp. 21–26, 265–274.
Much higher: three more steps higher on a ten-step ladder; somewhat higher: one or two steps higher; somewhat lower: one or two steps lower; much lower: three or more steps lower.
Data source: Wohlfahrtssurvey, 1980.

The welfare positions of the individuals in a domain such as income can be divided into groups: well off—people having high income and high income satisfaction; deprived—people having low income and less income satisfaction. These congruent types are dominant in the population. The inconsistent groups of dissonants (high income/low satisfaction) and of adapted (resigned) people (low income/high income satisfaction) are in a minority. The relationship between level of income and income satisfaction also holds if further variables (socio-demographic, socio-economic) are controlled. We found similar results in some other life domains. So I would venture to say that an improvement in living conditions will on average lead to a somewhat higher domain satisfaction. Satisfaction in different life domains can be used to explain satisfaction with life in general (Glatzer, 1984, p. 234).

However, the relationship between objective conditions and their subjective evaluation remains weak in many cases and has astonished most researchers who have a congruence thesis. So the search for "disturbing" factors began (cf. Chapter 3) and one of them seems to lie in the social comparisons that individuals use to evaluate their situation. People can make quite a number of social comparisons with their relatives, their neighbours, their colleagues, the average citizen, which can change from situation to situation. The result of our research on this point is that in the income area the average German is an important reference point. The relative position in respect to the imagination of an average German household influences satisfaction with income significantly.

Income position in relation to friends is less important. This holds again in complex multivariate analyses (Glatzer, 1984, p. 64). There, another influential factor for domain satisfaction is the expectation gap, the differentiation between what someone has and what someone expects. A conclusion that is evident from our research is that satisfaction in life domains depends on important factors, and the major part of variance cannot be explained.

We cannot be sure if the results from the income domain can be transferred to all life domains. For example, the determinants of social relations and the satisfaction they generate could be very different. Another question is how states of well-being can be explained when they do not have a clearcut objective counterpart such as income and income satisfaction. Happiness is one example to be explained in different ways (Argyle, 1987; Veenhoven, 1984, 1988).

Although something seems to be evident, no one should be afraid of our obtaining a wholly satisfied, immobile society. There are built-in factors that produce dissatisfaction in the production process of well-being as joint products. For example, most satisfaction in the income domain arises from an individual disproportionate increase. But this is unavoidably accompanied by a possibly disproportionate decrease for others who will react with dissatisfaction. Never will everyone be capable of maximizing their satisfaction at the same time, at least as long as social comparisons are strongly important for the subjective well-being. Additionally, a rise in expectations in accordance with a rise in conditions constitutes a further barrier against high satisfaction levels.

Well-being in small groups: Couples

Couples are a kind of institutionalized primary group in which living conditions are shared and well-being is mutually influenced. No doubt one expects rather similar definitions of the quality of life but different levels could also be possible because of partly separated life domains (e.g. the work-place) or privileges and subordination in the family.

There is much agreement between spouses. The similarity between spouses is strongest in respect to satisfaction with the household income and lowest in respect to satisfaction with work (Table 13.6). In the first, but not

TABLE 13.6. *Agreement between spouses in satisfaction and well-being*

	N	Agree-ment %	Husband is better off %	Wife is better off %	Agreement coefficient**
Satisfaction with household income	279	30.8	29.0*	40.1*	.60
Satisfaction with household management	287	40.1	44.3*	15.7*	.51
Impairment of well-being due to conflicts with neighbours	285	94.4	3.5	2.1	.51
Worries and problems in the family	289	74.7	12.8	12.5	.49
Loneliness	282	60.6	23.4	16.0	.44
Impairment of well-being due to conflicts with the spouse	287	78.0	14.6*	7.3*	.43
Satisfaction with domestic division of labour	278	34.2	46.0*	19.8*	.43
Life satisfaction	286	35.7	33.2	31.1	.42
Happiness	281	68.0	14.2	17.8	.40
Deficit of satisfaction with leisure time	278	55.0	16.2*	28.8*	.39
Deficit of satisfaction with the influence on political decisions	284	57.7	12.0*	30.3*	.39
Deficit of satisfaction with the family	286	65.0	18.9	16.1	.36
Deficit of satisfaction with success	284	49.7	21.8	28.5	.34
Impairment of well-being due to conflicts with friends	286	94.8	2.1	3.1	.33
Deficit of satisfaction with love	283	70.0	15.9	14.1	.28
Impairment of well-being due to conflicts with the children	239	73.6	13.8	12.6	.25
Deficit of satisfaction with work	283	50.5	20.1*	29.3*	.25

* Better position of husband or wife is significantly different (α ≤ 5%)
** The agreement coefficient shows the similarity between spouses in comparison to non-married people. A value of zero means that spouses do not agree more than unmarried persons. Negative values express less, positive values express better accordance between spouses than between other people. A perfect agreement is indicated by an index value of "1". (The index is described in Krippendorff, 1970: Bivariate agreement of coefficients for Reliability of Data. In: E. F. Borgatta and G. W. Bohrnsedt (eds.): Sociological Methodology 1970. Jossey-Bass Publ. San Francisco pp. 139–150).
Data Source: Wohlfahrtssurvey 1980—Sample of Spouses (N = 289 Spouses)

in the second case, the social condition is shared by the spouses, and this is a simple explanation of the differences. The general well-being is similar to a medium degree; it depends partly on common, partly on different life domains and experiences. The differences of well-being hint at gender-specific factors. In some dimensions the wife is better off than the husband, in some it is the opposite. We find that less satisfaction in wives can be explained by their special situation: they are less satisfied with household management and division of work in the household, domains in which they are burdened more than men. They also suffer more than their husbands from marital conflicts, but there is no difference as to conflicts with children. Wives feel less deficits of satisfaction in respect to their leisure time, political influence, household income and their work. The similarity of spouses grows according to the duration of the marriage.

The hypothesis that, besides the similarity of perceived living conditions, we find in couples similar standards of assessing and a mutual influence on the state of well-being is also proved. Interviewing both partners of a couple allows us to compare the mutual perception of states of well-being and role performance—how spouses view each other—and this allows for much more complex analysis (Berger, 1984, p. 321). This approach could be expanded to other "groups" too: for example to working groups, neighbourhoods or peer groups.

Cumulations of good and bad welfare positions

If welfare is conceived of as a constellation of good and bad positions in a number of life domains, including objective conditions and subjective perception and evaluation, then the crucial question is how often the individual will be better or worse off. There could be a high degree of consistency, e.g. an individual is on the same level in all life domains in objective and subjective respects. A high degree of inconsistency would imply that an individual has mostly different positions in respect of life domains and their objective and subjective dimensions. From a consistent combination of welfare positions at the individual level one would get a hierarchically stratified society; in the case of inconsistency one would get a pluralistic picture. This question has not often been addressed in quality of life research though it is a basic question in research on stratification and status inconsistency. Implicitly the problem has to be taken into account in approaches to building an index of well-being (Campbell, Converse and Rodgers, 1976, p. 49). Through a summing up of the individual's positions across different life domains, weights can be given to the more and the less important domains.

In the German population we do not find a clear-cut hierarchical structure of welfare positions but rather an inconsistent pattern of individual combinations of positions at various welfare levels (Berger, 1984, p. 249). There is almost no individual who, in all life domains, is continually in a good position and none who is continually in a bad position. One can interpret this as certain confirmation of the disparity theory of stratification and inequality. According to this theory, the market-based inequality is losing its importance for the stratification system because redistributioñ and the intervention of the welfare state are weakening the old, and creating new, disparities. In particular, for the position in the income distribution, it is of interest to see how far other "goods" are connected (Table 13.7). The result is that the position in an income group (income quintile) is not strongly related to the availability of goods, relationships or well-being. A striking exception is the lowest quintile of the population, which shows a cumulation of bad living conditions, lack of social relations and also deficits of well-being. This indicates that problem groups like the poor are somewhat separated from the mainstream of welfare.

TABLE 13.7. *Objective and subjective measures of welfare by level of household income*[a]*—1984*

		Income level (quintiles)					
		1 Low	2	3	4	5 High	Total
Dishwasher	%	13	23	20	34	42	27
Video recorder	%	12	16	12	16	22	16
Car	%	63	64	69	67	83	69
Telephone	%	84	92	90	93	97	91
Less than 1 room per person	%	21	15	5	4	1	9
Home ownership	%	51	44	47	46	46	47
Satisfaction with living standard[b]		6.0	6.9	7.3	7.9	8.2	7.2
Satisfaction with environmental protection[b]		3.8	3.7	3.9	3.9	3.7	3.8
No club membership	%	51	40	42	45	33	42
No close friends	%	37	35	35	20	18	29
Loneliness	%	23	17	13	17	17	18
Frightening thoughts	%	34	25	25	15	13	22
Overall life satisfaction[b]		6.9	7.5	7.2	7.8	7.6	7.4

[a] Weighted per capita income.
  Excluding respondents with no data on income question.
[b] Average on satisfaction scale 0–10.
Data source: Wohlfahrtssurvey 1984.

By defining five objective problem situations (belonging to the lowest decile of household income, having less than 1 room per person, no occupational degree, living alone, no close friends and chronic health impairment) and three subjective ones (often lonely, recurring frightening thoughts, usually unhappy or depressed) the cumulation profile of the affected population has the form of a funnel. Of the German samples 42 per cent are not affected by one of these measures and 2 per cent are affected by five or more (Table 13.8). Cumulations of a high number of problem situations are not very frequent, but more than 10 per cent of the population are affected by two or more deprivations on the objective and subjective side. Most frequently these cumulations occur among certain unprivileged groups such as working-class housewives, working-class retirees and unemployed people (Breuer, 1987, p. 142). Another large group which has on average poorer living conditions than the German workers is the guest-worker population. They rate their situation in the Federal Republic of Germany better than in their home country and are therefore not so very dissatisfied (Wiegand, 1987).

TABLE 13.8. *Cumullation of problem situations*

	Objective[a]	Subjective[b]	Total
		(%)	
Number of problem situations			
0	54	71	42
1	32	18	29
2	12	9	13
3	3	3	9
4	–		4
5 or more	–		2
Mean	0.65	0.43	1.10

[a] Five objective-problem situations.
[b] Three subjective-problem situations.
Data Source: Wohlfahrtssurvey 1984.

Structural stability and individual fluctuation

One of the main critical questions as to the measurement of satisfaction and well-being concerns the stability of the measurement results (see Chapter 3; Diener *et al.*, 1985). It could have been that satisfaction scores and other well-being scores are somewhat superficial and ephemeral without any significance for the individual's constitution. But when replication studies were carried out, and panel designs were also used, it was noteworthy that different degrees of reliability of the measure of well-being have to be taken into account. Structural stability, i.e. stability of the dispersion of the whole population is an outcome for the delectation of sociologists. Compared with this, individual stability is small, but allows, nevertheless, valid and reliable measurement.

The sixth main feature of the quality of life is that a high stability of structures is measured by distributions and correlations. Nevertheless, there is a broad fluctuation of individual cases through different welfare positions. The stability of structures can be shown by the almost ultrastability of satisfaction with life from 1978 and 1980 to 1984 (Table 13.9); there is no change in the average figure and only marginal changes in the dispersion profile. Happiness shows a small decreasing tendency from 1978 and 1980 to 1984, but on the whole the pattern is also quite stable. The same holds true if we look at the many domain satisfactions that were measured in 1978 and 1984 (Table 13.3); no change is monitored in most cases, a small positive change occurs in four domains (job, housing, education, public safety), a small negative change in three domains (marriage, family, household income) and a striking change in only one domain, which is environmental protection. Additionally, on the side of the negative concepts of well-being we also have a striking dominance of stability (Berger and Mohr, 1986, p. 27). But this stability pattern conceals a large number of fluctuations because it shows only the net balance of positive and negative changes (Brachtl and Zapf, 1984, p. 223).

TABLE 13.9. *Satisfaction with life in 1978, 1980, 1984*

Question[a]: "All things considered, how satisfied are you with your life as a whole these days?"

	Satisfaction scale							Total	Mean
	Completely dissatis- fied 0–4	5	6	7	8	9	Completely satisfied 10		
1978 %	4.2	5.6	7.3	15.4	31.5	18.0	17.9	100	7.8
1980 %	4.2	8.4	8.3	17.7	29.8	13.0	18.4	100	7.7
1984 %	6.0	6.6	6.2	14.4	32.0	17.3	17.4	100	7.7

[a] Slightly modified. For original question see J. Hall, "Quality of Life Survey", Urban Britain: 1973, Vol. 1: Distribution of Responses and Questionnaire, SSRC 1976.
Data source: Wohlfahrtssurvey 1978, 1980, 1984.

Fluctuations in the scores measuring the state of well-being can happen during the course of one interview (Table 13.10). If we compare life satisfaction at the beginning and at the end of an interview, we find changes in the positive and the negative directions (Glatzer, 1984, p. 187). That a change occurs is not astonishing because many life aspects and events are remembered during the interview. If we compare life satisfaction in two interviews from a panel over a two-year period, we find that two-thirds of the respondents change their life satisfaction, though only one-third change more than one point on the satisfaction scale. Life events explain some part of this change.

One can add that extreme positive or negative levels of well-being are unstable and that there seems to be pressure to change to a mediate level (Brachtl and Zapf, 1984, p. 329). Furthermore, a high expectation gap is reduced in the course of time.

TABLE 13.10. *The stability of life satisfaction*

Assessment of Life Satisfaction on a Scale from 0 to 10	At the beginning and at the end of the same interview 1978 All respondents	1978 and in the replication interviews 1980 Respondents on the panel	Respondents on the panel	Wife and Husband Respondents in the spouse interviews
2 and more points higher	13.6	16.3	19.4	15.7
1 point higher	19.8	19.0	19.0	17.5
On the same level	38.8	42.2	23.8	35.7
1 point lower	17.1	15.3	18.0	13.6
2 and more points lower	10.8	7.1	19.7	17.5
Respondents	1984	294	294	286
Pearson's r	.60	.60	.45	.42

Data Sources: Wohlfahrtssurvey 1978 (N = 2012 Respondents)
Wohlfahrtssurvey 1980 (N = 2396 Respondents)
Panel 1978/80 (N = 298)
Survey of couples (N = 289 couples)

The structural stability accompanied by individual fluctuation is a fact that has not been very well explained to date. The positive and negative changes must add up to the same amount if the mean is to have the same score. But how this is guided by attraction and rejection, by push and pull, by constraints and decisions, is a widely open question.

Optimistic and pessimistic views of satisfaction with life

Individuals exist in the present, but they are aware of their past and they take into account their future. Their life course could be experienced as stable, going up, going down or fluctuating. It has been shown for a long time that Americans on average view their life as going up (Watts and Free 1974, p. 205). This is somewhat different in West Germany and this depends perhaps on special societal developments.

The late 1970s are characterized by an increase in social problems. The "reform atmosphere" of the early 1970s differs considerably from the "problem atmosphere" of the transition to the 1980s. The term "problem atmosphere" relates to the increase in problem areas such as structural unemployment, sluggish economic growth, deterioration of the environment, overstrained public budgets, etc. The question is whether this increase in the number of problems, which is constantly emphasized by the mass media, has a corresponding effect on the level of individual well-being. As we have seen, life satisfaction has not changed from 1978 to 1984. But the assessment of life satisfaction in the past and the expected life satisfaction in

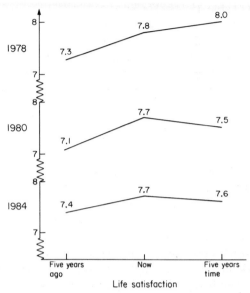

FIG. 13.1. Overall life satisfaction – individual comparison between past, present and expected life satisfaction.

the future varies somewhat. The upward trend reaches a ceiling (Figure 13.1). The share of respondents having a negative view of past developments has increased; a reduction in life satisfaction in the previous five years stood at 14 per cent in 1978, 18 per cent in 1980 and finally 23 per cent in 1984.

TABLE 13.11. *Comparative evaluation of past, present and future overall life satisfaction*

	1978	1980	1984
	(%)		
Comparison past-present 5 years ago—now			
Increase	41	34	31
Constant	44	48	46
Decrease	14	18	23
Comparison future–present Now–5 years time			
Increase	24	21	19
Constant	64	54	56
Decrease	12	25	25

Data source: Wohlfahrtssurvey 1978, 1980, 1984.

More remarkable is the decrease in expected satisfaction. The proportion of pessimistic respondents, who expected a lower life satisfaction than they had at the time of the survey, doubled: 12 per cent in 1978 and 25 per cent in 1980 and 1984 (Table 13.11). The level of overall life satisfaction did not actually decline during the transition into the 1980s; however, a pessimistic attitude in the area of subjective well-being became more prevalent. This was already apparent in 1980 and holds up tp 1984. It would appear that an increase in social problems does not immediately change the general well-being of the population, but there is a more direct reaction in regard to future expectations.

Summary

Looking back on the not very old tradition of quality of life research, it would be worthwhile balancing what we know and what we do not know. We have detected many unsolved problems about theoretical and method-ological issues in the course of research. But stock-taking in some areas shows that there are also substantial and important results. The starting point of this chapter is to lay emphasis not on the problems, but on the results. In my own work in the field I have received the impression of some basic features of well-being, similar in part to those in studies in different countries. They can be shown for the German population in particular, by use of the German Welfare Surveys. The shortest version of these seven hypotheses is as follows:

1. Subjective well-being is characterized by a high degree of differen-tiation and ambivalence.
2. Life domains constitute a hierarchy of satisfaction levels in which pri-vate domains are in the upper, and public domains are in the lower, parts.
3. The level of living and social comparisons are both among the deter-mining factors of the perceived quality of life.
4. In the small groups of couples similar perceptions of living conditions exist, similar standards of evaluation and similar well-being of the spouses.
5. Cumulations of continuously bad welfare positions are rather seldom, but there are special problem groups who are deprived on several dimensions.
6. Structural stability is accompanied by individual fluctuation.
7. The future expectations of life satisfaction are a more sensible indi-cator of societal problems than life satisfaction itself.

Of course this knowledge should be broadened and improved. The expla-nations of well-being and quality of life especially have to be elaborated. In this respect only a multidimensional approach seems to be adequate. Qual-ity of life and well-being are influenced by many factors, with the level of living and social comparisons being two of the somewhat stronger factors.

There is enough unexplained variance in the models to look for further influential factors.

References

ALLARDT, E. *About dimensions of welfare.* Research Report, Vol. 1, Research Group for Comparative Sociology. University of Helsinki, 1973.

ALLARDT, E. *Dimensions of welfare in a comparative Scandinavian study.* Research Group for Comparative Sociology, Research Report No. 9, University of Helsinki, 1975.

ANDREWS, F. M. and WITHEY, S. B. *Social indicators of well-being. Americans' perceptions of life quality.* New York: Plenum Press, 1976.

ANDREWS, F. M. and MCKENNELL, A. C. *Measures of self-reported well-being: Their affective, cognitive, and other components.* Institute for Social Research, The University of Michigan, Working Paper Series, 1978.

ARGYLE, M. *The psychology of happiness,* London: Methuen, 1987.

BERGER, R. *Angst und Entfremdung—Zur Eindimensionalität zweier Skalen im Wohlfahrtsurvey 1978.* Internal discussion paper No. 36, Frankfurt: Sonderforschungsbereich 3, 1980.

BERGER, R. Zusammenhänge und Abhängigkeiten zwischen Lebensbereichen. In W. Glatzer and W. Zapf (eds.), *Lebensqualität in der Bundesrepublik. Objektive Lebensbedingungen und subjektives Wohlbefinden.* Frankfurt: Campus, 1984.

BERGER, R. Übereinstimmungen und Unterschiede zwischen Ehepartnern. In W. Glatzer and W. Zapf (eds.), *Lebensqualität in der Bundesrepublik. Objektive Lebensbedingungen und subjektives Wohlbefinden.* Frankfurt; Campus, 1984.

BERGER, R. and MOHR, H. M. Lebensqualität in der Bundesrepublik 1978 und 1984. *Soziale Welt,* 1986; **37**(1).

BERGER-SCHMITT, R. *Antworttendenzen bei der Beantwortung der Zufriedenheitsfragen in den Wohlfahrtssurveys.* Working paper No. 259, Frankfurt; Sonderforschungsbereich 3, 1988.

BRACHTL, W. and ZAPF, W. Stabilität und Wandel individueller Wohlfahrt: Panelergebnisse. In W. Glatzer and W. Zapf (eds.), *Lebensqualität in der Bundesrepublik. Objektive Lebensbedingungen und subjektives Wohlbefinden.* Frankfurt: Campus, 1984.

BRADBURN, N. M. *The structure of psychological well-being.* Chicago: Aldine, 1969.

BREUER, S. Problem groups. In W. Zapf (ed.), German Social Report, living conditions and subjective well-being, 1978–1984. *Social Indicators Research,* 1987: **19**(1).

CAMPBELL, A., CONVERSE, P. E. and RODGERS, W. L. *The quality of American life.* New York: Russell Sage Foundation, 1976.

CAMPBELL, A. *The sense of well-being in America.* New York: McGraw Hill, 1981.

CANTRIL, H. *The pattern of human concerns.* New Brunswick: Rutgers University Press, 1965.

CARLEY, M. *Social measurement and social indicators. Issues of policy and theory.* London: Allen & Unwin, 1981.

DIENER, E., EMMONS, R. A., LARSEN, R. J. and GRIFFIN, S. The satisfaction with life scale. *Journal of Personality Assessment,* 1985; **49**, 71–76.

EUROBAROMETER. *Die öffentliche Meinung in der Europäischen Gemeinschaft,* No. 23, June 1985.

GLATZER, W. An overview of the international development in macro social indicators. *Accounting, Organizations and Society,* 1981; **6**(3), 219–234.

GLATZER, W. International actors in social indicators research. *Social Indicators Newsletter,* 1982; **16**, 1–16.

GLATZER, W. Determinanten subjektiven Wohlbefindens. In W. Glatzer and W. Zapf (eds.), *Lebensqualität in der Bundesrepublik. Objektive Lebensbedingungen und subjektives Wohlbefinden.* Frankfurt: Campus, 1984.

GLATZER, W. and MOHR, H. M. Quality of life: concepts and measurement. In W. Zapf (ed.), German Social Report, living conditions and subjective well-being, 1978–1984. *Social Indicators Research,* 1987; **19**(1).

HALL, J. *Quality of life survey, Urban Britain: 1973,* Vol. 1: *Distribution of responses and questionnaire.* SSRC: 1976.

HEADEY, B. W., HOLSTROM, E. L. and WEARING, A. J. Well-being and ill-being: Different dimensions? *Social Indicators Research,* 1984; **14**, 115–139.

KRIPPENDORF, K. Bivariate agreement of coefficients for reliability of data. In E. F. Borgatta and G. W. Bohrnstedt (eds.) *Sociological methodology*. San Francisco: Jossey-Bass, 1970.

MICHALOS, A. C. Satisfaction and happiness. *Social Indicators Research*, 1980; **8**, 385–422.

MOHR, H. M. Analysen zur Vergleichbarkeit von Zufriedenheitsmessungen. *Zeitschrift für Sozialpsychologie*, 1987; **18**, 160–168.

ROSSI, R. J. and GILMARTIN, K. J. *The handbook of social indicators. Sources, characteristics, and analysis*. New York: Garland Press, 1980.

STRUMPEL, B. (ed.). *Economic means for human needs. Social indicators of well-being and discontent*. Ann Arbor: Institute for Social Research, 1976.

VEENHOVEN, R. *The happiness revenues of economic wealth and growth*. Working paper No. 263, Frankfurt: Sonderforschungsbereich 3, 1988.

VEENHOVEN, R. *Conditions of happiness*. Dordrecht: Reidel, 1984.

WATTS, W. and FREE, L. A. *State of the nation*. Washington D.C.: Potomac Associates, 1974.

ZAPF, W. (ed.). *Lebensbedingungen in der Bundesrepublik. Sozialer Wandel und Wohlfahrtsentwicklung*. Frankfurt: Campus, 1977.

ZAPF, W. (ed.). German Social Report, Living conditions and subjective well-being, 1978–1984. *Social Indicators Research*, 1987; **19**(1).

Notes

1. The domination of the quality of life concept may be recognized in the title of the main journal in the field: *Social Indicators Research—An International and Interdisciplinary Journal for Quality of Life Measurement*, founded in 1974, edited by Alex Michalos.

2. The surveys were developed under the direction of Wolfgang Zapf, Wolfgang Glatzer and Heinz-Herbert Noll in the Special Research Group 3 (Sfb 3) of the University of Frankfurt and the University of Mannheim. The Center for Surveys, Methods and Analyses (Zuma) was consulted for the methodological approach, and INFRATEST (Munich) carried out the field work. The Welfare Survey data are available in the Central Archive in Cologne. The main publications (in German) are Glatzer and Zapf, 1985; Siara, 1980; Berger and Mohr, 1986; and Glatzer *et al.*, 1985. Zapf, 1987, is available in English.

Acknowledgements

The results presented here are a summary of the work of many colleagues over several years. In particular I would like to mention Wolfgang Zapf, who introduced this kind of research in Germany, Regina Berger-Schmitt, Roland Habich, Sabine Lang, Michael Mohr, Maria Muller-Andritzky, Heinz-Herbert Noll and Christian Siara.

Author Index

Page numbers in *italic* type are to Reference lists at ends of chapters

Duncan-Jones, P.   54, 66, fn69, *71*
Dunkel-Schetter, C.   221–222, *231*

Easterlin, R. A.   21, *25*, 27, *45*, 80, *98*, 116, *117*, 202, *211*
Eber, H. W.   176, 189, *191*
Eckenrode, J.   221, *231*
Eckes, T.   176, *191*
Edwards, J.   219, *231*
Eisenberg, D. M.   197, *211*
Eiser, J. R.   *71*
Ekman, W.   187, *191*
Elder   33, *45*
Elizur, D.   244, *257*
Ellis, A.   96, *98*
Ekman, P.   187, *191*, *192*
Embree, M. C.   222, *231*
Emmons, R. A.   30, *45*, 50, 52, 67, *70*, *71*, 77, *97*, *98*, 120, 124, 137, *138*, 142, 144, 163, *166*, 196, *211*, 273, *278*
Endicott, J.   147–148, *166*, *168*
Epictetus   132, *138*
Erbaugh, J.   78, *97*
Eurobarometer   265, *278*
Evans, G. W.   218, *231*
Ewert, O.   36, *45*
Eyman, A.   37, *46*
Eysenck, H. J.   53, *70*, 250, 251, 257, *257*, *259*
Eysenck, J. H.   186, *191*
Eysenck, S. B. G.   53, *70*

Fagin, L.   237, *257*
Faunce, W.   95, *99*
Feather, N. T.   112, *117*
Fellon, B.   249, *258*
Felner, R. D.   50, 67, *71*
Felton, B. J.   220–221, 224–225, 227, *231*
Fergusson, J. D.   20, *25*
Ferring, D.   223–224, 226, *232*
Fielder, K.   *46*
Field, T. M.   *99*
Filipp, S. H.   2, 33, *45*, 213, 215–216, 220–221, 223–224, 226, *231*, *232*
Fineman, S.   236, *257*
Fisher, E. B.   *25*
Fisher, S.   *97*
Fitzgerald, M. P.   88, *98*
Fletcher, B.   218, *234*
Flippo, J.   152, *166*
Flocco, R.   50, 67, *70*
Flügel, J. C.   130, *138*, 174, *191*
Fogarty, S.   50, *71*
Folkman, S.   152, *166*, 173, *192*, 215, 217, 220–222, *231*, *232*
Fordyce, M. W.   18–20, *25*, 52, *70*, 124, 125, 126, 128, 137, *138*, 139

Forgas, J.   *46*, 176, *191*
Fox, N. A.   *99*
Frank, B.   35, *45*
Franklin, J. F.   163, *167*
Fraser, C.   81, *97*
Fraser, J.   235, *257*
Frederiksen, N.   176, *191*
Free, L.   265, 275, *279*
Freedman, J. L.   11, *25*, 82, *98*
French, J. R. P.   88, *97*, 249, *257*
Freud, S.   130, 132–133, 136, *138*, 236
Freudenberg, E.   223–224, 226, *232*
Friesen, W. V.   187, *191*
Frost, R. O.   94, *98*
Fry, P.   142, *168*
Fryer, D.   89, *98*, 238, *257*
Furnham, A.   3, 83, 87–88, 92, *97*, 176, *190*, 246, 248–249, 253, *257*, *258*

Gallagher, D.   123, *138*
Ganster   253
Garrett, J.   253, *258*
Gaug, B.   179, 188, *191*
Gawron, V. J.   93, *99*
Geen, R.   251, *258*
Gorgoglione, J. M.   95, *98*
Gibson, S.   224, *233*
Gignac, M.   216, *232*
Gilmartin, K. J.   261, *279*
Glass, D.   218, *232*
Glatzer, W.   3, 14, *25*, 28, 40, *45*, 261–264, 269, 274, *278*, fn279
Glowacki, T.   66, *70*, 92, *98*
Goldberg, L. R.   144, *166*
Gorman, B. S.   133, *138*
Graef, R.   195, *212*
Graham, J. A.   176, *190*
Gray, J. A.   93, *98*
Green, M. L.   94, *98*
Greenberg, D. F.   51, 65, *71*
Greene, C.   251, *258*
Grice   30, *45*
Griffin, S.   2, 52, *70*, 142, *166*, 273, *278*
Grosscup, S. J.   95, *98*, 142, *167*, 195, *212*
Groves, R. M.   29, *45*
Gschneidinger, E.   29, 32, 41–42, *47*, 109–110, *118*

Haan, N.   215, *232*
Hackman, J. R.   87–88, *98*
Halisch, F.   *191*
Hammer, T.   251, *258*
Hampel, R.   187, *191*
Harding, S. D.   144, 163, *166*
Harpaz, I.   242, *258*
Harrell, A. V.   234
Harris, T.   86, *97*, 142, 157, 160, *166*

Subject Index